Automobiles of the World

by Albert L. Lewis
and Walter A. Musciano

WITHDRAWN

DRAWINGS BY
Björn Karlström, Gary W. Musciano,
Douglas Rolfe, Robert Godden

Simon and Schuster · New York

Copyright © 1977 by The Condé Nast Publications Inc.
All rights reserved
including the right of reproduction
in whole or in part in any form
Published by Simon and Schuster
A Division of Gulf & Western Corporation
Simon & Schuster Building
Rockefeller Center
1230 Avenue of the Americas
New York, New York 10020

Designed by Irving Perkins
Manufactured in the United States of America
Printed by The Murray Printing Company
Bound by The Murray Printing Company

1   2   3   4   5   6   7   8   9   10

Library of Congress Cataloging in Publication Data
Lewis, Albert L.
    Automobiles of the world.

    Includes index.
    I.   Automobiles—History.   I.   Musciano, Walter A.,
joint author.   II.   Title.
TL15.L48   629.22'2   77–7576

ISBN 0-671-22485-9

ACKNOWLEDGMENTS

The authors extend their sincere thanks to the following individuals for their kind cooperation in contributing information on many of the automobiles described herein: Henry Austin Clark, Jr.; A. Joseph Zawatski; Stanley G. Reynolds; Arthur G. Rippey; Harold Levy; Bill Dean; Björn Karlström; Richard Scherer; Hank Clark; Jill Rogers; Alexis Dawydoff; Dee E. Allen; Jim Williams; John Cameron; Paul Preuss; G. H. Rideout; and Ivan Mahy.

Special appreciation is also extended to the following museums and manufacturers for their assistance: the Long Island Automotive Museum; Reynolds Museum; Frederick C. Crawford Auto-Aviation Museum; and the Western Reserve Historical Society; the Chevrolet Motor Division, General Motors Corporation; Ford Motor Company; Lincoln-Mercury; Buick Motor Division; Rolls-Royce; American Motors Corporation; Chrysler Corporation; and Mercedes-Benz.

To Henry Austin Clark, Jr.

Contents

9

Introduction

THE AUTOMOBILE has revolutionized man's way of living more than any other invention, and it is quite possible that historians of the future will refer to our era as the "automobile age." The development of the motor vehicle is the result of visionary dreams, endless work and experimentation beginning not too long after the invention of the wheel. Countless self-propelled vehicles were built before the automobile evolved into its current form. What would we do without the car? Not only is it a most enjoyable convenience, but the auto industry provides employment for millions of workers in the steel, rubber, plastics, aluminum, petroleum, copper, and paint industries. The effect of this is now so widespread that the auto can be said to have altered the life-style of almost everyone on earth.

The cars themselves have been built in seemingly limitless variety. There have been limousines with inlaid paneling and mink lap robes, and then there is the Jeep. There have been sleek turbine-powered racing machines, and there are Mack Trucks. There have been cars that are absolutely one-of-a-kind, and there was the Model T Ford.

The over 1,000 examples that follow are a tribute to man's boundless ingenuity when it comes to providing for his comfort and convenience.

CHAPTER ONE

From Ur to Paris by Way of Watt 4000 B.C.—1783 A.D.

MAN'S LOVE AFFAIR with his motorcar has been traced back almost to the Garden of Eden. Near there, at the site of Ur, once one of the important Babylonian cities, were unearthed carvings of early wheeled carts which date back about six thousand years.

Artwork found in India indicates the wheel was in use there shortly afterward.

Before being applied to vehicles, the wheel was employed in a horizontal plane by the potters. Used vertically, it became the waterwheel. Soon heavier, solid, strengthened wheels were mounted on sleds or sledges which had previously been dragged along the ground by man or animal. These first wheels were fixed to their axles. The axle and wheel rotated together. Certainly a somewhat primitive arrangement, but, remember, this took place about 3000 B.C.

A thousand or so years later spoked wheels appeared in eastern Persia, then in Europe about 1400 B.C. The Scandinavian regions caught up with the wheel by 100 B.C. By then a wheeled vehicle had not only become the best way to go but also served as a status symbol of sorts.

Men in many countries began to devote time and money toward the improvement of propulsion systems. And the need for better roadways became obvious.

For power there were available such animals as camels, donkeys, elephants, horses, oxen, water buffalo, and other domesticated beasts—not forgetting man himself, who was frequently procured from the slave marts.

13

Roads consisting of compacted twin tracks about three feet apart to accommodate the average size cart were constructed by the Pharaohs, then later by the Chinese and the Greeks. Roadways were to be established, improved, or abandoned throughout the civilized world depending mostly upon the fortunes of war.

But man now had his helpful wheel, his basic cart, plus rough roadways over which he could travel with his trading goods or household effects.

Up to this point no one had been able to duplicate the vehicles described by Nahum and Ezekiel in their Old Testament accounts: magnificent carriages which featured some mysterious method of self-propulsion. Similar "horseless," fire-assisted chariots recurred in Oriental legends. To balance the many dreamers were a band of gifted inventors. The Chinese, for example, are credited with a keen knowledge of the power of steam—and this by 800 B.C.

Hero of Alexandria, a Greek scientist of the first century A.D., devised a primitive form of steam engine which was labeled an "aeolipile." It was a hollow sphere fitted with a nozzle. When filled with water and heated, it expelled a strong jet of steam. The basic principle was to appear centuries later in such turbine-powered cars as the Rover and the Chrysler, among others. Some scholars contend that one of Hero's steam machines was rigged up to move about under its own power. Others say, not so. Regardless, Hero's device was a significant step toward mechanical propulsion. Hero is linked to the modern automobile by another invention: the "hodometer," or as we know it, the odometer.

With most of the educational facilities controlled by the central Church/State or its representatives throughout Europe, it is not surprising that various visions of the motorcar should spring up among men of the cloth. An English Franciscan monk, Roger Bacon, who lived from 1214 to 1294, predicted horseless carriages, along with the airplane and self-propelled ships. Other church scholars thought or sketched along similar lines—usually until their superiors dismissed their doodlings as handiwork of the Devil.

While most mortals would be more than content to confine their talents to painting such masterpieces as the "Mona Lisa" and the "Annunciation," Leonardo da Vinci, the Florentine (1452–1519), also devised contrivances for converting reciprocating motion into rotary movement, and a means whereby two wheels on a common axle could turn in a circle at differing speeds. He pondered, too, about carts being propelled by the muscle power of their passengers. Leonardo undertook to improve upon the basic "slab" wheel by devising flared spokes which better resisted side loads and permitted the construction of lighter wheels. But here at least his ideas were not too different from wheels made by the Greeks in 400 B.C.

The military establishment, usually receptive to any improvement in devices of destruction, was approached by Roberto Valturio in 1472. Valturio's suggestion, typical of others of its time, called for a mammoth war chariot to be driven by windmill sails. Their power was to be transmitted to wheels through an intricate system of gears and cranks.

Less lethal in intent, still dependent upon wind power, but quite successful in its major test was Simon Stevin's large square-rigged sail-cart built to operate along the Dutch beaches. In 1599 a historic ride was recorded—in one direction, downwind! No reports on how the band of notable passengers returned to its starting point. Indeed, for such a unique mode of transportation vital statistics are woefully lacking. Some accounts contend that Stevin's *zeylwagen* was steered by its forward wheels; other reports depict a tiller aft which turned the rear wheels much as one shifts the rudder of a boat. In either configuration, it was an early example of man in motion across land without depending on human or animal muscle power. But Stevin's sail-powered land barge did set the stage for a series of stimulating advancements.

One of the first to propose steam as the means of propelling a carriage was Giovanni Battista Della Porta (1538–1615). This Italian physicist of Pesaro produced a pump capable of raising water by means of steam pressure. He observed that such a mechanism should be able to serve in some fashion as a means of locomotion. One of his pupils, Solomon de Caous, was to try out the propulsion idea later in France. Unfortunately, before De Caous could demonstrate anything he was hustled off to an asylum at the suggestion of French clergymen who professed to be shocked by such experiments.

It remained for another Italian, Giovanni Branca, to convert the Della Porta idea and the De Caous effort into a simple steam turbine. Steam from a boiler escaping via a nozzle pushed against the perforated rim of a wheel. As this wheel spun it actuated through a set of gears a mechanism that was employed to grind chemicals. Thus, the turbine! Branca's written report on his experiments appeared in 1629. Perhaps Rube Goldberg chanced upon this during his formative years.

Perfected by a priest, this same basic idea turned up next in Peking, China, where it was used to drive a car. True, the vehicle was undersized and unmanned—today it would be described as a "working model." But the little vehicle set heads wagging among the notables at the Chinese court. Europe first learned about Father Ferdinand Verbiest and his steam cart in 1687. That year his *Astronomia Europoea* appeared in Latin, translated from the Chinese.

Father Verbiest (1623–1688), a Flemish Jesuit missionary and astronomer serving in China, not only was instrumental in fixing the boundary lines between China and Russia, but also found time to construct such oddities as his four-wheeled, two-foot-long steam-driven wagon. Verbiest's steam cart, steered in a circle by a fixed-position trailing fifth wheel, could operate for about one hour with a single filling of its aeolipile. The dates of Father Verbiest's steam cart experiments are imprecise—apparently the demonstrations took place sometime between 1665 and 1680.

While considerable scientific interest was concentrated on steam power, a little-publicized development was taking place under the direction of the French Jesuit Jean de Hautefeuille (1647–1724). This "mechanician" put together an internal-combustion engine. De Hautefeuille's 1678 engine had a cylinder and piston. It depended upon the explosions of gunpowder for its source of motion. Father de Hautefeuille (or d'Hautefeuille) also produced another innovative device: the spiral spring for the movement of watches. Yet the spiral spring was patented by the older Christian Huygens (1629–1695), a Dutch mathematician and noted astronomer. Apparently there was an amiable and profitable exchange of ideas between De Hautefeuille and Huygens since Huygens is said to have suggested the explosive internal-combustion engine. Huygens, incidentally, was the first to use a pendulum to regulate the movement of clocks.

Stepping a safe distance back from the internal-combustion gunpowder engine—in fact, let us leave it to history and the local noise abatement committee—we encounter another of Huygens's pupil-assistants, the French physicist Denis Papin (1647–1712). Papin, in 1690, designed a machine that employed water vapor to move a piston inside a vertical cylinder. When heated by an external source, the water would expand as steam and drive the piston upward. Permitted to cool, the vapor condensed and the pressure of the atmosphere, plus a nudge from gravity, drove the piston downward. Rather a clever arrangement.

In 1707 Papin had his device working well enough so that he could install it aboard a riverboat. But, alas, success brought on the ruin of his invention. German boatmen who earned their wages by the power of their muscles viewed Papin's powered vessel as a threat to their livelihood. They destroyed Papin's test craft along with its powerplant and, at the same time, its inventor's ambition. Papin, disconsolate, moved to England and did little experimenting thereafter. But his contributions did not disappear. His earlier hermetically sealed saucepan of 1681 laid the groundwork for the pressure cooker found in food processing plants and home kitchens.

An English military engineer, Captain Thomas Savery (1650–1715), patented what has been labeled, and probably correctly, as the first commercially successful atmospheric steam engine. This was in 1698. A pistonless mechanism for raising water, it was called Savery's pump and soon became popularized as "the miners' friend." Captain Savery is said by some historians to have introduced the term "horsepower" to compare the abilities of his engine to the output of a horse. A larger group ascribes the term to James Watt of Scotland. Regardless, the ubiquitous, reliable steam engine was just around the corner, and Savery had shown the way.

Shortly afterward, in 1705, a brilliant innovator and skilled blacksmith who was also a Baptist minister, the Englishman Thomas Newcomen (1663–1729), drew upon both Papin's principle and Savery's ideas to produce a better atmospheric (i.e., low-pressure) steam engine. Newcomen formed a partnership with Savery and greatly improved the mine engine to the point where, by 1725, it was in use at every mine in England. Newcomen's atmospheric engine could raise 2½ tons of water a distance of 100 feet for every bushel of coal burned to heat water and create the necessary steam.

Not all the eighteenth-century experimenters were captivated by steam power. One Frenchman, Jacques de Vaucanson (1709–1782), with many improvements in silk-weaving machinery to his credit, revived an earlier proposal and turned out a coach propelled by steel springs. His king, Louis XV, intrigued by the contraption, ordered one for his own amusement in 1748. Although its range was limited and its performance marginal, the vehicle provided a fresh topic of conversation at court . . . just as Father Verbiest's steam cart had delighted the Chinese rulers more than a hundred years earlier.

At the time when Newcomen's steam pumps were keeping English miners reasonably dry, America was just beginning to do something about the low-pressure steam engine. The New World's first powerplant was installed in 1753 at a copper mine in Belleville, New Jersey.

On our main stage appears now James Watt. His influence on the entire industrial age was to be enormous.

Besides improving the Newcomen-type pump, Watt, a Scottish mechanical engineer (1736–1819), invented the modern "condensing" steam engine. For this he received a patent in 1769. By means of sun-and-planet gears, and other mechanical devices equally exotic for their time, he converted reciprocating action into rotary motion. Not the least of his ten major improvements to the steam engine was the centrifugal governor for regulating speed. With Matthew Boulton he produced steam engines at the Soho Engineering Works in Birmingham, England. From about 1765 on, Watt devoted considerable study to the possible use of steam engines as a means to propel road vehicles. Although his work inspired others along this route, Watt himself did not try to produce a "steam-mobile." That honor was to come, and across the English Channel, to Captain Nicholas Joseph Cugnot (1725–1804), a French army engineer.

Rudimentary as it may have been—ponderous, unwieldly—Cugnot's machine is considered the earliest predecessor of the automobile. It established Paris as the birthplace of the motorcar.

Captain Cugnot was forty-four years old in 1769 when his three-wheeled cart made its first brief, lumbering run at a speed of two and a quarter miles per hour. A huge steam-producing copper cauldron hung suspended in mid-air ahead of a single, steerable, fifty-inch-diameter front wheel. Steam supplied to two vertical cylinders actuated pistons which, by means of connecting rods and cranks, delivered power to that artillery-wagon front wheel.

This was Cugnot's second machine, and it was meant to tow heavy artillery pieces. Its unique, precision-machined cylinders were the result of manufacturing reforms introduced by General Jean Baptiste Vaquette de Gribeauval. The General's fight for better metalworking methods and machinery not only gave Cugnot superlative cylinders, but enabled French artillery to be the best in Europe.

Thus, from the first wheels of Ur to the first self-propelled road vehicle at Paris, man had traveled down a long road at a slow pace. But now advancements were to come with almost stunning speed.

HYKSOS CHARIOT   Ancient Egypt was invaded from the east and occupied, circa 1700 B.C., by a large combination of Semitic peoples called Hyksos or Shepherd Kings. Although the invaders brought sadness, they also brought the horse-drawn chariot to the land of the Nile. The chariots were primitively built of wood, wicker and iron. The Egyptian craftsmen improved the design and later exported these ideas of the wheeled chariot to Greece, Rome, and then into Western Europe. Although not a self-propelled vehicle, this historic event is important because, without the idea of the wheel, we would have no automobiles.

SAIL WAGON   Throughout the ages man has tried to develop a self-propelled vehicle, whether it be steam, electric, spring, or sail driven. In 1599, a mast and sails were fitted to a lightweight wagon in the Netherlands. Trials revealed that it could travel over forty miles in two hours. It was, however, at the mercy of the wind velocity and direction and could not move against the wind or travel at all when there was no wind. This vehicle was developed by Simon Stevin, a military engineer, and was probably the first self-propelled vehicle to carry passengers. It was reportedly developed for military purposes.

VERBIEST'S STEAM CART When Portuguese explorers reached the coast of China in the early sixteenth century, they were soon followed by Roman Catholic missionaries. One of these was a Flemish Jesuit, Father Ferdinand Verbiest, who worked in China from 1659 until his death in 1688. He was extremely well educated and is credited with surveying and establishing the borders between Russia and China! While in China, Father Verbiest designed and constructed a steam-powered cart. A water-filled metal retort was suspended over a fire and the steam that rushed out of the nozzle was directed against a turbine-like pinwheel which, in turn, transferred the power to the front axle by means of very primitive spoke gears. Steering was accomplished by setting a trailing rear wheel. Verbiest was in charge of the Chinese Imperial Observatory and possibly stumbled across a description of the "fire cart" of old Chinese legends. In fact, ancient Chinese writings of 800 B.C. mention steam power! Although Father Verbiest's experiment was small and could not carry humans, it must be considered an automobile in view of the fact that it was self-propelled.

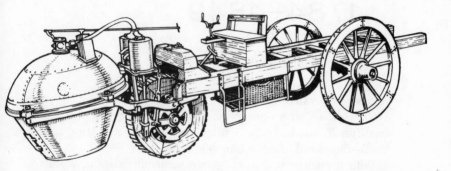

CUGNOT'S ARTILLERY TRACTOR   Acclaimed as the first self-propelled road vehicle, this steam-driven three-wheeler was constructed to tow heavy cannon. Depicted is 1771 version; designer was French army engineer Nicholas Cugnot. Unbalanced and top-heavy, its performance was marginal. One is displayed in Paris at the Conservatoire National des Arts et Métiers.

CHAPTER TWO

Trevithick and Evans and Those Road Locomotives 1784—1849

AMONG THE VARIOUS "firsts" established by Nicholas Cugnot in 1769 with his steam-propelled artillery tractor was that on its final run it smashed into a brick wall while attempting a turn. Voilà—the world's first automobile accident!

With a change in French government officials and a shift in army policy, support for Captain Cugnot's gun tractor was withdrawn. Soon he was forced to drop his work. However, a full-size Cugnot vehicle—either the repaired original or a carbon copy by one M. Brézin (authorities differ on this point)—remains today and is preserved in the Conservatoire National des Arts et Métiers in Paris.

With better knowledge of how to distribute a vehicle's weight, plus the use of a four-wheeled chassis, Captain Cugnot might have become "General" Cugnot.

Word of its performance, limited as it was, along with drawings of Cugnot's carriage, quickly crossed the Channel. One of James Watt's many talented assistants, William Murdock, who was Watt's representative in Cornwall, constructed a three-wheel, steam-driven model carriage which operated creditably. It was made prior to 1786, probably in 1784. Currently a copy is exhibited in the British Science Museum at South Kensington.

Murdock had to give up his experiments, however; as a worker for Boulton and Watt he was informed that the firm frowned on

24

such free-lance activities. Watt, who was busy mechanizing the textile industry by means of bigger and better steam power-plants, had subsequently dropped all thoughts of road machines. But in 1782 he had unveiled his version of the crank, which directly converted reciprocating movement into rotary power. That crank mechanism was to prove useful in countless applications, especially for self-propelled vehicles.

Richard Trevithick, ignoring Watt's public statements about the dangers of steam-propelled vehicles, installed higher pressure steam engines on full-size carriages. Trevithick's "road loco-motives" operated along the roadways of Cornwall in 1801 and through the streets of London by 1803. His single-cylinder steam plant ran at a pressure of about sixty pounds per square inch. For country operations and up and down hills he employed spur gears to give slow or high speeds. When additional financial backing could not be secured for bigger roadway machines, the inventive engineer from Cornwall turned his talents to railroad-ing, constructing the first steam engine to operate on rails. He also produced the first steam-powered threshing tractors.

Between the departure of Cugnot from the French scene and the start of the nineteenth century, two American advancements should be recorded. Jeremiah Wilkinson in 1776 perfected a method of handling material in a metalworking machine so that each resulting part could be interchanged with another. And Eli Whitney applied a similar system to the making of musket parts in 1799. From such knowledge were automobile dynasties to be established.

In other ways America was preparing for the horseless car-riage. The first U.S. toll roads were opened in Pennsylvania and Connecticut in 1792. Two years earlier a Salem, Massachusetts, inventor, Nathan Read, had been granted a patent for a four-wheel vehicle to be powered by a two-cylinder steam engine. A small operating model was tested. But there was no public (that is to say, financial) interest in his full-scale proposal.

Two significant patents issued in England near the turn of the century were forerunners of others that would combine one day to push steam out of the private transport picture. In 1791, John Barber patented a system that produced motion from the explo-sion of "inflammable air." Three years later Robert Street received a patent for an internal-combustion engine that operated on gas generated by the burning of tar or turpentine. Later Michael Faraday would identify this fuel as benzene.

While Trevithick's ponderous steam carriages were either captivating—or terrifying—Londoners, depending upon their spirit of adventure or their concern over a gigantic steam kettle dashing around on wheels, a quiet Swiss inventor, Isaac de Rivaz, was constructing the first vehicle to be driven by an internal-combustion engine. For this he received a patent from the French in 1807.

The De Rivaz four-wheeled machine mounted a single open-top vertical cylinder about sixty inches high. A crude electrical system known as a "Volta's pistol" was actuated by hand to provide the ignition. And the fuel which De Rivaz was igniting? Hydrogen!

Although De Rivaz's vehicle ran—fortunately without blowing him or itself to bits—its operation left much to be desired. Possibly the builder was a better chemist than a mechanic.

The early part of the nineteenth century saw steam carriages proliferating across England. Magnificent vehicles could carry up to twenty passengers and operate at speeds up to twenty miles per hour. Steam-driven tractors pulled even larger carriages. Trevithick, for example, towed joy-riding Londoners around in lavish sightseeing carriages at a more sedate ten miles per hour. But soon the railroads expanded and offered serious competition. Highway tolls for the steam carriages were increased sharply, sometimes with justification. After all, a 7,000-pound vehicle could easily chew up the light road surfacings of the day. So although the propulsion systems had improved enormously, and the carriages, too, by 1836 the best, the most advanced steam powerplants were busy working on the railroads.

William Murdock died in 1839; earlier he had been credited with the invention of the slide valve—that was in 1799. He was also said by some to have been the brains behind Watt's sun-and-planet gear movement.

At about the time Cugnot was expiring in near poverty and almost total obscurity in Brussels in 1804—his small government pension having been canceled—America was about to observe the operation of its first self-propelled land vehicle. This was to be no back-street, dark-of-the-night attempt, either. By means of advertisements in the local papers everybody was invited to witness the contraption perform in Centre Square, in the heart of Philadelphia. It was suggested that each onlooker help defray the cost of the demonstration by donating the magnificent sum of twenty-five cents. While a goodly number of witnesses did turn out, contributions were reported to be on the thin side.

Oliver Evans (1755–1819), born near Newport, Delaware, an inventor, engineer, and rare man of vision who has been called the "Watt of America," had tried earlier to convince investors that a steam-powered road cart could haul large loads great distances at less cost than horses. But in this he was unsuccessful even though he held a patent from the State of Maryland, dated 1787, for a high-pressure, steam-propelled wagon. (Prior to the establishment of a national patent system, patents were issued by the various states.)

A further attempt by Evans to drive a boat by steam power came close to succeeding, but he was thwarted in this instance by natural causes. A flood left his as-yet-untried experimental vessel grounded high and dry. Before it could be refloated, its engine was removed to power a mill.

The remarkable feature of Evans's steam engines was that they operated under pressures of up to one hundred pounds to the square inch. When informed of this practice, Watt, in England, was aghast. The famous James Watt had already made these two major pronouncements: (1) Steam power should not be employed for roadway vehicles; (2) Pressures greater than two or three pounds to the square inch were downright dangerous to workers and public alike.

Unable to find backing for his road vehicles, Evans secured a contract for the construction of a steam-powered dredge whose mission would be to clean out the muck from around the Philadelphia docks. Not only did Evans have a remarkably efficient powerplant, but by now he had a U.S. patent covering it. Evans's steam engines operated continuously and well in all kinds of mills. Sawyers used them to cut all types of material from wood to marble.

Evans had his dredge constructed at his own workyard which was a mile and a half inland from the Schuylkill River. Surely there was sufficient space somewhere along the waterfront to put together such a weighty barge?

It was in 1805 that his paddle-wheel barge with its scoop-bucket dredge equipment was completed. The inventive Mr. Evans had the barge hoisted atop a stout four-wheeled chassis. A front-mounted, smaller fifth wheel could be turned to guide the "Orukter Amphibolos" (amphibious digger), the name Evans had bestowed upon his vehicle-dredge. The flat-bottomed scow was thirty feet long and twelve feet wide; it weighed nearly 35,000 pounds. It was propelled through the streets of Philadelphia and around Centre Square on its heavy temporary chassis by one of Evans's amazingly small, very efficient, single-cylinder engines. The cylinder diameter was five inches; the piston stroke was nineteen inches.

One of the Orukter's axles was driven by a belt from the flywheel mechanism of the engine. When later launched, and freed of its land carriage, this power was applied to a stern-mounted paddle wheel. The scoop-buckets were also rotated in a continuous circle by that same powerful little steam engine.

So while the world's first "automobile" was an artillery tractor, America's first "automobile" was a steam-powered dredge which ran on temporary wheels.

Other road machines in the United States which followed Evans's effort included one attributed to two brothers named Johnson, also Philadelphians. Their experiments ended in disaster for their vehicle and near obscurity for themselves. But the Johnson machine was said to have proven its ability during a brief run.

Thomas Blanchard of Massachusetts turned out a steam carriage around 1825. Fortunately, Blanchard's work and road demonstrations were covered in detail by the Springfield newspapers. In addition, his accomplishments, luckily for the historians, were placed on the record by state officials.

With steam railroad locomotives and steam farm tractors no longer a novelty, a growing group of American inventors began to focus their attention on the internal-combustion engine. Some had access to the foreign press and overseas technical journals, and some exchanged news directly with European experimenters. But in all too many instances semi-skilled tinkerers duplicated one another's "breakthrough" efforts, often duplicating mistakes. Without too many realizing it, basic devices and systems were "reinvented" over and over.

On the more positive side, New Hampshire resident Samuel Morey secured a patent in April of 1826 for a two-cycle gas-and-vapor engine. It featured a somewhat crude carburetor, poppet valves, electric spark, and water cooling. A copy of the Morey engine, America's first internal-combustion powerplant, can be seen at Southampton, New York, in the Long Island Automotive Museum.

While trying their hand with the internal-combustion powerplant, some influential Americans were expressing concern over the lack of roadways, especially toward the west. In 1806, the Federal government launched a construction program for the "National Road." It was to stretch from the banks of the Potomac to the Mississippi River. But by 1837 money and enthusiasm had run out; the project was abandoned as a Federal undertaking; completed sections were turned over to the various states.

Although roadways came slowly, one helpful bit of news for internal-combustion experimenters was Michael Faraday's announcement, in 1825, of the substance benzene. He had detected it in tar derived from coal. The noted English chemist and physicist thus provided a dependable and stable fuel for the engine builder.

The 1830s produced another bonanza, a batch of infants who were one day to make significant contributions to the automobile. For instance, Siegfried Markus was born in 1831. And although the world lost sturdy Dick Trevithick in 1833, it gained a Studebaker, John M., that same year. Gottlieb Daimler made his appearance in 1834. This was the year in which England suffered a major steam bus accident with heavy loss of life. Apparently Watt was right, or perhaps it was because the roadways were in deplorable condition. Similar catastrophes were to follow with the result that restrictive British legislation affecting all powered road vehicles loomed over the horizon. France, with a better system of roads, the Routes Nationales, earlier sponsored by Napoleon, had inaugurated steam coach services, but there, too, the steamers' rise and decline would parallel British operations.

A determined inventor of note during the years 1830 to 1850

was the American Charles Goodyear. Considered something of an eccentric by his Massachusetts neighbors in Woburn because he placed more importance upon his experiments than the welfare of his family, Goodyear just would not give up a lengthy quest to tame rubber. By 1839 he had purchased patent rights to a sulphur treatment process. He carried this work forward, eventually making rubber permanently elastic and non-sticking. When he died in 1860 his name was known around the world. At the time of his death his business debts, resulting primarily from the over-zealous promotion of his product, amounted to several hundred thousand dollars. But this only meant, in the minds of those same neighbors, that Goodyear had achieved the status of genius.

During the first half of the nineteenth century some more very special infants arrived on the scene. This representative sampling is of particular interest to the American automotive picture.

Born 1843, Albert A. Pope—he would organize the U.S. bicycle industry, later help convert it to motorcar production.

Born 1843, Henry M. Leland—he would set up first the Cadillac, then the Lincoln motor firms.

Born 1845, Thomas B. Jeffery—he would become president of Nash.

Born 1846, George N. Pierce—he would establish the Pierce-Arrow concern.

Born 1849, George Baldwin Selden—he would apply for an all-inclusive U.S. patent for a road machine powered by an internal-combustion powerplant. He would be granted that patent by the Federal government.

Born 1849, twins, Francis E. and Freelan O. Stanley—after revolutionizing the photographic industry they would turn to steam-car manufacture.

Obviously the old order was changing. A new group of leaders was due on the automotive scene. True, much progress had been made, but major breakthroughs were still to come. To observe these vast changes we move on to the pensive French genius Jean-Joseph Étienne Lenoir.

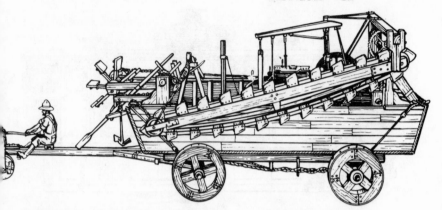

AMERICA'S CLAIM TO FAME This steam-powered dredge, designed by Oliver Evans to operate along the Philadelphia waterfront, was moved during July of 1805 from an inland construction site to water's edge on a temporary five-wheeled chassis propelled by the dredge mechanism's engine. Inventor Evans called it his "Orukter Amphibolos" (amphibious digger). The scow plus chassis and engine weighed a total of 40,000 pounds.

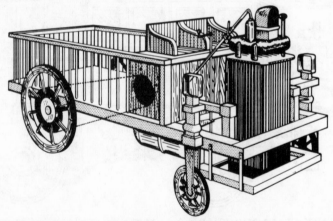

PECQUEUR STEAM VEHICLE In 1828 a French inventor, Onesiphore Pecqueur, constructed a steam-powered carriage that was even fitted with a differential on the rear driving axle. His steering mechanism also showed exceptional foresight because it was very similar to the mechanism used in the present-day automobile. Unfortunately, as is often the case, he was too far ahead of his time and died a poor man.

CHURCH STEAM CARRIAGE Put into operation between London and Birmingham, William Church's steam carriages of 1832 were soon outmoded by competition from a new railway line. Low ground clearance and ornate appearance were probably accentuated by artists of the time, and perpetuated over the years.

HANCOCK OMNIBUS Between 1832 and 1834, Walter Hancock became the most successful builder and operator of steam-powered highway carriages in Great Britain. His "Enterprise" carried sixteen; although its boiler blew up once there were no injuries. Hancock's nine machines carried about 4,000 passengers between London and Paddington.

CHAPTER THREE

Internal Combustion and the First "Real" Car 1850–1885

BEFORE RAISING the curtain on the talented Frenchman Jean-Joseph Étienne Lenoir (1822–1900) and his internal-combustion gaseous engine, let it be noted for the record that in 1823 Samuel Brown of London burned a mixture of alcohol and air in a large cylinder. When permitted to cool, this arrangement created a vacuum which actuated a piston. Brown's "patent gas vacuum engine" not only worked, but it propelled a small test vehicle in 1824. However, its power output must have been minuscule, because the carriage with its slow and labored operation attracted scant attention.

Two Italians had done somewhat better. Eugenio Barsanti and Felice Matteucci constructed a prototype engine at Florence in 1856, which featured two cylinders and worked on a three-stroke cycle. Fuel was a mixture of air and inflammable gas—there was no "compression" stroke (cycle). It is said that they anticipated switching to benzene fuel, but their studies terminated when Barsanti died in 1864. One of the Barsanti-Matteucci powerplants exhibited in England was viewed by a German, Nikolaus August Otto. It served to encourage Herr Otto to continue with his own experiments.

To have patented his gas engine in 1859, Étienne Lenoir must have been busy developing it through most of the 1850s. The engine he displayed in 1860 had one cylinder. A mixture of coal, gas, and air was fed alternately to opposite ends of a horizontal cylinder. An electric spark provided by batteries ignited the fuel.

The resulting explosions moved a piston back and forth. A large spoked flywheel was rotated in a vertical plane. There was no means of compressing the air-gas mixture.

The piston, as it traveled horizontally, moved a rod which could supply power by a chain or a belt to small machine tools, a saw, a pump, or other equipment. Running on illuminating gas, a substance readily available in many of the larger communities, Lenoir's two-cycle engine worked sufficiently well to be in commercial demand. It was duplicated under license outside of France. But it still lacked that all-important compression stroke.

With all due respect to Lenoir, it appears obvious that much of his operating mechanism had been borrowed from contemporary steam engine design. Lenoir used a governor much like Watt's to control the flow of gas to his cylinder. The motion of the piston was transmitted by connecting rod and crank just as in Watt's powerplants. At quick glance and while it was at rest, the casual observer might have passed by Lenoir's device as being just another steam machine. But it represented a most important milestone in i.c. (internal combustion) progress.

For reasons lost to posterity, M. Lenoir's road experiments in 1862, with one of his engines running off liquid fuel and utilizing a "surface vaporizer" or carburetor, have been little publicized. Perhaps because the test vehicle, a rather heavy-looking carriage as depicted in his drawings, required something like six hours to cover an estimated six miles. But those six miles would appear particularly significant even if the inventor had not pursued further his vehicle propulsion attempts. The carriage, incidentally, probably had full-elliptic springs in front, a chain drive to the rear wheels, and a vertical steering wheel. All this is according to M. Lenoir's artwork—his carriage did not survive the years.

The idea for a "four-stroke cycle" internal-combustion engine is credited to a French engineer, Alphonse Beau de Rochas. In 1862 De Rochas released a paper on his studies; this treatise sparked the imagination of numerous experimenters.

The town of Malchin, in East Germany, about 90 miles north of Berlin, currently identifies itself as the birthplace, in 1831, of Siegfried Markus, "inventor of the automobile." In 1865, in Vienna, Markus ran a four-wheeled cart propelled by a single-cylinder, two-cycle engine. He had developed a "jet" carburetor, probably the first, and had employed gasoline as his fuel. Markus's two-cycle motor ran for but a short distance. However, a second machine by Markus, called the "Strassenwagen," mounted a single-cylinder, four-cycle gasoline engine; it made numerous successful appearances in public during 1874 and 1875. The Technisches Museum für Industrie und Gewerbe in Vienna presently displays a Markus motor wagon.

While these powerplants and vehicles were progressing in Europe, America was involved in a Civil War (1861–1865) which drew the talents of most of her inventors, mechanics, scientists, and designers. But just before hostilities broke out, Sylvester Hayward Roper of Roxbury, Massachusetts, had started working with high-pressure steam road machines following Oliver Evans's example by utilizing lighter and stronger boilers. Roper's steam carriages from 1859 to 1863 seated two passengers forward, and were steered by a tiller bar. All the steam and driving mechanisms were positioned aft in place of any payload compartment. Roper's chassis appears to be from a work wagon. Follow-up refinements meant a smaller steam plant amidships under a single seat for two. The water tank was aft and looked much like a fancy trunk. The steam exhaust stack protruded downward from the center of the vehicle. Again, large carriage wheels and a wagon-like appearance. One of these machines is displayed at the Henry Ford Museum in Dearborn, Michigan.

From four-wheeled vehicles, Mr. Roper turned to steam-propelled, two-wheel velocipedes. He was killed in 1896 in Boston when one of these two-wheelers crashed. It was estimated that he was traveling about 30 mph. along the Charles River Race Track at the time of the accident. A Roper steam velocipede can be found in the Smithsonian Institution in Washington, D.C.

Other American steam pioneers busy during the 1860s included John A. Reed of New York City and Frank Curtis of Newburyport, Massachusetts. Henry Seth Taylor completed Canada's first steam-powered four-wheeler in 1867. The restored Taylor machine is now at the Ontario Science Center in Toronto.

Unfortunately for the long-term appeal of steam machines, back in the 1850s the first crude oil fields had been opened in Pennsylvania. In 1858 and 1859 around Titusville and Tidioute, special derricks were used to drill specifically for oil. Until this time natural mineral oil—petroleum, as we know it today—had been sold by traveling tent shows and by some pharmacies as "Seneca oil" (also called "snake oil") as a cure-all for various human and animal ailments. The oil, then, had been obtained by soaking it up from the surface of shallow ponds. This was usually done by Indians, who also had the custom of burning it on the waters during festival periods.

Petroleum gradually displaced whale oil for inexpensive illumination in the lamps of America. Even more importantly its availability encouraged experimenters to try it in the form of naphtha as a fuel for the newfangled internal-combustion engines. After these American "strikes," oil reserves were tapped next in Rumania and Russia.

Thus, we have arrived at a significant point in automotive progress. (1) Lenoir has invented the internal-combustion engine. (2) Otto has viewed the Barsanti-Matteucci engine. (3) Beau de Rochas has proposed the vital fourth function for the piston—the compression stroke.

Onto our stage now comes a group of gifted Germans: Nikolaus August Otto (1832–1891), Eugen Langen (1833–1895), Gottlieb Daimler (1834–1900), Karl Benz (1844–1929), and Wilhelm Maybach (1847–1929)—plus an assortment of well-financed friends, gifted associates, and cooperative relatives. These people would be associated with the first patented four-stroke ("Otto cycle") engine and the first "real" automobile.

It was in 1861 that the brothers Nikolaus and Wilhelm Otto of Cologne applied for a patent for a two-cycle engine. However, their powerplant was considered too much like Lenoir's by the examining authorities and their request was denied. Wilhelm gave up at that point, but Nikolaus continued his quest and secured the backing of Eugen Langen in 1864. The first Otto & Langen engine patented in 1866 was put into production and sold as a stationary powerplant. Though more efficient, it did not differ greatly from the earlier Lenoir unit.

When Gottlieb Daimler joined the Deutzer Gasmotorenfabrik enterprise in 1872 as chief engineer, he applied the De Rochas idea, redesigning the Otto & Langen illuminating gas engine to incorporate the four-cycle principle and to operate from a liquid fuel supply. Wilhelm Maybach entered the firm and helped raise production to unprecedented heights: upwards of 4,000 Otto engines were turned out in Germany and, under license, in England by 1875. During the next year Daimler and Maybach completed work on their four-stroke engine for Otto & Langen. It became known as the "Otto Silent Gas Engine"—silent, that is, in comparison to its two-cycle predecessor.

Six Otto & Langen two-cycle engines were displayed at the Philadelphia Centennial Exposition in 1876. They were the first European powerplants of the internal-combustion category to be seen in the United States. They were to have a profound effect on the growth of automotive interest in America. A lone U.S.-made engine, the Brayton, was exhibited at the same great fair.

Another maker of two-stroke engines was Karl Benz of Mannheim. Many authorities consider him as the one most responsible for the first "recognizable" motorcar. But even with an electrical ignition system, Benz decided his two-stroker was unsuited to drive a vehicle. Turning to a four-stroke unit, he mounted it on a three-wheeled tubular chassis in 1885.

Consider, for a moment, Herr Benz's revolutionary engine: four-stroke, single-cylinder, 400 revolutions per minute. Slide valve intake, poppet valve exhaust. Water-cooled with no recirculation of the coolant—as it boiled away it had to be replaced. Electric ignition via battery and *Ruhmkorpf* "tremble" coil. Surface carburetor. Envision his car: engine mounted at the rear with crankshaft in the vertical position. Large, horizontal, open-spoked flywheel with a diameter almost as wide as the chassis. Power drive was by crank-operated pulley, then via belt to a countershaft, thence by chains to the back wheels.

By 1887 Benz had more advanced vehicles which could whiz along at fourteen miles per hour. They employed a "low" gear for stall-free starting. Émile Roger became the exclusive Benz dealer in Paris. Both Benz and Roger were selling cars to the public between 1888 and 1890.

Daimler had operated a wood-frame motorcycle in 1885 powered by his single-cylinder, four-cycle gasoline engine. The machine was fitted with two small outrigger side wheels to keep it upright. Daimler also demonstrated a four-wheel *Motorwagen* in 1886. Yet the Benz three-wheel vehicle gets top honors from both historians and auto buffs as the world's first "real" car. Benz received German Patent DRP #37,435 in January 1886 for a "carriage with gas engine." Would you believe that Herr Benz and Herr Daimler never met?

During the years 1850 to 1881, the following made their first public appearance . . . babes in arms who were to be among those destined to make automotive history.

Born 1850, Edwin R. Thomas—he would win the New York to Paris race.

Born 1855, David Dunbar Buick—his brief contribution would mean the creation of the Buick Manufacturing Company and the development of the valve-in-head engine.

Born 1856, the Marquis Albert de Dion.

Born 1857, Charles Jasper Glidden—he would organize the famous Glidden Tours; Elwood G. Haynes—he would pioneer the use of aluminum in cars.

Born 1858, Rudolf Diesel, a German who would grow up in France and England.

Born 1860, William Crapo Durant—he would launch General Motors.

Born 1863, Henry Ford—on a farm near Dearborn, Michigan; James W. Packard—he would head the Packard Motor Company.

Born 1864, John Dodge—at one time he would own five percent of the Ford Motor Company; Charles W. Nash—he would head both the Buick and the Nash concerns; Ransom Eli Olds— the mass-production genius who developed both the Oldsmobile and Reo cars.

Born 1866, Windsor T. White—with brother Rollin he would produce the White Steamer; Giovanni Agnelli—founder of the Italian F.I.A.T. motor empire; Martin Fischer—Swiss builder of the Turricum cars.

Born 1867, Herbert H. Franklin—he would pioneer the air-cooled car.

Born 1868, Horace Dodge—with brother John he would receive $25,000,000 for this original $20,000 investment in Ford's third firm.

Born 1871, Harry C. Stutz—his Stutz cars would be made until 1919; Robert Samuel McLaughlin—he would build Canada's first production car.

Born 1875, railroadman Walter P. Chrysler; Alfred P. Sloan, Jr.—he would turn General Motors into the world's largest and most profitable auto maker; Henry A. Miller—developer of racing engines; Ferdinand Porsche of Volkswagen and Porsche car fame.

Born 1876, Charles F. Kettering—"Boss Ket" would head G.M. research.

Born 1877, Frederick Samuel Duesenberg.

Born 1878, Louis-Joseph Chevrolet.

Born 1881, Vincenzo Lancia—designer of elegant Italian cars; Ettore Isodoro Arco Bugatti.

In Germany, Benz had been credited with the world's first recognizable car. Daimler had been proclaimed as a worthy contemporary. What of progress in other countries?

ROPER STEAMER Sylvester H. Roper of Roxbury, Massachusetts, constructed many steam-powered wagons—this 1863 carriage could cruise at 20 mph. Boiler was mounted under the seat; tank at rear held water supply; hand crank pivoted the front wheel assembly. A similar Roper wagon is displayed at the Henry Ford Museum, Dearborn, Michigan.

DUDGEON ROAD "LOCOMOTIVE" With ten passengers seated over its horizontal boiler, Richard Dudgeon's steam-driven road machine was much like contemporary railroad engines. Main differences: solid wood wheels were unflanged, front axle pivoted for steering. This 1867 machine is on display at the Museum of Transportation, Larz Anderson Park, Brookline, Massachusetts.

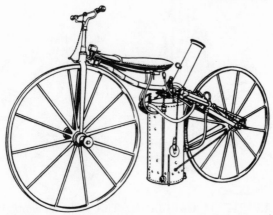

ROPER STEAM VELOCIPEDE Ingenious two-wheeler used for exhibitions and built by Sylvester H. Roper had vertical boiler and two oscillating steam cylinders with a "chimney" between. The water tank did double duty as the saddle. This is the oldest self-propelled road vehicle displayed by the Smithsonian. Roper was killed June 1, 1896, on a similar steam velocipede which is shown by Bellm's museum at Sarasota, Florida.

FIRST SUCCESSFUL CAR? Ninety miles north of Berlin in Malchin, now in East Germany, Siegfried Markus first operated this four-cycle, single-cylinder "petrol gas" car in 1874 or 1875. Earlier he had developed a jet carburetor and, in 1864, a somewhat undependable vehicle whose performance, if any, is shrouded in mystery. Markus did not follow up his pioneering automotive work. This vehicle is displayed at the Technisches Museum für Industrie und Gewerbe in Vienna.

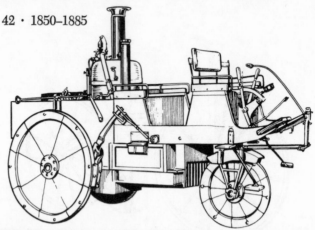

GRENVILLE STEAM CARRIAGE This early attempt at a self-powered vehicle took place at Newton Abbot, England, in 1875. The solid wooden-wheeled three-wheeler had an enormous boiler and steam engine that left room only for the driver and two passengers. It seems that many pioneers selected three in lieu of four wheels for their initial attempt at the automobile. Note the two levers, foot pedal and tiller steering. Only one instrument was provided, the boiler pressure gage. The design did not progress beyond the experimental stage and can be seen today in the Bristol City Museum, Department of Technology, Bristol, England.

AMÉDÉE BOLLÉE, "LA MANCELLE" In 1878, Amédée Bollée, père (or senior), a bellmaker of Le Mans, France, built this steam-driven vehicle which he named "La Mancelle." Notice the convertible top. The car can be seen today at the Musée de la Voiture et du Tourisme, Château de Compiègne, Oise, France. Bollée steamers were exported to Germany and a few were built there under license. One of these cars was taken on a demonstration trip to St. Petersburg, Russia!

SELDEN PATENT On May 8, 1879, George Baldwin Selden of Rochester, New York, an inventor and attorney, applied for a patent for a "cheap road-locomotive . . . propelled by a liquid-hydrocarbon engine of the compression type," which he had designed in 1877. With application held open and updated several times, Patent No. 549,160 finally was issued on November 5, 1895. In 1905 this second "latter-day" Selden car, which can be seen at the Henry Ford Museum, was constructed and tested.

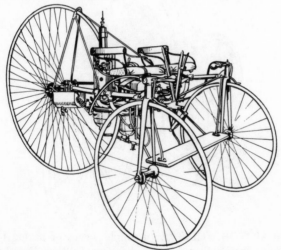

LONG STEAM TRICYCLE Around 1880, George A. Long of Northfield, Massachusetts, operated his steam-driven machine. The larger five-foot-diameter rear wheel was driven by a choice of two pulleys on the crankshaft. Gasoline was burned to generate steam pressure of 100 pounds per square inch. Mr. Long was granted Patent No. 281,091 on July 10, 1883, for this steam road vehicle. Restored tricycle is in the Smithsonian.

COPELAND STEAM BICYCLE Mating a Star bicycle with a one-cylinder steam engine, Lucius Copeland of Phoenix, Arizona, reached speeds of 15 mph. with his imaginative two-wheeler. From this Copeland moved on to tricycles, and even four-wheeled, steam-propelled configurations.

DAIMLER MOTORCYCLE As a simple means of testing his hot-tube ignition, single-cylinder gasoline engine, Gottlieb Daimler built this wood-framed cycle in 1885. Not much of a cyclist, he added small supporting side wheels. The vehicle was operated around Bad Cannstatt, Germany, near Stuttgart. Daimler, by inspiring Panhard-Levassor and Peugeot, became godfather to the French automotive industry.

CHAPTER FOUR

Motorizing the Buggy 1886—1899

WITH THE APPEARANCE of the internal-combustion-powered motor vehicle in 1885 in Germany and its subsequent improvement by Benz and Daimler, the steam-propelled road machine had encountered a formidable rival for public favor. There would be more steam cars built, primarily for personal transportation, even into the 1920s, but they were to be relegated to a very minor role.

In England, in fact, steam had been legislated off the highways back in 1865 by the restrictive "Locomotives on Highways Act." This law required a man on foot to precede any road machine; by day he had to carry a warning flag, by night a lantern. This regulation, which halted automotive progress throughout the British Isles, regardless of motive power, was not rescinded until 1896: thirty-one lost years for most English experimenters.

At America's Centennial affair at Philadelphia in 1876, along with the Otto & Langen internal-combustion engines, a single Brayton engine had been displayed—also an i.c. affair. George Bailey Brayton of Boston had patented his two-cycle gasoline engine in 1872. At the fair the Brayton powerplant operated an air pump for an aquarium. It had drawn the rapt attention of George Baldwin Selden, a patent lawyer from Rochester, New York, who had been experimenting with gasoline engines.

Attorney Selden realized that the Brayton Ready Motor, produced by the Pennsylvania Motor Company of Philadelphia, and a quiet-running affair compared to the Otto, could be the basis of an excellent powerplant for a horseless carriage. At the Centennial the Otto engines ran on illuminating gas. The Brayton used crude petroleum.

Nikolaus Otto was intrigued by the Brayton Ready Motor, too. While visiting the fair he placed an order for two motors with P.M.C. agents.

In 1876, Selden drew up plans for a three-cylinder motor and a vehicle on which to mount it. Then, in 1879, he applied for a patent on an automobile incorporating an improved version of the two-cycle Brayton. Under the patent office rules of the time he was permitted to keep his application "pending" by filing a series of updated amendments. Finally, his application was granted in 1895. By that time, as we shall see, there were to be many manufacturers as well as many assemblers of motorcars in America. Most came to believe that the Selden patent blanketed their efforts and put them in a position of infringement.

Interestingly enough the Selden patent drawings were witnessed by one "Geo. Eastman." Considering the inventive nature of Kodak's George Eastman and the fact that both he and Selden hailed from Rochester, it is reasonable to assume that the leading maker of photographic paraphernalia in the U.S. had been following Selden's efforts to design a "safe, simple, and cheap road-locomotive light in weight, easy to control, and possessed of sufficient power to overcome any ordinary inclination"—to quote the language of Letters Patent No. 549,160, dated November 5, 1895, as issued by the United States Patent Office.

While it has been popular to portray inventor Selden as a rapacious rascal scheming to defraud the auto makers of America of their hard-earned profits by means of a money-grubbing licensing plan, a closer look reveals him in a somewhat different light, at least to some researchers.

Four years after he was recognized as the inventor of the "road engine" (that patent title included the design for his vehicle and his version of an improved two-cycle powerplant), Selden assigned his patent rights for a payment of $10,000 and two percent of any possible profits to the Electric Vehicle Company of New York City. E.V.C. was a combine, a conglomerate, that expected to flood the cities of America with electric taxicabs. Yet it was from every maker of gasoline cars that the outfit intended to secure royalty payments. In the long run, Selden collected something under $200,000, which certainly was not all profit for him. His complete faith in the two-cycle engine would later turn out to be his downfall in the courtroom.

This was a time when America's automotive innovators had various powerplants available to them on the open market. For their four-wheel chassis they could pick from numerous makes and styles of light carriages, or heavier work wagons. The giant Durant-Dort concern (Flint, Michigan) and the Studebaker Brothers (South Bend, Indiana) were just two major wagon-carriage manufacturers who kept lowering prices and improving the durability of their horse-drawn products.

In some countries automotive progress was in a more advanced stage. In Denmark during 1886, A. F. Hammel and H. U. Johansen built the "Hammelvognen." Today it is displayed at the Danmarks Tekniske Museum in Helsingør. The car ran as recently as 1954 when it traveled fifty-six miles in just over twelve hours. Its water-cooled, horizontal, twin-cylinder engine put out 3.5 horsepower at 400 revolutions per minute.

Two other Danish car builders, both of whom rolled out four-wheeled vehicles in 1889, were H. C. Christiansen, who used a water-cooled, one-cylinder engine; and A. L. Brems, who employed an air-cooled, single-cylinder powerplant.

French rights to Daimler's engine were purchased by Édouard Sarazin on behalf of the firm of Perrin, Panhard & Cie. in 1887.

Two years later Émile Constant Levassor, who had married Sarazin's widow and consequently under French law automatically acquired rights to the Daimler powerplant, unveiled a wagon-like, rear-engined prototype. In 1891 the first Panhard-Levassor rolled out of the factory with the "Système Panhard & Levassor"—which meant that the motor was mounted at the front above the wheels for better roadability. It also featured a gearbox.

The Peugeot name appeared on the French motoring scene in 1891 when bicycle-builder Armand Peugeot displayed a quadricycle driven by a two-cylinder Daimler motor.

In Sweden, steam still occupied the attention of many. Jöns and Anders Cederholm, brothers, linked up as designer and builder, respectively, of a one-cylinder, steam-driven machine. Their "Cederholm" had only marginal performance, but an improved two-cylinder steamer made in 1894 did better and the machine can be seen now at the Kloster Museum in Ystad.

In England, the Daimler Motor Syndicate was formed in 1893 to secure British rights to Gottlieb Daimler's engine patents. The name of the firm was changed to Daimler Motor Company, Ltd., three years later.

In Grand Rapids, Michigan, the Sintz Machinery Company offered plans for a one-cylinder, two-cycle gasoline engine. They would also supply the completed unit ready to operate. There were comparable powerplants busily chugging away in machine shops, in boats, and in mining operations across America. Another outfit making Brayton-type engines was the Connelly Motor Company of New York City. And it was estimated that upwards of 18,000 Otto-type engines were in use in the United States before 1890.

"America's first workable gasoline-engine vehicle" is how government authorities label the four-wheeler designed by Charles E. Duryea and built, then driven on September 22, 1893, by his brother J. Frank Duryea. The key word in that description is *workable*. Actually, other American machines preceded the Duryea, but unlike it they did not win road races, nor, like the Duryea, did they ever go into series production. The first Duryea consisted of a used carriage and a single-cylinder, two-cycle, Otto-type engine much modified by Frank, who is credited with the first electric ignition and spray carburetor on a working U.S. vehicle.

Other gasoline cars in America during the early 1890s include one by Henry Nadig, which he built and operated in the Allentown-Bethlehem, Pennsylvania, area about 1891. Little survives in the way of specific details, and no artifacts.

But for some, the 1891 Lambert, which ran first indoors, then on the streets of Ohio City, Ohio, will always be "Number One." John William Lambert intended to produce his two-cylinder-engine-powered vehicle in quantity, but when orders were lacking, then the prototype car destroyed in a fire, Lambert dropped out of the automotive picture completely. Later, although strongly urged, he refused firmly to participate in any quest for "first" honors.

The Milwaukee, Wisconsin, Public Museum today displays the 1892 Schloemer motor wagon, which was constructed by Gottfried Schloemer and Frank Toepfer. A car completed by Charles H. Black in 1893 is exhibited in Indianapolis, Indiana, at the Children's Museum.

At a time when more than ten million Americans rode bicycles, the Chicago Fair of 1893 presented a small collection of electric and steam carriages. A display by Claude Sintz highlighted his small but reliable gasoline engine and attracted car builders-to-be. To further inspire them, piano-maker William Steinway showed a Daimler car. A Benz was also exhibited.

By 1893, James Ward Packard had the design work complete for his first car. Ransom E. Olds had already built, and sold for delivery overseas, a steam car. He had his first gasoline vehicle running in 1894. During that year the Benz European organization sold sixty-seven cars. In Kokomo, Indiana, Edgar Apperson operated his first car; it was built for Elwood G. Haynes by Edgar and his brother Elmer. Assisting them was Jonathan D. Maxwell, who ran a bicycle repair business with Elmer. Haynes operated the car publicly during a Fourth of July parade in 1894.

In Europe during 1894, city-to-city performance trials and outright road races whipped up great public interest in the motorcar. The Paris-Rouen Trial was the first of its kind, followed by the Paris-Bordeaux-Paris run in 1895.

Because of the popularity of racing events, the *Chicago Times-Herald* newspaper sponsored a combination testing trials and road competition. Entries were checked in a testing rack before and after an extensive street race. The racing portion of the contest was held on Nobember 28, 1895, which was a miserable Thanksgiving Day, over icy, snow-drifted streets. Entrants departed from Jackson Park in Chicago and headed northward, paralleling the Lake Michigan waterfront to Evanston, then returned by a more inland route.

Covering fifty-four miles in near-freezing, blustery weather, a Duryea machine, driven by J. Frank Duryea with umpire Arthur White as his passenger, was first across the finish line and ever since has been known as the "winner." But its $2,000 first-prize purse also included points for the range of speed it displayed during the static tests and for its pulling power, which was similarly recorded. The Duryea used a water-cooled, four-stroke engine. Weighing 700 pounds, it featured three forward speeds with a top of 18 mph., plus reverse. All machinery was concealed. It was an advanced, dependable car and, all things considered, deserved its victory.

Second money in the *Times-Herald* competition went to a

Benz, which crossed the finish line under the guidance of its umpire, Charles Brady King of Detroit. Its driver, Oscar Mueller, had collapsed from the biting cold. Because the car would be disqualified if both men were not aboard at the finish, King took over the driving duties while supporting Mueller.

The Chicago contest captured headlines across the country. Interest in automobiles quickened. New concerns jumped onto the motorized bandwagon. Soon, by rough count some 300 self-propelled vehicles were under construction or nearing completion. The Duryea Motor Wagon Company was formed in 1895. The Haynes-Apperson firm was organized and started to produce cars in 1896. Electric runabouts were being turned out by the Columbia Electric Company under the direction of Col. Albert A. Pope. Henry Ford operated his first car, a twin-cylinder, four-horsepower quadricycle on June 4, 1896. The first car by Alexander Winton was built the same year. It rode on pneumatic tires; these were the first in the United States and were made by Benjamin Franklin Goodrich. Eight years earlier the pneumatic tire had been "re-invented" by Dr. John B. Dunlop in Ireland for bicycle use.

In 1896, also, Charles B. King completed his first vehicle. The Stanley twins, Francis and Freelan of Newton, Massachusetts, sold their photographic plate business and turned their considerable talents to steam cars. On September 7, 1896, the first U.S. auto race on a closed course was held at the old Narragansett Park race track in Rhode Island. It was won by a Riker Electric Stanhope, but the affair was so dull that spectators took up the chant, "Get a horse!" It was a popular cry everywhere; any motorist experiencing difficulties with his vehicle could expect to be greeted by that admonition. In fact, that's what he usually did—get a farmer with a horse to tow his disabled vehicle back to town, or, if just mired down in a mudhole, to pull it free onto solid ground.

The first American buyer of a car, said to be George H. Morrill, Jr., of Norwood, Massachusetts, purchased a Duryea. Another Duryea went to the Barnum & Bailey circus, which ran it in street parades and during performances to generate publicity. Olds's first experimental gas car had two seats which held four passengers.

During 1897 the first Stanley Steamer appeared, and the Winton Motor Carriage Company sold its first machine. Mr. Winton set the motor world buzzing when he drove from Cleveland, Ohio, to New York City, a distance of 707 miles, in seventy-eight hours and forty-five minutes. The Olds Motor Vehicle Company was established in 1897 as the first Michigan auto maker. Automobile insurance was issued to a Massachusetts mechanic, Gilbert Loomis. He paid $7.50 for $1,000 worth of liability coverage. There being no official auto forms, the agreement was made out on a standard horse-drawn vehicle certificate—with numerous corrective amendments.

The first "independent" auto dealership was organized by William E. Metzger of Detroit in 1898. That same year a "franchised" dealership was created by H. O. Koller of Reading, Pennsylvania, so that in his area he could represent exclusively the Winton concern. In Chicago, Mrs. John H. Phillips made news by becoming the first American female driver to acquire an operator's license.

The Studebaker clan started making car bodies. The first auto parts supply house was opened in St. Louis, Missouri, by A. L. Dyke in 1899. The Packard car made its bow in 1899; it was produced in Warren, Ohio, by the Ohio Automobile Company. The Olds Motor Works, Ransom Olds's second company, moved from Lansing, Michigan, to Detroit and built the first U.S. factory for the making of motorcars. The Pope Manufacturing Company of Hartford, Connecticut, demonstrated its versatility, impartiality, and perhaps its indecisiveness, by manufacturing both electric and gasoline cars.

A little-publicized motoring show was held in Boston in 1898, another was conducted the following year in Philadelphia.

Outside the United States, the final years of the nineteenth century saw automotive developments similarly speed up. Some examples . . .

Australia—The "Pioneer" appeared in 1897, sponsored by the Australian Horseless Carriage Syndicate. It was powered by a kerosene motor.

Belgium—The "Vivinus," introduced in 1899, boasted a six-horsepower engine. It was built under license in England as the "New Orleans" and in France as the "Georges Richard."

Czechoslovakia—The "Nesselsdorf," which made its debut in 1897, was produced by a railway equipment firm, the Nesselsdorfer Waggonbau Fabrikgesellschaft. Its motor was a rear-mounted, flat-twin.

England—The first gasoline car on a public road was the 1895 three-wheeled "Knight," built by John H. Knight. It had a one-cylinder, one-horsepower engine and belt drive; later the machine was converted to four wheels. During the same year the Wolseley Sheep Shearing Machine Company constructed a two-cylinder, three-wheeled "Tri-Car," designed by Herbert Austin. Lanchesters appeared in 1895, British Daimlers in 1897, and Thomas Humber's three-wheeled "Sociable" in 1898. The latter was a modified Bollée with a Turrell engine.

France—The Société des Automobiles Peugeot was formed in 1897, the same year that Émile Delahaye showed his first car. In 1898 the Decauville made its bow by a builder who normally turned out locomotives. The Renault brothers, Louis, Marcel, and Fernand, constructed their first car. It had an air-cooled, single-cylinder De Dion engine of 1.75 horsepower.

Germany—Benz produced an eight-passenger omnibus in 1895. It was propelled by a rear-mounted, one-cylinder motor with belt transmission and a chain drive. The next year Friedrick Lutzmann improved and simplified the "Benz System," the result being the "Lutzmann System"; between 1895 and 1899 Lutzmann made cars and buses for up to sixteen riders.

Italy—Internal-combustion-powered cars were turned out by both Michele Lanza and Enrico Bernardi in 1895. Prinetti e Stucchi made a light car in 1898—Ettore Bugatti served his apprenticeship in their Milan plant. The first Fiat with a rear engine appeared in 1899; called the "3½-HP" model, it had a two-cylinder, water-cooled, 600-cc engine. Its maker was Fabbrica Italiana di Automobili Torino; one of its guiding lights was Giovanni Agnelli.

Norway—Paul H. Irgens, with the aid of his brother Jacob, built a four-wheeler having a one-cylinder gas engine in 1897.

Sweden—In 1897, while employed by Vabis (Vagnfabriks A.B. i Sodertalje), Gustaf Eriksson constructed a four-wheeled car fitted with a water-cooled, two-cylinder, two-cycle engine.

Switzerland—In 1897, Max Martini made a rear-engined car. Adolph Saurer, a constructor of internal-combustion engines, produced his first car in 1898; it was driven by one of his single-cylinder, five-horsepower motors.

And so, as a new century dawned around the globe, man was preparing to dispense with the horse. America would emerge as the world's leading producer of motorcars. One major reason for that leadership: a colossal phoenix which would rise from its ashes in Detroit.

DER ERSTE MOTORWAGEN   "The first!" proclaims the Deutsches Museum of Munich, which displays the original 1886 Karl Benz automobile—and so agree historians. Benz's own one-cylinder internal-combustion engine of ¾ hp. propelled his three-wheeler. The large horizontal spoked flywheel at the rear facilitated starting. Speed: 8 mph.

HAMMELVOGNEN   This was the very first automobile to be built in Denmark, in 1886. Powered by a two-cylinder, 3-hp., internal-combustion engine with hot-tube ignition, double-cone clutch, and chain drive, it included brakes and reverse, which many cars did not have in those early days. Speed: about 6 mph. Steering was opposite to that normally used today, i.e., you turned right for a left turn. Car was built by a blacksmith, Johansen, who worked in the shop of Albert F. Hammel. The original car can still be seen in the Danmarks Tekniske Museum, Helsingør.

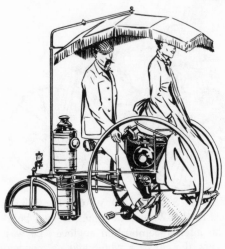

PHAETON MOTO-CYCLE   Lucius Copeland's steam tricycle with its 2-hp. steam engine was advertised as doing 10 mph. with two passengers and a driver. By 1888 the Moto-Cycle Manufacturing Company of Philadelphia had acquired the Copeland patents and started a sales campaign, but buyers were few. The machines ran well, one making a 120-mile round trip with passenger.

BENZ VELOCIPEDE   Built by Karl Benz of Mannheim, Germany, who was one of the pioneers in the development of the internal-combustion engine. Having first experimented with the two-cycle type, he soon changed to the more efficient four-cycle engine that powered this four-wheel, lightweight vehicle in 1888. It had a rear engine, chain drive, and crank-handle steering. He was the first designer to build and sell automobiles commercially, and in 1888 he had fifty men working for him in his shop.

DAIMLER-MAYBACH STAHLRAD WAGEN Wilhelm Maybach, later to be famous for his Zeppelin engines, helped build this car in 1889. Although an internal-combustion engineer, he was one of the first pioneers to view the car as a whole and not concentrate on the powerplant. This lightweight four-wheeler was chain-driven by the single-cylinder engine under the seat. This vehicle is often attributed only to Daimler, who was a friend of and worked with Maybach for many years. Maybach developed the jet carburetor, ancestor of the modern carburetor.

DE DION BOUTON QUADRICYCLE Marquis Albert de Dion and Georges Bouton built several steam-powered cars during the last dozen years of the nineteenth century. This four-wheeler was very advanced for the period, with engine hood and passenger protection, running board and full fenders. It was built and operated in 1891.

BENZ VIS-À-VIS   By 1892, Karl Benz had abandoned his earlier tricycle and developed this four-wheel convertible vis-à-vis with a rear-mounted internal-combustion engine. Much later, the Benz organization merged with the Daimler Company to form the famous motorcar and engine firm of Daimler-Benz, which set a fine example for the motoring world with their long line of Mercedes passenger and sports cars. The Vis-à-Vis can be seen in the Car and Carriage Caravan, Luray Caverns, Virginia.

BENZ VELOCIPED   Conservative Karl Benz built this model in 1893. Benz followed his previous successes by using his proven single-cylinder engine, vertical flywheel, chain drive, and rear-mounted engine. This car can be seen at the Henry Ford Museum, Dearborn, Michigan.

DURYEA CAR James Frank Duryea and Charles Edgar Duryea, brothers, ran their first vehicle on September 22, 1893, through the streets of Springfield, Massachusetts. It was America's first successful "gas" car, with a single-cylinder, four-stroke, water-cooled gasoline engine. An 1893 Duryea is in the Smithsonian Institution in Washington, D.C.

HAYNES'S FIRST An outstanding metallurgist, Elwood G. Haynes of Kokomo, Indiana, drove his original design on the Fourth of July, 1894. It was constructed by Edgar and Elmer Apperson in their Kokomo machine shop; assisting was Jonathan D. Maxwell. Initial power, a one-cylinder gas engine made by Claude Sintz of Grand Rapids, Michigan, sped the 820-pound vehicle along the Pumpkinvine Pike at 6 mph. The car is in the Smithsonian Institution, Washington, D.C.

BERNARDI   This car was the first car built in Italy and dates from 1894. Professor Enrico Bernardi built successful gasoline engines in 1883, and eleven years later used it to power this vehicle that he also designed and built. The three-wheeled two-seater boasted a very advanced powerplant. The engine was mounted in the rear and was a four-cycle, single-cylinder, water-cooled unit with a detachable cylinder head. It also had overhead valves, automatic lubrication, and a jet carburetor plus fuel and air filters! The engine turned at 800 rpm. and developed 2.5 hp. which drove the car at 20 mph. Construction rights were bought by S. A. Miari e Giusta of Padua in 1896, and they produced the car with minor variations until 1901.

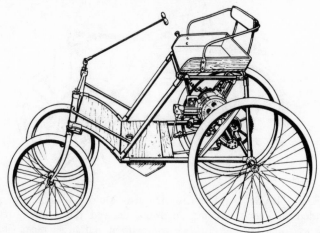

ROTARY-POWERED BALZER   Stephen M. Balzer made this remarkable lightweight in 1894. The Bronx, New York, builder produced his own powerplant—a three-cylinder, air-cooled rotary mounted vertically around a stationary crankshaft. As the cylinders and crankcase spun around, they turned a stub shaft connected to the driving gears.

BENZ VELO Karl Benz based much of this 1894 design of the Velo on his earlier Victoria. It had a single-cylinder internal-combustion engine and boasted of three forward speeds via clutch, as well as reverse. The car used a vertical flywheel rotating at about 450 to 500 rpm. It later developed into the Benz Comfortable. Benz sold sixty-seven cars in 1894.

GREAT "RACE" WINNER Duryea Motor Wagon Company, founded in Peoria, Illinois, in 1895, entered this winning car in America's first big performance competition and street race: Chicago to Evanston and return—fifty-four miles through snow-covered streets on Thanksgiving Day, 1895. J. Frank Duryea was the driver; his prize: $2,000 put up by the *Chicago Times-Herald*. Average speed: 7.5 mph.

EGG   This is the oldest existing automobile to be constructed in Switzerland. Built in 1895, it used the reliable Benz one-cylinder engine of two liters displacement and turning at 470 rpm. The cooling water was allowed to boil and evaporate as on many cars of this period. It is now on display at the Musée de l'Automobile, Château de Grandson, Lac de Neuchâtel, Switzerland.

BERLIET NO. 1 VOITURETTE   This tandem two-seater was built in 1895 as Berliet's first auto. It was fitted with a single-cylinder, horizontal internal-combustion engine under the rear seat, which was the driver's. The car used a conical clutch with a pinion driving a large gear that was attached to the rear axle. A metal fairing was fitted to the front of the car in an attempt at streamlining and to deflect the airflow upward and away from the passenger to keep him comfortable and clean. The engine bore was 80 mm.; stroke was 120 mm. It had tiller steering and battery ignition; two forward speeds.

EDISON EXPERIMENTAL ELECTRIC   It was inevitable that the prolific Thomas Alva Edison's attention should be directed to the automobile. He turned to electric power, which proved to be quiet and free from exhaust fumes. This three-wheeler was his first effort in the automotive field. Range was limited due to the short life of the storage batteries. This car can be viewed at the Henry Ford Museum, Dearborn, Michigan.

BENZ EIGHT-SEATER   As with most of the Karl Benz designs, this 1895 product was quite slow when compared with other cars of the period. Despite this, his cars were favored in Germany, England, America, and France. With his export business booming, he built 135 machines in 1895. Reliability was a big factor in this success. This car can be seen in the National Automobile Museum, Leidschendam, Holland.

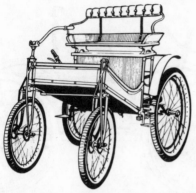

HERTEL Built in 1895 by Max Hertel of Chicago, this quadricycle was sold to John Pender in Melbourne, Australia, in November of 1897. It can be viewed today in the Science Museum of Victoria in Melbourne, Australia.

KING'S FOUR-CYLINDER, FOUR-CYCLE Charles Brady King, engineer and inventor, drove the first gasoline-powered vehicle on Detroit streets in 1896. It was his own design along with its remarkable engine: a four-cylinder, inline, water-cooled powerplant. The body was built by the Emerson and Fisher Carriage Company. Considering the car strictly experimental, King had it dismantled.

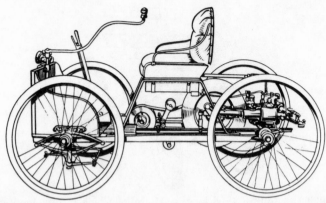

FORD'S FIRST   With Charles B. King as his passenger, Henry Ford made his first run publicly in a gasoline-driven car on June 4, 1896. The Ford Quadricycle was propelled by a two-cylinder, four-cycle engine built by Ford, who was a skilled mechanic and ex-farmer. Speed: 10 mph. in low; 20 mph. in high. The car is exhibited in the Henry Ford Museum at Dearborn, Michigan.

THOMSON STEAM CAR   Herbert Thomson of Armadale, Australia, was a steam engineer who decided to enter the automotive business. This is his first car, built in 1896 and shown to the public two years later. It had four-foot-diameter wheels in the rear and three-foot-diameter wheels in the front. These were fitted with 2½-inch pneumatic tires, especially made by Dunlop. The 5-hp. steam engine attained 1,000 rpm. The boiler measured only 14 x 18 x 18 inches and was tucked under the seat. Kerosene was used as the fuel and the range was thirty miles. In general, it proved to be a great step forward in steam car development, and the Thomas Motor Car Company, Ltd., was founded in Melbourne.

BENZ This Benz of 1896 used the reliable Benz single-cylinder engine, rear-mounted, as was his practice until 1902, when he was forced to make a front-engine car of increased horsepower to maintain his lead in a world gone horsepower mad. This car can be viewed at the Museum of Science and Industry, Chicago, Illinois.

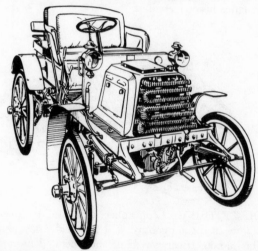

DAIMLER PHOENIX The name of this 1896 product of Gottlieb Daimler is derived from the four-cylinder, vee-type internal-combustion engine he had developed and called the Phoenix. Notice the finned coils in the front of the bonnet or engine hood which act as a radiator to cool the engine-cooling water. Many other designs of this period (including Benz's) merely allowed the water to boil away. The idea of a multi-cylinder engine was copied by many of Daimler's contemporaries. The original car can still be seen in the Automuseum, Nettelstedt, Lübeck, Germany.

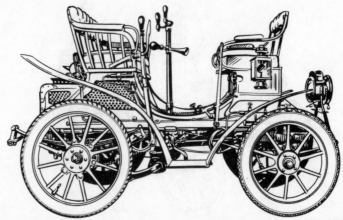

PEUGEOT VIS-À-VIS Armand Peugeot designed this vis-à-vis (occupants in separate seats facing each other) in 1896 and used Gottlieb Daimler's Phoenix engine, built under license. This four-passenger machine attained 10 mph. with the 4 bhp., 600 cc, two-cylinder engine. Two speeds and reverse were offered. After this, Peugeot designed his own engines.

LÉON BOLLÉE TRIKE Léon Bollée, eldest son of Amédée Bollée, joined his father in the automotive field and finally developed his own designs. This famous tricar was built and operated in early 1896. It was noisy and cranky but its speed exceeded 30 mph., which was phenomenal for that period. The Trike was a two-seater with the passenger in front of the driver.

FIRST EXPERIMENTAL RAMBLER English-born Thomas B. Jeffery sold bicycles in the U.S. that were assembled from parts made in England. In 1881 he became partners with Philip Gormully and they formed the G & J Manufacturing Company. The bicycles were called Rambler. After witnessing the first auto race in the U.S. in Chicago in 1895, the partners sold the firm to the American Bicycle Company and decided to enter the expanding automobile industry. Tom Jeffery designed and built their first car and tests were favorable. They then bought the Sterling Bicycle Plant and converted it to auto production, continuing to perfect the basic design. In 1902 they sold 1,500 Rambler automobiles, and thus became the second company in the world to mass produce automobiles; a year later than Olds and a year ahead of Ford.

CLARKE GASOLINE TRICYCLE   With a sturdy one-cylinder gasoline engine driving the rear wheels, Louis S. Clarke of Pittsburgh, Pennsylvania, fashioned his 1897 tricycle from readily available bicycle parts, with some modifications. Known as the first "Autocar," it led to the establishment of the Autocar Company in 1899. A restored tricycle is at the Smithsonian.

OLDS 1897 FOUR-PASSENGER   Progressing from steam, starting in 1886, to gasoline-engined vehicles in 1896, Ransom Eli Olds built this 6-hp., single-cylinder, four-placer in his Olds Motor Vehicle Company at Lansing. This sole remaining example is displayed by the Smithsonian. Organized on August 21, 1897, the Olds firm was Michigan's first incorporated auto maker.

PANHARD-LEVASSOR The Frenchmen Hippolyte Panhard and Émile Levassor decided that the engine should be placed in the front of the car instead of the rear, as was the vogue at that time. This 1897 model followed this practice, and the drive shaft can be seen running to the rear where it engaged a bevel-gear cross shaft which, in turn, powered the rear wheels via a chain drive connected to a differential live axle. This became known as the "Système Panhard," and was copied by other pioneers.

BERLIET NO. 2 VOITURETTE Berliet's second venture into the auto field was this side-by-side two-seater in 1897. The two-cylinder engine was rear-mounted and had a bore of 90 mm. and stroke of 150 mm. A steering wheel replaced the previous model's tiller. Drive was the same as the No. 1. A differential rear axle was fitted. It had two forward gears.

DE DION BOUTON VOITURETTE, Marquis de Dion and Georges Bouton have often been called the C. S. Rolls and Sir Henry Royce of France. The prolific pair made many successful automobiles, thanks to the mechanical genius of Bouton. This Voiturette of 1897 had a front-mounted, single-cylinder engine of 240 cc displacement. This fine car is exhibited in the Musée de l'Automobile, Château de Grandson, Lac de Neuchâtel, Switzerland.

VABIS The letters of "Vabis" stand for Vagnfabriks A.B.i Sodertalje —the firm that became interested in Gustav Eriksson's experiments and produced this car in 1897 based on Eriksson's designs. A rear-mounted, four-stroke, air-cooled, horizontal two-cylinder engine featured automatic inlet valves and low-tension magneto ignition and burned kerosene. Later a hot-tube ignition was tried, and finally gasoline was used in a two-cylinder in vee arrangement. The car had two forward speeds, chain final drive, epicyclic gearbox, and tiller steering. This was one of the first cars produced in Sweden and production continued on trucks and cars until 1911 when they joined Maskin A. B. Scania to form A. B. Scania Vabis.

GUSTAV ERIKSSON ÅKVAGN The Vagnfabriks A.B.i Sodertalje assembled railroad wagons for Surahammer Iron and Steel Works. Gustav Eriksson, an engineer for Surahammer, had studied automobile design in France. He built his employers an internal-combustion engine, burning kerosene rather than the more dangerous gasoline, for use in a road vehicle. After several attempts he arrived at a two-cylinder, four-stroke, 6-hp., horizontal engine. This powerplant was installed in the rear of a wagon supplied by C. A. Carlson & Sons of Stockholm. The kerosene engines he tried all ended in failure, and during one test the vehicle struck a wall. However, the experiments contributed to the development of a useful motor car. This car can be seen in the Tekniska Museet in Stockholm, Sweden.

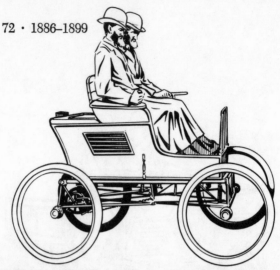

STANLEY BUGGY   The Stanley twins produced this steam-powered, chain-drive, Spartan-like simple automobile as their first effort. It was powered by a two-cylinder, vertical engine of 12 hp. at 400 rpm. The maximum speed was 25 mph. Bore and stroke were 2½ x 3½ inches. The chassis was wooden-braced. The brothers sold out to Mobile and Locomobile, and part of the agreement was that they promised to remain out of the automobile business for at least two years!

DE DION BOUTON TRICYCLE   This tricycle of 1897 featured high speed due to the improved De Dion Bouton engines, which ran even faster than those of Daimler: 1,500 rpm. compared with 800 rpm. They could often operate at 3,000 rpm. for short periods of time. The powerplant was a lightweight, air-cooled, single-cylinder affair. The 250 cc displacement developed 1¾ hp., which was an excellent ratio. It was double the power of the Daimler and quadruple that of the Benz. The De Dion trikes were winners in many races and were extremely popular in Paris during this time.

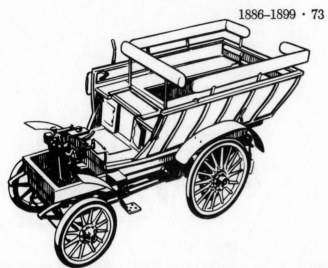

DAIMLER (BRITISH)   The English Daimler Motor Company was formed in 1896, having arranged for the use of Daimler's patents and construction rights. This car was built by the company in 1897, but the company had not yet been able to design a brand-new auto. The cars borrowed from many French designs, including those of Panhard & Levassor, and were known as the "Parisian Daimlers" by other manufacturers.

BENZ COMFORTABLE   In 1897, Karl Benz made 256 cars, and almost doubled that amount in the following year due to cars like his Comfortable of 1897. The conservative Benz stuck to his single-cylinder, horizontal engine of 3 hp., which drove a large spoked fly-wheel just behind the seat. The Benz ignition system utilized a spark with storage battery coil and spark plug which set the standard for the modern car. Engine speed was controlled by advancing and retarding the spark timing as well as by controlling the amount of fuel entering the engine. This car is now on exhibit in the Frederick C. Crawford Auto-Aviation Museum, Cleveland, Ohio.

EXPERIMENTAL HAND-BUILT FORD While still an engineer with the Edison Illuminating Company in Detroit and before he joined the Detroit Automobile Company, Henry Ford turned out his second car, in 1896, an auto buggy with a two-cylinder engine, chain drive, and planetary-gear transmission. Steering was by tiller.

DE DION BOUTON VIS-À-VIS De Dion Bouton & Cie., Paris, switched from their three-wheeled, gasoline-powered vehicles to heavier four-wheeled vehicles in 1898 because the sturdy four wheels were more stable and safer. This is one of their first four-wheelers, and it was powered by the very reliable and efficient single-cylinder, high-speed engine; 1,500 rpm. The firm sold this engine to many other auto manufacturers. The 2.75-hp. engine displaced 326 cc and had a water-cooled cylinder head but an air-cooled cylinder barrel.

LA CROIX DE LAVILLE   This trike car was made in France in 1898. The entire car was of wood, including the curved chassis and fenders. It was powered by a single-cylinder De Dion Bouton water-cooled, vertical engine placed in front of the radiator and water tank. Two speeds were available by slackening the extremely long belt drive and shifting it to the next pulley. Note the long tiller steering-handle. This car can be viewed at The Raben Car Collection at Aalholm Castle, Nysted, Denmark.

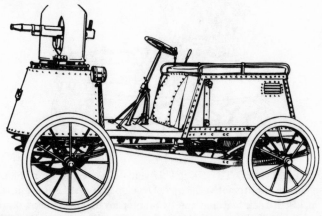

ARMORED STEAMER   During the years between the U.S. Civil War and the First World War, there was a constant search for an armored vehicle as protection against the newly developed machine gun, improved rifles, and artillery. This steam-powered carriage afforded protection for the vehicle but very little for the driver and gunner, who sat side by side. The armament was apparently a one-pounder. Engine was in the rear; solid tires. Experiments such as this led to the development of tanks and other armored vehicles which are commonplace today. It is on exhibition at the Museum of Science and Industry, Chicago, Illinois.

DURYEA TRAP   The Duryea brothers, Charles E. and J. Frank, built the first gasoline-engine-powered vehicle in the U.S. in 1893. As the years went by they built both three- and four-wheel designs. This 1898 product was one of the last three-wheelers. It was powered by a three-cylinder, 6- to 10-hp., rear-mounted engine. The price, new, was $1,600. This car can be viewed at the Henry Ford Museum, Dearborn, Michigan.

RIKER ELECTRIC TRUCK   This vehicle proved to be a milestone in the annals of automotive history. Developed by A. L. Riker in 1898, this enclosed truck featured the two-motor arrangement used on other Riker designs of the period. Each motor was geared to a rear wheel. The body was steel, and the roof and sides were steel mesh covered with a tight-fitting, painted-canvas tarpaulin. A rear gate was used that became a platform to assist in handling the load—an idea that set the pace for trucks for several decades.

FIRST WINTON SOLD Alexander Winton turned from bicycle manufacturing to cars; his first vehicle ran in public in September, 1896. In 1898 he built this gas-engine car, the Winton Buggy. It proved successful and was the first model sold by the Winton Motor-Carriage Company of Cleveland, Ohio. Twenty-five Wintons were built that year. Power was a single-cylinder, 6-hp., water-cooled, horizontal engine mounted in the rear. The transmission was connected by a chain to a cross shaft that was geared to a differential on the rear axle. It offered two forward speeds and reverse, tiller steering, and make-and-break ignition. Pneumatic tires were provided. Winton's last company became the Cleveland Diesel Division of General Motors. The original car can be seen at the Smithsonian Institution, Washington, D.C.

AUTOCAR NO. 2 The first United States Autocar designs were passenger vehicles, although the firm was later to become a successful truck manufacturer. This second model, built in 1898, was fitted with a 6-hp., two-cylinder engine mounted in the rear. The Autocar Company, Ardmore, Pennsylvania, was the first to feature shaft drive instead of chain. It also pioneered internal expanding brakes, the same as those used today. Price of this car was $825, when new. It can be seen in the Henry Ford Museum, Dearborn, Michigan.

PANHARD-LEVASSOR When Émile Levassor died as a result of injuries sustained when he lost control and overturned during the 1897 Paris-Marseilles Race, Hippolyte Panhard continued to build automobiles under their partnership banner. This model was constructed in 1898, and several of the firm's products were entered in the Paris-Amsterdam Race. Panhards finished in first and second place! Pneumatic tires aided steering considerably. A two-cylinder, water-cooled engine was mounted forward and developed about 6 hp. at 700 rpm.

BOLLÉE TRICAR–"THE COVENTRY MOTORETTE" So popular was the French Léon Bollée Tricar on the Continent that the Wolseley Company assigned the task of designing an English counterpart to Herbert Austin. Sold as the Coventry Motorette, it was obviously a copy of the Bollée and was the fastest auto for sale to the public for many years, attaining 30 mph. The burner for the hot-tube ignition was often extinguished by dust or water spray from the rear wheel, and in wet weather the brakes invariably failed. Despite these shortcomings, many people bought these flashy cars.

POPP PATENT MOTORWAGEN This vehicle was built in Switzerland in 1898. Lorenz Popp, an engineer of Basel, with the financial backing of Edouard Burkhardt, made two cars of this design. Burkhardt was the Benz agent in Switzerland and therefore the design borrowed considerably from Benz. The engine, however, was not Benz. The valves operated by a chain-driven overhead camshaft. It was more powerful than the Benz design because it developed 7 hp. and was a two-cylinder, water-cooled, rear-mounted model. Bore was 90 mm. with a stroke of 122½ mm. Displacement was 1,594 cc. The car can be viewed in the Verkehrshaus der Schweiz, Lucerne, Switzerland.

RENAULT VOITURETTE Designer Louis Renault was obsessed with small personal cars. This Renault product of 1898 was the first to have a sprung live rear axle with differential, driven from the gearbox by a jointed propeller shaft. Many other builders of light cars copied this design. This little one- or two-passenger design relied on a De Dion Bouton engine of 1.75 hp. that revolved at 1,500 rpm. and drove the car at about 13 mph. The following year Renault converted the car into the first all-enclosed automobile.

LÉON BOLLÉE TRICAR The French Léon Bollée Tandem Tricars of the late nineties were extremely popular because of their high speed and were considered sporty. The single-cylinder, air-cooled, horizontal engine was located on the left side of the rear wheel. No clutch was fitted; starting motion was directly from the crankshaft pinion to the wheel. The other speeds were accomplished by sliding the rear wheel, by means of a lever, to tighten or slacken the flat leather driving belt! Braking was accomplished by sliding the rear wheel, on its forks, all the way forward where the belt rims came into contact with a wooden block which eventually stopped the vehicle. Air-cooling was often diminished by the driver's left leg blocking the airstream.

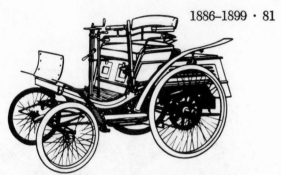

BENZ VELO This product of Benz & Company, Mannheim, Germany, cost $1,500 in 1898 when it was new. The single-cylinder, 110-mm. bore and stroke, 64-cubic-inch-displacement engine was behind the seat and connected via a two-speed belt drive to a jackshaft which, in turn, drove the rear wheels with twin chains and sprockets. The 3-hp. engine rotated at 600 rpm. and had a fuel consumption of about 22 miles per gallon. Ignition was via battery and vibrating coil. Solid rubber tires and elliptical springs were standard. This car can be viewed at the Museum of Automobiles, Morrilton, Arkansas.

BENZ PHAETON In 1898, Karl Benz produced this rear-engined two-seater with three forward speeds and reverse. It also had a transmission brake and two-wheel brakes! The 3-hp., single-cylinder engine was mounted horizontally and used a system of belts and chains to drive the rear wheels. Speed was varied by moving a lever on the steering column that shifted the belts from one pulley to another. One feature of this car was its hill-climbing ability due to an epicyclic gear, providing the third low gear; Benz called it his "cryptic" gear. Steering was rack-and-pinion, as in the present-day sports cars. A speed of 22 mph. could be attained with the 1,045-cc engine.

BAKER ELECTRIC Walter C. Baker was working for a ball-bearing manufacturer when he built his first electric car in 1898. In the following year the Baker Motor Vehicle Company was founded in Cleveland, Ohio, and the first Baker production vehicle was made. This 1899 car had three forward speeds and a one-horsepower motor. Speed was about 25 mph., and range was about 50 miles between battery charges. Ball bearings were used throughout the Baker. In 1915 the firm joined with Rauch and Lang to form Baker, Rauch and Lang.

DE DION BOUTON QUADRICYCLE In an effort to hold the interest of the type of customers who liked the De Dion Bouton dashing and speedy trikes, the partners developed this lightweight four-wheeler in 1899. The De Dion Bouton single-cylinder, 2.25-hp., water-cooled head engine was fitted, giving the four-wheel craft performance similar to the famous trikes.

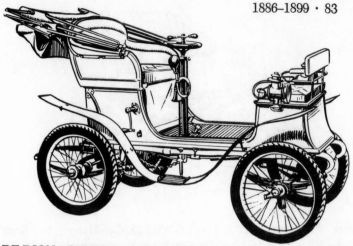

DE DION BOUTON MOTORETTE This vis-à-vis Voiturette Type E was made by De Dion Bouton & Cie. in 1899 and proved successful, being exported as far as to Australia. A 3.5-hp., single-cylinder, water-cooled engine of 3.14-mm. bore and stroke was located under the rear seat. The 400-cc engine gave the car a road speed of 25 mph. The steering-column gearshift gave two forward speeds but reverse was optional. Final drive was via spur gear. This car can be seen in the Gilltraps Auto Museum, Collangatta, Queensland, Australia.

MOBILE STEAMER After purchasing the Stanley Brothers' rights to their steam car, Mobile and Locomobile produced the Mobile Steamer, and it bore a strong resemblance to the Stanley. With a two-cylinder, 10-hp. engine, the car proved its climbing ability by climbing up a 45-degree stairway—a most successful demonstration that impressed many potential buyers!

KNOX "WATERLESS" THREE-WHEELER Harry A. Knox launched the Knox Automobile Company in Springfield, Massachusetts, to turn out air-cooled, one-cylinder, 4-hp. three-wheelers between 1899 and 1903. This 1899 Knox at the Smithsonian looks something like an advanced version of the 1886 Benz three-wheeler. Knox also turned to water-cooling and four wheels in 1901, starting a line of large, sturdy cars.

MORS KETTENWAGEN Émile Mors was a French electrical engineer who headed a business, founded in 1851, that made some gasoline railcars in 1893. His first car, in 1896, was based on the Benz designs, but he soon developed his own automobiles. This front-engined voiturette of 1899 featured a low-tension spark from a generator and battery; the first-known successful application of this principle. It charged the battery and supplied ignition spark, which became standard for automobiles all over the world for decades.

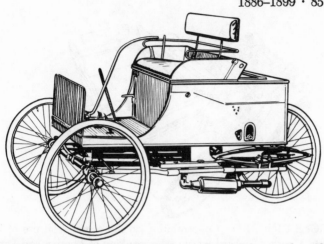

KELSEY & TILNEY "AUTO-TRI"   Carl W. Kelsey and I. Sheldon Tilney turned out this experimental water-cooled, one-cylinder, four-cycle-powered vehicle in 1899. Rear wheel was driven, having two forward speeds and reverse. Kelsey later produced his three-wheeled Motorette until 1912; some were exported to Japan as powered rickshaws. This original vehicle is at the Smithsonian Institution.

DE DION BOUTON VOITURETTE   This De Dion Bouton four-wheeler made by their company, De Dion Bouton & Cie. in Paris, in 1899, attained 25 mph. A vertical, single-cylinder, internal-combustion, water-cooled, 3½-hp. engine of 400 cc was fitted in the rear under the driver's seat. A column gearshift permitted two forward speeds and reverse. It was spur-gear driven. Notice the single headlamp. The price for this car, when new, was $250. This car is now in the Gilltraps Auto Museum, Collangatta, Queensland, Australia.

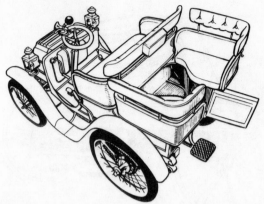

GEORGES RICHARD Concentrating on the commercial use of his products, Georges Richard became the taxi king of London and Paris. This is one of his early designs of 1899. Notice the rear entrance for the passengers. A two-cylinder, 10-hp. engine revolved at 1,500 rpm. and was located in the front, with finned cooling coils to act as a radiator. His company became the "Unic Cab," which later was absorbed by Simca.

JENATZY'S "LA JAMAIS CONTENTE" This French bullet-shaped auto was the first to exceed 60 mph., and Camille Jenatzy established a world speed record of 65.8 mph. on a measured course in April, 1899, at Achères, France. This Jeantaud-built vehicle was electric-powered, and the expensive batteries were not only exhausted but heavily sulphated due to overly rapid discharging. The record breaker weighed 2,200 pounds and had 25.6-inch-diameter wheels. It was the first auto to be built specifically for record purposes and it could attain 75 mph. "La Jamais Contente" means "The Never Satisfied." The car can be viewed in the Musée de la Voiture, Château de Compiègne, Oise, France.

DAIMLER (BRITISH) The English Daimler Motor Company of Coventry, England, produced this four-seater in 1899. It was powered by a 6-hp., two-cylinder engine with the Daimler hot-tube ignition. The engine was in the rear and drove through the gearbox to a cross shaft from which the rear wheels were driven via roller chains. The English Daimler cars had no relationship to the German Daimlers except for the basic engine.

RENAULT C 1 This four-seater auto, built by Louis Renault in 1899, was larger than most of his efforts during this period. It relied on a chain drive to a solid rear axle, while for his smaller cars he developed the sprung live rear axle and jointed propulsion shaft. The engine was of De Dion Bouton design, as on most of Renault's early projects, which was a single-cylinder affair developing 1.75 hp.

WINTON MAIL TRUCK The Winton Motor-Carriage Company built this mail truck in 1899. It was the first gas-powered car used in the United States Postal Service. It could attain a speed of 18 mph., and helped the mails get through.

MORS PETIT DUC Émile Mors was one of the early French auto manufacturers to be successful in racing his automobiles. Mors won the Paris-Bordeaux race in 1897. This 1899 product of Mors was intended for those who wanted a small vehicle but disliked the two-, three- and four-wheeled motorcycle types. The engine was a 5-hp., two-cylinder, water-cooled opposed type fitted in the front. The crankshaft extended to the rear to drive the rear wheels via a drive chain. Cone clutch was fitted, and three forward speeds were available from the gearbox. Speed was about 20 mph. The car is a two-seater with an additional collapsible "dicky" seat at the rear, forerunner of the rumble seat.

LOCOMOBILE This 1899 Locomobile bears a strong resemblance to the Stanley of 1897. The steam-powered vehicle had a wooden body mounted on two longitudinal steel tubes via leaf springs. The wheelbase was 58 inches and tread 53 inches. The 300-tube boiler developed 150 pounds per square inch of pressure to the two-cylinder double-acting engine, which developed about 400 rpm. and 3 hp. The engine could, however, develop 10 to 12 hp. for short periods. The car weighed 700 pounds. This car can be seen in the Smithsonian Institution, Washington, D.C.

CHAPTER FIVE

Mass Production Begins 1900—1904

THE MOST EXCITING ten years in automotive history were those from 1900 to 1910. But so great was the growth of the hobby-sport-business, and so fascinating the technical developments, both in the United States and abroad, that it is best to examine this period in two parts: 1900 through 1904, and 1905 through 1909.

It was during 1900 that James Gordon Bennett sponsored the first of many prestigious international cup races which were to bear his name. The first was held in France where Mr. Bennett ran the European edition of the *New York Herald*. A French Panhard won the 341-mile Paris to Lyon race at a speed of 38.6 mph. Entries were assigned colors to indicate their country of origin: blue for France, yellow for Belgium, white for Germany, red for the U.S.A. Each entry in its entirety was to be the complete product of the country it represented.

In America, Henry Ford's second major car concern, the Detroit Automobile Company, decided to close down. During 1900 there were at least four major showings of automobiles. A gathering at Bedford, Connecticut, included some track racing; at Chicago eighty vehicles were on exhibit, some of which ran; 95,000 spectators reportedly turned out for a show at Trenton, New Jersey. But it remained for the Madison Square Garden exhibit hall in New York City to capture top honors in the historical records and to draw the largest crowds with its First National Automobile Show. A Winton on display had been driven 810 miles from Cleveland at an average speed of 21 mph.

90

Some forty manufacturers exhibited three hundred vehicles at that old Garden under the sponsorship of the Automobile Club of America; longest surviving marque appearing there was to be Rambler.

At the time of the National Show a majority of the seventy-six million Americans still lived outside city areas, mostly on farms. For the most part they were little aware of what was going on in The Big City. The vast countryside had perhaps two million miles of crude roads. Only about 150,000 miles of these could be classed as "improved" surface—in most instances that meant loose gravel, although sand and shell topping was also used. In swampy areas felled trees laid crossways served as "washboard" roadways. In all America there was not much more than 150 miles of hard-surface roadway, and this was to be found in and around the larger cities.

While the American vehicle generally fitted one of two categories, high buggy wheels for rough and muddy country use, or light bike-wheeled buggies for the in-town dandies, the typical European machine appeared to be a much more advanced affair. In place of a tiller for steering, it offered a steering wheel; its body was likely to be custom-crafted and specially tailored to fit a standard chassis; there was a proven powerplant and reliable drive mechanism. Most of the French, German, and Belgian products had lost their earlier "motorized carriage" appearance. Renault, for example, offered an enclosed area which included the long-neglected driver.

In America, meanwhile, a muffler was not something to quiet the exhaust. It was a long wrap necessary to stave off asphyxiation from road dust and engine fumes, or a cold from the chilly breezes. The exposed motorist also required a mask and goggles, a cap or hat. Really cold weather called for a bearskin coat or its equivalent. And lots of extra blankets.

But though America lacked the improved roadways and some of the niceties of styling and mechanical advancements so common on the Continent, a valiant band of Yankee innovators and speculators, sometimes in competition with one another, often in cooperative ventures, were soon to push the United States into the world's Number One motoring spot.

One could contend, perhaps, that the initial impetus for the big leap forward came from Samuel L. Smith of Detroit. Mr. Smith did not have an overwhelming interest in cars; rather he was looking for a business in which he might invest that would be attractive to his sons once they finished college. Smith, a stockholder in the earlier Olds Motor Vehicle Company at Lansing, backed the new Olds Motor Works with the understanding it was to be located in Detroit. The new factory was the first designed specifically for car manufacture and was erected near the Belle Isle Bridge on East Jefferson Avenue. During the fall of 1900, when buyer interest in his larger cars appeared spotty, R. E. Olds built a small prototype vehicle with a curved dashboard. Olds's idea was that a mini-runabout that cost about $300 to manufacture could be retailed for about $650. It would appeal to city residents for local trips.

On a Saturday morning, March 9, 1901—a date that has tremendous significance for Detroit—the Olds Works, except for its foundry building, was destroyed by fire. The only car saved was the experimental curved-dash machine. A timekeeper, James J. Brady, pushed it out of the burning building. Later he was to become Mayor of Detroit. So he, Smith, and Olds all had a hand in the drama that turned Detroit into the motor center of the universe.

Until the fire decided matters, the Olds money men had been unable to agree on what size of car or propulsion system they should embrace. Now, suddenly, their entire future was tied up in their two-passenger, 800-pound, 20-mph. vehicle with its single-cylinder, four-cycle gasoline engine. This reliable little engine was water-cooled; it mounted horizontally at the rear. Ignition was by trembler coil. The lightweight car had leaf springs, a simple differential with epicyclic gear change, and a chain drive. Bicycle-type wire-spoked wheels with pneumatic tires supported a small open body with its single seat for two.

With the Olds plant gone, subcontracting of parts became an immediate necessity. This eventually resulted in the attraction to the Detroit area of many would-be suppliers. Soon Leland & Faulkner were making the Olds motor. John F. and Horace E. Dodge built the transmissions in their machine shop. Benjamin and Frank Briscoe, also brothers, supplied the radiators. Barney Everitt provided the bodies.

Everything went together rather well, a tribute to the car's designer, his associates, and the skilled subcontractors with their own talented engineering staffs. The assembled Olds had two forward speeds, plus reverse, and on a decent stretch could cruise along close to 14 mph.

Car tester Roy D. Chapin drove a Curved Dash Olds from Detroit, through Canada, and across New York State. Making various repairs en route, Chapin reached New York City in seven and a half days. When he found the main roads impassable between Syracuse and Troy, he took to the towpath of the Erie Canal—much to the consternation of bargemen along the way. The trip totaled 820 miles; his average speed was 14 mph. This feat helped promote orders for 1,000 of the machines. Some years later Chapin would become Secretary of Commerce. He always remained an advocate for good roads. Little wonder!

The year 1901 saw production of 425 of the C. D. Oldsmobiles. Subsequent annual records were: 1902, 2,500 cars; 1903, 4,000; 1904, 5,000; 1905, 6,500! By then the machine had a straight dashboard, the main assembly facilities were back in Lansing, and Mr. Olds had departed from the company.

But the United States was not the only country turning out cars in quantity. By the time the "Merry Oldsmobile" had reached the top of America's best-seller list, De Dion Bouton had sold more than 1,500 of their small voiturettes. Their tube-frame chassis featured the De Dion rear axle, which was separated from the drive shafts by universal joints. Thus, the final drive did not have to bear any of the car's weight—a decided improvement.

During this same period Henry Ford was very much involved with racing cars. At Grosse Pointe his first race car outran Alexander Winton's 70-hp. heavyweight. Ford used a two-cycle, 26-hp. motor. On the strength of his racing exploits the Detroit Automobile Company was reorganized as the Henry Ford Company.

In France the 1901 Gordon Bennett Cup Race covered 328 miles; a Mors with a 50-mph. average was declared the overall winner. A 12-hp. Panhard took the touring category, while Louis Renault's entry was crowned best among the lightweights. The white Mercedes, considered by many to be the most modern vehicle of its time because of its steel frame, made its bow. It was a Daimler designed by Maybach and named for Émile Jellinek's daughter. An Austrian banker, M. Jellinek was the Daimler sales representative for the Côte d'Azur in France, and held the sales rights for such far-flung areas as Belgium, Austria-Hungary, and the United States.

Thomas B. Jeffery of Rambler bicycle fame was turning out his first Rambler cars on a mass production basis at Kenosha, Wisconsin; Fred Duesenberg was his test driver. Henry B. Joy took over the direction of the Warren, Ohio, Packard outfit and soon moved it to Detroit. Other makers and marques proliferated. The Austin Highway King started up in Grand Rapids, Michigan; it remained in production almost until 1920. Some versions sold for more than $6,000. Although the Duryea Motor Wagon Company had turned out thirteen cars back in 1897, then ceased business, the Stevens-Duryea came along four years later.

Especially significant was the first gush of oil which on January 10, 1901, established the great Spindletop oil field in Texas. From its flow of crude oil came first kerosene, paraffin wax, naphtha, and various lubricants. Later, gasoline was to become its most important product.

With more than 150 known automobile companies active in the United States, developments came along rapidly. Ford left the Henry Ford Company and it was reorganized into the Cadillac Automobile Company under the leadership of Henry M. Leland of the Leland & Faulkner machine shops. Leland was a leading proponent of precision engineering and interchangeability of parts. Another ingenious industrialist, David Dunbar Buick, was working on the valve-in-head engine. The Studebakers rolled out their first car, an electric. On October 25, 1902, Berner Eli "Barney" Oldfield in Ford's "999" racer bested Winton in his "Bullet" during a second round of races at Grosse Pointe. Tom Cooper was Ford's partner in the "Arrow" and "999" racing cars endeavor. These cars had huge four-cylinder engines of 7-inch bore and stroke.

During 1902 the American Automobile Association was formed. Syracuse, New York, became the home of the Franklin air-cooled car and engine. Terre Haute, Indiana, saw the first Oakland make its debut. At Nice, France, Léon Serpollet drove a

6-hp. steamer to a record 75.06 mph. And all across Europe an over-supply of beets resulted in a number of ministry-sponsored "alcohol fuel" races. The first one of many was won by Henry Farman.

Ford's "final" firm, the Ford Motor Company, was organized during June of 1903. Except for bodies and wheels, all the early Fords were assembled from parts made by the Dodge Machine Shop to specifications drawn up under Ford's supervision by Childe Harold Wills and others. John and Horace Dodge each held fifty shares in the new company. The first Model A Ford-mobile weighed 1,250 pounds and sold for $850. Early Ford ads stressed "compactness, convenience, reasonable price, safety, and simplicity." The "A" had a Ford-designed two-cylinder engine; it offered two forward speeds and reverse, with a side-mounted hand-crank for starting. The first cash payment for an "A" came from a Chicago physician, Dr. E. J. Pfennig, on July 15, 1903.

By this time America had well over 200 automobile manufac-turers. The Buick Motor Car Company had been organized and sold sixteen vehicles in 1903, thirty-seven in 1904. Packard was operating full blast in Detroit; the Maxwell-Briscoe Company was turning out a two-cylinder runabout for $500.

The Association of Licensed Automobile Manufacturers, a group that eventually grew to twenty-six member firms, now con-trolled the Selden patent. The A.L.A.M. brought suit against Ford, its New York dealer, and other manufacturers, on October 22, 1903, for infringing on Selden's basic design.

While a long fight was shaping up in the courts between Ford and the A.L.A.M., nothing could hold back the ardent auto-mobilist of the day. The first coast-to-coast auto trip was made by Dr. H. Nelson Jackson of Burlington, Vermont, with Sewall K. Crocker as his chauffeur-companion. Jackson's machine was a two-cylinder Winton; purpose of the odyssey was to win a $50 bet. The pair left San Francisco on May 23, 1903, and arrived in New York City on July 26. Also in the automotive news of the day: the Columbia Electric Truck offered power steering. The Charter Water-Gasoline car operated on a fuel mix of 66 percent gasoline vapor and 33 percent atomized water which was drawn into a heated cylinder. The Newton, Massachusetts, fire depart-ment acquired a Stanley Steamer. The noted merchant John

Wanamaker was selling the new Searchmont in his New York City store.

For those who craved to build their own cars, Neustadt-Perry Company of St. Louis, Missouri, was prepared to ship any single part or the whole works in pieces, including the engine. Andrew Lee Dyke had been offering similar "kits" since the turn of the century. How many of these kit cars were completed to appear under various "private" labels, nobody knows. But we suspect the number was rather high since the sale of personal brand-name plates was brisk.

Europe was to capture the biggest headlines, all tragic, when more than three million spectators lined the roads between Paris and Madrid to see a big 750-mile race. The 175 starters were of varying skill, and some were driving machines of doubtful capabilities. There was precious little crowd control along the way. The casualty rate among onlookers, cars, and passengers was so high the competition was halted at Bordeaux. That pretty much ended city-to-city open-road racing in Europe.

The conservative British upped their national speed limit to a fast 20 mph. That mark was to be retained until 1930. Among the Continental favorites was the De Dion Bouton "Populaire," which put out 8 hp. at 1,500 rpm. with its single-cylinder, 864-cc engine. F.I.A.T. featured a somewhat larger plant: four cylinders, 4,181 cc; this "16/24-HP" car weighed 2,970 pounds.

If by 1904 you couldn't afford an automobile, at least you could read about them. Two hot sellers were both bylined by A. L. Dyke: *Diseases of Gasoline Engines and How to Remedy Them* and *Dr. Dyke's Anatomy of the Automobile*.

Two auto addicts, both with money, sought to improve the breed in somewhat different ways. Charles Glidden sponsored reliability tours; William K. Vanderbilt, Jr., called for speed and more speed via races. A former newspaperman and telegrapher, Glidden had retired full of honors and with a fat bank account after assisting Dr. A. G. Bell design, sell, and install telephone systems throughout New England. In 1904, Glidden headed up the Boston contingent that motored to the World's Fair in St. Louis. The famed Glidden Tours would follow; these were intended to be fairly sedate, over-the-road performance runs for a trophy that went to stock cars operated by their well-heeled owners. The tours were discontinued in 1914 because by then specially built and professionally tuned factory entries began to edge out the gentlemen drivers and their generally standard steeds.

An inveterate motorist and married to an auto-oriented wife, Glidden and Mrs. G. were the first, in 1904, to cross the Canadian Rockies by car. Their Boston to Vancouver trek consisted of 1,733 miles via roadway and 1,803 miles via railway track. To run along the rails they had their Napier equipped with flanged wheels. To meet railroading requirements they added a conductor, plus warning torpedoes and red flags to their equipment. Later Glidden took to free ballooning with Mrs. G. following along as best she could in the family touring car.

Autos operating along rail tracks were not unusual. Oldsmobile offered a flanged wheel special calling it the Olds Railroad Inspection Car. It sold for $450.

Bill Vanderbilt's premise was that an all-out quest for speed would be the quickest way of proving out new cars and equipment. The first Vanderbilt Cup Race was held on Long Island during 1904. It was won by a French Panhard driven by George Heath, an American residing in Paris. The course covered 284 miles; the winning speed averaged out to 52.7 mph. During the same year, Vanderbilt himself drove a Mercedes at 92.307 mph. at Daytona Beach. The 100-mph. mark fell to a French Gobron-Brillé machine operated by a M. Rigolly; precise speed was 103.56 mph. Fred Duesenberg by this time was designing his own racers; they were constructed until 1910 by the Mason Auto Company.

The biggest happening of 1904, though, was the production record; it was captured hands down by the American industry. U.S. firms turned out more cars than any other country. Of the more than 22,000 vehicles they made, about 700 were out and out trucks. Ford set up business in Canada, and soon every second Canadian car was destined to bear the Ford emblem. During November of 1904, the millionaire carriage-maker, William Durant of Flint, Michigan, after much persuasion, acquired control of the Buick concern. He built Buick quickly by turning his carriage dealers into auto dealers. Later he would go on to establish General Motors. Ransom Olds found a new home with the

REO Motor Company—"REO" being his initials. Both Buick and Ford were turning out "B" model cars—Ford's sold for $2,000, Buick's for $850. A Cadillac tourer was priced at $900.

Among the developments noted by the discerning tire-kicker of the day: the Pierce Great-Arrow had its gearshift on the steering column, following the Winton's earlier lead in the U.S.; windshields were offered as an accessory; in its factory, Olds was rolling car frames past assembly stations where workmen added successively more parts and pieces; the Sturtevant of Boston came with an automatic transmission and, along with the Fischer, air brakes; Rover of England was employing a tubular backbone-type chassis; Alexandre Darracq of France pressed out steel frames from sheet metal, a Darracq held the flying kilometer record (driver, one M. Baras) with a 100-hp. machine.

Europe continued to lead with its better roadways. But with its good roads and bad, America had embraced the motor vehicle for all time.

DANSK Built in 1900 for the Dansk Automobil og Cykelfabrik (Danish Automobile and Bicycle Factory) by H. C. Christiansen and Company, this car is one of the earliest built in Denmark and followed the design and construction of the early French cars. It had a Danish-built 3-hp., water-cooled engine, with a French carburetor, located in the front of the car. Bore was 85 mm. and stroke 100 mm. Displacement: 566 cc. A friction disc provided the primary drive and a single chain was the final drive. Steering was by tiller.

ARGYLL VOITURETTE This vehicle was built by Alexander Govan in 1900. He was working for the Scottish Cycle Manufacturing Company of Glasgow and from there he assembled a Renault, a De Dion Bouton, and a Darracq. This gave him enough experience to build his own design. The 2.75-hp. engine was front-mounted, driving through a cone clutch, sliding-pinion gearbox and drive shaft to the live rear axle, obviously of Renault influence. The Hozier Engineering Company was formed to manufacture the car, and at least 100 were built and sold. The car can be seen in the Museum of Transport, Glasgow, Scotland.

COLUMBIA MARK XIX ELECTRIC SURREY This U.S. automobile was built in 1900 as a result of the merger of the Electric Carriage and Wagon Company of Philadelphia with the Electric Storage Battery Company, which became the Electric Vehicle Company and further merged in 1899 with the Pope Manufacturing Company—America's largest bicycle builder. Columbia was the brand name given to their vehicles. The Surrey was slow but quiet, and the company soon turned to the gas engine.

RAMBLER STANHOPE This is one of the first cars built by Thomas B. Jeffery, founder of Rambler, in 1900. It was not a production car, but it led to the development of future Ramblers that were produced by his son, Charles T. Jeffery.

RIKER ELECTRIC AUTO It may appear strange but, at the beginning of the twentieth century, the electric motor was far better developed than the internal-combustion engine. The Riker Motor Vehicle Company, Elizabethport, New Jersey, produced this electric-powered car in 1900. Two motors were installed in front of the rear axle, each geared to the closest wheel with a ratio of about 10 to 1. Wheels were wood with solid rubber tires. The wheelbase was 82 inches and the tread 54 inches in front and 65 inches at the rear. The body was enclosed and made of wood. The driver sat high at the rear, in the open. A voice tube led from the enclosed passenger compartment to the driver. Motors were driven by 48 cells in four battery containers. Voltage was over 100. The car is now on exhibit in the Smithsonian Institution, Washington, D.C.

CLEVELAND ELECTRIC CAR The Cleveland Electric of 1900 was little more than a mechanical buggy. The rear-mounted motor was powered by accumulators. Three speed positions were provided: 2.5, 5, and 10 mph. A shovel or machine-gun-type hand grip was fitted onto the steering tiller. The brake was operated by twisting this hand grip. The company later converted to gasoline engines and built many motorcycles.

VIVINUS One of Belgium's early auto pioneers was Alexis Vivinus, who began building motor vehicles in 1899 when he introduced a small gasoline-powered car. In 1900 he produced a companion car that was much faster (25 mph. vs. 35 mph.). This is the car pictured here, and it used a vertical, twin-cylinder, 7-hp., water-cooled engine. It was fitted with a three-speed, sliding-pinion gearbox and shaft drive.

CLÉMENT PANHARD   Adolph Clément, who formed the Clément-Gladiator Company in 1896 and produced cars, owned the majority of shares in the Panhard-Levassor company. This lightweight vehicle was produced in 1900. The three-seater was fitted with a 5-hp., single-cylinder engine mounted in the rear. It was designed by the Panhard-Levassor chief engineer, Krebs, after Levassor's death.

PACKARD B RUNABOUT   The Packard brothers, James Ward and William Dowd Packard, decided to build their own cars when, during an argument with Alexander Winton, Winton taunted: "If you are so smart, Mr. Packard, why don't you build a car yourself?" James was a graduate mechanical engineer, and this Runabout was their second car in 1900. A single-cylinder, 9-hp. engine drove the 950-pound vehicle at 22 mph. Packard designs improved yearly so that Packard became one of the most respected names in motoring.

RAMBLER MODEL A This was another Thomas B. Jeffery experimental Rambler built in 1901. It had a water-cooled engine that was centrally located. The finned-coil radiator was mounted in front of the hood. Notice that a steering wheel instead of a tiller steering system was used.

BERLIET NO. 72 TYPE B PHAETON This four-cylinder-engine-powered two-seater Berliet design was produced in 1901. The engine was front-mounted as was the finned-coil radiator just below the single headlight. Cooling water reservoir was at the rear. Ignition was by means of a chain-driven magneto. Drive was via cone clutch, rear pinion and chain. The 16-hp. engine had a bore of 100 mm. and stroke of 120 mm. It had four forward speeds plus reverse.

ARROL-JOHNSTON DOG CART This British auto was built in 1901 by the Mo-Car Syndicate, which consisted of Sir William Arrol, George Johnston, T. Blackwood-Murray, and Norman Osborne Fulton. In 1899, Murray and Fulton left the group to make another car, the Albion. The early Arrol-Johnstons were single-cylinder powered, but in 1901 they transferred to a twin-cylinder, opposed-piston, 12-hp. engine. In this arrangement two pistons are fitted in each cylinder and two crankshafts are needed. The car was simple and strong and weighed 2,000 pounds. Speed was 20 mph. The type was manufactured until 1905.

BRASIER Brasier had been a designer for the Mors Company where he did an excellent job and seemed to concentrate on the larger types. Eventually he opened his own business. The 1901 model was one of his first and features a rear entrance for the back passengers. Of special interest are the spiral-spoked rear wheels that were fitted with very narrow tires. Note the side-mounted spare tire, windshield, and steering wheel.

COLUMBIA GAS RUNABOUT The Pope Manufacturing Company, builder of Columbia electric cars, hired Hiram Percy Maxim to design and produce gasoline-powered vehicles. His first gasoline-powered car appeared in 1901 and had a high-speed vertical engine and a three-speed, sliding-pinion gearbox. Power was 5 hp. and speed of the car was 35 mph. Maxim was the son of Sir Hiram Maxim, who had built a steam-powered airplane and invented the Maxim machine gun.

RENAULT VOITURETTE Following the pattern set by the Renault Brothers—Louis, Marcel, and Fernand—this 1901 product sported a live rear axle and drive shaft. This model was the Type "D" and was powered by a single-cylinder, front-located, water-cooled engine of 450 cc. The bore was 80 mm. and stroke was 90 mm. The car had three forward speeds plus reverse, and this two-seater could attain about 30 mph.

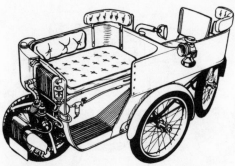

SUNBEAM MABLEY This most unusual vehicle was produced in 1901. There were four wheels: one each side of the car at the center; the remaining two were in front and rear but were not in line with each other. The front wheel was offset to make room for the single-cylinder, air-cooled, 2.75-hp. De Dion Bouton engine. Steering was by a machine-gun grip that controlled both front and rear wheels. The driver sat in the rear and the passengers sat at right angles to the car's direction.

DUMONT F This unusual and little-known French design of 1901 used the one-cylinder De Dion Bouton variomatic engine mounted in the front under the hood, which sported two modern-looking glassed openings. The body style was a tonneau that seated four with a rear entrance for the back passengers. This car is part of the collection of the Musée de l'Automobile, Château de Grandson, Lac de Neuchâtel, Switzerland.

MARSHALL BENZ DOG CART   This was small and very simple in appearance. Karl Benz preferred to concentrate on the mechanical operation of his cars rather than the outward appearance. This "dog cart" design of 1901 had a one-cylinder, 5-hp., water-cooled engine mounted under the seat. Speeds were shifted by means of a belt on loose pulleys. The belt was shifted from one pulley to another. Final drive was chain to the rear wheel. At this time Benz used a finned-coil radiator instead of an evaporation cooling system.

PACKARD ROADSTER MODEL C   This 1901 Packard was the first Packard with a steering wheel. It also had a convertible top for protection against the weather. Fitted with a single-cylinder, 12-hp engine, the light car had plenty of speed. In fact, one Alden S. Mc-Murtry was arrested for driving down a street in Warren, Ohio, at 40 mph.! During the summer of 1901, five Packards entered the New York to Buffalo endurance run and all five finished. Less than half of the eighty-nine entrants completed the course.

SEARCHMONT The Searchmont Motor Company, Philadelphia, Pennsylvania, produced this double phaeton with surrey top in 1901. It was called the Five Passenger Deluxe Type VII. The frame, made of hickory wood, was reinforced with steel. A 10-hp. engine powered the car with four-speed transmission forward plus reverse. Notice the right-hand drive, of European influence. The last remaining example of this car can be seen in the Forney Historic Transportation Museum, Denver, Colorado.

PIERCE NO. 1 MOTORETTE George N. Pierce was a successful manufacturer of bicycles and birdcages in Buffalo, New York, when he decided to enter the automobile manufacturing business. This is his first car, built in 1901. A single-cylinder, 2.75-hp. De Dion engine powered the vehicle. Pierce went on into the thirties producing cars of ever-improving characteristics.

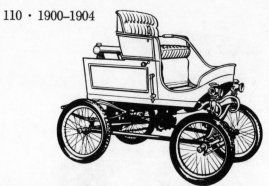

TOLEDO STEAMER STANHOPE MODEL A The American Bicycle Company of Toledo, Ohio, produced the Toledo Steamer Stanhope Model A in 1901. It was one of the heaviest steam carriages regularly manufactured in that period, weighing 1,450 pounds. The body frame was wood with aluminum panels, and the front of the body was an aluminum casting. Power was a two-cylinder, inline, rear-mounted steam engine with 3-inch bore and 4-inch stroke. The boiler was a water-tube, spiral-tube type with 38 square feet of heating surface. The 35-gallon water capacity could last for about thirty miles. Fuel was pressurized gasoline carried in two tanks of 4.5 gallons each, located under the footboard. Air pressure in the tanks was maintained via a pump driven from the engine. Pressure was necessary to feed the torch-like burner: water was forced into the boiler via an engine-driven pump. The engine was connected to the rear axle via a chain. This car is on exhibit at the Frederick C. Crawford Auto-Aviation Museum, Cleveland, Ohio.

NAPIER Montague Napier was the third generation of his family to practice engineering. He made his first road vehicle in 1900. In 1902 the racer shown here won the Gordon Bennett Race from Paris, France, to Innsbruck, Austria. This 45-hp., four-cylinder auto averaged 31 mph. over the entire 384-mile course, which was in rather poor condition. Its maximum speed was over 70 mph. The car was driven by Selwyn Edge.

RAMBLER MODEL C In 1902, Tom Jeffery sold his bicycle business and opened a factory in Kenosha, Wisconsin, where he offered his first production car during that year. The plant was placed in the hands of his son, Charles T. Jeffery. This Model C was a single-cylinder, 6-hp., 1,200-rpm., water-cooled, centrally located engine-powered "gas buggy" that could attain 30 mph. The hood was a dummy but doubled as a toolbox. About 1,500 Rambler Model C vehicles were sold in 1902. Rambler was the second U.S. auto manufacturer to employ quantity production methods. Note the tiller steering, which was commonplace during this period.

LOCOMOBILE This Locomobile of 1902 was the first United States gasoline-engine-powered vehicle with a four-cylinder, water-cooled, front-mounted powerplant. During the same year the Locomobile plant at Bridgeport, Connecticut, built the Locomobile Standard that was still steam-engine-powered, so this was a transitional year for Locomobile.

PEERLESS   This 1902 Peerless used the popular tonneau body style of the period with absolutely no protection against rain or wind. These were truly heroic days of motoring when all that mattered was to get the car started and keep it going. Later models of Peerless cars concentrated on more comfort for the passengers.

FRANKLIN   The H. H. Franklin Manufacturing Company built this design for sale in 1902. It had an angle-iron frame with a wooden body and a 71-inch wheelbase. The engine was a 7-hp., four-cylinder, air-cooled type mounted upright and transversely at the front. Each cylinder was individually cast with fins about $1/16$ inch thick. A planetary transmission at the left end of the engine connected to the differential via a long chain. The steering wheel was to the right of center, and on the column were mounted controls for the spark settings and mixture control. The muffler ran under the center of the frame for the length of the car. The gasoline tank also ran the length of the car on the right side. This auto can be viewed at the Smithsonian Institution, Washington, D.C.

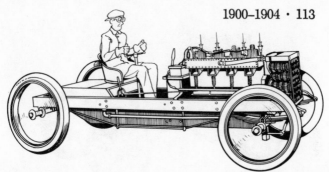

FORD 999 This sprint racer built by Henry Ford in 1902 had neither gearbox nor differential so that it had to resort to push starts and was restricted to straight runs. In January, 1903, it was driven to 91.37 mph., but the run was not officially timed for record purposes. Note the underslung body and steering grips instead of a wheel. With Barney Oldfield at the controls, the four-cylinder racer beat all competitors, including Winton and Packard at Grosse Pointe, Michigan. Oldfield took the turns wide open, not knowing how to operate the brakes, and ended the race a half mile ahead of second place!

HOLSMAN Holsman was a Chicago architect who decided to motorize a standard horse-drawn "high-wheeler," which was the classic buggy. The idea was to use the original large, thin wheels that could cut their way down through mud to firm ground and thereby never be caught in the mire. A two-cylinder, air-cooled, 64-cubic-inch engine was mounted under the seat and a belt was used to drive the rear wheels. The entire engine could be shifted to provide clutch action to the slackened belt. It was produced from 1902 to 1909.

SERPOLLET RECORD RACER Frenchman Léon Serpollet developed his flash boiler in 1885, and two years later used it to power his first vehicle. In 1890, he built a three-wheeler in conjunction with Armand Peugeot and drove the steam-powered vehicle from Paris to Lyon, a 290-mile distance that took two weeks. After this, his steam cars were placed in production. On April 13, 1902, Serpollet drove one of his steam cars to a world speed record of 75.06 mph. The engine was a four-cylinder model, 2.96-inch bore and 3.54-inch stroke, that developed 106 hp. at 1,220 rpm. The car weighed 3,960 pounds. The flash-boiler record breaker is shown.

OLDSMOBILE Ransom E. Olds made America's first mass-produced car in 1900. This 1902 model Oldsmobile followed the "curved dash" motif of many of his early designs. It was fitted with a one-cylinder gasoline engine and a two-speed planetary transmission and chain drive to the rear wheels. The finned-coil radiator was fitted under the curved dash.

SCANIA PHAËTON Maskinfabriks Aktiebolaget Scania, Malmö, Sweden, produced the Scania automobiles from 1902 to 1911, when they merged with Vabis. This is the 1902 model, and its sturdy construction helped in the firm's development of trucks, for which it earned a worldwide reputation. The firm originally made bicycles and is one of the oldest continuous auto manufacturers.

WHITE STEAM CAR This small automobile was made by the White Sewing Machine Company in Cleveland, Ohio, in 1902. Although gasoline was used as the fuel, the car was steam-powered. A semi-flash boiler made from multiple coils of seamless tubing was mounted under the seat. Several coils acted as a superheater; steam was reheated by the furnace, and this led to very efficient operation of the two-cylinder engine, which was also mounted under the seat. Water supply to the boiler was automatically controlled by the steam pressure. Water was carried in a 20-gallon tank near the boiler. Eight gallons of gasoline was carried in the front. It was pressurized by a hand-operated air pump to about 40 pounds per square inch. The engine connected to the split axle differential by means of a chain. This early auto can be viewed at the Smithsonian Institution, Washington, D.C.

ALBION When T. Blackwood-Murray and Norman Osborne Fulton left the Mo-Car Syndicate in 1899 they started their own automobile factory in Glasgow, Scotland. It was called the Albion Motor Car Company, and this car was the 1902 model. The body was of wood and it seated four. The two-cylinder, water-cooled, pump-circulated gasoline engine was located in the center of the body. An internal radiator was fitted. The 12-hp. engine had a bore of 4 inches and stroke of 5 inches with a displacement of 2,100 cc. Two forward speeds and reverse were made available via a sliding quadrant. Speed was 10 mph. The body was absolutely plain, called the "dog cart" style.

PRUNEL RUNABOUT This rare French 1902 Prunel Runabout was powered by a two-cylinder gasoline engine, mounted under the seat. The hood was a dummy to make the vehicle follow the accepted appearance of European cars of the time. Notice the finned-coil radiator and the starter crank running through it.

FORD EXPERIMENTAL   It was in 1899 that Henry Ford left the Edison Plant and helped to organize the Detroit Automobile Company. As chief engineer, Ford's idea was to produce a low-priced car that could be purchased by the average household. His associates had the opposite idea and wanted to build luxury autos for an exclusive clientele. As a result he left the company in 1902. The Detroit Automobile Company later became the Cadillac Automobile Company. This 1902 Ford Experimental was built in Ford's search for a real "people's car." It was utter simplicity in appearance and mechanics.

DARRACQ RUNABOUT Alexandre Darracq manufactured the very successful Gladiator bicycle until he sold the business in 1896. He soon turned to autos, and his first attempt was to hire Léon Bollée to design a car, but the venture was not overly successful. Darracq then turned to the Renault layout, and the design became more promising. This 1902 Runabout used a 6.5-hp., vertical, single-cylinder engine mounted in front. A three-speed gearbox and shaft drive to a live rear axle was used. Although the Darracq was noisy, it was lively and cheap. He soon became the French Henry Ford.

RENAULT K   This racer participated in the Paris to Vienna Race of 1902 and was driven by Louis Renault. During the race a Mors car sideswiped the Renault K and smashed a wheel. Louis pulled to the side, collected wood and whittled new spokes which he quickly fitted, and repaired the wheel. He reentered the race, but the lost time kept him from winning. This car had a four-cylinder, 3,770-cc engine with a bore of 100 mm. and three forward speeds plus reverse. It could attain 75 to 80 mph.

BERNA "IDEAL"   This car was built by Joseph Wyss, an ornamental iron worker from Berne, Switzerland, in 1902. It proved virtually identical to the De Dion Bouton designs of that time, especially the engine and transmission. The one-cylinder, 5.25-hp. engine propelled the car to 25 mph. The body was made by Geissberger of Zurich. The water-cooled engine of 785 cc had an automatic inlet valve and battery-and-coil ignition. Two forward speeds were available through an epicyclic-type expanding clutch gearbox with final drive to the live rear axle by means of gears. This auto can be seen in the Verkehrshaus der Schweiz in Lucerne, Switzerland.

WEBER   J. Weber et Cie. of Uster, Switzerland, were textile machinery manufacturers who decided in 1899 to enter the automobile business. First attempts were with three-wheelers, but the firm soon settled on the four-wheeled small car. This is their product of 1902, which was powered by a two-cylinder, horizontal, water-cooled, rear-mounted engine of 12 hp. Bore was 145 mm. and stroke 160 mm. and displacement 2,510 cc. Belt drive was used. A production averaging sixty per year was maintained until 1906. This car is on exhibition at the Verkehrshaus der Schweiz, Lucerne, Switzerland.

AMERICAN RUNABOUT MODEL A   The American Motor Carriage Company, Cleveland, Ohio, produced this Model A Runabout in 1902. It was powered by a single-cylinder, water-cooled engine of 5 hp. and 117.8-cubic-inch displacement that was built by Mudge of Milwaukee, Wisconsin. The car was 83 inches long on a 68-inch wheelbase, and the price was $1,000. The frame was angle iron with a wooden body. This car is part of the collection of the Frederick C. Crawford Auto-Aviation Museum, Cleveland, Ohio.

STANLEY After abiding by their agreement to remain out of the auto business for at least two years when they sold out to Mobile and Locomobile, the Stanley brothers returned to the business in late 1901. This is one of their first products and is of 1902–1903 vintage. Basically a two-passenger runabout, the folding footrest in front can convert to two additional seats. The 4.5-hp. engine was mounted on the rear axle and was the first to employ direct-gear drive. The wheelbase was 70 inches, and the car could maintain 30 mph. It was the first auto in the U.S. to be used as a police prowl car, and the first to be used by an American fire department. It can be seen at The Magic Age of Steam, Yorklyn, Delaware.

KNOX SEVEN-PASSENGER TOURING This car was built in Springfield, Massachusetts, for family transportation. The front seat was a folding type but sturdy enough to carry two adults. Power was a one-cylinder, air-cooled gasoline engine. The engine used a "porcupine" cooling system with corrugated stud pins driven into the cylinder walls to help carry off the heat. With this system, every square inch of block surface was multiplied to 32 square inches. Suspension, steering and motor mounts, and axles were of cast bronze. This car is now in the Car and Carriage Caravan, Luray Caverns, Virginia.

CADILLAC MODEL A   This is considered to be the first Cadillac automobile offered to the public, and the price was $800 in 1903. The design was developed in 1902 and was fitted with a single-cylinder, water-cooled, 98-cubic-inch-displacement engine that was built by Leland & Faulkner. It was centrally located, horizontally, with the cylinder facing to the rear. (A drawing of the Cadillac Model A engine is also shown here.) The finned-coil radiator was recessed into the front of the car in an effort to keep the heated air from flowing up and toward the passengers. The water was circulated by means of a pump. This car had planetary transmission with steel pinions and bronze gears. Two forward speeds and one reverse were available. A single chain connected the transmission to the divided rear axle. The car had a steel frame and wooden body and weighed 1,350 pounds. The car is now on view at the Smithsonian Institution, Washington, D.C.

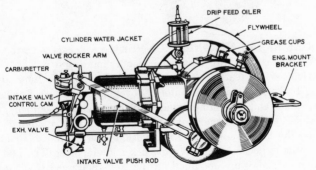

SPEEDWELL ROADSTER This lightweight car, intended for very personal transportation, was constructed in Manchester, England, in 1903. It was powered by a one-cylinder, water-cooled gasoline engine developing about 6 hp. The gas tank was located under the dash panel, and the driver's compartment was so small that a large man could not get his knees under the steering wheel, but an average-size woman could. Only one door was fitted and that was just 12 inches wide. Tires were 26 by 3 inches.

AUTOCAR REAR-ENTRANCE TONNEAU Autocars were the first U.S. production cars with more than one cylinder and the first U.S. production cars to feature shaft drive instead of chains. Internal expanding brakes were also an Autocar development. Lewis S. Clarke, vice president and consulting engineer of the Autocar Company, was responsible for these advanced design concepts. The company concentrated on the larger cars, such as this 1903 Rear-Entrance Tonneau, and eventually became a renowned truck manufacturer. The body of this car is of mahogany, mounted on the steel-reinforced wood frame by means of four full-elliptic springs. A two-cylinder, horizontally opposed engine was fitted.

HELIOS   This Helios truck of 1903 was made in Sweden by Soder-talje Verkstader AB from a German prototype. It was fitted with a two-cylinder, water-cooled gasoline engine. Wheels were wood with iron rims. Note the circular radiator below the hood or bonnet. Helios was the brand name for the truck, which continued to be produced until 1906.

WINTON BULLET NO. 2 RACER   This was Alexander Winton's third racing car and was one of the first automobiles to be fitted with an eight-cylinder, inline engine. The vehicle was constructed for the fourth Gordon Bennett Race in 1903. This was held in Ireland, and Winton drove his own car until minor mechanical failure forced him to drop out. The car was later raced in the U.S., and on January 28, 1904, the legendary Barney Oldfield attained a speed of 83.7 mph. on the sands of Daytona Beach. This was just short of beating the world's record. The eight-cylinder engine was made by bolting two four-cylinder engines together, a practice still used today. The cylinders were in a horizontal position to improve visibility, and the engine displaced 1,029 cubic inches. The engine was in the center of the chassis and was of the four-cycle type. The crankcase and intake manifold were aluminum as were the two water pumps. The radiator was the box type mounted at the front of the car. The wheelbase was 111 inches and the tread was 56 inches. This auto can be seen at the Smithsonian Institution, Washington, D.C.

PEERLESS REAR-ENTRANCE TONNEAU In this 1903 model Peerless the frame was pressed steel and the body of wood. As in previous years, it featured the tonneau style with a rear entrance for the back passengers. Seating capacity was five, and total weight of the car was over 2,000 pounds. A two-cylinder, water-cooled engine was located in front, vertically. The radiator was a series of finned coils, which can be seen in front of the hood or bonnet.

OLDS RACER With only the bare essentials placed on this 1903 Olds Racer, and no body at all, it covered a one-mile measured course at Daytona Beach, Florida, in 43 seconds. Note the box radiator and streamline water and fuel tank behind the radiator. The effectiveness of a streamline body was open to question in those days, and so Ransom Olds selected simplicity as the pattern for this speedster, as did Henry Ford with his 999 racer.

WOLSELEY By 1902, Wolseley was England's largest firm concentrating on motorcars. The company was started by Herbert Austin, later Lord Austin. He was a farmer's son and emigrated to Australia to work for the Wolseley Sheep Shearing Machine Company. He returned home to England in 1893 to manage the firm's Birmingham factory. After visiting Paris to examine the French autos, he built his first vehicle in 1895. The 1903 product shown here weighed almost 2,000 pounds, and was powered by a 10-hp., two-cylinder engine of 2,600 cc. The engine was very reliable.

FORD MODEL A In June, 1903, thirteen men organized the Ford Motor Company. Capital raised was $100,000, and Henry Ford placed his prototype car of 1903 as the equivalent of $25,000. The Model A of that year was an immediate success, and 1,708 cars were sold at $850 each. Ford was the third manufacturer to employ mass production methods in the construction of his cars, although he is often regarded as the first to do so.

MORS RACER   The Paris-Madrid Race of 1903 caused such loss of life due to crashes and spectator deaths that it was stopped at Bordeaux and no car was permitted to be operated back to Paris. They were all pushed or towed by horses back to Paris. Among the deaths was Marcel Renault, and the race was called the "Race of Death." Although there was no winner, the outstanding contender was this Mors Racer, driven by Ferdinand Gabriel. The car was very streamlined except for the underslung radiator. The four-cylinder, F-head, inline, 70-hp. engine gave the car a maximum speed of about 80 mph. The 342 miles of the race that were covered were made at an average speed of 65.3 mph. The engine displaced 10 liters.

STANLEY STEAMER RACER   This streamlined automobile, nicknamed the "Wogglibug," was the last steam-driven car to establish a record. It was designed and built in 1903, and on January 26, 1906, it established a world speed record of 127.66 mph. Frank Marriott was the driver in this record run. A two-cylinder steam engine was fitted, and the car body was of wood.

CRESTMOBILE D The Crestmobile was built by Crest Manufacturing Company, Cambridge, Massachusetts. This is the D model marketed in 1904 in a choice of two colors: red or green. The body was the tonneau type, constructed of wood on a tubular steel frame, and seated four. The 1,200-pound car had a vertical, single-cylinder, air-cooled gasoline engine mounted in front. The powerplant developed 8.5 hp., and connected to the rear wheels by means of clutch and friction bands and then a drive shaft to bevel gears. Two forward speeds and one reverse were fitted. A tonneau cover with windshield was offered as optional, at extra cost. Base car was $800; with tonneau cover $900; and with windshield and cover $1,050.

HUTTON NAPIER Using much of what was learned from the 1902 Gordon Bennett racer, Napier produced this 1904 version. It was fast and was offered as a sporty car to the public. He increased the engine to six cylinders, but other items were virtually the same as in the racer. This sporty roadster-type design was used by many manufacturers, and it proved popular during the next decade and later. It was built at Acton, England. In the following year a six-cylinder Napier, driven by Arthur MacDonald, set a world's record of 104.65 mph.

STEVENS-DURYEA STANHOPE   This runabout design was built in 1904. It is a typical three-seater of the period. The gasoline engine was of the two-cylinder, opposed type and was water-cooled. This particular model was known for its reliability and hill-climbing ability. A car of this type, under 1,000 pounds, sped the measured mile at Ormond-Daytona Beach in 57 seconds and beat the old record by 9 seconds. The 7-hp. engine had a bore of 4.75 inches and stroke of 4.5 inches, and revolved at 700 rpm. The front seat hinged forward for access to the engine.

WALTHAM ORIENT BUCKBOARD   The Waltham Manufacturing Company, Waltham, Massachusetts, marketed the Orient automobiles for many years. This was the 1904 model Orient Buckboard. It was the minimum car, not more than a double seat on the bare tubular frame. With an 80-inch wheelbase, the vehicle weighed 500 pounds. A 4-hp., air-cooled, single-cylinder engine was located in the rear. Two speeds via planetary transmission and spur-gear drive were provided; tiller steering was used. As shown here, without top, the price was $425. The purpose of buckboards was a cheap, quick method of transportation, but many customers used them as pleasure vehicles as they were considered sporty.

BERG This Berg tonneau of 1904 was sold by the Worthington Automobile Company, New York, New York. The body was constructed of wood covered with blue-painted aluminum and could accommodate five passengers. Total weight was 2,200 pounds, the wheelbase was 96 inches, and tread 56 inches. The powerplant was a four-cylinder, vertical, front-located, water-cooled engine. Four forward speeds and reverse were accomplished by means of a sliding-gear transmission. Final drive was double chain. Both wheel and differential brakes were provided. The gasoline tank held 14 gallons and the horsepower was 24. This advanced mode of road transportation was priced at $3,500 as shown here, but with a convertible top the price was $3,750.

NORTHERN REAR-ENTRANCE TONNEAU This Northern Touring Car was produced in 1904 and seated five. Body was wood on a steel angle frame. A 15-hp., two-cylinder, horizontal, opposed, water-cooled engine was located under the hood. The wheelbase was 88 inches on this 2,000-pound auto. Batteries and a jump spark provided ignition for the gasoline engine. Planetary gears provided two forward speeds and reverse. A drive shaft transmitted power to the rear wheels. One color was available: green. Brakes were on the rear drums. A fan was installed to draw air through the radiator. This car can be viewed in the Long Island Automotive Museum, Southampton, New York.

NORTHERN RUNABOUT   Produced by the Northern Manufacturing Company, Detroit, Michigan, the Northern automobiles were created by Charles B. King and Jonathan Maxwell, a pair of famous automobile pioneers. The Northern was said to make less noise than electric cars. This 1904 Runabout had a wood body on a steel angle frame. The two-seater weighed 1,100 pounds, and had a wheelbase of 67 inches. A single-cylinder, 6.5-hp., water-cooled, horizontal engine was installed under the seat. It had a planetary transmission with two forward speeds and reverse, and chain drive to the rear wheels. It came in one color: red. Brakes were on the differential. This car is on display at the Museum of Transportation, Larz Anderson Park, Brookline, Massachusetts.

SIDDELEY   J. D. Siddeley produced this two-seater in 1904. It participated in the old car run from London to Brighton, England. It was fitted with a 13-hp., water-cooled, two-cylinder engine. In 1910 the company became Siddeley-Deasy, and it eventually became a big name in the aircraft industry due to further mergers. This car can be viewed in the Cheddar Motor Museum, Cheddar, England.

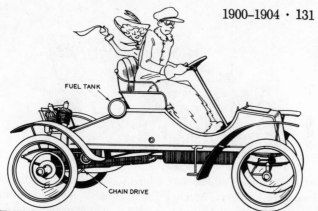

FUEL TANK

CHAIN DRIVE

ORIENT BUCKBOARD This runabout was produced by Waltham in 1907. A two-cylinder, vee-type, air-cooled engine was rear-mounted. Top speed was 40 mph., and the price of this very simple vehicle was $600. Chain drive was used to the rear wheels.

DARRACQ "GENEVIEVE" Alexandre Darracq was a successful bicycle manufacturer who turned to the automobile industry and became famous with his Société A. Darracq, Paris. His cars were reliable and featured every modern attachment of the day. This model was produced in 1904 and is now called Genevieve only because it was featured in the British film of that name in the 1950s! This is a two-seater runabout with a speed of 30 mph. It was fitted with a two-cylinder, water-cooled, 12-hp. engine, mounted forward. The gearshift lever was mounted on the steering column. Three forward speeds were of sliding-gear design. Foot accelerator, shaft drive and good brakes were added features. It is now on display in the Gilltraps Auto Museum, Collangatta, Queensland, Australia.

CADILLAC This Cadillac was built in 1904, five years before the company joined General Motors. The Cadillac Automobile Company was managed by Henry Martin Leland, a skilled engineer, who guided the general design of all models concentrating on passenger comfort and safety. This 1904 Cadillac was exported to many countries, and from 1904 to 1907 it was the most popular taxi in Stockholm, Sweden. A one-cylinder, water-cooled engine was centrally mounted and drove the rear wheels by a chain.

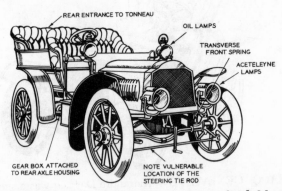

PACKARD MODEL L This product of the Packard Motor Car Company appeared in mid-1904 and was classed as a five-passenger tonneau. It weighed 1,900 pounds and had an aluminum body on a pressed steel frame. The detachable canopy was fitted with a glass front, which gave the passengers a great measure of comfort. The engine was four cylinders, water-cooled, vertical, 22 hp., located in front. Three forward speeds plus reverse were obtainable via sliding gear with a bevel-gear final drive. Brakes were fitted to the rear wheels and were the expanding type. The wheelbase was 94 inches and the tread was 56.5 inches. It was the start of the Packard luxury cars.

CLÉMENT-BAYARD TONNEAU   Adolf Clément's S.A. des Ets. Clément-Bayard, Paris, produced this car in 1904 after a short partnership with Panhard. A two-cylinder, water-cooled, 10-hp. engine was fitted forward, and a three-speed gearbox with cone clutch drove the rear wheels via an open propeller shaft. Note the radiator instead of finned coils. This car is on display at the Verkehrshaus der Schweiz, Lucerne, Switzerland.

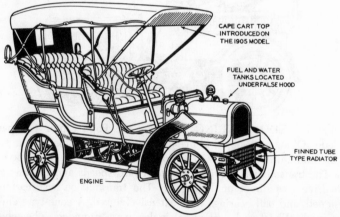

CAPE CART TOP INTRODUCED ON THE 1905 MODEL

FUEL AND WATER TANKS LOCATED UNDER FALSE HOOD

FINNED TUBE TYPE RADIATOR

ENGINE

BUICK MODEL B   The very first production Buick automobile was built in 1904 after David Buick had built sixteen experimental vehicles during the previous year. It was powered by a 22-hp., two-cylinder, valve-in-head, centrally located, water-cooled engine fitted with planetary gears. Two forward speeds and reverse were available. Final drive was by a chain to the rear wheels.

BAKER ELECTRIC RACER The Baker Motor Vehicle Company of Cleveland, Ohio, built this streamlined racer in 1904 to race at Daytona Beach. It was called the "Electric Torpedo" or "Torpedo Kid" and cost about $10,000 to build. It was clocked at 104 mph. in trying to establish a world's record.

POPE TOLEDO TOURING Built by the Pope Motor Company, Toledo, Ohio, in 1904, this five-passenger touring type had a steel frame and sheet-steel body. This gasoline-powered car developed 24 hp. The transmission provided three forward speeds and reverse, and the drive was direct on high gear. The transmission was carefully designed, and ball bearings were extensively used. A cone-type clutch was used. Wheel and differential brakes were provided. The wheelbase was 93 inches and tread 34 inches. It was one of the first automobiles to have a baked-on enamel finish.

BELLAMY This French roadster of 1904 is ultra modern in its basic configuration but did not bother to cover the straight eight-cylinder engine with a hood or bonnet. Also, no headlights were installed. The engine developed 200 hp., which surely made the vehicle one of the fastest production cars of the era.

RAMBLER MODEL K TONNEAU In 1904, Rambler sales soared to 2,342 vehicles due to enclosed cars like this Model K Tonneau. Many auto makers ignored the comfort of the passengers, who were at the mercy of wind, dust, rain, etc. The Model K provided a large windshield, overhead cover, with roll-down side curtains. Wheel steering returned from the experimental prototypes. The engine was a two-cylinder L type, mounted centrally.

OLDS This Olds was introduced in 1904 and was a five-passenger rear-entrance tonneau and featured wheel steering. Engine was a single-cylinder, 8-hp., water-cooled unit mounted in the front. Oldsmobiles were so popular that they inspired a popular song of that period. This was the first mass production car in the United States.

PACKARD GRAY WOLF RACER In 1903, two racing enthusiasts, Krarup and Fetch, crossed the United States in a Packard in 61 days. In the following year the company built this 1904 "Gray Wolf" racer. The four-cylinder, water-cooled machine was mentioned as a possible contender in the Gordon Bennett Race, but did not enter. The "Gray Wolf" did, however, gain fourth place in the 1904 Vanderbilt Cup Race. Packard, never really interested in racing, dropped out of the sport for a decade before trying again.

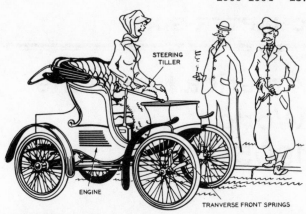

STEERING TILLER

ENGINE

TRANVERSE FRONT SPRINGS

OHIO PACKARD MODEL F   This Model F appeared early in 1904 and was the last type built by the New York and Ohio Automobile Company, Warren, Ohio. The Packard brothers and two former Winton employees formed another company, later in the year, to be known as the Packard Motor Company in Detroit, Michigan. This car was a typical gas buggy like most other U.S. cars of the period, but it had three forward speeds and reverse. It was powered by a single-cylinder gasoline engine. Displacement was 3,035 cc, and it was fitted with a jet carburetor and automatic inlet valve. An epicyclic gearbox with single chain to a live rear axle was installed. Suspension was by means of longitudinal springs in the rear and a transverse spring forward. Later in the year Packard switched to the heavier cars for which they became famous.

ROSS RACER   In the early days of motor racing the steam engine was, by far, preferred over the gasoline engine because it had many more years of development behind it, including flash boilers and direct drive to the wheels. Many steam racers actually geared the engine up to the wheels so that the driven axle rotated faster than the engine crankshaft. This Ross Racer of 1904 was exceptionally streamlined and earned the nickname "Steam Kettle."

CHAPTER SIX

America Leads the World 1905—1909

DURING THIS five-year span the United States not only retained production honors, but an American car won the longest race in history: 13,431 miles, New York City to Paris by way of Chicago, San Francisco, Yokohama, Vladivostock, St. Petersburg, and Berlin!

England, however, began to acquire a reputation for turning out fine cars. Much of this was due to the partnership between Frederick Henry Royce and the Hon. Charles Stewart Rolls, the latter a balloonist, car dealer, and auto racer.

During 1905, in America the Society of Automobile (later, Automotive) Engineers was formed; the president was A. L. Riker of Locomobile; one of the vice-presidents was Henry Ford. Many advocates of steam and electrical power began to drop by the wayside. A big debate raged over air-cooling vs. water-cooling. Cadillac's one-cylinder and four-cylinder offerings started to outsell both the Oldsmobile and Ford products. Ford's Barney Oldfield left to drive Winton's "Bullet No. 2" racer. But Ford did acquire a promising patternmaker by the name of C. C. Sorensen.

A White Steamer led the inaugural parade for President Theodore Roosevelt. Winton displayed an eight-cylinder motor. Percy Pierce, driving a Pierce Great-Arrow, was judged best in the first Glidden Tour by his participating peers. It was an 870-mile jaunt from New York City to Bretton Woods, New Hampshire, and return. The big Pierce machines sold from $3,500 to $5,000; the smaller topless Stanhope was $1,200. Winning the

138

Glidden Cup didn't hurt sales a bit. Sears, Roebuck & Company started selling cars, and a bus line was established on Fifth Avenue in New York City.

By now most American cars followed the European (i.e., Levassor) configuration: engine forward, next the transmission, then the drive. But breakdowns were more frequent here than overseas. Although Elwood Haynes had invented a process to produce tungsten chromium steel in 1884, many American-made components were still crafted from the less suitable carbon steel. All too often this meant too-weak springs, broken drive shafts and axles. Eventually vanadium and other special steels would help solve some of these problems.

In France, the Mors car offered a reliable self-starter that ran off compressed air. The Italian Fiat had pressure lubrication.

During 1906, Frederick Marriott, chief mechanic for the Stanley organization, drove a Stanley Steamer racer along the sands of Ormond-Daytona Beach, Florida, averaging 127.66 mph. for a world record. Fred was the first to exceed the two-mile-a-minute mark.

It was late in this year that the Rolls-Royce "Silver Ghost" with its special aluminum-painted touring body was developed. Without the body the car sold for 950 pounds, or almost $5,000. The six-cylinder R-R produced an extremely quiet 48 hp. at 1,700 rpm. It soon acquired the title of "best car in the world."

U.S. production for 1906 consisted of 33,200 passenger cars and 800 trucks for total sales of $62,900,000. Rather impressive. Gasoline storage facilities were being created for the motorists' use, even though new steam cars—the Doble, for example—continued to make their appearance.

While Fiat in Italy was going into production with detachable-rim wheels, it remained for Renault Frères to employ similar Michelin rims on their Le Mans racer with spectacular success. The first French Grand Prix race, Le Vingt-Quatre Heures du Mans, held over a two-day period, June 26 and 27, was captured by M. Szisz in a 13-liter Renault that averaged better than 63 mph. over the nearly 780 miles of quite miserable racing surface. Thirty-two cars entered: three German, six Italian, the remainder French. Each manufacturer was limited to three entries, none of which could weigh more than 2,200 pounds; horsepower was optional—with the sky the limit.

Our own Smithsonian Institution got into hot water during this period by giving the nod to Elwood Haynes as having pioneered the gasoline-engine car in America. Six years later the Institution corrected itself on the strength of documents provided by Duryea representatives. This controversy was to have its counterpart in the aeronautical section's decision on who was first to fly!

The Federal government, evidently deciding that roads were here to stay, unveiled its Office of Public Roads, known formerly as the Office of Road Inquiry. The annual budget for the department was a whopping $37,660. Henry Ford acquired the majority of the stock in his company and became its president. During the 1906–1907 model year, Ford became the world's largest manufacturer of motorcars by turning out 8,423 Model "N's." With small size tires, each of these sold for $550. The Ford company made a million dollars in profit. Henry was well on his way to industrial sainthood.

The former Oldsmobile jack-of-all-trades, Roy Chapin, organized the Thomas-Detroit Company with Howard Coffin. The latter would play a prominent part in World War I aircraft production.

John North Willys set up the American Motor Car Sales Company and was prepared to contract for the entire output of the budding Overland Company. He figured he could sell every Overland he could get his hands on.

Howard Marmon unveiled America's first air-cooled V-8 engine to utilize an aluminum block. Although it never went into production, it did lead to the use of aluminum alloys in powerplants. Most propulsion interest centered on the new six-cylinder engines offered by such concerns as Ford, Franklin, National, Pierce-Arrow, and the Stevens-Duryea. The latter car with all accessories sold for $6,000. Who said Rolls-Royces were expensive?

Buick dropped its basic price to $1,000 and sold 1,400 cars. The air-cooled Franklin light tonneau cost $1,650. The Chadwick was first in the U.S. to use a supercharger.

1907 was the year that Buick won the hill-climbing competition at Dead Horse Hill in Worcester, Massachusetts; the car had a four-cylinder engine and a sliding-gear transmission.

Even though a financial panic swept the United States, automotive sales increased sharply to more than $93,000,000. Willys took over Overland Motor Car Company and moved it from Indianapolis to Toledo. Fred Marriott took another crack at the absolute speed record in his Stanley racer. This time his steamer literally took off after reaching an unofficial speed of 190 mph. That was the end of the Stanley and very nearly the end of Fred.

France's Léon Serpollet died; in 1899 he had invented the flash boiler, which raised steam to operating levels within two minutes for the steam cars.

As a sort of warm-up run for the following year's New York-Paris Race, a French newspaper sponsored a Peking, China, to Paris dash. Prince Borghese drove a 40-hp. Italian Itala and completed the race in 60 days to win.

In 1908, George Robertson racked up a 64.39-mph. average in the Vanderbilt Cup Race driving the 120-hp. "Old 16" Locomobile. Operated along the privately owned Long Island Motor Parkway, this was the first victory by an American car in the competition.

The New York to Paris Race ended in victory for the six-cylinder, 70-hp. Thomas Flyer and its team of Montague Roberts and George Schuster. The winner averaged 151 miles per each running day and overall required 170 days to complete the awesome journey.

Vanadium-alloy steel was produced for Ford just in time for the new left-hand drive Model T, which made its bow on October 1—after having been announced to dealers in March. Initially the $850–$875 car came in red as a tourer, or in gray as a roadster. It had a four-cylinder inline engine of 20 hp. The car weighed 1,200 pounds, was ten feet long, and would do 35 mph. Anybody could drive it and most any man or boy could fix it. The T was an instant success.

The big four of U.S. motordom were now Buick, Ford, Maxwell-Briscoe, and REO. Each concern turned out 8,000 or more cars in 1908. Buick led with 8,487. Cadillac sold a modest 2,380 cars. Industry total was 63,500 passenger vehicles. By now about 400,000 cars were registered across the U.S.

The Royal Automobile Club in England awarded Cadillac the annual Sir Thomas Dewar silver cup for most meritorious performance in tests furthering the interests and the advancements of the automobile industry. The French decided to drive on the right side of the road and standardize the steering wheel on the left side of their cars.

Among American concerns getting under way was General Motors, headed by William Durant; it soon acquired Olds, also Buick, then a truck maker, the Rapid Motor Vehicle Company. Charles and Frederic Fisher set up the Fisher Body Company; they would be joined by their brothers Alfred, Edward, Lawrence, and William. Studebaker tied in with the Everitt, Metzger and Flanders Company, builders of E.M.F. cars, and arranged to take the firm's output of motors and chassis.

Chicago & Great Western Railroad's superintendent of motive power, Walter P. Chrysler, bought his first car, a white Locomobile, for $5,000—which he didn't have. But it was still a wise buy, for three years later he was plant superintendent of G.M.'s Buick Division.

Robert C. Hupp raised $25,000 to start the Hupp Motor Company and soon was selling a stripped-down machine for $750, later called the Hupmobile. Sears, Roebuck featured the Sears Motor Car in its catalog at a price range of $395 to $495; the car was made from 1905 to 1910. The "Brush" sold for $485.

By 1908 more than 500 concerns had entered the automobile manufacturing field; of these more than 60 percent had already gone out of business.

The first crossing of the American continent by a woman driver was accomplished by Mrs. John R. (Alice) Ramsey in a Maxwell. With three other ladies she departed from New York City on June 9 and arrived in San Francisco 53 days later.

Roy Chapin and Howard Coffin next set up Hudson Motor Car Company with the backing of department store owner J. L. Hudson. The subsequent Hudson car offered a sliding-gear transmission, quality workmanship, and a price tag of under $1,000.

G.M. next acquired Oakland and Cadillac. Kettering left National Cash Register to help form Dayton Engineering Laboratories Company (DELCO) to work on ignition problems. He was soon to receive an order for 4,000 self-starters from Leland at Cadillac.

The United States Circuit Court handed down a decision in favor of the A.L.A.M. against Ford. But Ford's lawyers were of the opinion that the judges just didn't understand the technical aspects of the case. So Ford fought on.

1909 saw President William Howard Taft and his family riding about in a White Steamer; he was the first President to order an official White House car.

Electric lamps appeared in the United States along with overdrive and easily converted tops. In Europe, Isotta Fraschini introduced four-wheel brakes. Among the magazines of the day were London's *Automotor Journal* and Denver's *Steam Motor Journal.*

In Detroit, Louis Chevrolet started work on a car of his own design. Nearby on Woodward Avenue the first rural mile of concrete pavement was poured. In all the U.S. there was a grand total of five miles of concrete roadway. Improved roads now added up to 190,476 miles; all roadways totaled 2,199,645 miles. And the Office of Public Roads received the grand sum of $87,390 as its twelve-month budget.

The international speed record had been raised to more than 125 mph. But something more important was just around the corner—standardization. We encounter it full force during the following five years and find that it took some of the romance out of motoring.

COLUMBIA ELECTRIC BROUGHAM Built by the Pope Manufacturing Company in 1905, this partially enclosed auto was powered by 88 volts from wet-cell batteries in the bottom. This electric-powered car permitted five forward speeds up to 18 mph. Pneumatic tires were fitted. The enclosed section was a great stride forward in providing for passenger comfort and safety. The car can be viewed in the Silver Springs Early American Museum, Silver Springs, Florida.

COURIER F Built in 1905 by the Sandusky Automobile Company, Sandusky, Ohio, the Courier F model was a 1,100-pound two-seater with a wood body and steel angle frame, and a wheelbase of 70 inches. This roadster type was powered by a single-cylinder, 7-hp., horizontal, water-cooled, front-located engine. Ignition was by means of jump spark, and the sliding-gear transmission permitted two forward speeds and reverse. Final drive was via chain to the rear wheels, and brakes were on the differential gear.

HAYNES MODEL L   Elwood Haynes was a metallurgical engineer who built a variety of automobiles for several years. He is the inventor of stainless steel and stellite, an alloy used where extreme durability is needed. The Model L was built in 1905 and Haynes designed and built not only the car but the engine, muffler, transmission, and steering wheel. This 1,500-pound vehicle could seat four and was priced at $1,350. The engine was two cylinders, opposed, water-cooled, 18 hp., and the very first gasoline engine fitted with roller bearings. Operation was extremely quiet. Three forward speeds and reverse were controlled by a single lever on the steering column. A single chain drove the rear axle. The gasoline tank and water tank were each six gallons. Lubrication was force-feed and ignition was a jump spark. This car is exhibited in the Elwood Haynes Museum, Kokomo, Indiana.

DUFAUX RACER   The brothers Frederic and Charles Dufaux of Geneva, Switzerland, built several large and powerful racing cars between 1904 and 1907. This is their 1905 water-cooled model. They also constructed an air-cooled racer during that year. Although this car did not win any races during the year, Frederic Dufaux covered a flying mile at Arles, France, at a speed of 97.26 mph. The four-cylinder engine could develop 150 hp. and displaced 26.4 liters.

RAMBLER SURREY This Surrey Type 2 was introduced by Rambler in 1905. It gave the passengers considerable comfort with the large windshield and top. President Theodore Roosevelt rode in a Type 2 in a parade in Louisville, Kentucky, on April 4, 1905. One of these cars entered and completed the Glidden Automobile Tour in 1905.

ROLLS-ROYCE GREY GHOST RUNABOUT In 1904 Henry Royce experimented with two-seaters based upon the Decauville. At that time he joined forces with the Hon. C. S. Rolls, and the famous Rolls-Royce name was founded. In 1905 a rakish two-seater was developed called "Grey Ghost." It was a basic runabout design with a four-cylinder, water-cooled engine. Forty of these automobiles were manufactured. The car is exhibited in the Resnick Motor Museum, Ellenville, New York.

PEUGEOT The Peugeot family had manufactured hardware in France since the French Revolution. Later, bicycles were constructed by the same firm: Les Fils de Peugeot Frères. Eventually they turned to the automobile. This is the company's product of 1905, the Type 68. It was a five-seater powered with a one-cylinder, 820-cc, water-cooled engine mounted in front. Bore and stroke were 102 mm. This car can be viewed in the Provinciaal Automobielmuseum Houthalen, Domaine de Kelchterhoef, Houthalen, Belgium.

DECAUVILLE This Decauville 24–28 was sold by the Standard Automobile Company, New York, New York, at a price of $7,900 with top as shown here. This 1905 model had a pressed steel frame and could seat eight. It weighed 2,250 pounds, and had a wheelbase of 110 inches. A four-cylinder, vertical, water-cooled engine was front-mounted. Four speeds via sliding gear were fitted, plus reverse and bevel-gear drive. Note the luggage rack and the trunk at the rear. This was considered a heavy, quality car at the time. It was available in any color.

MERCEDES   The Mercedes was born when Gottlieb Daimler agreed to build lower-slung modern cars and give them the name of his business associate Émile Jellinek's eleven-year-old daughter. This 1905 Mercedes was the fifth year of Mercedes production. It was a side-door model that seated five. Weight was 2,112 pounds, and the wheelbase 123 inches. The frame was pressed steel in four sections and had a large windshield and a rear window. A luggage rack was provided on the roof. A four-cylinder, vertical, water-cooled engine was front-mounted and developed 50 hp. Four-speed transmission via sliding gears and chain drive to each rear wheel was provided. A fan was attached to the flywheel to aid in radiator cooling. Three types of brakes were installed: on differential, countershaft, and on both rear wheels, which were water-cooled!

MARMON   Howard Marmon had been a flour-milling-machinery manufacturer since 1850 before he entered the automobile business in 1902 and founded the Marmon Motor Car Company in Indianapolis, Indiana. This 1905 model was powered by a vee-type, four-cylinder, air-cooled engine, mounted in front. What appears to be a radiator is really a screened air inlet to cool the engine. Marmon concentrated on simplicity of design and luxury automobiles.

MERCEDES RACER Mercedes products were racing since 1901 and most were specially designed cars. This 1905 model was powered by a 115-hp. engine of 14 liters displacement. The Mercedes team scored fifth and seventh in the 1905 Gordon Bennett Race; sixth in the Ardennes Race; ninth in the Coppa Florio; and fastest times at shorter races, such as Kesselberg, Semmering, and Gaillon. Tire trouble prevented first place wins during the year, however, but many other race drivers bought the Mercedes as well as the superb Mercedes engine for their own use.

REO The name REO is the initials of Ransom E. Olds, the American auto genius. The cars were built at the REO Motor Car Company, Lansing, Michigan. Some items that were stressed as an aid in sales were: freeze-proof radiator, perfect and positive lubrication, strength, jar-proof radiator. REO cars won the National Trophy and two prizes in the New York Motor Club's six-day Economy Test in 1905. The car shown here is the REO Buggy of 1905.

OVERLAND MODEL 17   The first Overlands were simple little two-seaters, built by the Standard Wheel Company, Terre Haute, Indiana, and marketed by the Overland Motor Car Company. This Model 17 was a two-cylinder, water-cooled-engine-powered two-seater of 1905. This was the first Overland with a steering wheel, and a conventional hood and radiator were fitted. This car cost $750 bare with no frills. John Willys took over the company three years later and the name changed to Willys-Overland.

FORD MODEL B   This Model B was Henry Ford's first touring design and it made its appearance in 1905. It was also Ford's first car with a four-cylinder engine. This 20-hp. engine sported copper water jackets. A planetary transmission with two forward speeds and reverse was fitted. This was also the first Ford torque-tube drive. Price was $2,000.

BLACK RUN-A-BOUT This true "horseless carriage" of 1906 was made by the Black Motor Company, Chicago, Illinois. It had solid tires, high buggy wheels, and externally greased hubs. A two-cylinder, transverse, air-cooled engine was rear-mounted. The entire car was wood except for some steel reinforcing.

ADAMS FARWELL STANHOPE The Adams Foundry, Dubuque, Iowa, built this seven-passenger Stanhope design in 1906. It was one of the first cars to use a rotary engine, not like the Mazda Wankel, but rather like the early form of rotary whereby the crankshaft is attached to the vehicle and the crankcase and cylinders are attached to the driving mechanism. They whirl around the crankshaft and this movement aids in their cooling. The engine was a three-cylinder radial type.

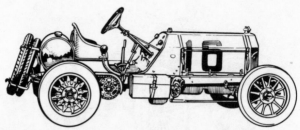

LOCOMOBILE CUP RACER   This car was specially constructed for the 1906 Vanderbilt Cup Race. It was powered by a 90-hp. gasoline engine of 976-cubic-inch displacement and still used chain drive. With Joe Tracy at the wheel it emerged first at the American Eliminating Trials and made the fastest lap of the race. Because of tire troubles, however, it placed tenth. The same car with the same number—"Old 16"—entered and won the 1908 Vanderbilt Cup Race with George Robertson at the wheel, averaging 64.39 mph. A virtual twin car, driven by Jim Florida, placed third in the race.

RENAULT 8CV AG   This Renault taxi was introduced in 1906 and had a four-cylinder, side-valve engine of 30 hp. It revolved 1,200 rpm. The design had shaft drive to a live axle. This automobile's claim to historic fame was that the Renault taxicabs of Paris were used to rush French troops to the Marne River to stop the German advance in 1914. They have, ever since, been called "Taxis de la Marne."

CADILLAC TOURING This 1906 Cadillac Model B touring car sold for $900 with the tonneau shown. More Cadillacs were sold than any other make at the New York Auto Show of 1904, which suggests that the auto-buying public wanted comfort and safety coupled with substantial performance. Cadillac concentrated on a superior muffler design to achieve quiet operation. The frame was pressed steel, and a propeller shaft was fitted to replace the old chain drive.

COLUMBIA MARK XLVII The Electric Vehicle Company, Hartford, Connecticut, was selling this double victoria in 1906 for $5,000. It was a large car for the time: weight 3,100 pounds; wheelbase 112 inches. Seating capacity was for five passengers in a pressed-steel frame. A four-cylinder, water-cooled, vertical, front-mounted, 45-hp. engine was fitted behind the radiator, and a fan was mounted on the engine, as is present-day practice. Four forward speeds and reverse were provided via sliding gears and a double side-chain drive.

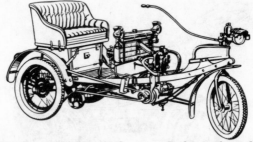

LA CROIX DE LAVILLE Without much change from their previous models, La Croix De Laville brought out this three-wheeler in 1906. A De Dion Bouton single-cylinder, water-cooled, 700-cc, front-mounted engine was fitted with a bore of 90 mm. and stroke of 110 cc. Body and chassis were of wood. It had a belt drive that permitted two speeds by slackening off the belt and transferring to another driving pulley. The original car is on exhibition at the Provinciaal Automobielmusuem Houthalen, Domaine de Kelchterhoef, Houthalen, Belgium.

PEERLESS MODEL 14 The Peerless Motor Car Company, Cleveland, Ohio, produced cars that were respected for thirty years, starting in 1902. This roadster was built in 1906 and was one of the firm's smallest cars. It seated five persons; three sat facing to the rear on an improvised "rumble seat." A 30-hp., four-cylinder, vertical, water-cooled engine was located under the hood. Four forward speeds and reverse were via sliding gears and then bevel gear to the rear wheels. The pressed-steel car weighed 2,500 pounds and had a wheelbase of 107 inches.

OLDSMOBILE MODEL S Ransom E. Olds designed this Olds-mobile in 1906. It was the first side-entrance Olds and seated five. This was also the first four-cylinder Olds of 26 hp. A cone-type clutch and three-speed gearbox plus shaft drive were features of this design. The car weighed 2,200 pounds and had a wheelbase of 106 inches. The price was $2,250.

RAMBLER Thomas B. Jeffery & Company produced this Rambler Model 15 in 1906. It was a five-passenger tonneau with a four-cylinder, water-cooled, 35-hp., front-mounted engine. Sliding-gear transmission gave three forward speeds and reverse. The name "Rambler" was stopped in 1914, and subsequent cars by the company were called "Jeffery" in honor of the founder. In 1916 the name changed again to "Nash."

FORD K   This 1906 Ford K touring car was fitted with a six-cylinder, 40-hp. engine. It weighed 2,000 pounds and the wheelbase was 114 inches, same as the 1949 Ford. This is considered to be Henry Ford's only mistake. The car was finely finished, but with the high power and weight the price was too much for the average man: $2,500.

FORD N   By 1906 Henry Ford owned 51 percent of the stock and became president of the growing Ford Motor Company. One of the models to appear that year was the "N." It was the first car ever driven by Edsel Ford. The Model N was a runabout two-seater powered with a four-cylinder, 15-hp., front-mounted engine. The car sold for $600 with oil lamps.

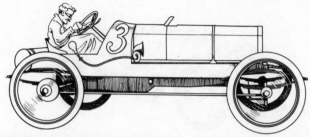

STANLEY STEAMER RACER Two of these Stanley steam cars were built for the Vanderbilt Cup Race in 1906 but did not enter that auto classic and never reached the Eliminating Trials. The speedsters were, however, frequently raced at Daytona and elsewhere, without success, by F. E. Stanley and Fred Marriott. This design was the basis for three models of roadsters offered to the public by Stanley during the years 1906–1908. The 20-hp. Gentlemen's Speedy Roadster claimed the title of Fastest Stock Car in the World after averaging over 68 mph. over a fifteen-mile handicap at Ormond Beach and attaining a maximum speed of 75 mph.

AUTO-CAR SIGHTSEEING BUS This open-air sightseeing bus was a novelty in 1907 and set the pace for future vehicles of this type. It was built in 1907 by the Auto-Car Equipment Company, Buffalo, New York, not to be confused with the renowned Autocar Company of Ardmore, Pennsylvania. It could seat ten.

LION-PEUGEOT In 1897 Peugeot established Société des Automobiles Peugeot and built many automobiles under this banner. In 1900 the separate Lion-Peugeot firm was established. In 1908, however, the two firms joined forces to become S. A. des Automobiles Peugeot. This Lion-Peugeot of 1907–1908 was a two-seater runabout powered by a single-cylinder, water-cooled engine, front-mounted, and with chain drive.

POPE WAVERLEY ELECTRIC MODEL 67 This victoria phaeton was produced by the Pope Motor Car Company, Waverley Dept., Indianapolis, Indiana, in 1907. Pope was a large concern with other plants in Toledo, Ohio, and Hartford, Connecticut. This electrically driven two-seater was powered by a 60-volt D.C. motor which was fed by accumulators. It could run about thirty miles between chargings. Pope also made gasoline-powered cars during this period.

THOMAS N.Y.C.-PARIS RACER The Paris newspaper *Le Matin,* in conjunction with *The New York Times* and the *Chicago Tribune,* planned an automobile race from New York to Paris! Virtually every country and auto manufacturer became involved in this stupendous undertaking. The sponsors originally planned the race to run from New York's Times Square to San Francisco via Chicago and then to Alaska and across the ice that they thought froze over the Bering Strait, across Siberia to St. Petersburg, and then on to Berlin and Paris. When it was discovered that the Bering Strait did not freeze over, the course was corrected so each car could be shipped to Yokohama and Vladivostock. George Schuster and Montague Roberts won the race in 1908, in a Thomas Flyer sponsored by the Thomas Company of Buffalo, New York. The car was a regular 1907 Model 35 taken right off the production line. It was a six-cylinder, 70-hp. model and cost $4,500 when new. It can now be seen in Harrah's Automobile Collection, Reno, Nevada.

TURRICUM In 1904, Martin Fischer of Zurich, Switzerland, began making the Turricum automobiles. This touring model was produced in 1907. A four-cylinder, water-cooled, front-mounted engine developed about 12 hp. and drove the car at about 30 mph. The bore was 80 mm. and the stroke 100 mm., with a displacement of 2,010 cc. It is on display in the Verkehrshaus der Schweiz, Lucerne, Switzerland.

INTERNATIONAL AUTOWAGON The International Harvester Corporation built this light truck in 1907. It was the very first of their long line of successful trucks. Of high-wheeler design, the rear area resembles the modern pickup truck. The body was wood on a steel chassis. A two-cylinder, 20-hp., air-cooled engine was installed.

BRASIER Brasier continued with his large luxury cars through 1907, of which year this car is an example. This five-seater was of tonneau styling with straps holding the collapsible cover in place. Only one door was provided for the driver and his partner, while two were provided for the rear passengers. The spare tire was mounted to the right side of the body, affixed to the circular frame shown. Note the large-diameter pneumatic tires, almost balloon types.

CARTERCAR MODEL E   This is the Cartercar tonneau for 1907. A runabout was also built during that year. The Model E was fitted with an Artz folding rear roof, which provided some protection for the five passengers. Price for this vehicle was $1,350. The Cartercar-patented friction drive induced W. C. Durant to incorporate Cartercar into the expanding General Motors.

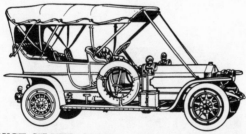

ROLLS-ROYCE SILVER GHOST   Frederick Henry Royce built his first car in 1904, at which time he met the Hon. Charles Stewart Rolls. In 1904 Rolls-Royce, Ltd., was founded, and in 1906 the famous Silver Ghost was born. The car was a strict luxury item: chassis price was $7,000 with body built to order. A six-cylinder, L-head, 430-cubic-inch, water-cooled engine was fitted. The wheelbase was 135 or 143 inches. It featured dual exhaust, full-floating rear axle, and magneto and battery ignition. The basic Silver Ghost remained in production, with very minor mechanical modifications, for nineteen years. The Ford Model T is the only car to rival this longevity.

ARGYLL   Front-wheel brakes and a single-sleeve-valve engine were features of this 1907 Argyll. The company never entered races and preferred to concentrate on the mechanical reliability of their machines. The four-cylinder engine was built under license from Burt & McCullion, which had designed it.

ELMORE   The Elmore Manufacturing Company, Clyde, Ohio, produced this double phaeton in 1907. It was unusual because it featured a three-cylinder, two-cycle, sleeve-valve engine in order to achieve simplicity and reduce maintenance, but neglected the more efficient four-cycle design. Two-cycle engines are sometimes used today for lawnmowers or cheap motorbikes where the lubricating oil must be poured into the fuel tank. The car was a success and sold for $1,750 F.O.B. the factory. The Elmore Manufacturing Company was incorporated into General Motors Corporation in 1909 because of its two-cycle engine.

RELIABLE DAYTON This five-passenger double phaeton touring car was manufactured by the Dayton Motor Company, Chicago, Illinois, in 1907. It was a high-wheeler with solid rubber tires. The engine was two-cylinder, transverse, water-cooled, and front-mounted. A solid rear axle was fitted, with the differential mounted ahead of it. Chain drive was used, as was tiller steering.

TENSION STYLE COIL SPRINGS

BRUSH This runabout design was made in 1907 by A. P. Brush, who had designed Cadillac's first one-cylinder engine. The suspension utilized coil springs instead of the standard leaf springs, which was considered a very progressive development. The engine was water-cooled and under the hood behind the radiator. Note the left-hand steering position, which is standard in the U.S.A. today.

STANLEY EX   This steam-powered car made money for the twin brothers, and the model remained in production from 1905 to 1908. It was the smallest and least expensive Stanley during this period: the price was $850, without lamps or windshield. The wheelbase was 90 inches. This car could not maintain the high speeds of the other Stanley products but had a high rate of acceleration with its 10-hp. engine.

OVERLAND   This Model 22 of 1907 was the last Overland car, because in the following year John Willys gained control of the firm, and subsequent cars were Willys-Overland. This roadster was the first four-cylinder-engine Overland. It seated two under a folding top and had full-elliptical springs. The gearshift lever was on the steering column. The price of this vehicle was $1,250.

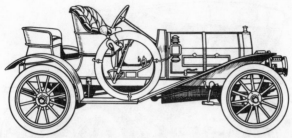

CRAIG-TOLEDO This sporty roadster of 1907 was a basic two-seater with a jump seat behind. This arrangement was popular during the period. The automobile sold for $4,000, a considerable amount for that era. Note the spare tire location, which kept the driver from falling out on rough roads because steering was on the right side of the car.

AMC This sleek, sporty-looking roadster was produced by American Motors Company of Indianapolis, Indiana, in 1907. The underslung frame gave it the racy appearance. A four-cylinder, water-cooled, 40-hp. engine was installed under the hood, which appeared longer than necessary. Note the spare tire location, right-hand steering, and spotlight.

F.W.D. BADGER TOURING   The Badger of 1908 was designed by Otto Zachow and William Besserdich and produced by the F.W.D Automobile Company, Clintonville, Wisconsin. The designers wanted to design a car that could negotiate the deep snows of that area of the United States, so they devised a four-wheel drive that proved practical. It was powered by a four-cylinder, 60-hp. engine, but was produced in limited numbers, probably because of its price of $4,500!

BAKER ELECTRIC MODEL V   This 1908 Baker Electric was very popular with the ladies because it provided conservative transportation at a moderate speed without noise and fumes. It was easy to operate with tiller steering. The car could run from sixty to seventy miles at 25 mph. on a battery charge. The driving motor required 48 volts from a 12-cell battery. This car is exhibited at the Car and Carriage Caravan, Luray Caverns, Virginia.

SCHACHT This little-known American high-wheeler appeared in 1908. It was powered by a water-cooled, two-cylinder, horizontal gasoline engine of 1,600 cc displacement. It was an L-head type with side valves. Coil and battery ignition were used, as well as a variable friction disc transmission. It had chain drive to the rear wheels. A single full-length spring on each side of the car was used for suspension. The firm was based in Cincinnati, and from 1914 until they went out of business in 1938, they concentrated on trucks.

IHC AUTO BUGGY SURREY The International Harvester Corporation, famous makers of farm machinery, entered the automobile manufacturing business in January, 1907. In 1908, this Auto Buggy Surrey was built in the Chicago plant. It was a high-wheeler carriage design seating five or six. The powerplant was an opposed, two-cylinder, overhead valve, air-cooled engine provided with twin fans for cooling at slow speeds. The firm later concentrated on trucks and, in October, 1907, the truck division was moved to Akron, Ohio.

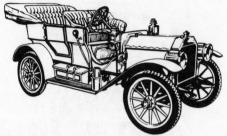

GREAT SMITH The Smith automobiles were made in Topeka, Kansas, from 1902 to 1910. This 1908 product was called Great Smith because it was the largest and most powerful of the line. This five-seater was fitted with a tonneau that provided some protection for the passengers. Note the right-hand drive, which was used on many cars of the period. The car can be viewed in the Kansas Historical Society, Topeka, Kansas.

DELAUNAY BELLEVILLE This car was constructed by Delaunay Belleville at St. Denis, France, in 1908. It was an HB6 Type Town Car with solid mahogany coachwork beautifully executed by Kellner & Ses Fils of Paris. A six-cylinder, water-cooled, front-mounted, 4,086-cc engine powered this luxury vehicle. The wheelbase was 10 feet 6 inches. Among the owners of Delaunay Belleville automobiles were the Russian Czar Nicholas II and Baron Rosenkrantz. The latter brought his car to the U.S. In all it traveled over 300,000 miles with very little trouble and is now on display at the Car and Carriage Caravan, Luray Caverns, Virginia.

CHRISTIE FRONT-WHEEL-DRIVE RACER   John Walter Christie was an American inventor who anticipated many naval, automotive, and armored military-vehicle concepts well before they became generally accepted. Christie was the first to use front-wheel drive and also the first to use a transverse engine installation. He pioneered the coil-spring, telescoping, and shock-absorbing suspension to replace the leaf spring. Another first was the vee-type engine application to the automobile. The 1908 car shown was a Christie demonstration racer that incorporated all of these advanced concepts. The "V-4" engine is tilted to the rear, and the front wheels are connected directly to the engine crankshaft, which took the place of the front axle. Clutch slipping was used to start rolling instead of a differential in turns. The radiator is in front of the driver. The engine was of 19 liters displacement.

AUSTIN LANDAULET   Herbert Austin designed this landaulet (differs from a limousine of the time in that the driver is protected) in 1908. It was a comfortable five-seater that was often used as a taxi or fashionable town car. A voice tube connected the passenger compartment with the driver. Power was either 18 or 24 hp. Later, Herbert Austin directed his talents toward much smaller vehicles.

AJAX LANDAULET The Ajax was a temporary designation for automobiles that were once called Rambler and wound up as the Nash with Jeffery in between. This landaulet appeared in 1908 and not only gave some comfort for the driver but the passengers had their choice of open air or enclosed protection from the weather via a folding top. The engine was a four-cylinder, water-cooled, front-mounted type of 3,420 cc. Bore was 100 mm. and stroke 104 mm., and the engine could develop 22 hp. and drive the vehicle at about 40 mph. Because of its rugged structure and well-arranged body it was often used as a taxi. The car can be viewed at the Verkehrshaus der Schweiz, Lucerne, Switzerland.

F.N. TYPE 2000A This automobile was manufactured in Belgium by Fabrique Nationale d'Armes de Guerre in 1908 and is very unusual because of the total enclosure of both driver and passengers which gave them a quiet, safe, and clean ride. A water-cooled, four-cylinder, inline engine of 1,545-cc displacement was fitted under the hood. A high-tension magneto ignition system was installed. Cylinders were of the L-head type. Three forward speeds plus reverse with shaft drive were fitted. Suspension was half-elliptic springs on all wheels. The F.N. Company began constructing automobiles in 1900.

S.P.O. RACEABOUT   This sport racer was built by Ste. Fse. de Petit Outillage, Seine, France, in 1908 and placed eighth in the first 24-hour race at the Brighton Beach, England, course on September 11 and 12, 1908. The car was driven by Juhasz and Kjeldsen, and they accumulated 955 miles in the race while the winner accumulated 1,107 miles in 24 hours. The S.P.O. survived a sideswipe accident by a disabled Renault, but this slowed the car. The power was a four-cylinder, water-cooled engine of 24 hp. and 241.7-cubic-inch displacement. The wheelbase was 104 inches. Notice the canvas-strip fenders that were used for racing because of their light weight. Cost of this car was $3,200. This car can be viewed at the Museum of Automobiles, Morrilton, Arkansas.

DÜRKOPP   Nikolaus Dürkopp of Bielefeld, Germany, began building automobiles in 1898, and some were sold in Britain as the Watsonia. This Dürkopp five-passenger touring car was built in 1908 and was powered by a four-cylinder, .6-liter, 24-hp. engine mounted in front. Automatic inlet valves and low-tension magneto and coil ignition were installed. This car can be seen in the Automuseum, Minden, Westphalia, Germany.

FORD S ROADSTER   This two-seater with an additional rear rumble seat was an improvement on the Model N and was deluxe appointed. The roadster sold for $750, while a more austere runabout cost $700. It was powered by a four-cylinder, vertical, front-mounted, water-cooled engine with shaft drive to the rear wheels. The wheelbase was 84 inches, and the car weighed 1,100 pounds. Speed was 45 mph. The car is on exhibition at the Long Island Automotive Museum, Southampton, New York.

WALTHAM ORIENT BUCKBOARD   Not to be confused with the Orient auto products of Germany, this Orient Buckboard was made by the Waltham Manufacturing Company, Waltham, Massachusetts. Although this 1908 product resembles the runabouts and roadsters of the period it was called a buckboard. The objective was to provide a very cheap automobile for the masses, but it was also a considerable improvement over previous buckboard types which were nothing more than a powered flatbed. Waltham was absorbed by the Metz Company in 1909.

PANHARD-LEVASSOR This 1908 product of Panhard-Levassor provided exceptional comfort for the three passengers but none for the driver and the fourth passenger. The car weighed 3,000 pounds on a 109-inch wheelbase. The frame was metal-sheathed wood with steel reinforcing. A four-cylinder, 35-hp., water-cooled engine was fitted with jump spark, battery and magneto. Sliding-gear transmission gave four forward speeds plus reverse. It was considered a luxury automobile for the period. The car can be viewed in The Raben Car Collection at Aalholm Castle, Nysted, Denmark.

DE DION BOUTON This product of De Dion Bouton was produced in 1908 and was the Type BG Tonneau. It was fitted with a single-cylinder, four-cycle, water-cooled, front-mounted engine of 924 cc. The rear axle design was the De Dion type that was so successful that many other manufacturers used it on their automobiles. The De Dion rear driving axle consisted of two half shafts and an axle tube to locate the rear wheels. This was patented in 1894.

PIC-PIC   This Pic-Pic was built in Geneva, Switzerland, in 1908. Pic-Pic was a luxury automobile and often called the Rolls-Royce of Switzerland because of its elegance and reliability. The car can be viewed at the Verkehrshaus der Schweiz, Lucerne, Switzerland.

JEWEL MODEL E STANHOPE   This Jewel Model E Stanhope was manufactured by the Forest City Motor Car Company, Massillon, Ohio, in 1908. Simplicity was the keynote of the design. It was powered by a two-cycle, one-cylinder, 10-hp., 63.6-cubic-inch-displacement gasoline engine with a bore of 4.5 inches and stroke of 4 inches. The car weighed 1,020 pounds on a 68-inch wheelbase and was priced at $800. The transmission was a two-speed planetary-gear design, and drive to the rear wheels was by chain. The body frame was steel angle, and the fenders were of patent leather, as was the side covering between the fenders and body. The gasoline capacity was five gallons. This car can be seen at the Frederick C. Crawford Auto-Aviation Museum, Cleveland, Ohio.

VULCAN   This Vulcan was built in 1908 in England. The body was a modified tonneau called "King of the Belgians" and was often decorated with vertical stripes that represented the ultimate in elegance in 1908. The engine was a four-cylinder, water-cooled, inline of 3,913-cc capacity. Three forward speeds plus reverse were fitted, which drove the rear axle with a shaft and bevel gears. A speed of 45 mph. could be attained. Price was close to $5,000.

MENARD AUTO BUGGY   The Windsor Carriage Wagon Delivery Works, of Windsor, Ontario, owned by Moses Menard, made this auto buggy in 1908. It was the first automobile to be made in Canada using all Canadian parts, i.e., the first all-Canadian car. It was fitted with a twin-cylinder, opposed, air-cooled engine. Friction drive was used for transmission with chain drive to the rear wheels. This car can be seen at the Western Canadian Pioneer Museum, Wetaskiwin, Alberta, Canada.

FORD MODEL T   The legendary Model T made its initial appearance in 1908. With only minor modifications the "Tin Lizzie" lasted for twenty years and was truly a "car for everybody." It was the first Ford with left-hand steering. Power was a four-cylinder, water-cooled, front-located engine with built-in flywheel magneto. The engine produced 20 hp. at 1,600 rpm. Displacement was 176.7 cubic inches. The wheelbase was 100 inches. Planetary gears were used, and two forward speeds plus reverse were standard. The price in 1926 was $260, the all-time low!

BUICK MODEL 10   This Buick double phaeton was built in 1908 and was the first Buick to have the engine located in front. Shaft drive was used from the gearbox to the differential. During this period Buick bodies began to assume their sturdy and heavy appearance, and it was cars like this Model 10 that caused Buick sales to exceed 10,000 cars in 1909.

RAMBLER 34-A This unusual runabout was produced by the Thomas B. Jeffery Company in 1908. It was a two-seater with an additional jump seat in the rear over the axle. The car was utter simplicity in order to reduce the selling price so as to be more attractive to the less affluent. No windshield or cover of any sort was provided.

HUDSON MODEL 20 The Hudson Motor Company was founded on February 24, 1909, by eight Detroit businessmen including Joseph L. Hudson, a famous department store owner, after whom the car was named. This 1909 Model 20, the very first Hudson offered to the public in July, 1909, was an immediate success. More than 4,000 of the roadsters were built and sold by the end of the year. The car weighed 1,900 pounds and was powered with a 22.5-hp., four-cylinder, L-head gasoline engine and a sliding-gear transmission. Notice the additional rumble seat behind the two regular seats. The automobile sold for $900 in 1909.

HUPP   The Hupp Motor Company was formed in 1908 in Detroit, Michigan, with the intent to produce an American automobile that would surpass the European models being imported. The cars were of medium size so as not to command a high price. The model shown here was produced in 1909. This five-seater was a side-entrance tonneau and on the large side for a Hupp. A four-cylinder, water-cooled engine was located under the hood. A runabout was also produced in 1909. The cars became known as Hupmobiles.

UNIC TAXICAB   French auto designer Georges Richard, of taxicab fame, built this landaulet taxi in 1909 to meet London Police regulations. Notice that the driver sat alone on a single seat while the passengers were well protected from the elements. French cars dominated the taxi trade in London for several years, and this style of body was used in London until the thirties. The engine was a four-cylinder, L-head type. The cars were extremely rugged, and one is reported to have traveled over 500,000 miles! One of the Unic Taxicabs can be seen in the Forney Historic Transportation Museum, Denver, Colorado.

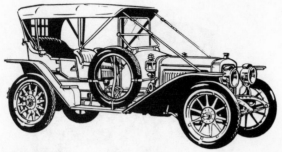

LOZIER MODEL H   H. A. Lozier sold his two bicycle factories in 1899 to enter the automobile business in Detroit. This five-place touring car was built by H. A. Lozier & Company in 1909. The auto was powered by a six-cylinder, water-cooled, T-head engine with the cylinders cast in pairs and with two plugs per cylinder. Displacement was 555 cubic inches which developed 50 hp. Bore was 4.5 inches and stroke was 5.5 inches. The wheelbase was 131 inches and the tread was 56 inches. A four-speed transmission was fitted. Price was $4,600. Quite often Lozier's customers bought two different bodies; a large touring type and a small sporting type! These could be interchanged on the same chassis. The car is on exhibition in the Frederick C. Crawford Auto-Aviation Museum, Cleveland, Ohio.

TURRICUM   The Swiss firm of Martin Fischer introduced this roadster in 1909, and it had a very advanced appearance. The two-seater was powered by a two-cylinder, water-cooled engine mounted under the hood. The car can be seen at the Musée de l'Automobile, Château de Grandson, Neuchâtel, Switzerland.

SPYKER   The Dutch Spyker Company is believed to have made the very first six-cylinder engine, in 1903, while some reports indicate that the engine was made by Mercedes. The Spyker shown here is the 1909 runabout. During later years the cars were active in competition: in 1922 S. F. Edge set a 24-hour record at Brooklands, England, at a speed of 74.7 mph., thereby beating the old record by almost 10 mph. The Spyker Company ceased automobile production in 1925.

CLÉMENT-BAYARD ROADSTER   Adolfe Clément's S.A. des Ets. Clément-Bayard produced good-selling cars for many years in his factory in Paris. His cars that were sold in England were known as Clément-Talbots, and his cars were exported as far as New Zealand. This 1909 roadster is typical of the light cars made by the firm. The most unusual visible feature of the car was the fact that two ear-type radiators protruded into the airstream behind the engine compartment. This was done in order to develop a more streamlined hood. Engine was four cylinders, vertical, water-cooled, front-located, 8 hp., and had a displacement of 1,200 cc. Three forward speeds and reverse were available with a drive shaft to the rear axle.

AMOSKEAG STEAM PUMPER   This steam pumper fire engine was built in 1882 as a horse-drawn vehicle. Due to the advances made in automotive development, an internal-combustion gasoline engine was mounted on the front of the vehicle in 1909 to drive the front wheels. A steering wheel and necessary controls were added to the existing driver's station. In the final analysis, a steam engine and boiler were used for pumping water while the gasoline engine was used to propel the vehicle.

MIDDLEBY ROADSTER   This two-seater was intended for personal transportation and was constructed in 1909 in Reading, Pennsylvania. The car was built from wood except for the hood and the fenders, and was powered by a four-cylinder, front-mounted, air-cooled engine. A large fan was fitted to cool the engine at slow speeds. The tires were made from white rubber. The Middleby Roadster sold for $850 in 1909.

NORSK Norwegian attempts to establish an automobile industry were destined to failure because of poor economic conditions and the geographical location. Several pioneers in many fields, such as marine engines, gas turbines, and automobile torsion-bar springing, did emerge. This Norsk of 1909 was made by the Norsk Automobil og Vognfabrik A/S and was one of several Norwegian attempts to manufacture an enduring line of automobiles. The Norsk firm was founded in 1907 and in the following year produced a five-seat double-phaeton type. This 1909 model is of typical runabout styling. Not many were built, but one can be seen in the Norsk Teknisk Museum, Oslo, Norway.

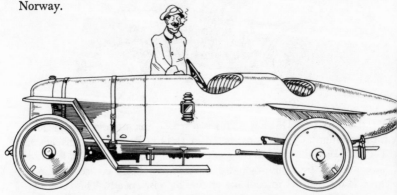

BENZ This streamline Benz street-sports model owes much of its design to the Blitzen Benz (Lightning Benz) racing car of 1909 that developed 200 hp. and could do a one-kilometer flying start at 126 mph. The street version was just as racy looking but had considerably less power. Note the twin cockpits and fenders, plus the underneath exhaust pipe to make it acceptable as a road car.

SEAGRAVE CHEMICAL FIRE ENGINE   This Chemical Fire Engine was made by The Seagrave Wagon Company, Columbus, Ohio, in 1909. In effect, it was a giant soda-acid fire extinguisher! Two sixty-gallon tanks contained a solution of bicarbonate of soda, and in the top of each tank was a container of sulphuric acid. When the two solutions were mixed, pressures as high as 300 pounds per square inch could be generated, thereby eliminating the need for steam pumps or hand pumps. The powerplant was developed by Lee A. Frayer and W. J. Miller. It was a six-cylinder, inline, air-cooled, 990-cubic-inch-displacement engine of about 45 hp. The Frayer-Miller engine was made by the Oscar Lear Automobile Company of Columbus, Ohio.

E.M.F. TOURABOUT 20   In 1905, Studebaker business was so good that they could not supply a sufficient quantity of cars for the demand. Three years later an agreement was made with the Everitt, Metzger and Flanders Company of Detroit, Michigan, for their assistance with Studebaker production. The agreement also called for producing their own cars under the name Studebaker-E.M.F., with Studebaker distributing the cars. By 1909 nearly 8,000 E.M.F. products were sold. Competitors claimed that the initials meant "Every Mechanical Fault." Studebaker bought E.M.F. in 1912. The E.M.F. Tourabout 20 of 1909 is shown here.

WILLYS-OVERLAND This 1909 Model 36 was the first car produced by the company after John Willys gained control. It was a side-entrance tonneau with no windshield or top on the standard models. The engine was a straight six-cylinder type, mounted under the hood, and produced 45 hp. Price was $2,250 in 1909.

PLYMOUTH This Plymouth of 1909 is not to be confused with the modern Plymouth of Chrysler Motors because it was made by the Plymouth Motor Truck Company. It was called the Plymouth Gasoline Pleasure Vehicle and was powered by a four-cylinder, water-cooled, 40-hp. engine. Price was $2,500. The body, a modified touring model, was called a Five Passenger Torpedo. The bump on the hood was a carburetor air-inlet filter.

GRÉGOIRE   This French Grégoire of 1909 is credited with being the first automobile to use electric lights instead of the usual gas or kerosene types then in common use. The two-door, two-seat body had side windows that were most unusual, being made with four panes each. The four-cylinder, water-cooled, front-mounted engine could propel the car at a speed of about 40 mph. It is on view at the Auto Museum, Leidschendam, Holland.

CHAPTER SEVEN

Standardization Sets In 1910–1914

By 1910 the General Motors Company owned outright, or controlled, twenty car and accessory makers, some fairly small. Benjamin Briscoe put together the United States Motor Car Corporation as a rival to G.M. Briscoe gathered 130 firms under his corporate umbrella—a few were worthy endeavors, but all too many were in declining health.

More than 170,000 spectators crowded in to see the exhibits at the Paris Salon de l'Automobile held in the Grand Palais. But few could afford to purchase or even operate the generally ornate and expensive cars on display. The Americans were already far ahead in registered vehicles in proportion to population.

Production in the U.S. in 1910 totaled 187,000 units; this figure included 6,000 trucks and buses. Registration of all types on U.S. roads was almost 470,000 vehicles.

It was the American ability to finance a large-scale manufacturing organization, establish networks of dealerships, and eventually provide thousands of local service facilities that meant world production records would now belong to the United States. No other nation, or geographical area, would be able to challenge the American car output for more than half a century.

At the New York Auto Show the White Steamer auto people showed their first gasoline-engined truck, a three-tonner. A typical passenger car at this American show carried five, was propelled by a four-cylinder gasoline-fueled engine of 40 or more horsepower, and came equipped with vapor gas headlamps and a

186

steering wheel. The more expensive vehicles also included a windshield, a top, running boards, and fenders. Overland, incidentally, was the first make selling at or near the $1,000 mark to provide a windshield and a folding "soft" top as standard equipment.

Electrics were still championed, especially by women, who appreciated their quiet, clean operation and the fact that no cranking was involved. Operating range for the typical 1910 electric was about seventy-five miles at a steady 25 mph. If you wanted to go faster it meant you traveled a shorter distance. The Baker Electric Coupé sold for $2,600.

The venturesome male driver, with money, demanded something more snappy, a car with real "pep." Oldsmobile introduced a large four-cylinder 40-hp. touring racer at $3,200, and an even bigger six-cylinder speedster at $5,000. One of these "sixes" beat the Twentieth Century Limited express train on a run between Albany and New York City.

For all-out speed Barney Oldfield took top honors, setting a land speed record of 131.724 mph. at Daytona Beach, Florida. His machine was a four-cylinder German Blitzen Benz of 200 hp. Barney's mark of 27.33 seconds for the mile would stand until 1922.

Harry Grant won the Vanderbilt Cup Race on Long Island's Motor Parkway driving a U.S.-made Alco. But four deaths during the competition resulted in the end of road racing there. The Glidden Tour covered 2,850 miles over a Cincinnati-Dallas-Chicago route. The first place award was presented to a Premier driven by Ray McNamara, but a Chalmers achieved a technical victory of sorts after a court ruling. Hugh Chalmers demonstrated his promotional flair by presenting baseball's Most Valuable Player with a Chalmers car. Ty Cobb of the Detroit team was a recipient in 1910. For the racing driver, Fred Duesenberg was busy designing new engines featuring horizontal valves.

Although General Motors was turning out about one out of every five cars made in America, all was not clear sailing for the big concern. Buick production and plant construction were both curtailed, and G.M. sales in general fell off. Nevertheless, Cadillac went ahead and ordered 150 enclosed bodies from the Fisher Closed Body Company. Cadillac would soon become the first

U.S. make to offer an enclosed, weatherproof body as standard equipment.

Among the pioneering American car men who died were Thomas Jeffery, George Pierce, and Byron Carter. The latter, of Cartercar fame, expired from injuries suffered when a crank kicked back on him. His death so disturbed his friend, Cadillac's Henry Leland, that Leland ordered an extensive program to develop a dependable starter.

New firms, and new faces at old concerns, included James J. Storrow of Boston's Lee, Higginson & Company taking over the presidency of General Motors; Studebaker buying out the E.M. F. Company partners—Barney Everitt, William Metzger, and Walter Flanders; establishment of the Four-Wheel Drive Auto Company—F.W.D. had been devised by a Clintonville, Wisconsin, blacksmith, Otto Zachow. After seventy-five years in the fire engine business American-La France offered its first motorized vehicle. The King Motor Car Company was set up. Harry Jewett assumed control of the Paige-Detroit firm.

Total vehicle production in the United States in 1911 increased by 23,000 units over 1910. The biggest news of the year came from the U.S. Appellate Court which decided that the Selden patent was "valid, but not infringed" (. . . upon . . . by Ford, and others) because it covered only two-cycle powerplants, not the four-cycle engines which were by now in general use. Ford celebrated by incorporating in England.

In August, 1911, experimental Cadillacs were displayed with Kettering's electric self-starter mechanism. Earlier, less successful starters had been operated by a variety of means including compressed air, powerful springs, or heavy, impractical electrical systems. Boss Ket's patented contribution was a new type of motor-generator that could provide brief 24-volt bursts of power that would not damage or run down a 6-volt battery.

Billy Durant formed the Chevrolet Motor Company by merging the Little and Mason motor firms. Louis Chevrolet was busy designing a new car for the concern. Also significant was Walter Chrysler, the former railroad superintendent, signing on with Buick as plant supervisor.

For the first Indianapolis 500-Mile Memorial Day Race Harry C. Stutz completed his first racing car in his nearby machine shop and drove it to the racetrack, where it placed eleventh in the competition. First place went to a Marmon "Wasp" driven by Ray Harroun at 74.59 mph. A rear-view mirror used by Ray during the race was heralded as a "first." Harroun used the mirror because he eliminated the usual "riding mechanic."

Automobiles acquired a more substantial standing in the financial community when G.M. shares were listed on the New York Stock Exchange. Trucks acquired a new status, too, with their first show at Madison Square Garden. The General Motors Truck Company was formed, also the International Motor Company. The Diamond T firm discontinued passenger cars to concentrate on trucks.

Probably the most striking vehicle abroad was the Panhard-Levassor "Skiff," built by Henri Labourdette, a French coachmaker. With a light three-ply wood sheathing and sparkling wheels it was a true beauty. It was emulated by a few near-copies in several countries.

Besides their electric self-starter, Cadillacs were offering electric headlamps, plus the first timing chain on a U.S. car. This latter feature, borrowed from the Europeans, helped reduce engine noise.

Although Rauch & Lang offered one of the largest electrics ever, a six-passenger town car, for $3,800, Cadillac's sensational starter meant the lady gas-buggy driver no longer had to contend with a crank-handle. And so electrics rapidly lost their primary appeal to all but a small segment of women automobilists.

California led the nation in instituting school bus service and marking traffic lanes on streets via white stripes. Charles Warren Nash, credited with developing the straight-line conveyor belt assembly system much earlier at the Durant-Dort carriage works, took over the presidency of General Motors in 1912. The other big conglomerate effort, Briscoe's United States Motor Car Corporation, collapsed. The Studebaker name, long famous among wagon makers, appeared for the first time on a car.

During 1912 the second Indy 500 was won by Joe Dawson in a National at 78.72 mph.; it would be the last American machine to take first until 1920. During 1912, Durant was producing both the Little (lowest priced six on the U.S. market) and the impressive Chevrolet. Ford was experimenting with a moving assembly line, inspired, it was said, by the overhead trolley systems employed by the beef packers. Ford's Model T was selling for $600. William S. Knudsen joined the Ford organization as manager of the company's more than two dozen factories.

The somewhat superfluous Association of Licensed Automobile Manufacturers became the Automobile Board of Trade. Later it would metamorphose into the National Automotive Chamber of Commerce, still later into the current Automobile Manufacturers Association.

Trucks, buses, and motorcar production in the U.S. for 1912 topped 355,000 vehicles. With something like 250 total miles of concrete highway in the entire country, hard-surfaced transcontinental roadways became the aim of the Lincoln Memorial Highway Association under the prodding of Carl Graham Fisher, who had founded Prest-O-Lite, the company that produced tanked compressed carbide gas systems for headlight illumination.

Most importantly for the industry, and ultimately for the buyer of mass-produced low-price cars, the Society of Automobile (later, Automotive) Engineers' first Standardization Committee had succeeded in reducing the kinds and sizes of various parts and materials that went into an automobile. One example: well over 1,000 different kinds of tubing were trimmed down to 17 sizes and 13 wall thicknesses.

About 1,200,000 passenger cars and almost 64,000 trucks were on the American roads in 1913. The Three P's—Packard, Pierce-Arrow, and Peerless—led the high-price, high-performance, top-quality parade. Yet it was Cadillac that was awarded the Dewar Trophy, and for a second time, in recognition of its reliable, compact electric starter.

Standard Oil of Indiana announced an advanced system of breaking down the heavier elements of crude oil, which resulted in a greater availability of gasoline for cars. The Glidden Tour trophy went to a team of Metz cars, manufactured in Waltham, Massachusetts, which turned in a perfect score. This was to be the last Glidden run until after World War I.

Sometime during the night of September 29–30, 1913, Rudolf Diesel disappeared while crossing the English Channel by steamer. He had created a dependable, heavy-duty powerplant that operated by compression-ignition and ran on low-cost "diesel oil." Herr Diesel had carried out his experiments in France, England, and Germany, and had found a wide market for his commercial powerplants in the United States and around the world.

Ford applied new construction techniques to every possible sub-assembly. His success increased magneto production fourfold via a moving assembly line. Behind America's mass production records were special-purpose tools, the like of which the world had never seen.

During 1913 the Willys-Knight made its debut with a patented Knight sleeve-valve engine that eliminated camshaft, springs, and valves. Instead, two sleeves between cylinder and piston moved almost silently up and down, admitting fuel and expelling exhaust gases.

The Duesenberg Motor Company went into business making engines as well as race cars. Harry W. Ford's Saxon Motor Company of Detroit brought out a stripped-down two-passenger roadster for $395. Harry, no relation to Henry, was an advertising man; the Ford-Saxon operation was bankrolled by Hugh Chalmers. It was not the only effort to trade upon the value of the Ford name. None succeeded. The Saxon, for example, was no match for the Model T, which was being rolled off the production lines at a rate of 1,000 each working day.

Another firm that emerged was the Stutz Motor Company. Its product would compete with the fantastic Mercer designed by Finlay R. Porter and built in Mercer County, New Jersey.

Few realized it when Archduke Franz Ferdinand von Hapsburg was assassinated in Sarajevo, Serbia, but a 1914 Austrian Gräf & Stift phaeton played a memorable part in the start of World War I. The Archduke was riding in the open vehicle when he was shot by a Serbian nationalist on June 28, 1914. The car is still displayed at the Museum of War History (Heeresgeschichtliches Museum) in Vienna.

In America the incomparable and unpredictable Henry Ford had already set agog the automotive world, as well as international business circles, early in January, 1914, by announcing that non-salaried Ford employees would earn not less than five dollars a day for eight hours' work and, furthermore, would participate in a profit sharing program. Then in August, Mr. Ford promised prospective buyers of his Model T that if 300,000 of the ubiquitous vehicles were sold during the following twelve months his firm would rebate between forty and sixty dollars to each purchaser. All this promotional-advertising hoopla, plus sound business acumen, helped raise Ford sales and production to where it was three times that of the nearest competition. Ford dividends totaled $12.2 million and employees divided up a $10-million bonus.

The Dodge Brothers finally went into the car business on their own. Their first offering had a four-cylinder, L-head engine of 35 hp. and sold for $785. Their touring car with its all-steel body, a first for America, was used by the American Expeditionary Forces in Mexico and won special acclaim from the military.

Cadillac became the first U.S. car maker to offer a high-speed V-8 engine. It was rated 60 hp. and was considered by many to be the ultimate in powerplants. The Rambler became the Jeffery . . . for a while. Steamers, although not numerous now, saw the introduction of a pilot light with its own separate fuel system. Providing you replenished your main water supply, this meant a steamer could operate continuously for up to four days.

In England, Humber cars sported steering wheels with a single spoke. Having seven cars for every mile of improved roadway, America boasted its first stop sign to control traffic in 1914 in Detroit. Later in 1914 electric traffic lights were installed in Cleveland, Ohio.

Reviewing historically the traffic go-stop systems, we note that in the 1870s a black American electrical scientist, Lewis Howard Latimer, invented a carbon filament for an electric bulb, and in 1881 he supervised the installation of electric lighting for the streets of New York, Philadelphia, and London. Needless to say, this had a profound effect on the use of the automobile, with improved street lighting very important because of the auto's relatively high speeds. In addition, the development of the incandescent bulb was most important to the automobile once the idea of electric headlights was conceived.

SEARS SURREY MOTOR BUGGY Sears, Roebuck & Company entered the automobile business in their fall 1908 catalog. They tried not to copy any existing vehicle and made simplicity of operation an important part of their advertising. Most of the Sears models were two-seaters; this Surrey of 1910 is unusual. A 14-hp. air-cooled engine used a friction-type transmission, and this friction surface required renewal every 3,000 to 4,000 miles; cost of this was $5. Solid rubber tires.

BERLIET In 1910, the Frenchman Marius Berliet made this sport-ster type that set the style for many other manufacturers. This two-seater was powered with a four-cylinder engine of about four-liter displacement. Speeds were in excess of 35 mph. This car is on exhibit in the Automuseum, Minden, Westphalia, Germany.

HUPMOBILE RUNABOUT By 1910 the Hupp name was changed to Hupmobile, and they produced this runabout during that year. Note the fuel tank, spare tire, and toolbox/trunk located behind the seats. The runabout and roadster two-seaters were favorite products of Hupp because the price was low and the sporty design made them very popular. A four-cylinder, water-cooled engine was installed.

MAXWELL RUNABOUT The late Jack Benny popularized the name "Maxwell" so that virtually everyone in the U.S. during the thirties and forties knew the name although it had ceased to be manufactured in 1924. This roadster was built in 1910 and was equipped with only the bare essentials—no top and no windshield. It was available only in red. The two-cylinder, horizontal, opposed, water-cooled gasoline engine developed 14 hp. In 1910 the car sold for $825.

ISOTTA FRASCHINI The Italian Isotta Fraschini firm was founded in 1899, and they were pioneers in four-wheel brakes and eight-cylinder engines. This Model IM Raceabout of 1910 was a distant relative of the Isotta Fraschini racing cars. It was powered with a four-cylinder, 12-liter, overhead-valve engine, and this was the year that the firm introduced four-wheel brakes. An enclosed oil-bath cabin drive was used.

FIAT In 1899, Count Biscaretti di Ruffia, Giovanni Agnelli, and Count Bricherasio founded the Fabbrica Italiana di Automobili in Turin, Italy. The initials of the firm's name plus the city's formed the name Fiat. The firm produced their first car in November of that year. In 1910, F.I.A.T. produced this tonneau seating seven persons. The basic configuration was that of a limousine with a full-height door for the passengers. It weighed about 2,500 pounds and had a wheelbase of 125 inches. A four-cylinder, water-cooled engine of 2,062 cc was front-mounted vertically. A Daimler-patented radiator was fitted. Four-wheel brakes were an outstanding feature.

DÉLAGE   Starting auto production in 1906 in France, Louis Délage went on later to develop some of the most beautiful cars as well as the fastest cars in many important races. This is his 1910 model roadster, Type T–Series 7. It was fitted with a four-cylinder, 1,320-cc water-cooled engine, with a bore of 62 mm. and stroke of 110 mm. The car is on exhibit at the Provinciaal Automobielmuseum Houthalen, Domaine de Kelchterhoef, Houthalen, Belgium.

BRUSH RUNABOUT   Alanson P. Brush, who designed the first Cadillac, started his own company in 1907. The Brush Runabout Company of Detroit produced this model in 1910. The car had wooden wheels, wooden body and wooden axles! The engine was a 10-hp., water-cooled, single-cylinder, vertical gasoline engine of 1,029-cc displacement. Two forward speeds, epicyclic gears, and chain final drive were used. The engine could reach 2,500 rpm. Suspension was by coil springs on all four wheels. A car of this type was the first to cross the continent of Australia, which was rugged, roadless terrain most of the way. This was in 1912.

WHITE "OO" STEAM TOURING CAR   This was one of the last steam-powered White automobiles. It was fitted with a flash boiler and kerosene burner. A two-cylinder, compound, double-acting, vertical steam engine was installed and developed about 30 hp. This car can be seen at the Frederick C. Crawford Auto-Aviation Museum, Cleveland, Ohio.

ALBION A-6   This side-entrance tonneau was built in 1910 by the Albion Motor Car Company of Glasgow, Scotland. A 24-hp., water-cooled, four-cylinder, vertical gasoline engine of 4,180-cc displacement was installed. Bore was 108 mm. and stroke was 114 mm. Four forward speeds plus reverse were available and final chain drive. This was the first Albion chassis made for passenger cars only; all previous models could accept either truck or passenger bodies. Half-elliptic front springs and full-elliptic rear springs were used. This car was available only during 1910 because it was too expensive for the company to produce a special passenger car which made the selling price prohibitive.

PEUGEOT Les Fils de Peugeot Frères was the first French auto manufacturer to place a gasoline-engine-powered car in production, in 1891. The company concentrated on reliable, standard practice to attract the average citizen. This five-seater tonneau was introduced in 1910. It was powered by a four-cylinder, inline, vertical, water-cooled, L-head-cylinder engine of 2,211-cc displacement that developed 16 hp. Side valves, high-tension magneto ignition, and a four-speed gearbox were all standard, as was shaft drive to the rear wheels. Half-elliptic springs were used front and rear. This car can be viewed at the Het Nationaal Automobielmuseum, Leidschendam, Holland.

AUTO-BUG This Model E was built in 1910 by the Auto-Bug Company, Norwalk, Ohio. It was a double phaeton high-wheeler with seats for five passengers. Tires were solid rubber. The Model E was fitted with a 22-hp., water-cooled engine, centrally located. It was built to sell at a reasonable price but to resemble the more expensive vehicles.

DELAUNAY BELLEVILLE This French company was making marine boilermakers of high quality when they decided to build high-quality automobiles. Their products were bought and used by the King of Greece, President of France, Czar of Russia, and the King of Spain. It has been said that no one ever drives his Delaunay Belleville, i.e., a chauffeur is always used! This is the 1910 touring model. The distinctive round radiator was copied by many other manufacturers. The car had a wheelbase of 11 feet 6 inches and a six-cylinder engine of 11,846-cc displacement. Bore was 134 mm. and stroke was 140 mm. A leather-lined cone clutch was standard as was high-tension ignition. Three forward speeds plus reverse were provided with chain drive to the rear axle. Some of the six-cylinder versions ran as much as 200,000 miles between overhauls.

HUDSON RUNABOUT In the early days of motoring many people bought cars as sport vehicles to get some excitement into their lives. This Hudson of 1910 had the open runabout or roadster design that preceded the modern sports car. The Model 20 enjoyed great popularity in those days when a sense of adventure was closely associated with a car of this type. It was powered by a four-cylinder, water-cooled engine of 23 hp. and sold for $900.

KNOX   The Knox Automobile Company, Springfield, Massachusetts, produced this five-seater side-entrance tonneau in 1910. The body was wood and steel on a steel frame. A 40-hp., four-cylinder, vertical, air-cooled engine was located under the hood, and four forward speeds plus reverse were provided in a sliding-gear transmission. The wheelbase was 112 inches and the tread was 56 inches. Chain drive was used. The auto weighed 2,800 pounds and was available in a variety of colors.

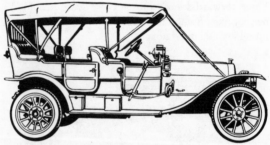

MITCHELL   Henry Mitchell, a Scottish wagon maker, came to the U.S. in 1834 and, after making wagons, bicycles, and motorcycles, he turned to the automobile in 1904 with the help of John W. Bate. This Model S was built in 1910 by the Mitchell Motor Car Company, Racine, Wisconsin. The detachable tonneau was optional and could be replaced by a surrey top or runabout deck at extra charge. Wheelbase of this five-seater was 130 inches. The engine was 50-hp., six-cylinder, water-cooled, with bore of 4.25 inches and stroke of 5 inches and displacement of 425 cubic inches. French gray was the most popular color available with red running gear. Price was $2,250. Body, fenders, and frame were all made from steel. Full-floating rear axle, three-speed transmission, and leather-lined cone clutch were standard.

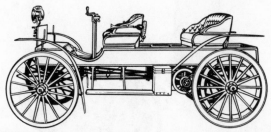

ÅTVIDABERG   The Åtvidabergs Vagnfabrik AB located in Åtvida-berg, Sweden, produced about thirty of these five-seaters in 1910. It was reported to be based on an imported prototype from the U.S. Power was a four-cylinder, air-cooled, rear-mounted gasoline engine. Transmission was of the sliding-gear type with two forward speeds and reverse. No tires were fitted and the result appears to be little more than a motorized wagon. This auto can be seen in the Tekniska Museet, Stockholm, Sweden.

CADILLAC GENTLEMEN'S ROADSTER   This rakish roadster was introduced by Cadillac in 1910. It had a four-cylinder, water-cooled engine with a rating of about 30 hp. Note the balloon tires and rumble seat behind the front seats, which were early versions of the popular bucket seat. Right-hand drive was still used on this model.

DE TAMBLE MODEL G RUNABOUT   E. S. De Tamble owned the Speed Changing Pulley Company of Anderson, Indiana, where Carrico and De Tamble engines were built. The De Tamble Motors Company was developed from this firm and produced this Model G Runabout in 1910. The car was powered by a four-cylinder, water-cooled, inline, 36-hp. engine. De Tamble cars were built only during a half dozen years preceding World War I.

RAMBLER   This Rambler touring five-seater was produced in 1910. Detachable wheels instead of detachable rims made changing tires easier. The engine was a four-cylinder, vertical, inline, water-cooled type with a 4,700-cc displacement. Bore and stroke were 114 mm. Each cylinder was individually cast, and side valves were fitted as well as high-tension magneto ignition. Three forward speeds and reverse were standard with a shaft final drive. Half-elliptic front springs and three-quarter-elliptic rear springs were used. In 1913 the company sold over 10,000 cars.

VELIE The Velie automobiles were manufactured from 1908 until 1923. The company produced luxury types until 1910 and then built this sportster/raceabout. It was powered by a six-cylinder Continental engine of about 45 hp. The two-seater was of conventional configuration for the type. Notice the absence of a windshield and the rather large spotlight mounted atop the hood.

SADDLE TYPE RADIATOR

MANUAL FUEL PRESSURE PUMP

BUICK RACER Since 1905, Buick had raced its stock cars with crack drivers such as Bob Burman, Louis and Arthur Chevrolet, and Lewis Strang. In 1909 Buick Racers placed first, second and third in the five-mile sprint and won first prize in the 250-mile event at the Indianapolis Speedway. In 1910 a special Buick Racer, called "The Bug," was timed at almost 106 mph. at Indianapolis. "The Bug" had a four-cylinder, water-cooled engine in a streamlined speedster that developed 57 hp. The engine displaced 550 cubic inches. Notice the saddle-type radiator, wrapped over the hood, to eliminate the resistance of a conventional front-mounted radiator.

OAKLAND This open-air sports roadster was typical of the two-seaters produced in 1910. It was the Oakland Model M, and was powered by a 40-hp., four-cylinder, water-cooled engine. The car sold for about $1,700 in 1910.

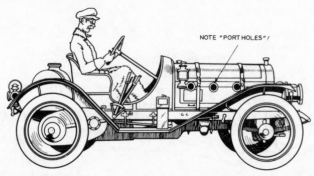

NOTE "PORT HOLES"/

CHADWICK GREAT SIX This 1910 product of the Chadwick Company, Pottstown, Pennsylvania, was called the "speediest stock car in the world" because it was produced in both racing and street models. The Great Six was introduced in 1907 and was very successful in hill-climbs when driven by a Chadwick test driver, Willy Haupt. To increase the 60-mph. speed, Haupt suggested the use of three carburetors and the speed jumped to 85 mph. Haupt then recommended an engine-driven compressor to force air into the engine. This was the world's first supercharger and made the car even more successful in hill-climbs. While practicing for the 1907 Vanderbilt Cup Race the car exceeded 107 mph. Willy Haupt led the field in the 1908 Vanderbilt classic for a while, but then was in tenth place when the race was stopped. In 1909 Chadwick set a record for a ten-mile sprint in 8 minutes 23 seconds, beating a 200-hp. Benz! In 1910 Len Zengle won the Fairmount Park Race in Philadelphia, setting a new record for the course. After 1910 the company could no longer support racing machines. The sports model cost $6,500 F.O.B. Pottstown. The portholes were really engine exhaust outlets.

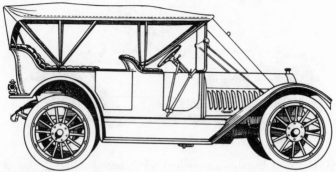

OLDSMOBILE LIMITED Ransom E. Olds introduced six-cylinder engines in his cars in 1908. In 1910 he produced the "Limited," which was a large car for the time with a price tag of $4,000. It was capable of 75 mph.—very fast for a five-passenger tonneau. An even larger Limited appeared two years later and cost $5,000.

STEVENS-DURYEA When J. Frank Duryea left the Duryea Motor Wagon Company of America in 1898, he left his brother, Charles, in charge. After association with several other firms he contracted to design and build cars, under the name Stevens-Duryea, for the J. Stevens Arms and Tool Company of Chicopee, Massachusetts, in 1901. The first car, in 1904, was an instant success, and the Stevens Duryea Motor Company evolved. In 1905 they introduced the first six-cylinder car in the U.S. The model shown here was their 1910 five-seater. It has a six-cylinder, water-cooled engine with each cylinder separately cast. They were of L-head design, bolted to the crankcase. Bore was 3.9 inches and stroke 4.75 inches with a displacement of 337 cubic inches. The car had a 114-inch wheelbase and 56-inch tread. Three forward speeds plus reverse were provided in a sliding-gear transmission.

REGAL   Most Regal roadsters had rakish lines because the company specialized in the underslung chassis design. This is the Model N-25, produced in 1910, and it steered from the left as is present U.S. practice. A four-cylinder, water-cooled, vertical engine of 25 hp. was located under the hood. The car weighed 1,900 pounds and sold for $900 in 1910.

HISPANO-SUIZA   This famous Spanish firm began in Barcelona in 1904, making luxury cars. The chief designer was Marc Birkigt, who in 1909 designed a sports racer that came to be known as Type Alfonso XIII. In 1910 the version shown won the Coupe de l'Auto race. Power was a four-cylinder, long-stroke, T-head, water-cooled engine of 3.6-liter displacement. It developed 64 hp. In 1911 a factory was opened in France.

CADILLAC LIMOUSINE The first four-cylinder Cadillac was introduced in 1905. This 1910 Model 30 luxurious Cadillac limousine was fitted with a four-cylinder, water-cooled, 30-hp. engine, located under the hood. It was fitted with a three-speed conventional transmission. Cadillac discontinued planetary gears in 1908. Cost was $3,000.

MAXWELL The Maxwell automobiles were built in Tarrytown, New York, by Maxwell-Chalmers from 1904 through 1924. Maxwell won the Glidden Reliability Tour, the early standard of automotive achievement, in both 1911 and 1912. The Maxwell shown here is a five-seater tonneau and was produced in 1911. A roadster was also made during that year. The two-cylinder, opposed, water-cooled, gasoline-engine-powered automobiles stressed economy and reliability. They were extremely popular. In 1925 Maxwell-Chalmers was reorganized into the Chrysler Corporation.

HUPMOBILE ROADSTER This Model "20" was introduced in 1911 and was also called the Raceabout. The two-seater was powered by a gasoline four-cylinder, water-cooled, 17-hp. engine. The bore was 3.25 inches, and the stroke was 3.5 inches, giving the powerplant a displacement of 1,900 cc. Top speed was about 30 mph. Two forward speeds plus reverse were available, and final drive to the rear axle was via drive shaft. This auto can be viewed at the Car and Carriage Caravan, Luray Caverns, Virginia.

CHEVROLET NO. 1 This touring five-seater was the very first Chevrolet to be produced. In 1909 William C. Durant, one of the founders of General Motors, sponsored some automotive experiments. Among them was the design and testing of a new automobile being conducted in Detroit by the famous Swiss engineer and racing driver Louis Chevrolet. Their combined efforts resulted in the first "Chevy," called the "Classic Six," which was offered to the public in March, 1911. It was also offered as a "Light Six."

MARMON WASP   Howard Marmon entered serious racing with his cars in 1909 with considerable success. The Wasp was his special racing design of 1911. This six-cylinder, water-cooled racer was unusual for its time because it was a single-seater with no riding mechanic. Ray Harroun and Joe Jawson drove Marmon Wasps in the very first Indianapolis 500-Mile Race. Harroun took first place with an average speed of 74.59 mph., while Dawson came in fifth. A few sports car versions of the racing Wasp were made, but Marmon never followed up on the initial success. Marmon racers competed until 1920 and placed second at the 1914 Grand Prix at Santa Monica, California. Notice the wide rear-view mirror, on braces above the steering wheel, a necessity in any race.

LE ZÈBRE   The little-publicized Le Zèbre was built in France by S.A. Le Zèbre. The firm specialized in very small voiturettes, which they introduced in 1909. This is the A4 model that made its appearance in 1911. It was powered by a single-cylinder, water-cooled, side-valve gasoline engine of 600 cc. A two-speed sliding-pinion gearbox and a plate clutch were fitted with shaft drive. Half-elliptic springs were used all around on this two-seater. The designer, Salomon, later designed the post-World War I Citroën machines.

FORD T LIMOUSINE The Ford Model T is generally considered to be a simple car for the common man and to learn of a Model T limousine certainly surprises many. The limousine made its appearance in 1911 and provided an enclosure for the passengers while the chauffeur was semi-protected from the elements by an enormous windshield and the roof. The basic chassis and powerplant were the same as the other Model T bodies. The chief designers of the "Tin Lizzie" were Joseph Galamb and C. H. Wills under the direction of Henry Ford.

PEERLESS "60-6" This sporty Peerless Speedster made its appearance in 1911. The dashing two-seater owed much of its design to the Peerless racing cars driven by Barney Oldfield and Louis Mooers, who set new records for sprints, beating such cars as Renault, Fiat, and Richard-Brasier. This commercial version was, of course, toned down for safe road driving. Notice the monocle windscreen, which was popular on many sporty cars of the period, and also the fuel tank behind the seats and double spare tires. This was definitely a man's car, rugged and rough. A car of this type can be seen at the Frederick C. Crawford Auto-Aviation Museum, Cleveland, Ohio.

RAMBLER 63C   The Rambler Model 63C seated four passengers in a totally enclosed cab. Three faced forward and one faced aft. The car's appearance was deceiving because it looked very much like the electric-powered cars of that period, 1911. It was, however, gasoline-engine-powered with a four-cylinder, water-cooled powerplant. An outstanding feature was a tilting steering column that could be adjusted at any angle to suit the comfort of the driver!

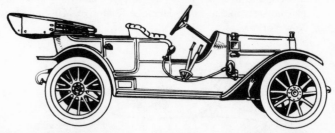

HUDSON 33   This Hudson touring car was produced in 1911. Four models were offered that year: a pony tonneau, a torpedo, a roadster, and this touring model. The auto was designed by Howard E. Coffin, who was often called "the master builder of automobiles." The wheelbase was 114 inches. The car was painted blue with gray wheels. Hudson sales totaled 6,486 vehicles that year.

WHITE OPERA COUPÉ This White Opera Coupé Model G-A was made in 1911 by the White Company, Cleveland, Ohio. The car weighed 3,010 pounds, had a 110-inch wheelbase, and was fitted with oil lamps. Power was a White four-cylinder, water-cooled, inline, 30-hp. gasoline engine of L-head design. Bore was 3.75 and stroke was 5.13 inches. Force-feed lubrication was used. A four-speed transmission, plus reverse, of the sliding-gear selective type was installed. Cone clutch was used, and final drive was by propeller shaft and bevel gear. This car can be seen in the Long Island Automotive Museum, Southampton, New York.

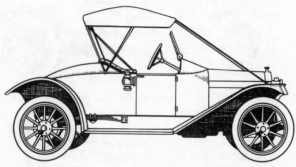

KING ROADSTER Charles Brady King started building automobiles in 1896 and then supplied Ford with valves and later worked for Oldsmobile and Northern. He resumed car manufacturing from 1910 until 1924. This 1911 product of the King Motor Company was the Silent 36 Roadster. The car had a very quiet four-cylinder engine of King's design. Other progressive mechanical developments included semi-cantilever rear springs. The company is now but a memory, as with many other firms.

REGAL   Regal produced automobiles from 1910 to 1915. This is the Regal two-door, five-passenger, enclosed coupé of 1911. Enclosed cars that protected the occupants were a rarity, even in 1911 when this model was produced. Note the visor-like extension of the roof over the windshield. The engine was a four-cylinder, water-cooled affair, front-mounted.

PACKARD LIMOUSINE   This luxurious totally enclosed limousine was introduced in 1907 as the Model 30 and continued in production for several years. The 1911 version is shown here and was priced at $4,350. A 30-hp., four-cylinder, T-head, water-cooled engine was fitted that rotated at 650 rpm. The wheelbase was 123.5 inches and the gasoline tank capacity was an enormous 27 gallons. Three forward speeds plus reverse were fitted, using an internal expanding clutch. This car can be seen at The Museum of Automobiles, Morrilton, Arkansas.

SEARS MODEL L Despite cars that were technically behind the times, Sears remained in the auto manufacturing business until 1912 when they produced this, their last car. The friction drive was abandoned and chain drive substituted. The wheelbase was 72 inches and the track was 56 inches. The weight was 1,000 pounds and gasoline capacity 6 gallons. At extra charge the following optional items were available: magneto, speedometer, odometer, combination acetylene and kerosene front lamps with generator, extra switch key, and extra set of six dry-cell batteries. Cost of the basic car was $494 F.O.B. Chicago. After Sears stopped auto production, they remained in the business with their comprehensive auto parts, accessories, maintenance and service.

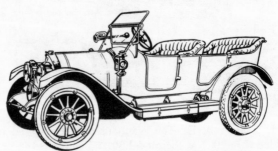

OVERLAND TOURING This product of the Overland Motor Company, Toledo, Ohio, made its appearance in 1912. Gas headlights and kerosene sidelights were standard equipment. This five-passenger tonneau had right-hand drive and two spare tires—but not wheels—mounted in the rear. The four-cylinder engine had each cylinder cast separately, plus a cast aluminum crankcase, oil pan, and water jackets. A Bosch magneto and a bulb horn were standard.

OPEL   By 1909 Opel was Germany's foremost manufacturer of well-built, moderately priced small cars. One thousand had been built by 1908, and by 1912 the figure jumped to ten thousand. This 1912 Opel was powered by a four-cylinder, vertical, water-cooled, L-head engine of 1,540-cc displacement. Bore was 70 mm. and stroke was 100 mm. A high-tension magneto ignition system was used. It was fitted with four forward speeds plus reverse with shaft drive to the rear axle, and had half-elliptical springs all around.

GRÄF & STIFT   Karl, Heinrich, and Franz Gräf started a bicycle business in Vienna in 1896. They built their first car the following year. Wilhelm Stift provided financial assistance in 1902. The firm concentrated on conservative, well-built automobiles. This 1912 product was powered by a four-cylinder, T-head, water-cooled engine of 5.8 liters. When turning at 1,400 rpm. it developed 32 hp. which drove the car at a maximum of 50 mph. It was in a car of this type that the Archduke Franz Ferdinand and his wife Sophie were assassinated in Sarajevo in 1914, the incident that precipitated World War I.

CLÉMENT-BAYARD   Adolphe Clément established the S.A. des Établissements Clément-Bayard, Paris, in 1903. It was named after a famous French knight of the sixteenth century, Chevalier Bayard, who was a national hero. This 1912 product of the firm was the Type 4M, fitted with a four-cylinder, water-cooled, vertical, inline engine with side valves and of 1,354 cc. Bore was 60 mm. and stroke was 120 mm. High-tension magneto ignition was used. Three forward speeds and reverse were provided with shaft drive to the rear axle. Notice the dash-mounted radiator with ears protruding from behind the hood.

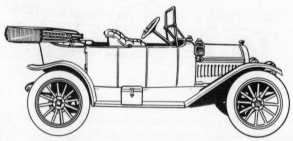

ELMORE   This five-passenger Elmore was called the "Light Torpedo" and made its appearance in 1912. A product of the Elmore Manufacturing Company, Clyde, Ohio, the car continued to be powered with the two-cycle, valveless engine as in previous models. The advertisements stressed simplicity and smooth operation. Price was $1,250 for this automobile.

ARROL-JOHNSTON MODEL 15-9   The Arrol-Johnston Company of Glasgow produced this five-seat touring car during 1911–1912. Notice the dash-mounted radiator with ears protruding from behind the hood, which seems to have been the vogue during this period. Power was a four-cylinder, water-cooled, vertical, inline engine of 2,414-cc displacement, fitted with high-tension magneto ignition, and developed 16 hp. Four forward speeds and reverse were installed. Half-elliptic springs in front and full-elliptic springs at the rear comprised the suspension.

SIMPLEX   This sporty two-seater was built in 1912 on a 128-inch wheelbase. One of the outstanding features was that, in addition to four half-elliptic springs and the rear springs with JM shock absorbers, telescopic airplane-type "jounce preventers" were fitted to the front wheels. The car weighed 4,000 pounds and cost $5,000. The 50-hp., four-cylinder, T-head, water-cooled engine, with cylinders cast in pairs, drove the car to 80 mph. Final chain drive was used. An externally mounted fuel tank was behind the seats.

PIERRON TYPE 1   This little-known French car was built by Louis Pierron in 1912. It was of two-seat roadster design with a four-cylinder, water-cooled engine of 1,460 cc. Bore and stroke were 65 mm. and 110 mm. The car can be seen at the Provinciaal Automobielmuseum Houthalen, Domaine de Kelchterhoef, Houthalen, Belgium.

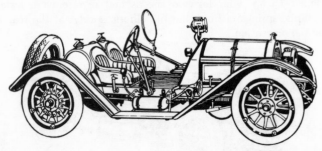

MERCER 35C RACEABOUT   The Mercer Automobile Company of Trenton, New Jersey, was founded in 1910. It started racing during the following year. In 1912 a Mercer placed third at the Indianapolis 500-Mile Race, with the smallest engine in the race, at an average speed of 76.3 mph. 1912 Mercers won the 300-cubic-inch class of the Santa Monica Road Race and placed first, second, and third in their class at Elgin. These were stripped-down racers, but the 1912 model shown here was no slowpoke on the road, with monocle windscreen, fenders, etc. It was named after the county in which the factory was located, Mercer, and was owned by the Roebling family of engineers (who designed the Brooklyn Bridge). The fuel tank held 40 gallons, which was enough for 500 miles. Last Mercer was built in 1925.

STELLA This Swiss-made Stella five-seater enclosed auto made its appearance in 1912. It used half-elliptic springs for both front and rear suspension. A four-cylinder, water-cooled, vertical gasoline engine of 4,073 cc was installed. It was fitted with side valves and high-tension magneto ignition. Four forward speeds plus reverse and shaft drive to the rear axle were standard. Notice the circular radiator that was apparently copied from the exclusive Delaunay Belleville.

NATIONAL RACER Joe Dawson won the 1912 Indianapolis 500-Mile Race while driving a 1912 National Racer, and Howard Wilcox placed ninth in another National. Nationals placed second and third at Elgin with Livingston and Greiner at the wheels in 1910, and Zengle placed first at that race in 1911 in a National. The National racing career was short, and they were not very active after 1912.

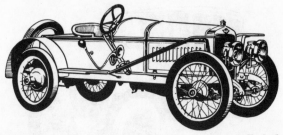

HISPANO-SUIZA 15T   This Hispano-Suiza is often called the Type Alfonso XIII because an earlier version was given to King Alfonso XIII of Spain by his wife as a birthday present in 1909. The Type 15T was entered in numerous racing events and placed as follows: 1910 Catalan Cup—third; Coupe des Voitures—first, second, and sixth; 1912 Imperial Russian Automobile Club, Czar's Cup—first prize. The engine was a four-cylinder, water-cooled T-head, monobloc, overhead-valve design of 3.6-liter displacement. Speeds were in the neighborhood of 90 mph.

FLANDERS MODEL 20   Walter E. Flanders learned much about automobile production when he worked for Henry Ford. He left Ford and produced basically the same car from 1909 through 1912. The Flanders Model 20 shown here was built in 1912 and was marketed for Flanders by Studebaker. It had a four-cylinder, inline, vertical, water-cooled engine with a three-speed transmission.

ALCO The American Locomotive Company became interested in the designs of Marius Berliet and secured the rights to build his designs in the U.S. This is the 1912 seven-passenger touring car produced by Alco. It was almost a twin to the Berliet of 1911. A four-cylinder, water-cooled, four-liter-displacement, 40-hp. engine was fitted to the 126-inch wheelbase. Alco cars were built for a very short time.

MOON RACEABOUT The Moon Motor Company of St. Louis, Missouri, built automobiles from 1905 to 1930. This Raceabout was introduced in 1912 and followed the sports car styling of the period. It had, however, an electric starter and electric lights, which were brought out by Moon in 1911. This car is on exhibition at the Long Island Automotive Museum, Southampton, New York.

SWIFT   After making bicycles Swift began auto manufacturing in England in 1899 and continued until 1931. This Swift of 1912 was a cyclecar design, very light and seating two. The engine was of side-valve design, developing 10 hp. Note the absence of the running board and the hoe-shaped step for convenience. The car can be viewed in the Danmarks Tekniske Museum, Helsingør, Denmark.

THOMAS FLYER TOURING   This seven-passenger open touring car owed much of its design to the New York-Paris Race winner of 1908. The E. R. Thomas Company of Buffalo, New York, introduced this car in 1912. Most Thomas cars were known for their reliability. The frame was pressed steel on a 118-inch wheelbase. A four-cylinder, water-cooled, vertical, inline engine of about 50 hp. was fitted.

OLDSMOBILE AUTOCRAT This open sport/speedster was introduced by Oldsmobile in 1912. It followed the trend of that era for speedsters: two bucket seats, monocle windscreen, no passenger protection, fuel tanks behind the seats, and plenty of power. A six-cylinder, water-cooled engine with 5-inch bore and 6-inch stroke was installed and displaced 707 cubic inches. Note the strap holding the hood closed.

NYBERG Only a very few Nyberg automobiles were built from 1912 to 1914. The firm was Nyberg Hy. Autos Le Works Anderson in Chicago, Illinois. This was the eight-passenger limousine, built in 1912. The front and rear seats each held three passengers, while two jump seats were installed in the rear compartment. The only remaining Nyberg limousine can be seen at the Forney Historic Transportation Museum, Denver, Colorado.

PACKARD In 1912 Packard produced its first six-cylinder engine of 60 hp. The company also introduced the electric starter, which was a very welcome feature because cranking a car by hand was not only exhausting but dangerous. Electric lights were also introduced in this year by Packard. The 1912 model shown is a two-seater roadster with an added jump seat in the rear, and used the new six-cylinder engine.

MATHESON The Matheson Motor Car Company, Wilkes-Barre, Pennsylvania, produced this semi-enclosed automobile in 1912. It was called the "Silent Six" because the company spared no expense to produce a quiet car. One year later the company went out of business, possibly because most of their automobiles were in the $6,000 plus range.

MORRIS OXFORD   Like many other automotive pioneers, William Richard Morris was in the bicycle business when his attention turned to powered vehicles. First came motorcycles and then the car. In 1910 he designed his own car. It was announced in October of 1912 and was first sold in 1913. It was called Oxford in honor of that English city, on the outskirts of which it was built. The car was a small two-seater and was powered by a four-cylinder, inline, water-cooled, gasoline engine of 1,018-cc displacement. This model was produced until 1917, by which time 1,475 cars had been sold.

SCRIPPS BOOTH CYCLECAR   James Scripps Booth designed cars with considerable originality and inventiveness although many of his efforts never emerged from the experimental stage into production. This 1912–1913 Scripps Booth small-size cyclecar was inspired by the little-known French Bedelia design. The tandem two-seater was powered by a two-cylinder, vee-type, air-cooled motorcycle engine. An extremely long vee belt was used to drive the rear wheels. The bullet-shaped tank in the nose contained the gasoline and the oil compartments. Wire wheels were fitted, and steering was from the rear seat.

OAKLAND MODEL 42   This five-passenger touring car was produced by the Oakland Motor Company, Pontiac, Michigan, in 1913. It was one of four models made by the company that year. The Model 42 was powered by a six-cylinder, inline, water-cooled, gasoline engine and fitted with electric lights and electric starter. An oil sight was provided on the dash panel so that the oil level could always be checked. Price of this car was $1,750.

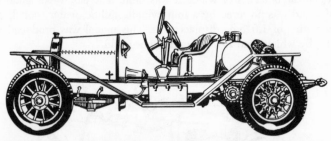

FIAT TYPE 55   This Fiat sports raceabout made its appearance in 1913 and much of what was learned from the early successful Fiat racers was incorporated into this automobile. Many Fiat wins were attained with stripped-down sports models that won thirteen first places in seven years. A four-cylinder, overhead-cam, water-cooled engine of 10.5-liters displacement could propel the stripped version to nearly 100 mph.

GARFORD SIX TOURING The Garford Six was made by the Garford Company, Elyria, Ohio, and introduced in 1913. This six-cylinder, inline, water-cooled, gasoline-engine-powered car developed 60 hp. Bore was 3.75 inches and the stroke was exceptionally long at 6 inches. Wheelbase was 128 inches. The body was one piece, all steel. Electric lights, electric horn, and electric starter were standard. The price was $2,750.

HUDSON MODEL 37 The Hudson Model 37 Coupé made its appearance in 1913, and a total of 6,401 Hudson cars were sold that year. The interior of this enclosed two-seater was very luxurious with "hand-buffed pebbled leather upholstery." All Hudson 37 models were painted in medium-blue with a light-gray as optional. The chassis, fenders, and wheels were painted blue-black on all production cars.

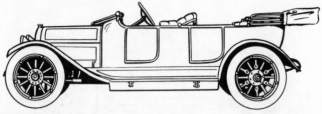

MICHIGAN 40   Introduced in 1913 by the Michigan Motor Car Company, Kalamazoo, Michigan, the Model 40 was designed by W. H. Cameron, an experienced automotive engineer, while the body was styled by John A. Campbell. About $16 million worth of the Model 40 was exported to Europe in 1913. The 46-hp. engine was fitted with a four-speed transmission. This four-door tonneau or touring car was equipped with electric lights, electric horn, and a gas starter as standard. An electric starter could be had as an "extra." The left-hand, adjustable steering wheel was standard.

BÉBÉ PEUGEOT   This diminutive product of Peugeot made its appearance in 1913, and some models continued to be manufactured for several years. The car shown here is the voiturette or roadster design, but the basic vehicle was also made in a totally enclosed version in wood and steel. A four-cylinder, water-cooled, inline engine of 856-cc displacement powered this small but extremely popular auto. Bore was 55 mm. and stroke was 90 mm. A two-speed transmission was fitted. The car was designed by Ettore Bugatti, who became a very famous designer and builder of sophisticated automobiles. It can be seen at the Automuseum Nettelstedt, Lübeck, Germany.

LOZIER MEADOWBROOK   Lozier was one of the highest quality cars built in pre-World War I U.S. This runabout made its appearance in 1913. Lozier had been active in racing since 1907, and this commercial product was merely the road version of some of the more successful machines. In 1907 Harry Michner won the 24-Hour Race at Breeze Point, Pennsylvania, and in 1908 Harry Cole and Ralph Mulford won the Brighton Beach 24-Hour Race; the race was won again by a Lozier in 1909! In 1910 Loziers won at Elgin, Atlanta Speedway, and Santa Monica. In 1911 Mulford won the Vanderbilt Cup, beating two 90-hp. Mercedes! In the same year a Lozier placed second in the Indianapolis 500-Mile Race. Naturally, the racing types were fenderless and without windshield or jump seat or lights. Power was a four-cylinder, inline, water-cooled engine of 735 cubic inches.

PEUGEOT 145   This full-size sport touring car was introduced in 1913 by Peugeot. It could seat five and was powered by a four-cylinder, water-cooled, inline engine. The car is on display at the Museum of Transportation, Larz Anderson Park, Brookline, Massachusetts.

BERLIET In 1913, this luxurious landolet was produced by the French firm of Berliet. As can be seen, the two or three passengers rode comfortably enclosed and entered via a rear entrance. The engine was four cylinder, vertical, inline, of 2,408-cc displacement and with side valves. High-tension magneto ignition was used. Four-speed transmission and shaft drive were fitted. Half-elliptic front and three-quarter-elliptic rear springs were installed. The car is exhibited in The Raben Car Collection at Aalholm Castle, Nysted, Denmark.

ARGYLL TYPE G The Argyll Company in Glasgow, Scotland, produced this Type G touring car in 1913. A four-cylinder, single-sleeve-valve, water-cooled engine of 160 cubic inches developed 16 hp. The car had magneto ignition and a multi-disc-type plate clutch running in oil. Four-wheel brakes that were diagonally compensated rounded off all these advanced engineering features. The single-sleeve-valve idea was a patent held by Burt and McCullion. During this year a Captain Kelsey attempted to travel from Capetown to Cairo in an Argyll, traversing the length of Africa, with a few associates. Several mechanical problems developed, and the expedition came to an end when a leopard killed Captain Kelsey.

DARRACQ TYPE 13 Alexandre Darracq produced this Type 13 roadster in 1913. It had a four-cylinder, sleeve-valve, water-cooled, vertical engine of 1.4 liters displacement. The general design was conventional for the period, but it may have inherited something from Darracq's racing machines because this car could attain about 50 mph. The car is exhibited in the Automuseum Nettelstedt, Lübeck, Germany.

STUDEBAKER TYPE 45-AA The Studebaker brothers, Henry, Clem, Peter, and Jacob, began as blacksmiths in 1852 and built wagons in South Bend, Indiana. The Studebaker Brothers Manufacturing Company was formed in 1868 and they continued to turn out horse-drawn wagons until 1920, despite the fact that they built their first automobile in 1902! The Type 45-AA open touring design made its appearance in 1913. This seven-passenger auto featured folding seats, right-hand drive, and electric lights. A four-cylinder, inline, water-cooled, 4.27-liter-displacement engine that developed 27.2 hp. was installed. The car's price was $1,290 and, in 1913, 9,800 automobiles were sold; 1913 was the first year that Studebakers were also built in Canada. A fine example of this car can be viewed in the Provinciaal Automobielmuseum Houthalen, Domaine de Kelchterhoef, Houthalen, Belgium.

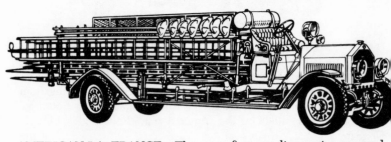

AMERICAN-LA FRANCE The very first gasoline-engine-powered vehicle designed and built for fire-fighting was the American-La France fire truck made by the American-La France Fire Engine Company, Inc., Elmira, New York, in 1910. The 1913 hook and ladder is shown here. It was powered by a 105-hp., six-cylinder engine with two spark plugs per cylinder, and it had an asbestos-lined plate clutch. A sliding-gear transmission provided three forward speeds, and roller chains connected to the rear wheels. Speeds over 50 mph. could be attained. Electric headlights plus electric searchlights were installed. A hook and ladder vehicle was usually combined with a pumper vehicle when fighting a fire; however, sometimes the hook and ladder vehicle was fitted with a rotary gear pump that was powered from a secondary gearbox bolted to the transmission and driven from the engine when the truck was at rest. This fire truck can be seen at the Long Island Automotive Museum, Southampton, New York.

ENFIELD NIMBLE NINE   This clean-looking sport roadster was produced by the Enfield-Allday firm in 1913. The British company engaged A. C. Bertelli to design the car. Bertelli later became the designer for Aston Martin. The Nimble Nine was a two-seater powered by a four-cylinder, inline, water-cooled, side-valve engine that produced 9 hp. The slender hood, spare tire recessed into the running board, and streamlined pointed radiator were progressive styling features later used by many manufacturers. Notice the wire wheels (not of the bicycle type) that became a feature of later sports cars. The last of the Nimble Nines can be seen at the Cheddar Motor Museum, The Cliffs, Cheddar, England.

AUSTRO-DAIMLER "PRINCE HENRY"   In 1906 Dr. Ferdinand Porsche became the designer for Austro-Daimler where he designed the "Prince Henry" sportster/competition automobiles of which the 1913 version is shown. At the 1909 Prince Henry Trials, stripped versions of this car, driven by Porsche, Fischer, and Hamburger, placed first, second, and third. In 1911 in the Austrian Alpine event the design took the first five places plus the team prize! This model had a four-cylinder, water-cooled, overhead-camshaft, inline engine of 5.75 liters. Valves were inclined. Notice the pointed radiator and the jump seat behind the two bucket seats. The body of this car was custom-designed by Donald Healey. This car can be seen in the Frederick C. Crawford Auto-Aviation Museum, Cleveland, Ohio.

FISCHER   The Swiss firm of Fischer produced this five-place touring car in 1913. Martin Fischer designed the valveless, four-cylinder, water-cooled engine of 2,720-cc displacement that developed about 30 hp. Bore was 85 mm. and stroke was 120 mm. The four-speed gearbox was of patented design with internal toothing. The clutch was a multiplate type. The footbrake operated on the differential while the handbrake operated against the rear wheels. Half-elliptic springs were used in front with full-elliptic springs in the rear. It is truly strange that despite the large number of Swiss automotive pioneers, there is not one auto company in Switzerland today. This car can be viewed at the Verkehrshaus der Schweiz, Lucerne, Switzerland.

CHENARD WALCKER   Chenard Walcker automobiles were first introduced in France in 1900 and progressed in design until this 1913 Type T2. The design followed the standard two-seat roadster style of the period and was powered by a four-cylinder, water-cooled engine of 1.59 liters. Bore was 65 mm. and stroke 120 mm. Chenard Walcker continued to build cars well into the twenties and, in fact, won the first Le Mans 24-Hour Race in 1923. A fine example of the Type T2 can be seen in The Raben Car Collection at Aalholm Castle, Nysted, Denmark.

MINERVA LANDAU   Since 1900 the Belgian firm of Minerva made motorcycles and in 1905 started building automobiles. This landau made its appearance in 1913, and it gained some prominence due to the fact that it was the first automobile to be owned by King Haakon VII of Norway. Minerva concentrated on large, high-quality cars until they went out of business in 1939. This 1913 landau was fitted with a four-cylinder, sleeve-valve, water-cooled engine. The advantages of the sleeve valve over the more conventional poppet valve is quieter operation and over 10 percent more power. A 1913 Minerva Landau can be seen in the Norsk Teknisk Museum, Oslo, Norway.

HISPANO-SUIZA 3.5 LITER   This is generally considered to be the world's first sports car. Designed by the Swiss engineer Marc Birkigt in 1913 and built at the Barcelona works, the car owes much to the famous "Alfonso XIII." The competition versions of this design did well in Continental hill-climbs, and a Hispano-Suiza won first prize in the Czar's Cup event. The 3.5-liter, water-cooled, T-head, overhead-cam, four-cylinder engine could propel the car at about 80 mph. The car can be seen at the Automuseum Nettlestedt, Lübeck, Germany.

ADLER   Heinrich Kleyer of Frankfurt, Germany, started making bicycles in 1886, and he fitted engines to his products after a few years. In 1899 he made his first automobile, using a De Dion Bouton engine with a Renault transmission. He continued to improve the design of his automobiles, which he called Adler (Eagle). This is his 1913 four-place touring model. It was fitted with half-elliptic leaf springs all around. It had a four-cylinder, side-valve, water-cooled, vertical engine of 14-cubic-inch displacement. Bore was 65 mm. and stroke 65 mm., and a four-speed transmission with shaft drive was installed. Speed was about 35 mph. Notice the hexagonal shape of the trio of rear windows, called "cathedral" by the manufacturer. This motif was later copied by a few other auto manufacturers. This car can be seen in the Jysk Automobilmuseum, Gjern, Denmark.

FORD T TOURING   By 1913 the Model T was four years old and was destined to remain in production for fifteen more years with plants in the U.S.A., Canada, and England. Over fifteen million were made and sold! Although the Model T was produced in a wide variety of bodies from roadsters to buses and trucks, the favorite seems to have been the touring style of which the 1913 version is shown here. The Model T was one of the first cars to use left-hand steering, the first to employ a monobloc cylinder casting and detachable cylinder heads cast as a unit. The use of vanadium steel allowed a slimmer chassis structure, which proved its ability to endure unlimited punishment.

BUFFALO ELECTRIC The Buffalo Electric Vehicle Company of Buffalo, New York, also had plants in New York, Philadelphia, Boston, and Montreal. At a time when gasoline cars were overpowering both steam- and electric-powered cars, the Buffalo continued to produce quality electric-powered automobiles, successful because of their silent propulsion. Electric cars and trucks were built through the immediate post-World War I period.

ROCHET-SCHNEIDER This Rochet-Schneider coupé de ville made its appearance in 1913 and was a product of Établissements Rochet-Schneider, Lyon, France. The firm concentrated on automobiles for the middle class, starting at the turn of the century and, although their cars contained few novel features, their 1903 design was made under license in the U.S., Belgium, Italy, and Switzerland by other manufacturers. This 1913 model was powered with a four-cylinder, water-cooled, vertical engine that displaced 4.8 liters, making it the largest of the Rochet-Schneider four-cylinder engines. Side valves, high-tension magneto ignition, four forward speeds and shaft drive were standard. It had half-elliptic springs in front and three-quarter-elliptic springs in rear. The car could seat five, the back three in extreme comfort in an enclosed cab. This car can be seen in the Provinciaal Automobielmuseum Houthalen, Domaine de Kelchterhoef, Houthalen, Belgium.

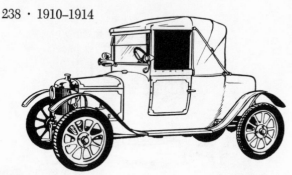

LAGONDA An American, Wilbur Gunn, went to England before the turn of the century to further his career as an opera singer. However, his interests changed radically, and by 1905 he had established an automobile plant in Staines, Middlesex, England. His first products were motorcycles, then tricycle cars. In 1907 he switched to four wheels. Lagonda autos were exported to Russia in large numbers. The two-seat roadster shown was introduced in 1913. Its body and chassis were of integral construction, thereby saving considerable weight. The engine was a 1,100-cc, four-cylinder, water-cooled type with overhead-inlet valves and side-exhaust valves. The autos were considered very sturdy and combined good performance with economy. Lagonda continued in the production of cars until 1939. The name was taken from a tributary of the Mad River in England.

HUMBERETTE Thomas Humber manufactured high-quality bicycles in England as early as 1868. In 1896, H. J. Lawson absorbed the company and began the manufacture of automobiles of questionable quality. Four years later Humber, Ltd., was formed in Coventry, England, as an independent firm and concentrated on small cars. Their first auto was the Humberette of 1903. Soon another factory was established in Beeston to concentrate on more expensive and better-equipped versions. The model shown is the 1913 Humberette two-seat roadster. It was powered by a two-cylinder, air-cooled engine of about 8 hp. The car was simple in appearance and operation and was exceptionally well constructed. An example of this car can be viewed at the Cheddar Motor Museum, The Cliffs, Cheddar, England.

WANDERER This unusual but little-known auto was built in Germany in 1913. It appeared to be a four- or five-seat touring car, but actually the car was very diminutive. Due to the narrow body it could seat only two in a tandem arrangement; one passenger in front and the other in the rear. The car was called *Puppchen,* which in English means "little doll." It was powered by a four-cylinder, water-cooled 1.298-liter engine that developed about 15 hp. Speed was about 40 mph. The car was made of steel except for the running board, which was a plank of finished wood. Doors were on the left side only because a spare tire occupied the right side. Wanderer created Auto Union along with Audi, DKW, and Horch in 1932. This car can be seen in the Automuseum, Minden, Westphalia,Germany.

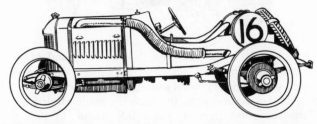

DELAGE RACER Louis Delage was racing before he became an auto manufacturer. In 1908 his cars were successful at the Coupe de l'Auto and the French Grand Prix and, in 1914, René Thomas won the Indianapolis 500-Mile Race in the 1913 Delage Grand Prix Racer shown here. This type finished fourth and fifth in the 1913 French Grand Prix. At Le Mans the Delages finished first and second! The engine was a four-cylinder, horizontal-valve, water-cooled affair with a displacement of 6,234 cc and developing 130 hp. A five-speed transmission was installed.

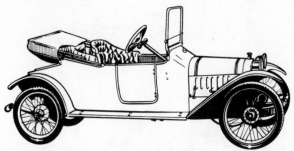

WOODS MOBILETTE   The few years of peace before the outbreak of hostilities of World War I ushered in an utterly simple and very light type of auto called the cyclecar. The pace had been set by Peugeot and Bugatti. The cars were so simple that any engineering workshop could build them. They usually had a motorcycle-type engine, light wire wheels, chain or belt drive or friction discs, and a very light chassis, often made of wood. This English Woods Mobilette Cyclecar made its appearance in 1913. Although at first glance it appeared to be a large touring type, it could seat only two.

RUSSELL-KNIGHT   In 1899 the Canada Cycle and Motor Company was formed through a merger of five other companies. Thomas A. Russell, soon hired as general manager, added ice skates to the line of products. For several years the company made electric autos and had Canadian selling rights to many U.S. makes. In 1905 the first Russell was produced. Two years later Tom Russell went to see the famous automotive inventor Charles Y. Knight in England, and brought back the rights to manufacture Knight's silent sleeve-valve engine. The first Russell-Knight was built in 1910 and in the following year a separate firm was formed, the Russell Motor Car Company. The 1913 Russell-Knight is shown here in the Touring Model 28 that sold for $3,500. It was fitted with electric starter, electric lights, full-floating rear axle, left-hand drive, heater, electric starter, and a powered tire pump! The car can be viewed at The Manitoba Automobile Museum, Elkhorn, Manitoba, Canada.

PAIGE TOURING Fred Paige was in the insurance business when he decided to try automobile manufacturing. He took H. M. Jewett into the business because he needed an engineer. This is the 1913 Paige Touring that could seat seven passengers and was fitted with advanced features such as an electric horn, electric lights, and an electric starter.

COMMERCIAL ELECTRIC TRUCK During the early days of the automobile, the gasoline engine was noisy and troublesome to operate and maintain. As a result, many commercial houses turned to the electric truck, which enabled the drivers to switch with ease from the horse to the motorcar. This is the commercial Electric Truck produced in 1913 by the Commercial Electric Truck Company of America, Philadelphia, Pennsylvania. The truck weighed seven tons and was powered by four General Electric, 16-ampere, 85-volt motors, one driving each wheel. The batteries were stowed in compartments on each side of the truck. One of these trucks remained in continuous service from 1913 to 1963! A cover was often fitted over the driver's seat. Four-wheel steering was optional!

SCRIPPS BOOTH "BI-AUTOGO"   The two-wheel automobile has always been a fascinating engineering challenge. Only one is known to have been built and operated although the idea still intrigues automotive designers. The Detroit artist-engineer James Scripps Booth built this cycle-type, two-wheel automobile in 1913. In general, his designs were highly original but rarely progressed past the experimental stage. Although the idea was sound, the technology of 1913 was inadequate for success. It was very difficult to straighten the front wheel after making a turn, and it required superhuman physical effort to raise and lower the "landing wheels" on each side of the vehicle so the project had to be dropped. Power steering and hydraulic operation of the wheels plus gyroscopic stabilization could have spelled success for this experiment. Many automotive designers feel that the two-wheeler would require a less powerful engine and could maneuver more easily than the conventional four-wheeler. Mr. Booth was ahead of his time.

KEETON   This very little-known Keeton double phaeton of 1913, a virtual copy of the 1911 Arrol-Johnston double phaeton, owed much of its design to Renault. Notice that the car featured the sloping hood with the radiator between the hood and passenger compartment. The advantage was improved forward visibility plus added streamlining. A four-cylinder, water-cooled engine was used to power this five-seater. The Keeton was made in Detroit, Michigan, from 1908 to 1914. This 1913 model had chrome vanadium gears, imported ball bearings, and a 136-inch wheelbase.

OPEL SPORTS CAR Opel had been active in racing since 1899, and a spinoff from the 1909 and 1910 racers was this streamlined sports car of 1913. It was fitted with a 1,950-cc, four-cylinder, inline, water-cooled engine. The car was a four-seater with the spare tire stowed vertically in a compartment behind the rear seat. The opening was covered with a leather boot. Notice the headlight faired into the leading edge of the fender. The car was not an immediate success, but sales mounted as people became accustomed to its advanced styling.

CADILLAC ROADSTER The development of this 1913 Cadillac resulted in the award, to the company, of the Dewar Trophy for automotive progress. The roadster featured an electric starter and electric lights as standard equipment. It was the last four-cylinder-engine-powered Cadillac. Another feature was an electromagnetic gearshift.

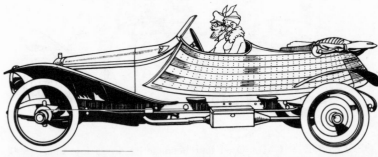

PANHARD-LEVASSOR This polished, wood-planked, boat-like body belonged to the rakish 1913 Panhard-Levassor "Skiff." Notice the duplex curved-front fenders instead of the flat type. The rectangular box beside the chassis is the engine muffler. A four-cylinder, inline, water-cooled engine of about 2,700 cc powered this custom-made beauty.

PACKARD COUPÉ This 1913 Packard was one of America's first luxury cars with comfort and silence for the two coupé passengers. Notice the single taillight atop the tip of the rear fender. This automobile sold for between $4,150 and $5,000.

WILLYS-OVERLAND   This Model 79-T touring car made its appearance in 1913 and cost $950 with a hand-crank starter, folding top, and windshield. Electric lights and self-starter were extra; the price of the car was $985 with the self-starter. A 35-hp., four-cylinder, water-cooled, inline engine powered the car. Notice that the steering wheel was still on the right side, following European practice. Eight thousand workers were employed in the Toledo, Ohio, factory at that time.

JEFFERY J-6   This Jeffery J-6 RD made its appearance in 1914. The two-seater, wire-wheeled roadster was powered by a water-cooled, flat-head, six-cylinder, inline engine that developed 34 hp.

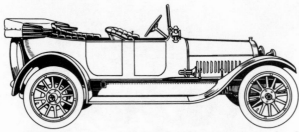

BUICK TOURING This 1914 Buick Touring car was the first six-cylinder car produced by the company. It contained such progressive items as electric lights, electric horn, running board aprons, demountable wheel rims, and a convertible top that could be raised and lowered by one person. Big features in 1914.

STUTZ BEARCAT Harry C. Stutz is considered to be one of America's greatest automotive engineers. He built his first car at the age of twenty-one in 1897 and then worked for various firms until he designed the American Underslung. He then became chief engineer for the Marion Motor Car Company. In 1910 he began producing his own cars and formed the Ideal Motor Company, Indianapolis, Indiana. To prove the worth of his car he entered the first Indianapolis 500-Mile Race. His car finished eleventh. In 1912 Stutz cars finished fourth and sixth in that race. Third place was earned in the 1913 race. This 1914 Bearcat was a typical open raceabout and was powered by a four-cylinder, T-head, water-cooled engine that developed 60 hp. Bore was 4.75 inches and stroke 5.5 inches. Three-speed transmission and shaft drive were standard. Dual ignition, double distributor, and a forced-feed lubricating system were features. The wheelbase was 120 inches. The car, weighing over 4,000 pounds, was capable of speeds over 80 mph. A Stutz Bearcat is on exhibit in The Museum of Automobiles, Morrilton, Arkansas.

HEADLIGHTS

SAXON The Saxon Four Roadster was a very popular small and inexpensive light U.S. car. It was powered by an 18-hp., L-head Continental water-cooled engine. The Saxon could seat four passengers on an eight-foot wheelbase. Wire wheels and transverse front springs were fitted. The price was only $395.

DODGE NO. 1 The Dodge Brothers, John and Horace, made their first production automobile in 1914 and placed it on the market early in 1915. The car was of open touring design. Before this they had established a reputation as builders of automotive parts and even supplied engines to the Ford Manufacturing Company. This first car was simple but extremely rugged and reliable. It was powered with a 35-hp., four-cylinder, L-head, water-cooled engine. The five-seater was priced at $785.

JEFFERY ROADSTER In 1914 the Thomas B. Jeffery Company developed a six-cylinder, inline engine and built this snappy roadster/raceabout around it. The engine was water-cooled. The design followed the popular arrangement of the day for sporty cars: two bucket seats, fuel tank behind the seats, and space for a strap-on luggage trunk between the spare tire and tank.

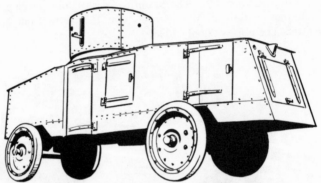

JEFFERY ARMORED VEHICLE A son of the founder of the Thomas B. Jeffery Company, Harold W. Jeffery, was instrumental in developing this experimental armored vehicle in 1914 when hostilities appeared inescapable. The occupants were well protected with armor plate, and a rotating turret was fitted. Tires were solid rubber to prevent deflation from enemy fire. The basic design set the pattern for many armored cars in the future.

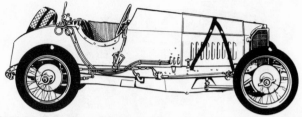

MERCEDES GRAND PRIX RACER This Mercedes racer was designed in 1914 for the Grand Prix races. Several were built for the Mercedes Team effort. The cars were four-cylinder, water-cooled, with overhead valves and camshaft. Dual-magneto ignition and four spark plugs per cylinder were installed to develop 110 hp. which drove the cars at a top speed of 110 mph. In the French Grand Prix one blew up its engine, but the remainder of the team finished in first, second, and third places! In 1915 Ralph De Palma won the Indianapolis 500-Mile Race in a Mercedes. Three 1914 Mercedes were entered in the 1922 Targa Florio, and the old cars scored first and tenth places.

DETROIT ELECTRIC BROUGHAM This Detroit Electric Brougham was made by the Anderson Electric Company, Detroit, Michigan, in 1914. It was powered by an 80-volt, 10-hp. motor mounted in the center of the car. Final drive was shaft and bevel gears. It had five forward and five reverse speeds, the highest of which was 25 mph. Batteries could be charged without removing them from the car. A battery charger was available from the manufacturer and a receptacle was provided at the rear of the car to plug in the charger.

ROLLS-ROYCE SILVER GHOST   The Rolls-Royce Silver Ghost earned the undisputed title of "The finest car in the world." It was designed in 1906 by The Hon. C. S. Royce, and the model was continued for twenty years without major changes. Only the chassis, engine, and drive were made by Rolls-Royce. Each car was built to order and the body was then assigned to an approved coach builder. This 1914 "Colonial" touring body was made by Kellner of Paris and featured two windshields, one for the rear passengers as well as one for the driver. The design was similar to the 1913 "London-Edinburgh" type, which exhibited superb performance in a 15,000-mile trial. The 1914 "Colonial" is on display at the Briggs Cunningham Automotive Museum, Costa Mesa, California.

HUDSON MODEL 54   This 1914 Hudson Sedan Model 54 featured a totally enclosed passenger compartment on a 145-inch wheelbase. It was the first U.S. six-cylinder car of moderate weight, tipping the scales at 2,680 pounds. A four-speed overdrive transmission was standard. An open touring model was also offered in 1914. Price of the sedan was $3,100. Hudson sales in 1914 were over 10,260 cars, making Hudson sixth in total sales among United States auto firms. The Detroit factory comprised 26 acres. The sedan was available only in blue with black moldings and gold striping.

LOCOMOBILE SPEEDSTER The Locomobile Company of America, Bridgeport, Connecticut, manufactured this Gentleman's Speedster in 1914. It was the equivalent, in those days, of a Jaguar or a Corvette today. The six-cylinder, T-head, water-cooled engine with three blocks mounted on a bronze crankcase had a displacement of 525 cubic inches and propelled the car at over 70 mph. Bore was 4.5 inches and stroke was 5.5 inches. Four-speed transmission was fitted. The car can be seen at the Car and Carriage Caravan, Luray Caverns, Virginia.

CRETOR POPCORN WAGON Charles Cretor and Company of Chicago, Illinois, produced nine Popcorn Wagons in 1914. They were built almost entirely by hand, and the body was constructed integrally with the chassis as a single unit. The wagons took about eight months to build. A four-cylinder, water-cooled Buda gasoline engine was located under the hood, which extended into the driving compartment. The wheelbase was 132 inches, and half-elliptic springs were installed all around. A low-pressure steam boiler was also installed, using butane for fuel. It supplied steam to a small one-cylinder steam engine that turned the popcorn popper and peanut roaster. It also heated these items as well as the hot-dog-bun warmer and kept the popcorn hot after it was popped. The wagon was, therefore, much more than a popcorn wagon. Price of this luncheonette on wheels was $4,600. Now on view at The Museum of Automobiles, Morrilton, Arkansas.

BRISCOE TOURING This little-known Briscoe Touring car was made in Jackson, Michigan. It was a light auto of 1914, weighing only 1,700 pounds. It sold for $785. The body was French, designed by Carrosseries Industrielles of Paris. It was powered by a four-cylinder, water-cooled, L-head, gasoline engine that developed 15.6 hp. The car was sold with Ajax tires that were guaranteed for 5,000 miles! Note the single headlamp.

CRANE-SIMPLEX Smith & Mabley, Inc., were the New York distributors of foreign cars around 1900, after which time they formed the S & M Simplex Company, producing their own cars. Then the firm declared bankruptcy. In 1907 Henry Lockhart, Jr., and associates reorganized the firm and renamed it Simplex Automobile Company, with the factory on Long Island, New York. They engaged the services of Henry M. Crane, one of the most capable automotive engineers in the U.S., to design this 1914 touring model. In the following year they bought the equipment and plant of the Crane Motor Company of Bayonne, New Jersey. The name Crane-Simplex remained. A four-cylinder, water-cooled engine was fitted under the hood. A 1914 Crane-Simplex can be seen at the Heritage Plantation of Sandwich, Sandwich, Massachusetts.

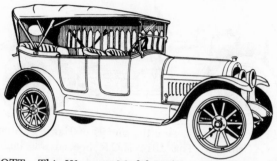

WESTCOTT This Westcott Model U-50 open touring was built in Richmond, Indiana, and made its appearance in 1914. The seven-passenger car was powered by a six-cylinder, water-cooled, gasoline engine that made the car an excellent hill-climber. All brass parts, such as light-rims, were nickel-plated. The car can be viewed at the Car and Carriage Caravan, Luray Caverns, Virginia.

RAUCH AND LANG The Rauch and Lang Carriage Company of Cleveland, Ohio, built this car in 1914. It was electric-motor-powered, and the designer, John H. Hertner, claimed that the car could travel 100 miles on a single charge of the batteries. The 2½-hp. motor, rated at 80 volts, was located near the center of the frame and connected to the rear axle by means of a short shaft and a worm gear. The rear axle was of the floating type. Suspension for the 100-inch-wheelbase vehicle was via full-elliptic springs in the rear and half-elliptic springs in the front. The optimum speed was 13 mph. and top speed was 19 mph., which made it ideal as a city vehicle. The car weighed 4,000 pounds and could be controlled from either the front or rear seats. A car of this type can be seen in the Smithsonian Institution, Washington, D.C.

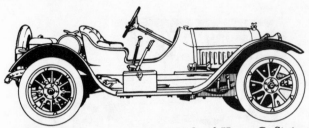

H.C.S. SPECIAL H.C.S. were the initials of Harry C. Stutz of the Stutz Motor Company. This 1914 H.C.S. Special was built by the company as a companion car to the Stutz Bearcat. It was powered with a four-cylinder, L-head engine and was priced at $1,475, which was cheaper than its more famous brother. It was very similar in general appearance but did not have the stamina of the Bearcat.

PIERCE-ARROW TOURING The George N. Pierce Company, Buffalo, New York, had manufactured birdcages, refrigerators, and bicycles before it entered the automotive field in 1901 with a Motorette. The first Pierce-Arrow was made in 1909. The seven-passenger Pierce-Arrow Touring shown is the 1914 Model 48. It was a big car with a 147-inch wheelbase and was powered by a 60-hp., six-cylinder, water-cooled engine. Price was in the $6,000 range. The name Pierce-Arrow became a household word with auto enthusiasts after World War I because of the innovations and design of the Pierce-Arrow.

TRUMBULL COUPÉ Two of the seven Trumbull brothers, Alexander H. and Isaac B. Trumbull, began building automobiles in their American Cycle Car Company, Bridgeport, Connecticut, in 1913. The following year saw the company name changed to Trumbull Motorcar Company. This is the Trumbull Coupé built in 1914 and advertised as the "Little Car That Looks Big." The wheelbase was 80 inches and the tread was 44 inches. The car weighed 950 pounds and was priced at $600. It was powered by a thermo-syphon, water-cooled, four-cylinder, inline, L-head engine of 104-cubic-inch displacement and 18 hp. This could propel the car to 50 mph. No water pump or fan was fitted to the engine, manufactured by the Herrmann Engineering Company, Detroit, Michigan. Of the 2,000 cars built, about 1,500 were sold in Europe, especially England. Production stopped in May, 1915, when Isaac B. Trumbull went down with the *Lusitania*.

CHAPTER EIGHT

War and Peace 1915—1919

To ASSIST in viewing this brief but turbulent five-year period of peace-war-peace in some perspective, especially as it relates to the American car, we should keep three dates in mind.

1914—August 2; Germany invaded Luxembourg and France.

1917—April 6; the United States declared war on Germany.

1918—November 11; World War I ended.

During 1915, as the war in Europe continued, total truck and passenger car production in the United States reached close to the million mark—falling short by only about 30,000 units. These vehicles with their total value of more than $700 million almost doubled the previous year's output. *Most significantly, this meant that motor vehicle production, then, and for all time in the foreseeable future, was tightly locked into the national economy.*

With Europe's war gradually becoming "our" war, car fanciers found themselves "financing" army trucks and staff cars instead of family vehicles. The poorer man had to put aside his dream of owning a flivver while he and the richer man's chauffeur drove or marched off to war, leaving the town-car owner with the task of learning to maneuver his own machine.

Obviously these turbulent times were destined to have a profound effect on the auto makers, the bypassed car buyers and drivers, and on the products, too.

True to his earlier promise, Henry Ford, in mid-August of 1915, refunded fifty dollars to the more recent purchasers of his Model T. The Ford empire turned out its millionth car; by now the "T" was selling for $440 and boasted an electric horn in place of the earlier bulb-type honker. But General Motors matched the

256

magic fifty-dollar figure in a different fashion. If you owned a share of G.M. stock your initial cash dividend was fifty dollars.

The Chevrolet Model 490 touring car carried a price tag of $490 F.O.B. Flint, Michigan, or at franchised plants across the country. It had a four-cylinder, valve-in-head engine, an electric starter, and an electrical lighting system—all representing very serious competition to the Ford product. Chevrolet had something else up its sleeve, too. The firm was acquiring, in great secrecy, vast chunks of G.M. stock.

The Dodge organization was moving into full swing and the word "dependability" was coined by its promoters; fifteen years later and after extensive advertising the word would begin to find its way into dictionaries. The 1915 Dodge eliminated the standard hardwood body frames still in general use throughout the industry (and a carry-over from the carriage industry) and produced instead an all-steel body.

Packard unveiled a fantastic V-12 engine featuring aluminum pistons, truly a spectacular "first." This 900-pound "Twin-Six" powerplant utilized two banks each of six cylinders canted 60 degrees apart. For more conventional power, numerous V-8 powerplants were in production led by Cadillac's earlier offering.

Number Two in the production race at this point was Willys-Overland. Ford, of course, was first by a country mile. "Sociable" bodies were a highlight of the 1915 National Automobile Show; they offered a passageway between the front seats to the rear section. But turning out a good car was not exactly easy . . . the war in Europe began to make itself felt through shortages of many vital materials.

For General Motors 1916 was a momentous year. Charles W. Nash made his departure after William Durant assumed command and the presidency; then the firm incorporated in Delaware.

Chevrolet turned out 63,000 vehicles. Willys-Overland production at Toledo more than doubled that with 141,000 cars. However, Ford's 1916–1917 output exceeded 730,000 vehicles and the T's price dropped to a remarkable $345.

Dodges continued to serve the Army with distinction in its Mexican campaign. An early motorized attack there by a small force in Dodge cars was led by one George S. Patton, Jr., Lt., U.S.A. Doorposts in some Dodges, as well as on the Hudson

Super-Six, could be removed to provide a more "racy" appearance. Hudson offered the first counterweighted crankshaft.

The Federal Aid Road Act encouraged the creation of state highway departments by offering matching Federal funds for the construction of better roads.

Mr. Nash took over the Thomas B. Jeffery Company and out of it he formed the Nash Motors Company. The Stanley Steamer engine was pared down to only 32 moving parts; the car sold for $1,975 F.O.B. Newton, Massachusetts. But for $775 less you could buy a 246-cubic-inch internal-combustion Olds V-8. During 1916 more than a million and a half passenger cars were produced and nearly one hundred thousand buses and trucks.

A long distance away from its original Long Island setting, the final race in the original Vanderbilt Cup series was run off at Santa Monica, California.

The American industry, through its National Automobile Chamber of Commerce, embarked on a reciprocal exchange of patents. This meant fewer lawsuits and a trend toward standardization in general. And as for the mass-produced vehicle, externally, at least, originality of appearance began, ever so slightly, to give way to a sort of discernible Detroit "sameness"—beloved by banks, dealers and stockholders, but bewailed by the connoisseur.

When America entered World War I in April, 1917, many industry facilities, but not all, turned quickly to the making of war items. Total car production for the year topped 1,700,000 units. Additionally, more than 128,000 trucks and buses were built. The first Nash emerged powered by a six-cylinder, valve-in-head engine. The Lincoln Motor Company was set up by Henry Leland, who had resigned from the Cadillac organization. He was a super-patriot, and G.M. did not plunge into the war effort fast enough to suit him; his Lincoln outfit, among others, produced Liberty aircraft powerplants. The Essex Motor Car Company was created by Hudson. And the Dodge appeared on a new battlefield; one in Europe was chauffeured by ex-racing driver Eddie Rickenbacker. His boss in the back seat: General Pershing.

To aid in vital farming operations in England Ford started producing tractors, and his company also turned out its first specialized truck chassis. The Indianapolis 500 was run, war or no war. And in a series of match races Ralph De Palma and Barney Oldfield met at six different tracks. Oldfield took three of these affairs in Harry Miller's enclosed-cockpit "Golden Sub" racer; De Palma won three in his 120-hp. Packard Twin-Six. Over a twenty-seven-year period De Palma was to enter 2,800 races and win 2,000 of them!

Also during 1917, the Stanley twins retired from the Stanley Motor Carriage Company. Maxwell leased the Chalmers Motor Company facilities. John M. Studebaker died. The Federal government allotted $5 million toward the construction of improved roads.

Although America was deeply embroiled in the "war to end all wars," 1918 opened with the 18th National Automobile Show. Held at New York City's Grand Central Palace, most of the "new" cars had an austere and military-like appearance, as was to be expected, with few mechanical innovations. On a few of the closed-body models exhibited a bit more glass was in evidence. The Federal Aid Road Act, inaugurated two years earlier, brought forth its first tangible result: 2.55 miles of "super" highway in the Oakland, California, area. Upon completion it was immediately labeled as inadequate for its needs, thus presaging almost all urban highway construction ever since. "Motorless Sundays," which had been instituted to save motor fuel and conserve equipment, came to an end in mid-October of 1918.

As its part in the war effort the American automobile industry produced a plethora of weapons, tractors, trucks, staff cars, aircraft engines, subchasers, many other massive items, plus vast quantities of smaller, but highly specialized matériel for all branches of our military and our allies. For anyone interested in following up the fantastic part automotive men played in all this, his or her attention is directed to such stellar performances as the Dodge boys', who turned out mechanisms for French field guns, which nobody thought could be mass produced . . . including the French; Knudsen's remarkable work for Ford cranking up a complete shipbuilding operation from uncertain blueprints; and the famous Liberty engine and the part the Lelands played in its perfection.

Total 1918 truck and car production topped 1,170,000 units, with most of this earmarked, of course, for the military.

Although Cadillac had lost the Lelands, Henry and Wilfred (father and son), G.M. had gained the Chevrolet company. Better than an even swap because Cadillac quality continued high, and Chevrolet would one day become the tail that wagged the G.M. dog. Pioneering car maker Francis Stanley died.

With the cessation of hostilities on November 11, 1918, the world in general, as well as the auto industry in particular, hoped to return to the good old days. Translated: high output, high sales, high profits. But prices for raw as well as finished materials in America, particularly, remained abnormally high. Inflated wartime wages in the production plants and mines had left their mark. Trouble, big trouble, was ahead.

In January, 1919, the Hudson firm unveiled its new line of Essex cars; these were the only really all-new vehicles displayed at the 19th National Automobile Show, although internally most makers had improved their offerings structurally and mechanically as the result of wartime production refinements, knowledge of better fabrication methods, and an understanding of metal fatigue.

At the Paris Salon in 1919 the genius of the Swiss engineer Marc Birkigt was most obvious in the new luxurious French version of the Hispano-Suiza. The stunning 37.2-hp., overhead-camshaft car incorporated techniques perfected through the wartime design and use of lightweight aircraft engines. Originally a combination of Spanish financing and Swiss technology, and previously considered a product of Spain, the car and its marque would now acquire a French allure and worldwide reputation.

In America the single biggest change at this time was the acquisition, in its entirety, of the Ford Motor Company by the Ford family. For their original one-tenth joint ownership John and Horace Dodge collected $25 million. And a schoolteacher who had invested $100 in 1903 for a single share of Ford stock received $355,000. One sign of change—gradual as it was and certainly long overdue—became evident on the Model T. Henry and Company now offered electric starting as an extra-cost option. Regardless, Ford continued to dominate the industry, producing more than one-third of all cars made in America. Harold Wills left Ford at this time to develop the Wills Sainte Claire car.

General Motors, under Durant's direction, acquired various outfits. One was Fisher Body. Another was a rather small outfit which many of Little Billy's colleagues considered of dubious value. It was called Frigidaire. A lending operation, the General Motors Acceptance Corporation, was launched, and the G.M. Building—originally intended to be designated the Durant Building—was started in Detroit to house top G.M. offices. By now Delaware's Du Pont firm controlled more than a quarter of all General Motors stock.

Also in 1919, the Studebaker clan gave up its long-time carriage-making activities. The first state gasoline tax was imposed by Oregon, one cent on every gallon sold. All states now qualified for assistance under the Federal Highway Act, and no wonder. During 1919 Washington allotted $65 million for roadway construction. Some three million miles of roads offering varying degrees of permanent or semi-permanent surfacing existed in the United States. Fort Smith, Arkansas, became an outstanding Saturday shopping mecca for Oklahoma and Arkansas farm families with its extensive twenty-seven miles of concrete roadways.

A new land speed record was established in 1919 by Ralph De Palma. Driving a special Packard V-12 Twin-6 at Daytona Beach, the famous driver set a mark of 149.80 mph. Overseas, the dangerous Targa Floria road race over the wild mountain roads of Sicily was won by André Bollot in a 2.5-liter Peugeot.

Fred and August Duesenberg, doing business as the Duesenberg Brothers, Inc., tuned their machines to rack up international marks for distances of up to 300 miles in all official classes for powerplants ranging from 161- to 450-cubic-inch displacement.

As the 1920s loomed on the horizon, the vast majority of passenger cars (90 percent) still continued to be open touring models or roadsters. But designs would change drastically, and automotive fortunes would rise and wane as critical times would come to affect both men and machines.

WOODS ELECTRIC The Woods Motor Vehicle Company of New York, New York, and Chicago, Illinois, concentrated on electric vehicles from 1900 to 1919. "No fumes, no flats, no fuss" read the Woods advertisement. This was made possible, because the electric power eliminated the exhaust, the tires were solid, and starting and stopping were accomplished by the movement of a lever. The car shown here is the Woods of 1915. Speed was about forty miles per hour, and range was about 100 miles before recharging of the batteries was necessary. As gasoline engines became popular, Woods offered a combination gasoline-engine, electric motorcar in 1917, but very few were sold. Notice the holes in the front tires to make them softer and more resilient.

JEFFERY ROADSTER The Thomas B. Jeffery Company produced this medium-priced roadster Model 96-2 in 1915, and it was the last two-seater to be built by the firm for a half-dozen years. In 1916 the company was sold to Charles W. Nash, retired president of General Motors, and thereafter all their cars were called Nash.

HUDSON MODEL 40   The Hudson Landolet Model 40 made its appearance in 1915 and gave the rear passengers their choice of fresh air or protective enclosure. It was six-cylinder-engine-powered, as were the other three models offered that year. The engine developed 30 hp. Hudson sales in 1915 were 12,864 cars, which was a 300 percent increase in six years!

FORD STATION WAGON   The Ford Model T Station Wagon has a fond place in the memories of many of the older generation. The "woody," as it later became known, had a wooden body with a hand-rubbed finish that today would be a prized possession to many automobile enthusiasts. The "woody" could seat six, and the propelling machinery was the same as other Model T body styles.

FORD FIRE CHIEF Of the fifteen million Ford Model T autos produced, some were used as commercial vehicles and by municipalities because of their initial low price and economical operation. In 1915 the Sandy Hollow Fire Department used a Model T roadster as the Fire Chief's car. The car was painted bright red and had a large brass bell mounted forward of the windshield.

GRANT COUPÉ The Grant was a very little-known automobile made in Cleveland, Ohio, from 1913 to 1923. The 1915 two-passenger enclosed coupé is shown here. Although fairly dependable, the Grant was also comfortable but lacked distinguishing characteristics and innovations.

MOON TOURING Joseph W. and John Moon began building automobiles in St. Louis, Missouri, in 1905. A few years later they hired Louis Mooers, an engineer from Peerless, who designed a fine overhead-valve, four-cylinder engine. By 1914 Moon switched from their own engines to Continental in order to meet production demands. This is the Moon touring car of 1915 that was powered by the Continental six-cylinder engine. The Moon was one of the most successful of the so-called "assembled" cars due to Moon's insistence on all parts being built to their rigid specifications. Note the radiator crescent ornament.

REO TOURING Ransom E. Olds left Oldsmobile in 1904 but continued to manufacture automobiles, concentrating on passenger types, under a new name, REO, made up of his initials. This is the REO touring model of 1916. REO continued production until 1936.

JEFFERY CHESTERFIELD One of the few pleasure vehicles made by the Thomas B. Jeffery Company, of Kenosha, Wisconsin, during 1915 was this Chesterfield touring car. It was powered by a six-cylinder, water-cooled engine of about 35 hp. Production of this model was discontinued the following year due to the war and the need for military vehicles.

JEFFERY QUAD TRUCK Although they produced automobiles as well, the Thomas B. Jeffery Company concentrated on commercial vehicles in 1914–1915. In 1915, automobile sales totaled 3,100 vehicles while truck sales totaled 7,600 vehicles. This Quad Truck of 1915 was one of the greatest in demand at that time. It had a steel frame and wooden open cargo area and is generally considered to be the company's contribution to the Allied efforts in World War I. About 20,000 were built up to the time of the Armistice! The biggest feature of the Quad Truck was the four-wheel drive, which was indispensable in the muck and mire near the front lines.

CHEVROLET ROADSTER This 1915 Chevrolet roadster was called the Amesbury Special. It was one of three models that sold well over 13,600 cars in 1915. It was powered by a 24-hp., four-cylinder, water-cooled, inline engine. The car weighed 2,300 pounds, and the price was $985.

SCRIPPS BOOTH ROADSTER When James Scripps Booth designed conventional automobiles they were invariably successful. This Scripps Booth roadster made its appearance in 1915 and it was one of the most popular U.S. light cars during that period. It was a three-seater powered by a four-cylinder, overhead-valve, water-cooled engine. Price was $775.

WILLYS-KNIGHT   For an enclosed car of 1915 this Willys-Knight Model 79-C coupé had unusually good visibility due to a rather high body design and large windows. This two-seater was equipped with an electric starter and electric lights. Price was $1,150.

WILLYS-KNIGHT TOURING   In 1914–1915 John Willys bought many Knight automotive patents, and this Willys-Knight touring car was introduced during 1915. It was powered by the sleeve-valve engine taken over under the Knight patents in 1914. This made the car run very silently at a time when the average automobile was notoriously noisy.

METZ TOURING The light or compact car movement began in Europe about 1910 because, at that time, European roads were superior to those in the U.S., where heavier cars were the vogue. One of the few U.S. light car manufacturers, the Metz Company, introduced this four-place touring model in 1915. The car had wire wheels and full-elliptical springs. The company built their last automobile in 1921.

OLDSMOBILE TOURING The Oldsmobile Touring Model 42 made its appearance in 1915 and was powered with a four-cylinder, water-cooled, inline engine, fitted with overhead valves. Electric starter and electric lights were standard on this five-seater. The wheels were fitted with demountable rims which facilitated tire changes. In addition to these advanced features the convertible top could be operated by one person, which was a great step forward.

CADILLAC SEDAN In 1910 Henry M. Leland's Cadillac Company became part of General Motors. His preoccupation with quality cars continued the name Cadillac. This Model Type 51, introduced in 1915, had the very first 90-degree, vee-type, eight-cylinder engine. The powerplant was water-cooled and developed between 60 and 70 hp. The engine was so successful that it remained basically unchanged for twelve years. This 1915 sedan was the car that first made Cadillac famous.

PULLMAN DELUXE COUPÉ The Pullman Company of railroad fame produced this coupé in 1916. The outstanding feature of the car was the hand-hammered all-steel body which had a well-rounded passenger compartment, a refreshing departure from the squared-off cars of that era. Note also the small window forward of the door to improve visibility. This gasoline-engine-powered car featured a pushbutton gearshift.

PIERCE-ARROW "66"   This Pierce-Arrow "66" Raceabout was made in 1916 and was powered by a T-head, six-cylinder engine that developed 60 hp. at 856 rpm. and 100 hp. at 1,500 rpm. Pierce was very conservative in its advertising and avoided the 100-hp. ability! The car followed the raceabout pattern of the era except that the fuel tank was buried in the frame. Note the triple spare tires. Horn, starter, and lights were electric. The car is on display at the Long Island Automotive Museum, Southampton, New York.

HUDSON SUPER-SIX   In 1916 Hudson developed a new six-cylinder engine called the "Super-Six." It had the first fully balanced crankshaft and the first high-compression, non-detonating cylinder head. The compression ratio was 5 to 1. This was a modification of an earlier design which boosted the power from 48 hp. to 76 hp. and provided smoother operation, longer engine life, and increased running economy. Hudson's 1916 sales exceeded 26,390 cars. One of the most popular models was this open touring five-passenger model, one of which traveled round-trip from San Francisco to New York with no major problems.

JACKSON WOLVERINE   The Jackson Automobile Company, Jackson, Michigan, produced this Wolverine model, five-passenger touring car in 1916. It was built on a 118-inch wheelbase and cost $1,295. Powered by an eight-cylinder, inline, water-cooled engine, the car had a high power to weight ratio and the company claimed seventeen miles to the gallon of gasoline under touring conditions. Suspension was by means of four full-elliptic springs. The car was upholstered in genuine leather and was supplied with a mechanical tire pump that required no effort from the operator.

STANLEY MODEL 725   The vee-type radiator on this 1916 Stanley steam car was really an air-cooled condenser for the steam that was exhausted from the engine. In this way the water could be used several times, requiring very little make-up. This is a five-passenger touring model. The engine was 20 hp., twice the power of the 1914 engine.

CHEVROLET TOURING MODEL 490   The 1916 Chevrolet model 490 was offering in touring or roadster types at the same $490 price. The touring type is shown here. The powerplant was a four-cylinder, water-cooled, 24-hp. engine. In this year, Chevrolet took over the Mason Motor Company, which had been making Chevrolet engines. Chevrolet sales reached 70,701 automobiles in 1916, more than fourteen times the 1914 auto output! The model 490 was the main Chevrolet production car until 1923.

OWENS MAGNETIC   Produced between 1913 and 1920 by Baker, Rauch and Lang Company, the Owens Magnetic had many advanced features. The 1916 touring model shown was powered by a six-cylinder engine of 45 hp. that was fitted with a helical gear-driven camshaft and a semi-pressurized lubricating oil system. All six cylinders were cast in a single block instead of in pairs as was the normal practice. The engine drove a generator that supplied electric current to an electric motor that drove the rear wheels, thereby achieving a gearless transmission. Pushbuttons were used to control the speed of the car.

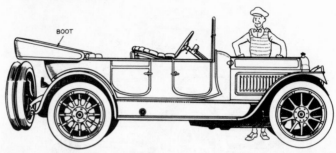

BOOT

PACKARD TWIN-SIX TOURING   Jesse G. Vincent became Packard's chief engine in 1910, and this brilliant man soon developed a "Twin-Six" engine at a time when most companies were arguing about the qualities of fours versus sixes. The engine was the first American twelve-cylinder automotive engine and the first auto engine with aluminum pistons. The powerplant was a vee type at 60 degrees between banks of cylinders producing 85 hp. at 3,000 rpm. The engine was exceptionally smooth and could idle down to 3 mph. in high gear and then accelerate to 30 mph. without changing gears! Prominent personalities and the social elite enhanced the Twin-Six prestige, both in the U.S. and abroad, including Czar Nicholas II and Grand Duke Michael of Russia; the Maharajah of Alwaar of India had several, and Viscount Jellicoe of New Zealand used a Twin-Six Touring as his official car. Packard showrooms were forced to open twenty-four hours a day because of the crowds that wanted to see the new "marvel."

WILLYS ROADSTER   Willys-Overland brought back its L-head, six-cylinder, inline engine in 1917 for this chummy roadster. The engine was a standard poppet-valve powerplant of 45 hp., which gave this light car a more than average speed.

STUTZ BEARCAT MODEL R With the same basic powerplant and some styling changes, Stutz introduced the Bearcat Model R in 1917. A full windshield replaced the monocle type, and the cylindrical fuel tank was faired into the rear of the body, which was mounted on a 120-inch wheelbase. A four-cylinder, 16-valve, T-head engine operated with a pressurized gasoline system. Electric starter, horn and lights were added. The Model R can be seen at the Museum of Transportation, Larz Anderson Park, Brookline, Massachusetts.

CHEVROLET Produced in 1917 and 1918, this almost forgotten "chummy roadster" sported a V-8 engine with overhead valves and dual carburetors. It was a two-door, four-passenger auto. It never gained the popularity of the Model 490.

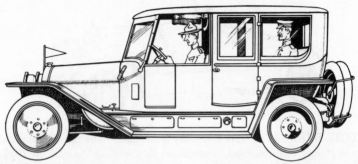

LOCOMOBILE LIMOUSINE Locomobile continued to build cars until 1929. This gasoline-engine-powered limousine was made in 1917 and was used by General John J. Pershing as his staff car during World War I. Note the disc wheels and squared fenders. An innovation was the vee-type windshield which reduced wind resistance.

DODGE SEDAN Dodge was an early exponent of the totally enclosed car when many U.S. makers were still adhering to the open-touring designs. Dodge produced two- and four-door versions of this sedan from 1917 to 1919. The chassis was basically the same as their first production model of 1914 but was fitted with wire wheels. Cost was $1,295 in 1917.

COLE ROADSTER   The Cole Motor Car Company of Indianapolis, Indiana, often had the bodies of its cars made by Cole-Springfield, Springfield, Massachusetts. Although the company concentrated on larger cars, this is the Cole Tuxedo Roadster of 1917. It was a four-passenger auto powered by one of the earliest V-8 engines used in automobiles.

HUDSON AMBULANCE   The Hudson Motor Car Company built a variety of vehicles for the U.S. Army during World War I. This 1917 military ambulance was one of them. The fine riding qualities of the Hudson cars plus the powerful super-six engine contributed to the success of this ambulance.

NATIONAL TOURING   The National Motor Vehicle Company of Indianapolis, Indiana, made an enviable reputation on the race courses which advertised its passenger cars. This touring model of 1917 had a 128-inch wheelbase and an engine-powered tire pump! Electric starter, electric horn, and electric lights were standard. Full-floating rear axle, dual double-magneto and multi-jet carburetor were also fitted.

WHITE SPORT TOURING   Rollin H. White changed the name White Sewing Machine Company to White and Company in 1905. In 1910 he decided to change to gasoline-powered cars, although his steam cars had been successful. The firm concentrated on touring models, which were very popular. The 1917 Sport Touring shown here had smooth lines, as can be seen. This auto can be viewed in the Museum of Transportation, Larz Anderson Park, Brookline, Massachusetts.

PREMIER The Premier automobiles were made from 1903 to 1925 in Indianapolis, Indiana. This is the 1917 seven-passenger touring model. In 1912 a dozen Premiers driven by their owners, and not professional drivers or mechanics, crossed the United States in a group. They took their families along and all arrived on schedule. No mechanical difficulties were experienced. Needless to say, the company used this trip to illustrate the dependable qualities of their product.

STUDEBAKER TOURING This Studebaker Phaeton Touring made its appearance in 1917. It was in that year that the company developed and used an inlet manifold with a "hot spot" to vaporize the fuel mixture more efficiently. The basic car was designed in 1915 as the Series 16 Model F and was sold through 1916 into 1917 with minor modifications, such as this touring model. It was powered by a four-cylinder, water-cooled, 24-hp. engine. Almost 20,000 vehicles were sold at $885.

NASH MODEL 671/681   The Nash Model 671 was the first car of the Rambler/Jeffery firm to bear the name "Nash"—after Charles W. Nash. The 671 made its appearance in 1917 and was available in coupé or sedan bodies. The five-passenger sedan is shown here. Model 671 and the succeeding Model 681 were fitted with an advanced overhead-valve, six-cylinder engine, which basic design was continued for many years by Nash. Notice that the window columns are not visible when the windows are in the down position. The columns were removable to give the passengers the advantage of an open and unobstructed view similar to the modern-day "hardtop."

OLDSMOBILE MODEL 37   By the end of World War I Oldsmobile was moving into the higher-priced market. This Model 38, four-door, five-passenger touring car was introduced in 1918. It was powered by a vee-type, eight-cylinder, water-cooled engine.

FRANKLIN BROUGHAM The H. H. Franklin Manufacturing Company, Syracuse, New York, sold its first automobile in 1902. This is the 1918 brougham four-seat coupé. It was powered with a six-cylinder, air-cooled, 25-hp. engine with an approximate 3,500-cc displacement. Road speed was about 45 mph. In addition to air-cooled engines, Franklin featured wood chassis and aluminum body work. The resilient wood chassis is reported to have provided a very comfortable ride. Price was in the $3,000 range.

BIDDLE H TOWN CAR This little-known Biddle H Town Car was made in 1918 in Philadelphia, Pennsylvania. It was of classic landaulet body style with an open driver's seat and enclosed passenger compartment. Note the wire wheels, which were becoming fashionable around this time, and the elegant coach-type lights on the passengers' cab. The engine was made by Duesenberg and was of four cylinders with four valves per cylinder. Biddle cars were built from 1917 to 1922. This car can be viewed in the Long Island Automotive Museum, Southampton, New York.

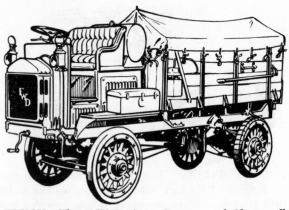

F.W.D. TRUCK   The F.W.D. Auto Company of Clintonville, Wisconsin, was developed from the Badger firm in 1910 under the leadership of Walter Olen. F.W.D. concentrated on trucks and produced this model in 1918. They were especially proud of its economical upkeep. During 1918 the company made a total of $65 million worth of F.W.D. trucks, and 3,000 were exported to England! The truck weighed three tons and could carry from two to five tons of cargo. The F.W.D. truck featured four-wheel drive, which proved to be invaluable in France during World War I.

U.S.A. LIBERTY TANK TRUCK   Prior to the United States' entry into World War I, the U.S. Army visualized the advantages of several standard specialized vehicles rather than a dozen various commercial models. In the early fall of 1917, approximately fifty automotive engineers from many companies met in Washington, D.C., to design vehicles in accordance with Army specifications. The parts were made by several manufacturers. The trucks made their appearance in 1918 and came in several varieties: troop-carrying, cargo-carrying, and tank trucks that were designed to carry a variety of liquids from gasoline to fresh drinking water. They were called Liberty trucks.

CHEVROLET TRUCK NO. 1   The first of what was to become a long line of Chevrolet trucks was produced in 1918. It was an open truck with roll-down curtains to protect the payload. The basic chassis was from the Chevrolet passenger cars.

G.M. COLUMBIA AMBULANCE   G.M. has been associated with cars and trucks since 1902, and they produced the first heavy-duty gasoline-powered truck to enter production in the United States that year. This ambulance was produced in 1918 for the U.S. Army to aid in the war effort and used a standard G.M. light truck chassis. The vehicle can now be seen at the Long Island Automotive Museum, Southampton, New York.

DODGE TRUCK This was the first Dodge commercial vehicle, a light panel truck, introduced in 1918. It proved to be immensely popular because it was very rugged, dependable, and low-priced at $885. The truck could carry a 1,000-pound payload. Note the screened sides of the cargo area and the rolled curtains which could be lowered during bad weather.

AUSTRALIAN SIX The F. H. Gordon & Company, Ltd., Sydney, Australia, made this four-seat touring model in 1918. Their cars were well made and in a class with the better U.S. cars, such as Packard. This Australian Six was powered by a vertical, six-cylinder, water-cooled engine of 23 hp., with a displacement of 3,800 cc. It had a three-speed transmission plus reverse, and used a drive shaft to the rear wheels. Speed was about 50 mph. The car can be seen in the Gilltraps Auto Museum, Collangatta, Queensland, Australia.

DODGE SEDAN Dodge, an early exponent of the closed car, produced two- and four-door sedans. This enclosed sedan of 1918 featured a "California Top," which consisted of glass panels in the steel roof to admit light, and keep out the rain and snow. The car had wood-spoked wheels and a split-hinged windshield. Price was approximately $1,300.

BUICK TOURING This five-passenger Buick Touring Model E-35 made its appearance in 1918 on a 106-inch wheelbase. Power was a four-cylinder, water-cooled, inline, 170-cubic-inch-displacement engine that developed about 18 hp. Bore was $3\frac{3}{8}$ inches, and stroke was $4\frac{3}{4}$ inches. In addition to the touring model, Buick produced roadster, sedan, and light delivery models, including a series built on a 118-inch wheelbase with 27-hp. engines in 1918. This was the beginning of the luxurious Buicks of succeeding years.

SLIDING SEAT
RUMBLE SEAT
STEP
FOOTREST FOR SLIDING SEAT

KISSEL-KAR SILVER SIX   Kissel began building cars in the United States in 1906. This Silver Six roadster made its appearance in 1919, and was an outstanding contribution to U.S. sport types because of its innovations. Although a basic two-seater, it featured a rumble seat in the rear which could accommodate two passengers. In addition, two more seats could be pulled out of the side of the car, one on each side, thereby converting the two-seater into a car for six people! What appears to be a step for entering the car also served as a footrest for the side passengers. Many outstanding personalities bought Kissel-Kars, including the famous aviator Amelia Earhart.

ESSEX SEDAN   In 1917 the Hudson Motor Car Company organized the Essex Motor Car Company to manufacture a lightweight car with a lower price than the regular Hudson auto. This made the Essex one of the most famous automobiles built in the United States. The Essex line was introduced in 1919, and this sedan was one of the 1919 Essex cars. It was a five-seater, totally enclosed with the body built in Detroit by Fisher. From 1919 to 1932 a total of almost one and a half million Essex automobiles were sold! This sedan was powered with a four-cylinder, water-cooled, 18-hp. engine with overhead valves and a displacement of 2.9 liters.

FORD COACH In keeping with the trend toward closed cars, the Ford Motor Company produced this two-door, four-seat "Coach" (sedan) in 1919. The basic engine and chassis were the faithful Model T that was to continue in production for another eight years. In 1919 Ford produced 750,000 cars, which was more than all other U.S. automobile manufacturers combined.

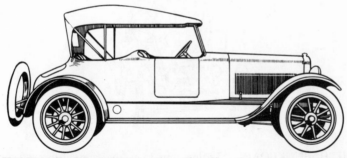

CHANDLER ROADSTER The Chandler Motor Car Company, Cleveland, Ohio, produced automobiles from 1912 to 1929. This is the Chandler four-seat chummy roadster for 1919. Price was $1,795. The manufacturer claimed fourteen to sixteen miles per gallon of gasoline and promised approximately 8,000 miles per one set of tires! Note the spare tire, but no spare wheel.

KISSEL-KAR SPORT TOURING This Kissel-Kar Sport Touring model was produced in 1919. Kissel automobiles were never without some innovation. On this car the front seats were able to slide on rails for adjustment. Other automobile manufacturers and modern aircraft manufacturers have copied this idea. A car of this type can be viewed at the Forney Historic Transportation Museum, Denver, Colorado.

SMITH BUCKBOARD Little more than the present-day go-cart, this Smith Buckboard enjoyed a brief period of popularity in 1919. It consisted of four bicycle wheels, a flatbed of wooden planks, two seats, and a simple air-cooled engine. A fifth wheel was located between the rear wheels and was connected to the engine thereby providing power for the car. The vehicle had absolutely no protection and was used as a fun vehicle by the younger set.

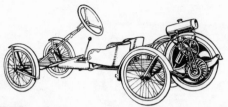

AUTO-RED-BUG   The younger generation enjoyed speeding about in buckboards like this Auto-Red-Bug of 1919. Many vehicles of this type were made in bicycle shops because they were little more than two bicycles tied together. This Auto-Red-Bug buckboard was powered by a single-cylinder, air-cooled, Briggs and Stratton engine. One of the vehicles can be viewed at the Silver Springs Early American Museum, Silver Springs, Florida.

STANLEY STEAMER COUPÉ   The Stanley Motor Carriage Company, Newton, Massachusetts, had the longest run of any steam car— from 1895 to 1931. Much of this popularity is credited to the use of a pot boiler that was very simple but required about twenty-five minutes to reach the operating pressure. This two-door, four-seat coupé made its appearance in 1919. It was powered by a two-cylinder steam engine which operated with steam at about 400-pounds-per-square-inch pressure. The radiator was really a water-condenser. However, some make-up water was required after every 100 miles. It was fitted with a 12-volt electrical system and an engine-driven generator. There were only 32 moving parts on the Stanley engine. Cranking or shifting of gears was not required to operate the car.

PIC-PIC TOURING   The Swiss Pic-Pic firm of Geneva produced this three-door touring model in 1919. The driver had access to one door only because of the spare wheel location. A four-cylinder, water-cooled engine of about 16 hp. drove the car to a maximum speed of about 70 mph. The Pic-Pic is often called the Rolls-Royce of Switzerland. The car can be seen in the Verkehrshaus der Schweiz, Lucerne, Switzerland.

HUDSON PHAETON   This seven-passenger Hudson Phaeton touring model was one of the most popular cars made available by the company in 1919. It was powered by the famous Super-Six engine, and the Hudson catalog claimed that "Today there is a Hudson Super-Six for each six miles of improved roadway in America."

CHAPTER NINE

Free-wheeling Through the Twenties 1920—1929

AMERICA'S "ROARING TWENTIES" began with a financial "Panic" and ended with a full-fledged economic "Depression." During these years, 1920 through 1929, a great many lesser-known car makers emerged, then disappeared, while a handful of the larger firms continued to grow. Makes and models that fell by the wayside were not all bad; as a matter of fact, some very excellent designs just couldn't weather the economic storms.

"Bad times" in the American automotive industry reared its head in 1920 when lines of credit throughout all segments of the automotive business started tightening in May. This was at a time when some other countries were already deep into the worldwide postwar doldrums. Japan, as one example, experienced its financial panic on April 17, 1920.

Nevertheless, passenger car output in the United States during 1920 was a bit more than 1,900,000 units . . . a truly impressive total. The Duesenberg Model A deluxe family car made its debut featuring a straight-eight engine and hydraulic brakes on all four wheels. The latter had been developed by Malcolm Loughhead (later the family name would be changed to "Lockheed").

The flamboyant, high-living Dodge Brothers, John and Horace, both died in 1920, as did another pioneer, Elmer Apperson. After Billy Durant departed as the head of G.M., for the second time, the Durant Motor Company was set up; it would give birth to the Flint, the Durant, and the Star marques.

America's best and most expensive steam car, the Doble, along

291

with Abner Doble, shifted its facilities westward, from Detroit to Emeryville, California. But during 1920 the most significant moves as far as the future of the American auto was concerned were these two: Walter P. Chrysler left Buick to head up Willys-Overland and Charles ("Boss Ket") Kettering became head of the General Motors research laboratories. Under Ket's prodding would come quick-drying body "paints" and ethyl gasoline.

Although public interest in formal racing waned somewhat, the Indianapolis 500 continued with national and international fanfare. Gaston Chevrolet driving a Monroe racer built by his brother Louis Chevrolet won the widely publicized Indy race at a speed of 88 mph.; his engine had twin camshafts, overhead valves, and hemispherical combustion chambers.

About nine million Americans were on the roads in 1920; the motorcar business was now the largest U.S. industry. The government allotted $75 million for roads and a new numbering system was devised for Federal highways. North-South routes were assigned odd numbers; East-West roadways received even numbers.

Even though the American railroads reached a passenger-carrying peak during 1920, the public was being wooed to the road and away from the rails. Signs of the times: 15,000 gasoline stations in operation across the land. Significantly, the Ford T touring model was priced at $440. Nearest in cost to it among its mass-produced competitors was the $895 Overland. Generally, cars were better engineered and structurally improved over earlier models.

Expensive European cars, mostly handcrafted in small quantities and at high prices, offered a greater variety of bodies than American machines. For the less affluent, tiny cars with small, economical powerplants were in demand on the Continent and in England. In France, the biggest sellers were Citroën in the Number One spot, Peugeot next, then Renault. But Peugeot, with a less up-to-date line, would soon find the going hard.

In 1921 the magnificent, massive, and expensive Lincoln car was unveiled by the Lelands. It was a classic example of the right car at the wrong time. With its V-8 engine the Lincoln sold for about $4,600.

On March 4, 1921, Warren G. Harding became the first U.S.

President to ride in an an automobile to his inauguration. He was transported in a Packard Twin-Six.

Although car sales fell off generally, forty-five new concerns took a crack at the American market during 1921. Among them was the Rickenbacker Motor Car Company, promoted by Walter Flanders and Barney Everitt, both from the earlier E.M.F. outfit. Wills Sainte Claire got into production. But it was Henry Ford who best weathered the financial storm by dropping his "T's" price to $355 and loading up his dealer's inventories. More than a million Fords were sold, and they represented a bit more than 55 percent of all the U.S. cars and trucks turned out. Chevrolet production dropped to fewer than 65,000 units.

Although the "Panic" was over by late 1921, the Maxwell Motor Car Company had gone into receivership; it was reorganized with Walter Chrysler in charge. The Maxwell name on its cars would be retained for four years.

In English races the original Chitty Chitty Bang Bang was introduced by the irrepressible Count Louis Zborowski. "Chitty I" was powered by a 300-bhp., 1,500-rpm. Maybach aero engine of six cylinders, each cylinder having four overhead valves. The chassis was from a 1913 Mercedes 75. The fantastic contraption was a delight to spectators and a terror to its competitors. The Count followed up the first Chitty by later wheeling out Chitty II and Chitty III.

In France the Le Mans winner was Jimmy Murphy's three-liter, straight-eight Duesenberg. At Indianapolis a Frontenac designed by Louis Chevrolet and driven by Tommy Milton took first place.

A Super Fiat limousine was conceived to attract rich Americans. It had a V-12 engine with overhead valves and servo-assisted four-wheel brakes.

During 1922, Ford acquired the Lincoln Motor Company. Hudson introduced its Essex closed-body sedan. Rickenbacker cars reached waiting buyers. These three events were of special significance since it now put the Ford empire into the deluxe field, the Essex led a parade to low-cost closed "coach"-bodied cars (i.e., under $1,000), and the Everitt associated with Rickenbacker harkened back to the B. F. Everitt carriage shop which had supplied early Ford bodies.

The longer-lasting, low-pressure "balloon" tires became more common, and Nash was first to utilize rubber-mounts for its engines. Another Ford alumnus, former business manager Frank L. Klingensmith, helped set up the Gray Motor Company with its cars aimed at the low-price end of the market. But, as usual, Ford led all others in a continuing workingman's "revolution": a five-day work week and a six-dollar-per-day minimum wage.

In 1922 America had about three million miles of roadways, along with 15,000 deaths attributed to the automobile. Employment at the auto factories was about a quarter million; there, wages reached $400 million.

A speed mark of 133.75 mph. was set by K. C. Guinness in a Sunbeam at the Brooklands track in England. At Indianapolis Jimmy Murphy won the "500" driving his own car.

In 1923 the Durant Motor Company's touring car, an "assembled" machine directed at the Model T buyer, was selling for $443. In addition, the Durant line included America's first production station wagon. But apparently nothing could top the yearly Ford truck and car output, which passed the $2-million mark; and little wonder, the very basic Ford Runabout was selling for $265.

America had 108 automobile manufacturers in 1923, and could count two-thirds of a car per family. More of the new cars had enclosed, rather than open, bodies. Ethyl gasoline could be bought in Dayton, Ohio; it represented the culmination of seven years of research by Tom Midgley and Boss Ket.

Buick joined the parade with four-wheel brakes, and turned out more than 200,000 cars. Dodge made news on several fronts. It produced the first all-steel, closed body. And General Pancho Villa was killed in Mexico while chugging along in his Dodge.

A small midwestern city, chosen as a typical test locality, was found to have 6,221 autos. Fords comprised 41 percent of this total. In descending order came Chevrolet, Oakland, Dodge, Maxwell, Buick, Studebaker, Overland, Willys-Knight, Nash—then 87 other makes!

During 1923 Alfred P. Sloan, Jr., became president of General Motors. Under him at Chevrolet William Knudsen took charge, and that division jumped its output to 454,968 units. That total did not include 759 "experimental" Chevrolets powered by a special air-cooled engine which employed copper fins to dissipate motor heat. All were recalled and scrapped when the air-cooling feature failed to perform as expected. But another, much smaller outfit had all the bugs out of their air-cooled engines. In 1923 11,000 highly prized air-cooled Franklins were turned out. The industry produced 12,000 school buses. Walter E. Flanders died.

Jimmy Murphy again appeared in the winners' listings, taking the Indy 500 in an H.C.S. (Miller) car. This Miller was Henry A., a former carburetor specialist. At Le Mans, France, over the old Sarthe circuit, the first "Le Vingt-Quatre Heures du Mans" (Le Mans 24-Hour) race got under way on May 26 at 4 P.M. The greatest distance run was by a Chenard-Walcker; fastest lap was by a Bentley.

Two great unveilings, one new, one old, marked the year 1924. Near Luxor, Egypt, the tomb of King Tutankhamen was opened. And at the Commodore Hotel in New York City, near the Grand Central Palace exhibit hall, home of the National Automobile Show, Walter Chrysler exhibited his exciting 70-mph. Light-Six Chrysler car with a high-compression engine and numerous other innovations. The car was barred from the auto show on the grounds that it was not in production at the time.

The new Chrysler attracted 32,000 buyers from across the country and $5 million from Wall Street banks and investment houses, which made that sum available to Maxwell-Chalmers, its maker.

With four-wheel brakes commonplace on most American cars, regardless of their price, the luxurious Rolls-Royce Silver Ghost finally adopted a four-wheel braking system in 1924. This same year saw the last Stanley Steamer. Also suspending production was the Winton Motor Carriage Company, which had been organized in 1897.

The Indy winner was a Duesenberg. Racing there, too, were three Model T entries which had been modified into Barber-Warnocks. But even more interesting was the front-wheel-drive Miller racer built for Jimmy Murphy. It would lead later to the L-29 Cord passenger car.

In Europe, the first Italian vehicle meant for a mass market, the 990-cc Fiat 509, was introduced. It was offered in four body styles: Torpedo, Spider, Cabriolet, and Salon.

Killed at Monza during the Italian Grand Prix while driving his Mercedes entry was Count Zborowski of Chitty Chitty Bang Bang fame.

In America, G.M. and Standard Oil of New Jersey set up the Ethyl Corporation. The Ford concern turned out its 10-millionth vehicle; the 1924 T was being sold for under $300.

By 1925, spray-finishes, synthetic and quick-drying, were in general use. They brought with them a variety of high-gloss colors. Also in 1925, the Maxwell-Chalmers Company was reorganized as the Chrysler Corporation. In its first year of operation the Chrysler firm secured orders for $50 million worth of cars, so now the "Big Two," Ford and General Motors, had become the "Big Three."

The Dodge Brothers Company was purchased by the New York financial house of Dillon, Read & Company, for a record $146 million.

By now most of the "electrics" had left the scene, and 1925 also marked the end of production for the Stanley Steamer. With more than 17 million cars registered in the United States, 75 percent of all new or used cars were sold through dealers via installment-plan purchasing.

Ford, for the first time since 1912, offered his Model T in a body color other than black. Big changes, too, on the other side of the Atlantic Ocean—Rolls-Royce, after an eighteen-year run, dropped its outdated Silver Ghost model, replacing it in 1925 with the R-R Phantom I.

The big races of 1925 included the Indy where Peter de Paolo won in a Duesenberg at 101.13 mph., becoming the first to break the magic 100-mph. mark in the famous "500" competition.

Antonio Ascari won the Belgian Grand Prix over the Spa course in an Italian Alfa Romeo, only to be killed during the subsequent French Grand Prix conducted for the first time at Montlhéry. Winner at Montlhéry was a Délage V-12 with two superchargers, driven by Albert Divo and Robert Benoist. The twelve-cylinder motor turned 7,000 rpm. to deliver 190 bhp. This was the year that the requirement for a "riding mechanic" was eliminated.

In America, Floyd Clymer drove an Olds "6" to the top of Pikes Peak in Colorado, a distance of twelve miles and a climb of 4,959 feet, in a record 28 minutes, 49 seconds.

The final Haynes car was made in 1925. That same year Elwood G. Haynes died; his first car had been tested in 1894.

Although the Apperson brothers, Elmer and Edgar, had been associated with Haynes back before the turn of the century, they had been on their own for many years. Among their notable cars was the Jackrabbit. The last Apperson vehicle appeared in 1926. Elmer had died in 1920; Edgar lived almost forty years longer.

Ford production in 1926, while astronomical to most folks, was down by a quarter million units from the previous year. Even though it was priced at $290, the lowest price ever for any mass-produced, full-size vehicle, the Model T tourer was beginning to lose favor with the buying public. New makes such as the Pontiac by G.M.'s Oakland division, the Ajax by Nash, and the Diana by Moon were among those attracting attention, and buyers. The Essex coach cost only $765—compared to the "T" it was elegance itself. The first Pontiac was ticketed at $825 for six cylinders, 25 hp., and an L-head engine. Studebaker announced the Erskine Six, a six-cylinder machine named after the firm's president, Albert R. Erskine. REO's newest line included the Flying Cloud. During 1926, Dr. Graham Edgar presented the octane scale for rating gasoline and General Motors acquired the Fisher Body Works.

The biggest news of 1926, and it really swept across the nation, came from the Ford firm—the Model T would be dropped in the near future. Although the "T" coupé, for instance, had been considerably improved through various refinements, many not obvious to the average eye, it still bore an unmistakable resemblance to its 1917-edition ancestor.

A general trend in 1926 was toward the use of pressed-steel wheels; by now wire wheels were confined mostly to sports, or "sporty looking," cars. As the Maxwell continued its career as the Chrysler "50," it joined a total U.S. car output for 1926 of nearly 3,700,000 vehicles. School bus production reached nearly 33,000 units.

During the following year, 1927, total car production in the United States was down some to just under three million vehicles. Of these, Ford produced a bit over 350,000 machines. The last Model T rolled from the assembly line on May 31. Various "totals" have been proclaimed for the "T," from 15,007,033 to 15,754,292. But nobody disputed the fact that between 1908 and

1927 Ford had turned out something more than fifteen million of the ubiquitous "T's"!

By November 1, 1927, Ford had its new four-cylinder, three-speed, sliding-type-gearbox Model A rolling off the assembly lines priced at $385. Helped by the Ford hiatus, Chevrolet enjoyed sales of just under 750,000 units.

Also in 1927 the Paige-Detroit firm which had been making the Paige and Jewett cars was taken over by three brothers—Joseph, Ray, and Robert Graham—who launched the successful Graham-Paige line. Willys-Overland offered the Willys-Knight and the less expensive Overland Whippet. The latter sold for $495. The La Salle V-8 was unveiled by the Cadillac organization. Oldsmobile applied chrome plating to all its external "brightwork." The Rickenbacker went off the market.

During 1928 the most momentous move in the American automobile industry was made by Walter Chrysler when he purchased the Dodge Brothers concern for a paper transaction of $225 million. Along with its manufacturing facilities, marques and models, Chrysler had his eye on the very valuable network of Dodge dealerships. Soon he was able to roll out the $725 four-cylinder Plymouth sedan which replaced the lower-priced Chryslers, and to follow up this good-looking offering with the six-cylinder DeSoto, which helped broaden his combined Chrysler company line.

Ford, in 1928, got back into reasonably high gear with his Model A car and truck production. More than 750,000 "A's" were rolled out.

Studebaker introduced its "President" line in 1928, including the Dictator and Commander series. One President car covered 30,000 miles in less than 26,500 minutes at the Atlantic City, New Jersey, speedway. The car ran continuously from July 21 to August 8. Small airplanes were busy setting similar endurance records, too.

James W. Packard died in 1928; back in 1902 he had sold the Packard car and name to Henry B. Joy.

The following year, 1929, brought the death of David Buick. Like Packard, he had left the auto business early (in November, 1904). Unlike Packard, his name lives on as a division of G.M.

Also, 1929 saw a new production mark: 5,337,087 cars and

trucks. This figure would not be exceeded for another twenty years! In 1929 there were at least 400,000 auto factory workers who received something like $800 million in wages. Three times that number found employment outside the factories, above and beyond the manufacturing enterprises, and in allied automotive parts and service operations.

Two significant milestones of 1929: taxes and trailers. Every state now had a tax on gasoline. It averaged out to be three cents on each gallon of fuel. And house trailers were on the market.

On March 11, 1929, Major (later Sir) Henry O. D. Seagrave drove his 900-hp. "Golden Arrow" along the sands of Daytona Beach, Florida, to a record 231.36 mph. It was powered by a Schneider Trophy-type Napier Lion twelve-cylinder aero engine. The car had been designed by Captain J. S. Irving.

Although the bottom dropped out of the stock market on October 29, car sales for the year had already racked up substantial totals. General Motors, during 1929, took over Opel in Germany; four years earlier it had acquired the British Vauxhall auto maker. In 1929, for the first time, Great Britain produced more cars (235,000) than any other European country; France had formerly been the leader. The Rolls-Royce Phantom II appeared in this year.

In the United States nine out of every ten passenger cars produced were closed-body types. This ratio was the exact reverse of ten years earlier.

Cars were at a point where they were more plentiful; they were beginning to play a vital and permanent part in changing the face of America. The American automobile was about to spawn the American suburb.

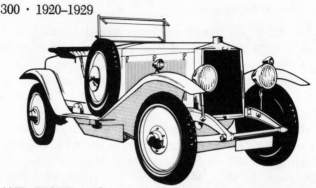

LEYLAND EIGHT When Leyland Motors, Ltd., instructed their chief engineer, Parry Thomas, to design a perfect automobile and not worry about cost, the Leyland Eight was the result. The Leyland made its sensational appearance in 1920 and was the first British touring car to be powered by an eight-cylinder engine. The inline engine was water-cooled with hemispherical heads and two inclined valves operated by a single overhead camshaft. Displacement was 6,967 cc and the powerplant developed a maximum of 145 bhp. at 2,200 rpm. Vacuum-servo brakes were fitted. The steering column did not enter the engine compartment; instead steering was via two gearboxes that ran down the driver's side of the dash. The tilt angle of the column was adjustable. Overall length was 16 feet 1 inch, with a wheelbase of 11 feet 9 inches. Track was 4 feet 8½ inches. Between 1922 and 1926 the Leyland Eight won 27 first places at Brooklands. It also established several world records for production automobiles.

ESSEX PHAETON This Essex Phaeton touring model was produced in 1920. It proved to be an important asset to Essex when the United States Postal Service bought a large fleet of Essex Phaetons for rural delivery of the U.S. Mail. The low price of the car as well as its reliability were favorable factors. In order to publicize this sale, the Hudson Motor Car Company, parent firm of Essex, sent four Essex cars on a transcontinental trip from San Francisco to New York. The best time was four days, 14 hours, 43 minutes by the Phaeton.

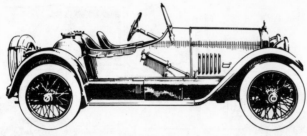

MERCER RACEABOUT The Mercer was a thoroughbred sports car, and this is the 1920 "Series 5." It was not only fast but had fine road handling qualities. Power was a four-cylinder, water-cooled, L-head, 70-hp. dual-ignition engine. The large cylindrical gasoline tank located behind the seats gave the car a 500-mile range. This tank was pressurized by means of a hand pump on the side of the car. Mercer went out of business in 1929. A 1920 Mercer can be seen at the Frederick C. Crawford Auto-Aviation Museum, Cleveland, Ohio.

AUTOCAR BUS In 1921 the Autocar Company in Ardmore, Pennsylvania, envisioned the possibilities of mass transit via the automobile and therefore developed this ten-passenger bus. It was used mainly by hotels to transfer their guests to and from railroad stations. A two-cylinder, water-cooled engine powered the vehicle at moderate speeds.

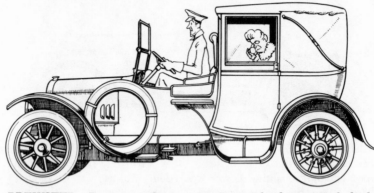

BREWSTER Brewster & Company on Long Island, New York, built cars to order for celebrities between 1915 and 1935. Their automobiles were custom-built with superb craftsmanship. The firm had built "Prairie Wagons" for the American pioneers. This is the 1920 Brewster landaulet or town car—the last word in beautiful coachwork. The cars were very expensive, and only the wealthy could afford the price. Continental engines were generally fitted.

PIERCE-ARROW In 1920 Pierce-Arrow finally moved the steering wheel to the left side to conform with the American standard. This is a 1920 custom-built Pierce-Arrow phaeton specially constructed for a Hollywood personality. It was the last word in luxury-car design at the time. The dual-valve, six-cylinder engine was powerful enough to move the big car from 3 mph. to 75 mph. in high gear. Despite this, the public became "eight-cylinder happy" and Pierce business began to decline.

ROLLS-ROYCE   This sporty Rolls-Royce Silver Ghost was produced in 1920 as a sports phaeton. As with most of their cars, Rolls-Royce built the chassis and the six-cylinder engine. The purchaser decided on the type of body and had it ordered elsewhere. We are led to believe that Brewster built this body.

NASH LAFAYETTE   The Nash Motor Company built the Lafayette automobiles between 1920 and 1929. The Lafayette became one of the top contenders in the fairly high-price field. This is the four-place sedan of 1920 which inaugurated the line. It was powered by a six-cylinder engine. Lafayette Motors Company was at Mars Hill, Indianapolis, Indiana. The make was reintroduced in 1935 for the low-price market.

PAIGE The Paige was often called "the most beautiful car in America." This is the 1920 touring model featuring long, low lines plus uncluttered styling. It was priced just lower than the luxury types. The firm was later taken over by Graham, and then became known as the Graham-Paige.

APPERSON JACKRABBIT The Apperson Brothers Motor Car Company was associated with Haynes at the turn of the century. As an independent firm, however, they produced cars between 1905 and 1924. This is the touring model of 1920, advertised as the "Eight with eighty less parts" in an effort to focus attention on the car's simplicity. The eight-cylinder, water-cooled engine easily drove the lightweight body, hence the name "Jackrabbit."

VELIE LIMOUSINE Velie automobiles were made in Moline, Illinois, from 1908 to 1929, and this limousine was built around 1920. Most Velie cars were fitted with Continental engines, as was this model, which had a six-cylinder, 40-hp., inline, water-cooled powerplant of 190-cubic-inch displacement. Price of this car was $2,000. Velie conceived the idea of "hardtop" styling about this time.

NASH 685 This unusual two-seater coupé was manufactured by Nash in 1920. The narrow cab accommodated two persons: the driver in the front left and the passenger in the rear right side. The car was often referred to as the "stagger seat."

BENTLEY Walter Owen Bentley exhibited his 3-liter sport car at the 1919 London Car Show but did not make it available to the public until 1921. The car was a high performance roadster, and the first production car won the 1921 Brooklands at an average of 72.5 mph. The following year it placed thirteenth at the Indianapolis 500-Mile Race and second in the Isle of Man Race at a 55.2-mph. average. The 1921 car shown was powered by a four-cylinder, water-cooled, 3-liter-displacement, 16-hp., overhead-valve engine. The wheelbase was 9 feet 8 inches. Four forward speeds plus reverse were fitted.

BERLIET TORPEDO VF Marius Berliet founded Automobiles M. Berliet, Vénissieux, France, in 1900. Production of well-built automobiles continued until 1939. This Berliet Torpedo VF of 1921 was a sturdy, totally enclosed, four-door sedan that proved to be very popular. The powerplant was a four-cylinder, water-cooled engine with thermo-syphon circulation. Bore was 80 mm., stroke was 130 mm., and a Zenith carburetor was installed. Three forward speeds plus reverse were fitted, tires were pneumatic and easily demountable, and an electric horn, starter, and lights were provided.

NASH 682　The average car of 1921 was cold and drafty in winter, so Nash engaged the Seaman Body Corporation of Milwaukee, Wisconsin, to design and build a special padded winter-top for the seven-passenger Nash Model 682 touring car of 1921. Seaman started as a furniture company and then moved into the auto body business. The model 682 was very comfortable and quiet, and cost $2,600.

STANDARD EIGHT　The Standard Steel Car Company's automotive department built this "Vestibule" sedan at the Pittsburgh, Pennsylvania, factory in 1921. In addition to this model, Standard built other models in that year: touring, sport, roadster, sedanette, coupé, and conventional sedan. This auto was large and comfortable. Its name was derived from the fact that when the rear doors were both open the passengers' feet were barely visible because of a "vestibule" which could be used for packages or for a jump seat.

BJERING SLEIGH-CAR   In the developing days of motoring many ideas were tried to solve the numerous problems that arose. Winter snows in Norway can be quite heavy, and the cars of the early twenties were often stuck fast in the snow. This 1921 Norwegian auto tried to solve this problem by using the design with four conventional wheels in summer. In winter, however, the front wheels were replaced by heavy steerable skis and the rear wheels wrapped in chains for traction. A good idea, not needed today, due to the availability of advanced automobiles.

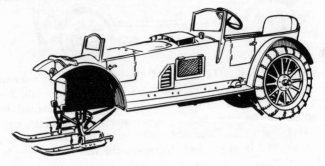

HALLADAY FALCON   This unusual Falcon sportster, built in 1921 by the Halladay Motors Corporation, was designed and custom-built by Donald Healey, and represented the contemporary ideal for a sport model. Note the second seat, without doors, which appears to have been an afterthought. A four-cylinder, water-cooled, 20-hp. engine drove the car to 60 mph.

RUMPLER SEDAN   The Edmund Rumpler Flugzeugwerke built some of the best German reconnaissance aircraft during World War I. The company entered the automobile business with this car in 1921. It was extremely advanced, with a rear engine, teardrop body, fins, and a streamlined windshield.

OVERLAND ROADSTER   This low-priced Overland of 1921 is considered to be the ancestor of the world-famous Jeep. It was powered by a four-cylinder, water-cooled engine. The wheelbase was 100 inches and suspension was by transverse leaf springs. This light car was built in Toledo, Ohio, home of the larger Willys-Knight cars. The car was a two-seater. During the same year a four-seat sedan was produced on the same chassis.

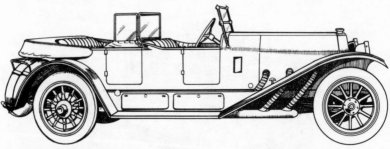

LOCOMOBILE PHAETON MODEL 48   The Locomobile was the first U.S. automobile to mount spare tires on the rear, in 1911. This Locomobile Sport Phaeton was produced in 1921 in Bridgeport, Connecticut. The smooth lines, double windshield, and 90-hp. six-cylinder gasoline engine made it a very popular car. Notice the flexible exhaust stacks from the hood, piercing the fender and collecting in the muffler header. Locomobile became part of Durant Motors, which was dissolved in 1929.

AUSTRO-DAIMLER SASCHA RACER The genius of Ferdinand Porsche revealed itself at the Austro-Daimler plant in Vienna for the last time in 1922 when he designed this light two-seater. It was named Sascha after Count Sascha Kolowrat, who entered one of the cars in the 1922 Targa Florio in Sicily. The engine was a 1,100-cc displacement, four-cylinder, water-cooled, overhead-cam, short-stroke powerplant. Four Saschas were entered in the 1922 Targa Florio, and Alfred Neubauer won with an average of 35 mph. One car was timed at 89 mph. through one kilometer. Austro-Daimler claimed no less than 43 first prizes that year! Versions of this car were being raced as late as 1926. The car shown here is one of the four 1922 Targa Florio entries. Each sported one of the playing card suits—spades, diamonds, clubs, and hearts—for insignia!

ROLLS-ROYCE SILVER GHOST This Pall Mall Phaeton, another of the famous line of Silver Ghosts, was made in 1922. The double-windshield, touring-type body was made by Brewster. The Silver Ghost was one of the most successful Rolls-Royce designs.

ARROL-JOHNSTON MODEL M This Scottish Arrol-Johnston Model M, Type C was produced in 1922. It was a closed touring type with glass windows and was powered by a four-cylinder, overhead-valve, water-cooled engine. Bore was 80 mm., stroke was 120 mm. and displacement was 2,412 cc. Note the disc wheels, the side spare wheel, and the three-sided windshield.

MARMON Marmon was a pioneer in the use of the rear-view mirror and the V-8 engine. This Marmon touring car was made in 1922 and was powered by a six-cylinder, overhead-valve, 74-hp., water-cooled engine of 5,721-cc displacement. Aluminum was used for many of the engine components. Speed was about 70 mph.

CASE MODEL X   The J. I. Case T.M. Company of Racine, Wisconsin, had been in business since 1842 and began building autos in the early twentieth century. This 1922 Case Model X, a luxurious touring sedan moderately priced, had a low center of gravity on a 122-inch wheelbase. With twenty-two miles per gallon of gasoline possible, this five-passenger car could idle along at 2 mph. in high gear, and without shifting, increase its speed to 70 mph. Price was $2,790.

MAXWELL   This Maxwell open touring model was in production from 1920 to 1925 after which time the firm was merged with the Chrysler Corporation. This is the 1922 production model. It was powered by a four-cylinder, water-cooled, side-valve, 3-liter-displacement engine of 21 hp. Three forward speeds were fitted. The wheelbase was 9 feet 1 inch.

HANDLEY-KNIGHT   Patents taken by the Englishman Charles Yale Knight in 1905 and 1908 for an engine with double-sleeve valves instead of the normal poppet valves were used by many European and U.S. manufacturers, including Daimler, Mercedes, Rover, Nash, and others. The little-known Handley-Knight made its appearance in 1922 with five models: the five-passenger touring at $2,250; the deluxe seven-passenger touring at $2,650; the four-passenger coupé at $3,750; the seven-passenger touring at $2,450; and the seven-passenger sedan at $3,750. The five-passenger touring is shown here. Note the thermometer built into the radiator cap. The Handley-Knight Company was located in Kalamazoo, Michigan.

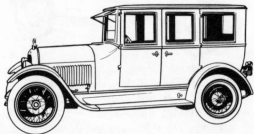

KLINE-KAR   The Kline Car Corporation, Richmond, Virginia, was the maker of the Kline-Kar in the twenties. The 1922 four-door sedan is shown. The company stressed economy and value in its advertisements, but the car never made an impact on the automobile market. A roadster, tourer, and coupé were also offered in 1922.

OGREN Another little-known automobile manufacturer of the twenties was the Ogren Motor Car Company of Milwaukee, Wisconsin. This is the Ogren Seven-Passenger Touring of 1922, priced at $4,350. Continental engines were used in all seven Ogren models produced in 1922. The cars were designed for upper middle-class customers.

FORD T DEPOT HACK The long-lived Ford Model T was certainly a versatile auto, fitted with numerous bodies. This 1922 Depot Hack had room for six passengers plus luggage and was designed to transport passengers to and from railroad stations. The same design could be transformed into a light truck by removing the rear seats.

STEARNS-KNIGHT TOURING Automobiles were made by the F. B. Stearns Company, Cleveland, Ohio, starting in 1904. In 1922 the firm produced this touring model which was fitted with the Knight sleeve-valve engine. The engine was six-cylinder, water-cooled, with a 12-volt ignition system. The top could be raised and lowered by one person. The car weighed 3,450 pounds.

ANDERSON TOURING John Anderson founded the Anderson Motor Company of Rock Hill, South Carolina. The Anderson was the only automobile produced in that state. This is the Anderson Touring Model of 1922.

VAUXHALL OE TYPE This English Vauxhall OE Type Tourer 30/98 of 1922 was the first sports car to guarantee a speed of 100 mph.! It was powered by a four-cylinder, water-cooled, overhead-valve engine that produced about 115 hp. at 3,300 rpm. The connecting rods were made of stamped Dural aluminum alloy to reduce the reciprocating weights. Displacement was 4,224 cc. The body was of aluminum on this four-seater and was made by Vanden Plas. The wheelbase was 9 feet 8 inches, the tread was 4 feet 6 inches, and the suspension consisted of half-elliptic springs plus shocks. This car can be seen at the Briggs Cunningham Automotive Museum, Costa Mesa, California.

TEMPLAR ROADSTER This wire-wheeled, two-place touring roadster was made in 1922. It followed the standard roadster design except that it had no doors. A step was provided, placed beneath the insignia, to assist one in stepping into the car! A sample of the Templar can be seen at the Frederick C. Crawford Auto-Aviation Museum, Cleveland, Ohio.

PIERCE-ARROW   This snappy two-seat roadster was introduced by the George N. Pierce Company in 1922. It was powered by a dual-valve, six-cylinder engine. Despite the fact that it was an excellent powerplant, it was not as acceptable to the public as were the straight and V-8 cylinder engines used in other cars at that time. Pierce business went into a temporary slump in 1923. This car can be viewed in The Raben Car Collection at Aalholm Castle, Nysted, Denmark.

WALTHAM TOURING   Another little-known auto manufacturer of the twenties was the Waltham Manufacturing Company of Waltham, Massachusetts, which produced automobiles from 1902 into the Depression. This Waltham four-door touring car of 1922 could seat five. The wheels were wood-spoked. Notice the wind deflectors at each side of the windshield. Waltham claimed they offered an expensive car at a low price! This car cost about $1,000.

DIXIE FLYER   This Model HS-70 Dixie Flyer four-seat touring car was produced in 1922. It was powered by a four-cylinder, water-cooled, L-head, 40-hp., inline engine. Note the portholes on the side of the hood which took the place of air-outlet louvers. Price was $1,385. The firm went out of business two years later.

NASH CARRIOLE   Although Nash had perfected a successful six-cylinder engine, this low-priced sedanette made its appearance in 1922 with a four-cylinder engine of about 30 hp. The car could seat four in a coupé-type body that was designed to lend itself to quantity production due to the elimination of curved surfaces. Price was $1,350 F.O.B. factory.

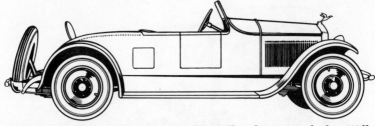

WILLS SAINTE CLAIRE Harold Wills, designer of the Wills Sainte Claire, was a perfectionist. Therefore, many enthusiasts consider the 1922 Model A-68 to be one of the technically finest cars made in the U.S. It was powered by an overhead-camshaft, V-8 engine of 68 hp. and 267-cubic-inch displacement, patterned after the Hispano-Suiza powerplant. The two-seater was fitted with a rumble seat and sported twin exhausts. The Wills Sainte Claire Company of Marysville, Michigan, produced cars between 1921 and 1926. An example of this car can be seen at Harrah's Automobile Collection, Reno, Nevada.

RICHELIEU This little-known U.S. automobile made its appearance in 1922. It sported domed fenders instead of the flat open type. The Richelieu was powered by a Duesenberg-made engine of 85 hp. This touring model had a long wheelbase for comfortable riding.

STAR TOURING The Durant Motor Company was formed when W. C. Durant was forced out of General Motors in 1922. He produced a rival, low-priced, competitive auto in the same year—the Star Touring—which sold for $350! It was a five-passenger car with a four-cylinder Continental engine, a three-speed transmission, and wheels made with demountable rims.

HISPANO-SUIZA SIX-WHEELER This luxury automobile was built in Spain in 1923 and was bought by D. W. Griffith, the famous motion-picture producer of that time, for $35,000. Eventually it was used in many motion pictures as an officer's staff car. Later it was leased to a Hollywood studio for $100 per day. It can be seen, today, in the Forney Historic Transportation Museum, Denver, Colorado.

CITROËN VOITURETTE   This French company concentrated on inexpensive, reliable automobiles in the twenties. This 1923 Citroën Voiturette shown was very similar to what would be called a two-seat roadster in the United States. The car was small with an 88½-inch wheelbase. Power was by a 7.5-hp., four-cylinder, water-cooled, side-valve, vertical engine of 0.9-liter displacement. Bore was 55 mm. and stroke was 90 mm. Three forward speeds were fitted. One of the remaining cars can be seen at the Provinciaal Automobielmuseum Houthalen, Domaine de Kelchterhoef, Houthalen, Belgium.

GRÄF & STIFT SR3   This large four-door sedan was made by Gräf & Stift, Vienna, Austria, in 1923. The engine was an eight-cylinder, water-cooled powerplant of 7.8 liters. Notice the single windshield wiper for the driver only. The car is on display at the Science Museum of Victoria, Melbourne, Australia.

FIAT 501   Fiat production in the twenties concentrated on economical family-type autos. This four-place Fiat 501 open touring model is from 1923. It was powered by a four-cylinder, water-cooled, 23-hp., 1.46-liter-displacement engine, which gave it a top speed of approximately 50 mph. An example of this car is on exhibit at the Automuseum Nettelstedt, Lübeck, Germany.

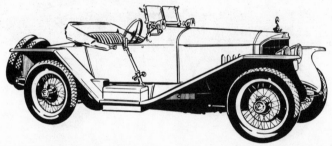

MERCEDES "28-95" RUNABOUT   The German Daimler firm introduced the 28-95 Mercedes in 1923 which was intended for luxury coachwork. In addition to this runabout, a five-place touring type was also constructed during the year. This two-seater sports car was powered by a four-cylinder, water-cooled, supercharged engine of 2.6-liter displacement. A Roots-type supercharger was used. Instead of placing the unit between the carburetor and engine, Mercedes pumped the air into the carburetor. The supercharger was activated by depressing the accelerator beyond full throttle. A speed of about 75 mph. was attained. This was the first supercharged auto to be sold in any quantity to the public. A car of this type is on display at the Briggs Cunningham Automotive Museum, Costa Mesa, California.

RENAULT TORPEDO   In 1923 Renault was the best-selling automobile in France. This Renault Type KJ1 Torpedo two-door sport touring car was made that year. The smooth hood lines were made famous by Renault. Power was with a four-cylinder, water-cooled engine of 951-cc displacement. The radiator was located behind the engine with air scooped into the front-facing louvers, and therefore discharging below. Three forward speeds were fitted, and the car could travel about 50 mph.

CADILLAC SPORT TOURING   Cadillac was the first automobile manufacturer to apply chrome-plating on grilles and bumpers, in 1922. During this time, they were the first manufacturers to ventilate the engine crankcase. This 1923 Cadillac Sport Touring car was fitted with both of the above-mentioned innovations and a V-8 cylinder engine. This six-seater cost $4,440. Note the covered side spare tire.

BUGATTI TYPE 30 The famous auto designer Ettore Bugatti was born in Italy and worked and lived in France, although he was a German citizen. He produced this sportster/raceabout in 1923 which was quite successful in hill-climbs and short race competitions. Power was from an eight-cylinder, overhead-valve, water-cooled, 18-hp. engine of 2 liters displacement. Bore was 60 mm., stroke was 88 mm. Four forward speeds were fitted. The wheelbase was 9 feet, and speed was about 85 mph. A Type 30 can be seen in the Automuseum, Minden, Westphalia, Germany.

DELAUNAY BELLEVILLE This two-seater Delaunay Belleville convertible coupé was a departure from the usual products made by the company because of its sporty design. The car was produced in 1923 and 1924. Note the rumble seat in the open position. The bodywork was performed by the French coach builder Salmons and was up to the standards set by the larger Delaunay Bellevilles.

WOLSELEY SPORTSTER The Wolseley Sheep Sheering Machine Company of Birmingham, England, made this two-place Sportster in 1923. The firm had made aircraft engines during World War I, and developed a good engine for this car. It was a four-cylinder, water-cooled, 1,270-cc displacement powerplant that developed 10.5 hp. Bore was 2.5 inches and stroke was 3.75 inches. Road speed was about 45 mph. The car did well in several 200-mile races in 1923.

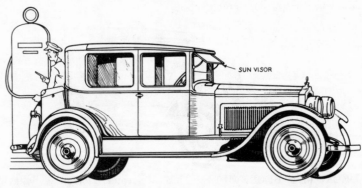

PACKARD Although Packard had introduced the "Twin-Six" years before, they entered the straight-eight-cylinder field in 1923. This straight-eight proved to be one of the smoothest powerplants to come off a production line. The crankshaft was fitted with nine bearings! This is the sedan coupé four-seater of that year. Disc wheels and low-pressure tires were featured on this model. Packards also had four-wheel brakes in 1923.

CHEVROLET COUPÉ   In a bid for the low-price market, Chevrolet introduced the Model M Superior Utility Coupé in 1923. It was a two-seater featuring large trunk space as a selling point for salesmen and other businessmen. Price was $680. Wheelbase was 103 inches. Note the sun visor and artillery-type spoked wheels. What appears to be a radiator is really a shuttered air scoop to cool the experimental four-cylinder engine. The engine block was surrounded with copper fins to cool the engine without the use of the water radiator. It was often called the "Copper Cooled" model.

M.G.   The first M.G. was a handmade conversion of the popular Morris Oxford in 1923. In fact, M.G. bears the initials of Morris Garages as a tribute to Sir William Morris and the company from which M.G. car company had evolved. Using the Oxford chassis, a Hotchkiss engine with overhead valves was installed, plus the barest minimum of body. Wire wheels, no windshield, and handbrake outside the body turned into a car that could top 80 mph. In the 1925 English Lands End Race it won a Gold Medal with Cecil Kimber at the wheel. Although the car created considerable attention, no production models of M.G. sports cars were made until 1929.

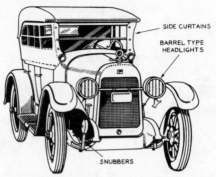

SIDE CURTAINS

BARREL TYPE HEADLIGHTS

SNUBBERS

BUICK TOURING SEDAN   The Buick Touring Sedan Model 23-4-38 five-passenger automobile of 1923 weighed 2,750 pounds on a 109-inch wheelbase. The top of this car was solid and did not fold; the framework was covered with hardened and weatherproofed leather. The side curtains were removable. In a way, the car could be called a hardtop. Power was a four-cylinder, inline, water-cooled, 170-cubic-inch-displacement engine that developed 35 hp. Three-point engine mounting was used, as was electric starting. A multiple disc, dry-plate clutch was fitted. About six thousand Model 23-4-38 cars were made in 1923. Price was $1,325.

DODGE TYPE A   The first closed Dodge with an all-steel body made its appearance in 1923. This was the Type A four-door sedan which could seat five and had plenty of window area for both driver and passengers. This was the highest-priced Dodge of the period; it sold for about $1,400.

FRANKLIN The H. H. Franklin Manufacturing Company of New York produced this four-door, five-seat sedan in 1923. The car was powered by an air-cooled, six-cylinder, front-located, vertical, 25-hp. engine of 3,871-cc displacement that gave the car a road speed of 45 mph. The body was of aluminum and the chassis of wood. The Franklin was produced from 1901 through 1935.

BEARDMORE 12-8 TYPE D Beardmore Motors, Ltd., of Glasgow, Scotland, built excellent aircraft engines, tanks, guns, and other important war matériel during World War I. Later it produced high-performance roadsters as well as family types. This touring sedan with a soft top and glass windows was made in 1924. It was powered by a four-cylinder, 14-hp., water-cooled engine of 2 liters displacement. Bore was 74 mm., stroke 114 mm. and overhead valves were installed. The car, accommodating five, was produced in limited quantity.

AMILCAR GRAND SPORTS   The Amilcar firm was established in Paris, France, by former Le Zèbre engineers when the Le Zèbre firm went out of business. The first Amilcar was introduced in 1921. This Grand Sports was made in 1924, and the light sports car scored 102 first prizes in hill-climbs and minor races in that year! The car was designed as a single-seater, and the second seat seems almost to have been an afterthought. Power was a four-cylinder, side-valve, water-cooled, 985-cc displacement engine of 23 hp. at 3,200 rpm. The cylinder block and crankcase were cast in one piece. The car could attain 60 mph.

BENTLEY CUSTOM SPORTS TOURER   Bentley has, for many years, been one of the finest sports cars. Their successes at Brooklands and Le Mans proved Bentley's speed and stamina. This Custom Sports Tourer four-seater was produced in 1924. It was powered with a four-cylinder, water-cooled, 65-hp., 3-liter, inline engine. The fixed cylinder head block had four valves per cylinder, operated by an overhead camshaft. Bore was 80 mm. and stroke 149 mm. The wheelbase was 9 feet 8.5 inches. Four forward speeds were fitted. Despite a quality product, Bentley went into liquidation and was acquired by Rolls-Royce.

CHRYSLER PHAETON   After helping Buick and Willys-Overland become solvent and increase their production and sales, Walter P. Chrysler answered a call by the Maxwell-Chalmers Company. This marked the formation of the Chrysler Corporation. In 1924 the first cars were produced bearing his name. The Chrysler Model B Six was mechanically unusual with four-wheel hydraulic brakes and steel bodies made by Fisher. The six-cylinder, water-cooled, side-valve engine of 22 hp. and 3 liters displacement had a bore of 3 inches and stroke of 4.5 inches. Three forward speeds were installed. The engine had seven main bearings! This Open Touring Phaeton Model B had a 112-inch wheelbase. Note the glass wind deflectors. By the end of 1925, when a new model was introduced, over 100,000 Model B Chryslers had been sold! A Model B Phaeton can be viewed at the Provinciaal Automobielmuseum Houthalen, Domaine de Kelchterhoef, Houthalen, Belgium.

PANHARD-LEVASSOR TOURING   The French pioneering auto firm of Panhard-Levassor produced this five-place open touring car in 1924. The wheelbase was about 144 inches. It was powered by an eight-cylinder, sleeve-valve, 6.4-liter, 36-hp., inline, water-cooled engine. Four forward speeds were fitted.

HISPANO-SUIZA Produced at the French factory of the Spanish firm, this Hispano-Suiza open touring car was known as the Boulogne. It became one of the oustanding cars of the mid-twenties. Power was a six-cylinder, water-cooled, inline, 37.2-hp. engine of 615 liters displacement. The cylinder block was of light alloy and the compression ratio was 6 to 1. Note the twin windshields and hinged decking over the forward end of the rear passenger compartment. Hispano-Suizas like this were in a class with Rolls-Royce, Mercedes-Benz, Lincoln, and Packard. This body was made by Bligh Brothers of Canterbury, England. The car could exceed 80 mph.

GALLOWAY 10-5 The Galloway automobiles were built in Glasgow, Scotland, from 1921 to 1928. The firm, somehow, was associated with Arrol-Johnston. This Galloway 10-5 roadster was built in 1924 and followed the standard medium-priced roadster designs.

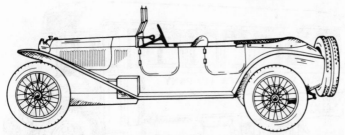

LANCIA LAMBDA Introduced in 1922, the Italian Lancia Lambda was the first automobile to combine independent front suspension, monocoque construction, and a vee-type engine enabling the car to make greater average speeds than many more powerful autos. The Lambda was made until 1931 in nine modifications or series as they were called. The 1924 four-place Torpedo shown here had a wheelbase of 10 feet 2 inches and an overall length of 14 feet 4 inches. Track was 4 feet 4 inches and width 4 feet 5.5 inches. Power was a four-cylinder, water-cooled, vee-type, 2,120-cc displacement engine that produced 50 hp. at 3,000 rpm. Final drive was via drive shaft and spiral bevel gear with crown and pinion. Notice the height of the bottom of the doors which was necessary in order to leave enough solid steel to provide adequate strength for this very advanced automobile. The car was fitted with white rubber tires.

OLDSMOBILE This Oldsmobile Light Six Sports Touring, produced in 1924, boasted as standard equipment: steel disc wheels, trunk, running-board scuff plates, and adjustable windshield wings. The car could seat five. Power was a six-cylinder, water-cooled, 19-hp. engine of 2.6 liters. Three forward speeds were fitted.

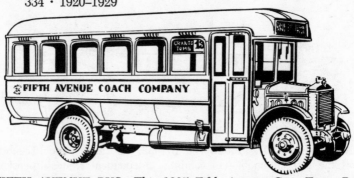

FIFTH AVENUE BUS   This 1925 Fifth Avenue Cross-Town Bus was operated in New York City during the late twenties and into the thirties. It was built by the New York Transportation Company, New York, New York, and the make was known as FACCO (Fifth Avenue Coach Company) Type J. The bus could seat twenty-four passengers and had a wheelbase of 174¾ inches. The brakes were mechanical with a vacuum booster. Power was a Moline Knight sleeve-valve, four-cylinder, inline, water-cooled engine of 301-cubic-inch displacement that developed 40 hp. at 1,400 rpm. Bore was 4 inches and stroke was 6 inches. Top speed was about 35 mph. This bus is on exhibit in the Long Island Automotive Museum, Southampton, New York.

FRANKLIN BOAT-TAIL   The H. H. Franklin Manufacturing Company of Syracuse, New York, produced this sporty roadster in 1925. It was called Boat-Tail because the body sides met at the rear to form a point like the bow of a boat, thereby giving the car a very streamlined appearance. Basically a two-seater, the Boat-Tail had a folding rumble seat for two more passengers. An unusual feature was the top extension for protection of the rumble seat occupants from the weather. As with all Franklin cars the engine was air-cooled. It was a six-cylinder, inline, 25-hp. engine of 3,871-cc displacement. Speed was over 50 mph. A three-speed transmission and sliding-plate clutch were standard. A Boat-Tail is on view at the Heritage Plantation of Sandwich, Sandwich, Massachusetts.

SALMSON GRAND PRIX RACER Salmson was one of the most successful small sports-car builders in France during the twenties. Under the direction of Émile Petit, the competition cars were developed and proved themselves on the circuits. The 1,100-cc displacement, overhead-cam, four-cylinder engine of 33 hp. made its appearance in 1922 and was used for several years in competition. In that year, André Lombard drove the car to victory in the French Cyclecar Grand Prix and placed second in the 200-Mile Race at Brooklands. The St. Andrew's Cross on the radiator is in honor of André (Andrew) Lombard. The car won numerous competitions during 1923 and 1924. The 1925 car shown here won at Brooklands and San Sebastian.

MILLER JUNIOR 8 RACER Harry Armenius Miller designed some of the most famous U.S. racing cars of all time with a tremendous string of victories at the Indianapolis 500-Mile Race. In 1925 he designed and built a front-wheel-drive racing car. The second front-wheel-drive racer was sold to Cliff Durant, son of William C. Durant who had just acquired the Locomobile firm. The car, named Junior 8 after one of the Locomobile models, had an eight-cylinder, 121-cubic-inch-displacement engine. Dave Lewis and Benny Hill drove the car to second place in the 1925 Indy with rear-wheel-drive Millers in fourth, fifth, sixth, seventh and ninth places.

ADLER TYPE 10/50   This Adler (Eagle) four-door open touring car was produced in Frankfurt, Germany, in 1925. It was powered by a six-cylinder, water-cooled inline engine of 2.6 liters displacement which could propel the car to a speed of approximately 60 mph.

MAYBACH W5   This large and luxurious, quality four-door sedan Model W5 was produced by Maybach in Germany in 1925. It was powered by a six-cylinder, overhead-valve, water-cooled, 7-liter-displacement engine of 120 hp., which gave the car a top speed of about 85 mph. at 2,400 engine rpm. It will be recalled that Wilhelm Maybach was a friend of Daimler in the early days of automotive experimentation. Maybach automobiles were intended for the wealthy and commanded prices of up to $25,000!

RICKENBACKER America's leading air ace of World War I, Edward V. Rickenbacker, began manufacturing automobiles in Detroit in 1922. The insignia emblem that he used was the Hat-in-the-Ring of his former 94th Aero Squadron. Rickenbacker was the second manufacturer to fit four-wheel hydraulic brakes on U.S. cars. This is the 1925 Rickenbacker four-seat club coupé. The Rickenbacker featured shatterproof glass by sandwiching a layer of transparent celluloid between two layers of glass and bonding them together. This technique is still in use for automobile glass. The car was well-constructed, but Rickenbacker could not beat the bigger companies and ended production in 1927.

OVERLAND This two-door sedan was made by the Willys-Overland factories in England and Canada. It could seat five on a 106-inch wheelbase. Power was from a four-cylinder, 1.8-liter, side-valve, 14-hp., water-cooled engine. Three forward speeds were fitted. Bore was 75 mm. and stroke was 102 mm.

BENJAMIN TYPE R   Benjamin automobiles were built from 1921 through 1927 by Maurice Jeanson, Asnières, France. The 1921 production model was powered by a 750-cc-displacement, four-cylinder, overhead-valve engine with the gearbox combined with the rear axle. By 1924 two- and three-cylinder two-cycle engines were used. The Benjamin Type R of 1925, built on a 110-inch wheelbase, is shown. Power was a four-cylinder, inline, water-cooled, four-cycle engine of 1,100-cc displacement. The design was a four-door, four-seat voiturette. The company continued to build cars in 1928 and 1929 under the brand name of Benova, which replaced Benjamin. Engines had up to eight cylinders.

CHEVROLET SEDAN   Chevrolet was created in 1914 to sell against the Ford Model T. By 1922 Chevrolet was faring poorly and was about to be dropped, when W. S. Knudsen left Ford and took a leading position with Chevrolet. He improved the design and built up sales until Ford dropped the Model T in 1927. This Chevrolet five-passenger, four-door sedan was one of Knudsen's first projects. He enclosed the entire passenger compartment with steel and glass, thus giving it the appearance of a much larger car, plus the added comfort. The car also featured steel disc wheels with detachable rims. The engine was a four-cylinder, water-cooled, 22-hp., inline powerplant of 2,800-cc displacement. Three forward speeds were fitted. An approximate speed of 45 mph. could be reached on the road.

STANLEY TOURING   Stanley was still a believer in steam-powered cars well into the twenties. This four-door fixed-top touring of 1925 looks just like the conventional gasoline-engine-powered car of the period. It had a two-cylinder, double-acting, 14-hp., 2,000-cc displacement, horizontal steam engine mounted in the rear, driving the rear axle via a 1½ to 1 spur gear and giving the car a speed of over 50 mph. The boiler was located under the hood. This four-seater was easy to drive because there was no changing of gears. It was made by the Steam Vehicle Corporation of America, Newton, Massachusetts.

WILLYS-KNIGHT SEDAN   Willys-Overland, Inc., of Toledo, Ohio, had expanded by 1925 to include a Willys-Overland Sales Company, Ltd., in Toronto, Canada. During this year the company used the Knight-patented sleeve valve for the engine design and advertised it as the car "with an engine you will never wear out." The engine was extremely smooth-running and virtually silent. The company used four-cylinder engines in their coupé ($1,495), coupé-sedan ($1,495), and touring model ($1,295). Six-cylinder engines were fitted to the brougham ($1,695), and the sedan shown here ($1,575).

FRAZER NASH SPORT Captain Archie Frazer Nash and H. R. Godfrey stopped producing the Godfrey Nash in 1924, and the Frazer Nash firm was started at that time. This was the 1925 Frazer Nash sports car on which the company concentrated. Power was a four-cylinder, water-cooled, 40-hp. Anzani engine that could propel the car to a cruising speed of 60 mph. and a top speed of over 70 mph. Chain transmission was used. Features of all Frazer Nash cars were lightness, simplicity, high speed, and accurate steering.

DAIMLER DOUBLE-SIX The English Daimler Company was founded in 1896 and reorganized in 1904. In October of 1926 the Daimler Double-Six was introduced as a 7.1-liter-displacement, sleeve-valve (Knight patent), vee-twelve-cylinder engine of about 50 hp. Two Daimler four-jet carburetors and full-pressure lubrication were fitted. The engine was cast in four blocks of three cylinders each. This landaulet with an enclosed driver area was a large car that was bought by the wealthy, the nobility, and the King of England himself. The car is fitted with three doors, with the driver's door on the other side. The car could attain 80 mph. and was extremely quiet, due to the multiple cylinders and sleeve valves. Notice the cooling fins on the top of the radiator.

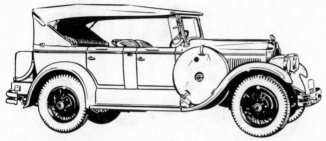

IMPERIAL   Chrysler initiated its higher-priced quality car in 1926 and called it the Imperial. The wheelbase was 136 inches on this Imperial Phaeton Touring. This four-door car could seat five and was fitted with wire spoked wheels. The engine was essentially the same as the 1925 Chrysler except that the fuel mixture was electrically heated for improved combustion.

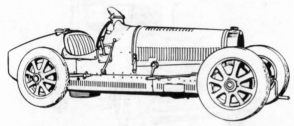

BUGATTI 35 GRAND PRIX   In 1924, Bugatti designed the Type 35 Racer. The Bugatti-patented aluminum wheels created a sensation. The car was, however, plagued with tire troubles. In 1925 the car won the Rome Grand Prix and the Targa Florio as well as the Italian Voiturette Grand Prix. In 1926 a supercharger was added and the design won the European championship by winning the Rome GP, the French GP, the Targa Florio, the Spanish GP, the Italian GP, the Milan GP, and was second in the British GP with Malcolm Campbell at the wheel. The 1926 racer is shown. The engine was an eight-cylinder, inline, water-cooled powerplant, attaining 35 hp. at 5,500 rpm., with the cylinders cast in two blocks of four cylinders each. An overhead camshaft was fitted and driven by bevel gears. Three valves were installed on each cylinder, two inlet and one exhaust. Two car-buretors were fitted. The wheelbase was 94.5 inches, and the overall length was 12 feet 1 inch.

ESSEX SEDAN   The Hudson Motor Car Company introduced this Essex four-door sedan in late 1926 as a lower-priced companion to the Hudson Super-Six Coach. It was powered by a six-cylinder engine and was advertised as costing $1,000. This was $500 less than the Hudson.

PONTIAC NO. 1   The first Pontiac automobile was introduced in 1926 by General Motors. It was to eventually replace the Oakland, which was terminated six years later. This two-seat coupé was fitted with a six-cylinder, inline, water-cooled engine that was rubber-mounted to reduce noise and vibration—a relative innovation at the time. The car started—and remained—in the medium-price class. Note the Indian chief motif on the radiator cap.

CROSSLEY   The British firm of Crossley Brothers had long been noted as the builder of engines. The company made automobiles from 1904 to 1937. This two-seater sports convertible coupé was introduced in 1926. It was fitted with a spacious rumble seat which increased the seating capacity to four. Power was a six-cylinder, inline, water-cooled, 18-hp. engine. Bore was 69 mm. and stroke was 120 mm. This car should not be confused with the American Crosley cars.

GRAY TOURING   One of the very light cars of 1926 was this Gray built by a famous manufacturer of marine engines. It was very conventional but most economically priced at $490. A 25-hp., four-cylinder engine was noted for its fuel economy. The company went out of business in 1926.

AJAX   The Ajax Auto Parts Company of Racine, Wisconsin, began production of a limited line of phaetons and sedans in 1923. The firm ran into financial problems in 1925 and was absorbed into the Nash organization. This is the first Nash-built Ajax of 1926, designed to make a dent in the low-priced car field. It failed to live up to expectations, however, and later emerged as the Light-Six and later Standard-Six Nash.

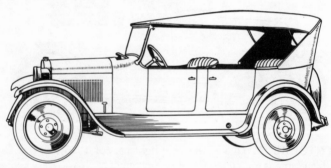

DODGE WB 126 TOURING   Over 300,000 Dodge WB models were sold in 1926. Much of this success was due to this Dodge WB 126 touring car. The design was lower than in previous years, and the one-piece windshield, straighter hood, and elegant appearance contributed to the popularity of the car.

BUICK ROADSTER   The Buick Motor Division of General Motors Corporation introduced this Master-Six Roadster in 1927. A six-cylinder, inline, water-cooled engine of 4,493-cc displacement powered the car. Bore was 89 mm. and stroke was 120 mm. The two-seater was very sporty yet heavy enough to provide a comfortable ride. Note the wind-deflecting adjustable side panes attached to the windshield, and the single windshield wiper for the driver only. A Buick Master-Six Roadster can be seen in the Provinciaal Automobielmuseum Houthalen, Domaine de Kelchterhoef, Houthalen, Belgium.

NASH 260 COUPÉ   Nash offered four coupé designs in 1927. This is the 1927 Model 260 Advanced Six Coupé and was the finest of the four. The car weighed 3,580 pounds on a wheelbase of 127 inches, and was priced at $1,775. It was powered by a six-cylinder, inline, water-cooled engine of 35 hp. and 4 liters displacement. Three forward speeds were fitted. A rumble seat and side-door luggage compartment were features.

PAIGE-DETROIT SEDAN   The Paige-Detroit firm made automobiles from 1908 to 1927 and this four-door sedan was one of the last to be built by that company. The car was powered by a six-cylinder, inline, water-cooled engine. The Paige was first built in 1909 in an old drug factory, and by 1925 sales were 50,000 per year. It was a sturdy, well-built car, but the firm expired in its nineteenth year.

GRAHAM PAIGE   In late 1927, the Graham Brothers bought the Paige-Detroit firm and renamed the cars Graham Paige at once. Power of this car was an eight-cylinder, L-head, water-cooled, Lycoming 80-hp. engine of 299-cubic-inch displacement. The wheelbase was 131 inches. The cars were very successful in stock car races at the Atlantic City Speedway. The four-door sedan is shown here.

DELAGE 1500 GRAND PRIX RACER Frenchman Louis Delage raced his first car before it went into production and finished second in the 1906 Coupe de l'Auto Race. Delage cars were constantly competing in most of the important European races and took their share of prizes. By 1927, the cars had rakish lines, and Delage racers placed first, second, and third in the French Grand Prix. They also won the British, Spanish, and the Italian Grand Prix races. The cars were powered by an eight-cylinder, double-overhead-camshaft, water-cooled, inline, 1.5-liter-displacement, 170-hp., supercharged engine that drove the car to 130 mph. A five-speed transmission was fitted. This type was still winning races nine years later!

ARGYLL 12-5 This Scottish Argyll was produced in 1927. The open touring car was powered by a single-sleeve-valve engine, which was different from the Knight design that employed a double-sleeve valve. The single sleeve had a spiral motion as it opened and closed the ports to the cylinders. The engine was of four cylinders, water-cooled, 16-hp. and with a 2.6-liter displacement. Four forward speeds were fitted. The wheelbase was 120 inches, and brakes were installed on the front wheels only.

WHIPPET Willys-Overland introduced the Whippet as a successor to the Overland in 1926, and production continued in the Toledo, Ohio, factory until 1931. A four-cylinder, L-head, water-cooled engine of 212-liter displacement powered this snappy roadster with rumble seat. The 1927 model is shown.

LA SALLE PHAETON The Cadillac Motor Car Company, a division of General Motors Corporation, introduced in 1927 a companion luxury car of lower price, the La Salle. While Cadillac prices ranged from $3,200 to $7,000, the La Salle cost from $2,200 to $2,800. Both cars had bodies by Fisher and Fleetwood. The 1927 Dual Cowl Phaeton is shown. Note the double windshields and hinged steel cover over the rear passengers' laps.

FORD MODEL T TOURING   After producing more than fifteen million Model T cars since 1908, the Ford Motor Company stopped production in late 1927. This touring model proved to be one of the most popular types, although the Model T was produced in roadster, sedan, station wagon, and coupé models. The car shown is of 1927 vintage.

CHANDLER SEDAN   The Chandler Motor Company, Cleveland, Ohio, produced this four-door sedan in 1927. It was powered by a six-cylinder, inline, side-valve, water-cooled engine of 55 hp. and 289-cubic-inch displacement. Maximum speed was about 80 mph. The car was excellent in "stop and go" traffic because it had a semi-automatic transmission. The body was made by Fisher at this time. During the following year, Hupmobile took over the Chandler Motor Company.

STUTZ BLACKHAWK This Boat-Tail Stutz Blackhawk was produced from 1927 to 1929. It was a touring-type roadster that was a radical departure from the previous designs due to the revised policies of the Stutz new president, Frederick E. Moskovics. This is the 1927 model, and it was powered by an eight-cylinder, inline, water-cooled, 95-hp., 419-liter-displacement engine. The engine was fitted with an overhead camshaft and two spark plugs per cylinder! It used an underslung worm gear drive to fit a low body to the chassis. Note the step plate instead of a running board. A Black Hawk averaged 96.3 mph. in the 150-mile stock car race at the Atlantic City Speedway on September 5, 1927, with two more Black Hawks in second and third places!

MERCEDES-BENZ SS The Mercedes-Benz SS Super Sports design was based on the S design that won the Nürburgring Race in 1927. The SS was introduced in that year and was powered by a six-cylinder, water-cooled, inline, 115-hp., 7.1-liter-displacement supercharged engine with a magnesium block and single overhead camshaft. Maximum speed was about 115 mph. The supercharger was started when the accelerator pedal was completely depressed. A four-speed transmission was fitted. The car weighed about 5,000 pounds on a 136-inch wheelbase. The touring body is shown.

MERCEDES SEDAN   This large four-door sedan was produced by Mercedes-Benz in 1927. It was built on an enormous 149-inch wheelbase and was intended for rich buyers. The weight was over 5,000 pounds. The six-cylinder, overhead-camshaft, water-cooled engine produced 100 hp. The car could seat six in comfort.

ISOTTA-FRASCHINI BROUGHAM   The finest of all Italian cars was the Milan-built Isotta-Fraschini. Production began in 1900 when Cesare Isotta and Oreste Fraschini started the firm. In 1907, the make won the Coppa Florio with an overhead-camshaft racer. In 1910, the company was the first in the world to fit production models with four-wheel brakes. They soon directed their efforts to luxury automobiles and produced some of the most elegant and expensive designs for rich patrons. Many Hollywood stars, including Rudolph Valentino, bought several! This 1927 Isotta-Fraschini had a straight-eight engine of 7.4-liter displacement on a 145-inch wheelbase. The car cost about $8,000 with coachwork extra. This elegant automobile can be seen at the Frederick C. Crawford Auto-Aviation Museum, Cleveland, Ohio.

VOLVO P-4 *Volvo* is the latin word for "I Roll" or "I Rotate." The company, the result of a combined effort, was organized by Assar Gabrielson. It consisted of such Swedish companies as Bofors, Svenska, Pentaverken, Kugellagerfabriken, and Kopings Mekaniska Verkstad. This is their first product, introduced in 1927. Power was a four-cylinder, water-cooled, inline engine of 119-cubic-inch displacement. Bore was 3 inches and stroke was 4⅜ inches. This open tourer was designed by Mas-Ole. The Volvo company grew slowly during the thirties and became a major automobile manufacturer in the forties.

FRANKLIN SEDAN This Franklin four-door sedan was produced in 1928 and was the Model 130 on a 119-inch wheelbase. As was usual with the Franklin, the engine was air-cooled. It was a six-cylinder, inline, 30-hp., 4.5-liter-displacement powerplant with overhead valves. Four forward speeds were fitted. The car sold for about $2,100. It featured hydraulic brakes, a shatterproof windshield, and a seven-bearing crankshaft. A car of this type can be seen at The Raben Car Collection at Aalholm Castle, Nysted, Denmark.

DURANT SEDAN When William Durant was forced out of General Motors due to financial problems, he started his own company with four plants in Elizabeth, New Jersey, Lansing, Michigan, Oakland, California, and Toronto, Canada. After he introduced the low-priced Star auto, he produced a larger and more expensive line. The Durant four-door sedan of 1928 had four-wheel brakes, balloon tires, and sold for about $1,500.

OPEL RAKETE I Fritz von Opel was the owner of a large factory in Germany building inexpensive automobiles. He was sometimes called the German Henry Ford. In early 1928 he became interested in rocket propulsion and contacted Friedrich Wilhelm Sander to design rockets to propel an automobile. Sander owned and operated a rocket factory near Bremen which built marine line-throwing and navigation rockets. At Opel's test track in Russelheim the test driver, Kurt Volkhart, tried with a variety of solid rockets to attain success with this new powerplant. The results were unimpressive, so Opel converted a standard racing car by removing the engine and fitting it with a battery of twelve Sander rockets behind the cockpit. This test was called, officially, the First Test Run and took place in the spring of 1928. With Volkhart at the wheel, the car began to move emitting smoke and flame and sped along the test track at more than 70 mph., even though five of the twelve rockets had failed to ignite! This was the first rocket vehicle in the world. Opel built two more rocket cars that year which attained speeds of 125 mph. and 180 mph. But this car was the pioneer.

HUDSON COUPÉ The coupé style of auto was in vogue during the pre-Depression years. In 1928, the Hudson Motor Car Company engaged the Walter M. Murphy Company of Pasadena, California, a famous custom-body-building firm, to design a series of special bodies. This Hudson Coupé of 1928 is one of the results. Note the long, low lines that made the car look very expensive. The Super-Six was used for power.

ALVIS COMPRESSOR The British firm of T. G. John, Ltd., of Coventry, England, made their first auto in 1920. They produced this Alvis Super Sportster Roadster in 1928. It was powered by a four-cylinder, inline, water-cooled, overhead-cam, supercharged engine of 1.5-liters displacement, developing 75 hp. The Alvis cars were among the first British designs to employ front-wheel drive. Alvis entered many competition events including Brooklands, Le Mans, and Grand Prix. This car had all four wheels independently sprung. One of the 1928 cars can be seen at the Automuseum Nettelstedt, Lübeck, Germany.

DeSOTO ROADSTER   In May, 1928, the Chrysler Corporation took over the DeSoto Motor Car Company of Auburn, Indiana. This lightweight Model K was one of the first DeSotos manufactured by Chrysler. It was powered by a six-cylinder, inline, 55-hp., water-cooled engine of 175-cubic-inch displacement. By the end of 1928, over 34,000 DeSotos had been shipped to 1,500 new dealerships!

CHRYSLER IMPERIAL 80   This 1928 Chrysler Imperial 80 Roadster was advertised as "America's Most Powerful Car." In 1927, a Chrysler Imperial 80 sped from coast to coast in 168 hours, averaging 40 miles per hour for 6,721 miles. Top speed of the car was over 75 mph. In 1928, Chryslers finished in third and fourth places in the Le Mans 24-Hour Race. The 1927 Chrysler sales of 192,083 automobiles placed fourth among United States auto makers. An Imperial 80 can be seen at Pettit's Museum of Motoring Memories, Natural Bridge, Virginia.

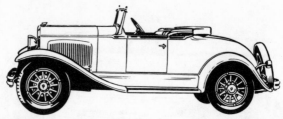

PLYMOUTH NO. 1 The first Chrysler-made Plymouth came into being on June 11, 1928. It was so successful that by the end of the year 58,000 had been sold. This is the roadster model that had a wheelbase of 109 inches and was powered by a four-cylinder, L-head, water-cooled, 45-hp., 170-cubic-inch-displacement engine.

LINCOLN SPORT PHAETON MODEL L Henry M. Leland, who helped found Cadillac, also founded the Lincoln Company in 1917. He sold the company to Henry Ford in 1922 and remained as general manager. Ford enlarged the cars a bit and maintained the high standard of craftsmanship set by Leland. This is the 1928 Lincoln Sport Phaeton Model L that was powered by a 284-cubic-inch-displacement, 60-degree vee, eight-cylinder, 90-hp., water-cooled engine. The car proved extremely reliable. This open car featured an aluminum Locke-bodied sport phaeton with a rear-passenger cowl and windshield. Seven passengers could be accommodated. The car weighed 4,950 pounds and could cruise at 75 mph. for hours on end.

CUNNINGHAM   James Cunningham & Sons of Rochester, New York, manufactured fine, luxury-type automobiles from 1907 to 1936. This 1928 five-passenger convertible was powered by a vee, eight-cylinder, water-cooled engine that developed 100 hp. at 2,400 rpm. Many celebrities such as Mary Pickford, Harold Lloyd, and William Randolph Hearst were Cunningham enthusiasts. This car sold for $9,000! One of these cars is on exhibit at the Pioneer Auto Museum, Murdo, South Dakota.

MERCEDES-BENZ SS   The major difference between this 1928 Mercedes-Benz SS and the previous 1927 model was the external flexible exhaust pipes emerging from the side of the hood and entering a collecting chamber. A double-bar bumper had also been fitted. This car can be seen at the Automuseum Nettelstedt, Lübeck, Germany.

DODGE VICTORY SIX SEDAN   Dodge Brothers, Inc., of Hamtramck, Michigan, became part of the Chrysler Corporation on July 30, 1928. This is the Victory Six four-door sedan which was produced that year. Beginning in 1928 all Dodge cars were fitted with six-cylinder engines. The Victory Six had a 112-inch wheelbase and was powered with a six-cylinder, water-cooled, 58-hp., 208-cubic-inch-displacement engine.

FORD MODEL A   The Ford Motor Company introduced the Model A in 1928 to replace the Model T that had left the production lines during the previous year. This 1928 Tudor sedan had a wheelbase of 103 inches and was 152 inches overall. Weight was about 2,375 pounds. It had a four-cylinder, water-cooled, inline engine of 24 hp., with a displacement of 200 cubic inches. Four-wheel brakes were fitted as were balloon tires. A three-speed sliding-gear transmission was standard. By March, 1932, almost a half million Model A Fords had been built.

MERCEDES STUTTGART   The newly formed merger of the Daimler and Benz firms became known as Mercedes-Benz and introduced a car aimed at lower-middle-class buyers in 1926. It was known as the Mercedes Stuttgart 200. This was a five-passenger sedan with a six-cylinder, water-cooled, overhead-camshaft, 38-hp. engine with a 2-liter displacement. The wheelbase was 112 inches. This was the first car to bear the Mercedes-Benz name, and production continued into 1928 when the larger Mannheim model replaced it. The 1928 Stuttgart is shown here. A car of this type is on exhibit at the Automuseum Nettelstedt, Lübeck, Germany.

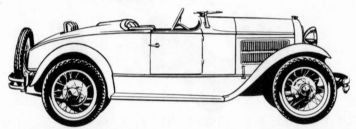

ESSEX SPEEDABOUT BOAT-TAIL   The Hudson Motor Car Company produced this Essex Speedabout Boat-Tail Roadster from 1927 through 1931. This is the 1929 model, which was fitted with a rumble seat. The Essex Speedabout was so successful that a heavier, more powerful Hudson Boat-Tail Roadster was also made available in 1931. This was an attempt to bolster the poor Hudson sales of only 113,898 cars in 1930.

HUPMOBILE SEDAN The Hupp Motor Corporation, Detroit, Michigan, produced this four-door sedan in 1929. Hupmobiles were large users of aluminum in the construction. At times the bodies were made by the Pullman Company. Power for this five-seater was a six-cylinder, water-cooled, 23-hp., 3.2-liter-displacement, side-valve engine. Three forward speeds were fitted. The wheelbase was 9 feet 6 inches.

FORD MODEL A ROADSTER The Ford Model A replaced the veteran Model T. This 1929 Ford Model A Roadster was 155 inches long with a 103-inch wheelbase. Weight was 2,155 pounds. It was primarily a two-seater with two more places in a folding rumble seat. A four-cylinder, water-cooled, 200-cubic-inch-displacement, 24-hp., side-valve engine was used to power all eleven body types in the Model A series. In addition to the roadster, a phaeton, coupé, deluxe coupé, sport coupé, Tudor and Fordor sedan, deluxe sedan, town sedan, cabriolet, and station wagon were offered in 1929.

SINGER JUNIOR ROADSTER The English Singer factory built bicycles, and in 1902 added automobiles to the line. By 1914 the make had many successes at Brooklands and the Alpine Trials. This is a 1929 model of the Singer Junior Roadster that was introduced in 1927. Power was a four-cylinder, overhead-camshaft, 8-hp., 848-cc-displacement, water-cooled, inline engine. The wheelbase was 90 inches. The little car was an excellent performer. In 1927, a stock Junior won the Montlhéry Marathon Race by driving for six days and nights at an average speed of 39.4 mph.!

STUDEBAKER COUPÉ The Studebaker Automobile Company of South Bend, Indiana, developed the first soundproof direct-flow muffler, modern fuel pump, overdrive and hill-holder mechanism. They also produced this President Coupé in 1929 with a wheelbase of 120 inches. Power was an eight-cylinder, inline, water-cooled, side-valve, 30-hp., 4.1-liter-displacement engine. Bore was 3 inches and stroke was 4.25 inches. In 1929, two stock Studebaker Presidents established records in the Atlantic City 24-Hour Race, both averaging 85 mph. for 24 hours! In 1929, the Pikes Peak Hill-Climb was won by stock Studebakers in the first, second, and third places!

DODGE STATION WAGON The Dodge division of the Chrysler Corporation produced this station wagon in 1929. It was the Dodge Brothers Standard-Six, which sold for $995. The wheelbase was 112 inches. A six-cylinder, water-cooled, inline, 208-cubic-inch-displacement, 58-hp. engine was installed. Note the drop-type heavy-framed passenger windows on this six-seater. The body was a combination of steel and wood, and wire wheels were standard.

MERCEDES-BENZ SSK Based on the outstanding supercharged Mercedes-Benz SS, the SSK was developed in 1928. The K meant *Kurz* or "short" and referred to the 116-inch wheelbase. The car was fierce and powerful with 225 hp. and a top speed of 130 mph.! At the 1929 Grand Prix at Nürburgring the SSK scored third. This was repeated at Monaco. First, second, and third prizes were won by the SSK at Weisbaden-Rennen and another placed third at Monza. The SSK also dominated the Central European hill-climbing season.

ROLLS-ROYCE PHANTOM II   This sport touring Phantom II was produced by Rolls-Royce in 1929 with a wheelbase of 144 inches. The five-passenger auto was powered by a Rolls-Royce six-cylinder, inline, water-cooled, overhead-valve, 7,668-cc-displacement, 120-hp. engine that gave the car a 95-mph. speed. A four-speed transmission was fitted and power brakes were standard. The weight of the chassis, without the body, was about 4,000 pounds.

WILLYS-KNIGHT OPEN TOURING   This Open Touring Willys-Knight was produced in 1929 and sold for $1,195. It boasted a one-man operatable convertible top, running board step plates, hand rubbing plates at the tops of the doors, plus the quiet running Knight double-sleeve-valve, six-cylinder engine. The engine had seven crankshaft bearings and was exceptionally smooth-running. Knight engines consumed more lubricating oil than was usual.

M.G. MIDGET TYPE M The first M.G. Midget was the Type M and was produced in 1929. It proved to be an immediate success with the public. In May, 1930, the Type M won first and second prizes at the 24-Hour Race at Brooklands. Other Type M cars won five other places in that race. The car had a 78-inch wheelbase and a 42-inch track. The engine was a four-cylinder, water-cooled, 847-cc-displacement, 20-hp. powerplant with a bore of 57 mm. and a stroke of 83 mm. Speed was over 80 mph. This was the first of a long line of sports cars.

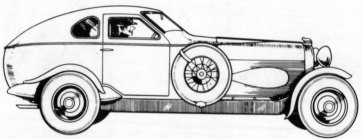

AUBURN CABIN SPEEDSTER This Auburn Cabin Speedster was the sensation of the 1929 New York Automobile Show. It featured a streamlined aluminum body containing two seats, and was built on a 120-inch wheelbase. The bottom of the car was covered by a pan in the interest of streamlining, and the very low body reduced head resistance. Airplane-type wicker seats were installed for lightness. A Lycoming eight-cylinder, inline, water-cooled, 298.6-cubic-inch-displacement engine developed 120 hp. at 3,300 rpm. The car weighed 3,000 pounds, and guaranteed a speed of 100 mph. The price was $2,195.

NOTE UNDER-PANNING

DU PONT MODEL G   The Du Pont firm of Wilmington, Delaware, had a considerable financial interest in General Motors. The Du Pont company also built cars from 1919 to 1931. This is the well-known Du Pont Model G Speedster made in 1929. It was powered by an eight-cylinder, inline, water-cooled, L-head, 114-hp., 322-cubic-inch-displacement Continental engine. The two-seater body was mounted on a 122-inch wheelbase. A Warner four-speed transmission was fitted, with the fourth gear direct to the rear axle. Speed was about 100 mph.

CHAPTER TEN

Millions Take to the Open Road 1930—1939

ALTHOUGH 1930 was a depressed period financially, enough Americans still took to the roads to push the death toll that year to 32,000. Car-owning families were on the move to the suburbs, not knowing that just ten years earlier Henry Ford had predicted that the old-fashioned city was doomed.

As banks closed down across the nation, almost two million fewer vehicles were manufactured than during 1929. Yet the Cadillac V-16 with a Fleetwood body was finding buyers who would pay $8,000 or more per car.

During September of 1930 Hitlerites won 107 seats in the German Reichstag elections.

In America the Winton Engine Company, which had been set up by Alexander Winton to manufacture industrial diesel, railroad and marine powerplants, was acquired by General Motors. It became the G.M. Cleveland Diesel Division.

Plymouth went "big-time" overnight in 1930 when sales franchises were granted to all Dodge, DeSoto, and Chrysler dealers. The Austin Bantam, a derivative of the English Austin Seven, was made in the U.S. by the American Austin Car Company (the English car was also made by French, German, and Japanese concerns—the latter, Datsun).

Total vehicle production in the United States—and that includes passenger cars, trucks, and buses—was down *another* one million units during 1931, yet the 50-millionth American motor

366

vehicle was rolled out. It is interesting to note that during this same year the Ford assembly lines produced their 20-millionth vehicle.

Despite the Depression everything called for high figures: Federal expenditures on roads, over $200 million. Number of passenger cars registered, 23,000,000! Buses and trucks on the roads, 3,550,000!

During 1931 in England the Bentley business and marque was taken over by Rolls-Royce and the Lanchester was absorbed by Daimler (itself a part of B.S.A.—Birmingham Small Arms Company).

In America the Oakland nameplate on cars was replaced entirely by its stablemate, Pontiac. Studebaker replaced its Erskine with the Rockne Six; the new car, selling for as little as $585, was named after the famous Notre Dame University football coach, Knute Rockne. Buick stepped up to a straight-eight engine. Plymouth employed a three-point suspension system in mounting its engines to dampen vibration.

Vehicle production in the United States in 1932 was a bit more than 1.3 million units, the fewest that had been rolled out in seventeen years. The biggest news from Ford confirmed rumors of a 65-hp. Ford V-8 engine. A V-8 Ford roadster was priced, free-on-board Detroit, at $600; the V-8 convertible sedan was $650 F.O.B. A choice of fourteen body styles was offered.

But Chevrolet was treading on Ford's heels; in August G.M. turned out the 8-millionth Chevrolet. Louis Chevrolet, long away from G.M., was working with Glenn L. Martin and had been granted a patent for a ten-cylinder radial aircraft engine. Franklin revealed its air-cooled V-12, which it installed in a $4,400 broughham model. Buick hailed its vacuum-operated clutch.

Dead in 1932 were pioneers Alexander Winton and Henry Leland. In Italy, Benito Mussolini announced he would rule for thirty years. America elected its first woman senator, Hattie Caraway (D., Arkansas).

The depth of the American Depression was reached during 1933, but still the automobile chugged along. The "dust bowl" farmers of Oklahoma and surrounding regions followed Horace Greeley's advice by driving West . . . and making memorable scenes of overloaded cars, farm trucks, and homebuilt trailers piled high with meagre household goods, wind-honed humans, and high hopes.

In the East, at Camden, New Jersey, a drive-in theater opened. F.D.R. launched his "fireside chats" on March 12, 1933. In August, the N.I.R.A. (National Industrial Recovery Administration), its N.R.A. Code and the "Blue Eagle" emblem burst upon the public scene.

During 1933 Fisher Body "No-Draft Ventilation" was introduced on all G.M. cars. Hudson presented the new Terraplane and Plymouth moved up from four to six cylinders. Nash came out with twin ignition on its OHV powerplants. G.M. began impact-testing and the scientific examination of crashes. John N. Willys died during 1933.

Total vehicle production in the United States jumped by almost a million units during 1934. Nash turned out its 1-millionth car at Kenosha, Wisconsin, while the last Franklins were rolled out and that car factory closed at Syracuse, New York. The final Franklin brougham was priced at $2,885.

Biggest automotive sensations of 1934 were the "Airflow" models by DeSoto and Chrysler. The first truly streamlined production cars in America, they brought out the lookers and tire kickers, but not the buyers.

During 1934, two big-car fanciers got together for the first time. Hitler and Mussolini met in Venice.

Refined elegance for 1935 was represented by the first Lincoln-Zephyr with its twelve-cylinder engine. Esthetically, at the other end of the appearance scale, was an all-steel station wagon by Chevrolet. It looked much like an enclosed delivery truck with some extra windows and seats added on. The "coffin-nosed" Model 810 Cord appeared featuring disappearing headlights and a Lycoming powerplant; a patent was granted to Gordon Miller Buehrig for its configuration. The car had its operational drawbacks, still it quickly established itself as a classic.

The National Automobile Show, the 36th, was shifted to an earlier (November) date to help even out employment within the automotive industry. Production and sales rose for 1935.

The United Automobile Workers formed and linked up with the Congress of Industrial Organizations (U.A.W./C.I.O.). Nash embraced overdrive and showed a prototype whose seats converted to beds. G.M. featured all-steel "turret-tops" on its closed cars.

In Europe Daimler-Benz was busy experimenting with fuel-injection engines, with fuel injected directly into the cylinders or indirectly into the inlet manifold.

One of the most famous cars throughout Europe in 1936, and one of the smallest, was the Fiat 500A Coupé. This two-seater, just 11 feet long, would give its owner about 55 mpg. at 55 mph.; power was provided by a four-cylinder, 570-cc engine.

In America in 1936 more than half of all American families (54 percent) now owned a car, or cars. REO, nevertheless, gave up on its passenger car efforts, turning its full attention to commercial vehicles. The Auburn Automobile Company of Auburn, Indiana, closed its doors after thirty-three years. Once again an auto manufacturer, this time Nash, merged with a refrigerator firm, Kelvinator, to form the Nash-Kelvinator Corporation. Earlier, much earlier, in 1919, it had been a wedding of General Motors and Frigidaire.

Vanderbilt Cup racing was revived in 1936 at Roosevelt Field on Long Island. Traveling over what the racing fraternity would later describe as a "Mickey Mouse circuit," Tazio Nuvolari, the Italian wonder driver, placed first in an Alfa Romeo.

Automobile commutation got a great assist around the San Francisco bay area in 1937 with the opening of the Golden Gate Bridge. Traffic-wise, it was the Western equivalent to the George Washington Bridge, which had been finished six years earlier; the GW spans the Hudson River between Fort Lee, New Jersey, and New York City.

General Motors recognized the U.A.W. as a bargaining agent for that union's members on February 11, 1937. Chrysler followed suit two months later.

During 1937 Nash dropped its Lafayette, Stutz went bankrupt, and Hupp went downhill rapidly. Total vehicle output, however, was up by almost 400,000 units for the year even though the financial recession had sent stocks tumbling in early fall of 1937.

Honors for the most unusual automobile went to Waldo Waterman's "Arrowbile," one of the first workable flying autos.

Business generally was in the doldrums across the nation during 1938. This was reflected in a further drop within the auto/

truck industry: down 2.3 million units to a 2.5-million total. Most car makers emphasized their lower-priced merchandise. Ford, however, solidly entrenched in the low-price field, introduced its medium-priced V-8 Mercury. Studebaker was busy planning a smallish car.

Pontiac moved its gearshift control from the floor to the steering column. Chevrolet boasted a vacuum-operated gearshift. Nash offered heated and filtered fan-driven fresh air, designating the final product as "conditioned air."

Hudson decided to drop its Terraplane, a move considered by many as a bit of unfortunate timing. Pierce-Arrow was out of business. Detroit Electric quit making battery-operated "electrics." Pioneers Charles Duryea and Roy Chapin died in 1938; Henry Ford suffered his first stroke.

With war clouds gathering over Europe many Americans in 1939 figured it was time to acquire that new car. Thus, passenger vehicle production jumped by more than 800,000 units. Studebaker released its jaunty little Champion with a six-cylinder, 78-hp. engine. Packard offered air conditioning, a remarkable feature for the time. Powell Crosley, Jr., introduced his mini-compact, the air-cooled 580-cc twin Crosley—not to be confused with the English Crossley which had gone off the market several years earlier.

Hitler's legions invaded Poland on September 1.

During October, 1939, the "Continental Cabriolet" model of the Lincoln-Zephyr was shown at Dearborn, New York City, and Los Angeles. But it would be produced as a 1940 model car.

As indications of things to come, Packard started making marine engines for U.S. Navy PT boats and White turned out "scout" cars for the U.S. Army.

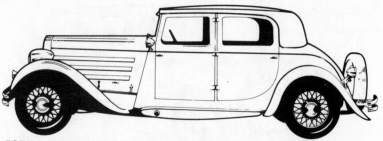

JORDAN SPEEDWAY SPORTSMAN   With the Depression gnawing away at auto sales, the Jordan Motor Car Company decided to capture a portion of the apparently unaffected luxury car market with the Speedway Series in 1930. This four-door sedan was called the Sportsman. The wheelbase was 145 inches, and power was an eight-cylinder, inline Continental engine. Notice the streamlined taillight and running board and the lack of a radiator figure. Jordan went out of business shortly after the introduction of the Speedway Series.

PLYMOUTH ROADSTER   This Plymouth Model 30-U Roadster was produced by the Plymouth Division of Chrysler Corporation, in 1930. Production lasted until mid-1931. With a 109-inch wheelbase, the two-seater was powered by a four-cylinder, L-head, water-cooled, 196-cubic-inch-displacement, 48-hp. engine. The compression ratio was 4.6 to 1. New vibration-proof engine mountings and shock absorbers made the car quite comfortable for its size. Hydraulic four-wheel brakes were standard.

VOISIN SEDAN The French Voisin firm were famous builders of military aircraft during World War I. This four-door sedan was made in 1930. The five-passenger auto was powered by a six-cylinder, sleeve-valve, water-cooled, inline engine of 5,830 cc and about 100 hp. Speed was about 90 mph. A V-12 engine was an available option.

MARMON ROADSTER Col. Howard Marmon's Marmon Motor Company of Indianapolis, Indiana, began building automobiles in 1904. This roadster was produced in 1930 and sold for about $1,500. Although Marmon had developed a superb V-16 aluminum engine for his more expensive cars and for racing, this roadster was fitted with an eight-cylinder, inline engine. Marmon advertised that his cars were fitted with eight-cylinder engines for the price of a six. The firm went out of business in 1933 after twenty-nine years of auto-making.

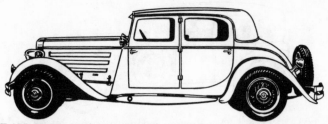

JORDAN SPORTSMAN   The Jordan Motor Car Company, Cleveland, Ohio, built cars from 1916 to 1931. This four-door Sportsman of 1930 was one of the company's last designs and was an attempt to attract the luxury sporting market. A roadster version of this car was also produced and was called the Speedway Ace. The wheelbase was 145 inches and power was a 114-hp., Continental, inline, eight-cylinder, water-cooled engine. The price was $5,500.

RUXTON ROADSTER   In 1930, New Era Motors of New York City merged with Kissel, Moon, and Gardner auto manufacturers. Ruxton had already been introduced by Moon Motor Car Company to the order of New Era Motors. This is the 1930 Ruxton Roadster. Ruxton cars were underslung and very well appointed, which led to the rumor at the time that they were produced in Europe. This roadster was fitted with a rumble seat and could therefore carry five persons. This custom body was made by Budd. Notice the most unusual headlights. The car was front-wheel driven by an eight-cylinder, inline, water-cooled Continental engine. About 600 were built.

RUXTON SEDAN   This Ruxton Sedan was made by Moon Motor Company, for New Era Motors of New York City (Moon, Kissel, and Gardner) in 1930. It featured a front-wheel drive which was not much appreciated at that time. The car was extremely well appointed. Power was an eight-cylinder, inline, water-cooled Continental engine that was reversed so the gearbox pointed forward. Despite a good product, New Era Motors became involved in numerous lawsuits that closed the company in 1931. The rival front-wheel-drive Cord was introduced that year.

PONTIAC SEDAN   This Pontiac Model 6-30, two-door sedan was produced in 1930. The car weighed about 2,700 pounds on a 110-inch wheelbase with an overall length of 168 inches. The car could seat five passengers and had a turning circle of 39 feet. Power was a six-cylinder, L-head, water-cooled, inline, 200-cubic-inch-displacement, 60-hp. engine with a bore of 3.312 inches and stroke of 3.875 inches. The engine was rubber-mounted and used two cylinder heads and three main bearings. The car was a leader in the medium-priced field and was called the "Chief of the Sixes."

BENTLEY LE MANS SPEED SIX TOURING   This 4.5-liter Bentley touring car was developed in 1929 and almost seventy were sold to the public. The model won the 24-Hour Le Mans Race, the Six-Hour Brooklands Race, and placed second in the Irish Grand Prix and in the 500-Mile Brooklands Race. The 1930 Speed Six was virtually identical except for strengthened connecting rods, new-design valve rockers, and an increased compression ratio. About 170 were sold to the public. In 1930 the Speed Sixes placed first and second in the 24-Hour Le Mans and first in the Double-Twelve Race at Brooklands. After this the car was often referred to as the Le Mans. The 1930 Le Mans Speed Six is shown here and was powered by a 200-hp., 4.5-liter, water-cooled engine. It was equipped with two carburetors as well as a pressurized fuel system. The wheelbase was 11 feet and overall length was 15 feet 1 inch. The body was a touring style and designed by Vanden Plas to seat four. The engine was supercharged by an engine-driven blower located in front of the radiator. Top speed was about 135 mph. In 1931 Rolls-Royce, Ltd., took control of Bentley and in that year a Speed Six won the 500-Mile Race at Brooklands! This car can be seen in the Resnick Motor Museum, Ellenville, New York.

HUDSON CLUB SEDAN   Hudson produced this Club Sedan in 1930. The four-door, five-passenger auto was built on a 119-inch wheelbase. The coachwork was done by the famous firm of Le Baron. The car had a Great-Eight inline, water-cooled engine that provided power and economy. A sedan of this type averaged 25.5 miles per gallon on a 480-mile run in Australia.

MORGAN AERO   The Morgan three-wheeled cars were built in England from 1910 to 1936, at which time they changed to four-wheel designs. At one time, in England, four-wheeled cars were taxed more than three-wheelers. Therefore, Morgan decided to make three-wheelers. The Morgan Aero of 1930 is shown. The car had an excellent power-to-weight ratio, good handling, economy and low price, but it was noisy and rough riding. Power was one of a variety of two-cylinder, vee, water-cooled, 1,096-cc-displacement engines. Two forward speeds were fitted with a chain final drive. The car featured independent front suspension. The rear wheel was the driver, while steering was conventional via the front wheels. It was England's most popular three-wheeler and could attain 80 mph.

AUSTIN BANTAM COUPÉ   The American Austin Company started building modified versions of the diminutive English Austin Seven in 1930. The car was extremely popular and was produced in two-seat coupé and convertible models. This is the coupé of 1930. It was powered by a four-cylinder, water-cooled, inline engine of 13 hp. The wheelbase was only 75 inches. The car was economical to operate as well as to buy. Price was $425. Upon its introduction, the car was called the American Austin, but the name soon changed to Bantam.

ASTON MARTIN INTERNATIONAL   Although in the automobile business since 1913, Aston Martin, Ltd., Feltham, England, produced the first Aston Martin car in 1926. At that time the firm had reorganized with Augustus C. Bertelli, formerly of Enfield and Alldays, heading the design staff. The International design was introduced to the public as the "11.9 Super Sports" in 1928. The 1931 Aston Martin International two-four seater is shown. It was powered by a four-cylinder, overhead-camshaft, 12-hp., 1,495-cubic-inch-displacement, water-cooled engine. The engine used a magneto, two fuel pumps, and two carburetors. It featured a dry-sump lubrication system, whereby an engine-driven pump fed the engine from a lubricating oil tank via a filter. As the oil drained into the sump, it was picked up by another pump and cooled before it was pumped back to the tank. The wheelbase was 8 feet 6 inches with an overall length of 12 feet. The fenders were attached to the rear of the brake drums on all four wheels so they rose and fell with the wheel. The Aston Martin International placed seventh and eighth in the 1930 Irish Grand Prix, sixth in the Brooklands Double-Twelve of 1931, and fifth in the 1931 Le Mans 24-Hour Race. The cars placed first and second in the 1931 Tourist Trophy.

CORD SEDAN   The Cord was the first mass-produced automobile in the U.S. with front-wheel drive. The Ruxton and Christie preceded it but they were not produced in volume. Errett L. Cord took over the ailing Auburn Automobile Company, and introduced his first front-wheel-drive car in 1929, the L-29. The 1931 Cord Sedan is shown. It was powered by a Lycoming, eight-cylinder, inline, water-cooled, 299-cubic-inch-displacement engine. The engine developed 125 hp. at 3,600 rpm. The wheelbase was 137 inches, and the car was only 61 inches high because of the front-wheel drive, while most automobiles of the period were over 70 inches. The Cord L-29 could reach 80 mph. Production was stopped in 1932, after 4,429 Cords had been sold, to make way for a new model.

STUTZ DV-32   In 1931, the Stutz Motor Car Company reworked their eight-cylinder SV-16 engine by adding two more valves per cylinder, making each cylinder equipped with two intake and two exhaust valves. The engine was also fitted with double-overhead camshafts. This water-cooled, inline engine could develop 156 hp. at 3,900 rpm., and had a displacement of 322 cubic inches. A single spark plug was used in the center of each cylinder. Bore was 3⅛ inches and stroke was 4½ inches. This engine was installed in the Stutz Sport Tourer of 1931, and the chassis cost $1,000 more with the DV-32 than with the SV-16. It is believed that this five-seater body was built by Weymann.

M.G. C-TYPE MIDGET RACER   George Eyston drove this car to a World Class H speed record of 100 mph. on February 16, 1931. This 746-cc-displacement-engine-powered car became the smallest car to attain that speed. Two weeks later the racer was in production. C-Type Midgets took the first five places at the Brooklands Double-Twelve Race, first three places in the Saorstat Cup Race, and first and third in the Irish Grand Prix! The successes continued in 1932. The car was built on a 6-foot-9-inch wheelbase and a track of 3 feet 6 inches. The four-cylinder, water-cooled, inline engine developed 37 hp. and had a bore and stroke of 57 mm. and 73 mm. This car was often called the Montlhéry Midget.

CHEVROLET ICE CREAM CAR   During the twenties and thirties, the tasks required of the automobile increased immeasurably. This Chevrolet of 1931 was designed to sell ices, ice cream, and other goodies. What is today considered commonplace was at that time a most unusual idea. The chassis was the standard type AE with a six-cylinder engine that was fitted with overhead valves. Displacement was 2,960 cc. This ice cream car can be seen at the Provinciaal Automobielmuseum Houthalen, Domaine de Kelchterhoef, Houthalen, Belgium.

DUESENBERG J TOURSTER   The Duesenberg brothers, Fred and August, were born in Germany and came to the United States in 1880. By 1905, Fred worked as a mechanic in his own garage and raced cars. The brothers built race cars until, in 1921, they showed their first passenger car to the public. In 1929, the Duesenberg Motors, Inc., Indianapolis plant introduced the "J." The 1931 Duesenberg J Tourster is shown. The car was a very high-performance machine, capable of accelerating from 10 mph. to 80 mph. in high gear in 22 seconds and from 5 mph. to 25 mph. in 5 seconds! The wheelbase was large— 142.5 inches. The price of the chassis with engine, fenders, bumpers, and six wheels was $8,500. Coachwork or body was extra as it was with the Rolls-Royce! Power was an eight-cylinder, inline, water-cooled, 420-cubic-inch-displacement engine of 265 hp. It was the largest straight-eight engine to power an American production automobile. Four valves per cylinder were fitted. The chassis weighed about 4,500 pounds and the completed car about 6,000 pounds. A model J Tourster can be seen at the Heritage Plantation of Sandwich, Sandwich, Massachusetts.

ROLLS-ROYCE CONTINENTAL ROADSTER   This Phantom II Continental Roadster, introduced by Rolls-Royce in 1930, was equipped with a higher compression engine and shorter wheelbase of 144 inches. This is the 1931 model with a body built by Young of Bromley. A great deal of engine smoothness was sacrificed in order to insure a 90-mph. speed.

PIERCE-ARROW TOURING Pierce-Arrow of Buffalo, New York, produced this beautiful touring car in 1931, and it is considered to be one of the finest U.S. cars. Notice the headlights built into the fenders and the bowman radiator insignia. The powerplant was an eight-cylinder, inline, L-head, water-cooled engine that developed 124 hp. Bore was $3\frac{7}{8}$ inches and stroke was $4\frac{3}{4}$ inches. The vertical vanes in front of the radiator were thermostatically controlled, opening when the engine was hot and closing when the engine was cold. This car can be seen at the Car and Carriage Caravan, Luray Caverns, Virginia.

FORD MODEL A PHAETON The Ford Model A for 1931 was basically the same as 1930, except that the windshield wipers were changed from electric to vacuum operation. The engine supports were heavier, the steering gear ratio changed from 11 to 1 to 13 to 1, and the brake drums were rolled instead of ground to shape. The Model A Phaeton as shown here was 153 inches long on a 103-inch wheelbase. It was available in any of five standard colors, which was a refreshing departure from older Fords which were available only in black. Engine and drive were the same as previous Model A cars.

NASH UTILITY SEDAN This 1931 Nash Utility Sedan was a standard eight-cylinder, two-door sedan with an added rear door, and the rear seats replaced by a wood-slat floor. It was the ancestor of the modern delivery van. The model was used for delivery of flowers, clothing, food, and other lightweight commodities.

BUICK SEDAN MODEL 90X This stately Buick 90X four-door sedan was produced in 1931 on a large 132-inch wheelbase. The seven-passenger car was powered by an eight-cylinder, inline, water-cooled, 345-cubic-inch-displacement engine that developed 35 hp. Bore was $3\frac{5}{16}$ inches, and stroke was 5 inches. The design, epitome of elegance in its time, featured wire spoke wheels, a fender-mounted spare tire, and a sun visor.

MERCEDES-BENZ TYPE 720 SSKL   The fiercest Mercedes-Benz was the SSKL, which made its appearance in 1929 and was made until 1934. The S meant supercharged, the K meant *Kurz* or short, and the L meant *Leicht* or light. The car could exceed 140 mph. and won the Mille Miglia in 1931. It also won the German Grand Prix and the Eifelrennen as well as the Polish Grand Prix in that year. The car finished in second place in the 1931 24-Hour Le Mans Race. The blown engine developed 300 hp. at 3,500 to 4,000 rpm., and the chassis was drilled to make the car lighter. Mercedes-Benz took the European Hill-Climb Championship in 1931 with the SSKL!

FORD B DIRT TRACK RACER   When the Ford Motor Company developed its V-8 engine, the firm again became interested in racing. Collaborating with racing car designer Henry A. Miller, several designs, including this front-wheel-drive racer, were developed using the new engine. This is the 1932 Ford B Dirt Track Racer that used a flathead V-8 and was successful in minor races in the U.S. during that period.

MILLER-HARTZ SPECIAL Miller-engined cars won every Indianapolis 500-Mile Race from 1930 to 1938. This Miller Hartz was developed by H. A. Miller and Harry Hartz and won the 1932 Indianapolis Race with Fred Frame at the wheel. This car featured front-wheel drive and was powered by an eight-cylinder, inline, water-cooled engine of 183-cubic-inch displacement.

TERRAPLANE SEDAN In July, 1932, Hudson introduced the new Terraplane line of cars to replace the regular Essex series whose sales had sagged. For some time both names were used for the same car until the full Terraplane line could be developed, and the transition was so gradual that the Terraplane was often called the Essex Terraplane. This Terraplane Sedan used many Essex parts and was aimed at the economy market with prices as low as $425. A Terraplane Roadster won the annual Pikes Peak Hill-Climb in September of 1932, and established a stock car record of 21 minutes, 21 seconds.

ESSEX TOWN SEDAN   The Depression was a bad time for automobile manufacturers, and 1932 was the last year for Hudson's Essex series. This Essex Town Sedan of 1932 was one of the last to bear the Essex name. In an attempt to recoup its losses between 1929 and 1932, Hudson management decided to replace the Essex with the new and sportier Terraplane in 1932.

AUBURN BOAT-TAIL SPEEDSTER   E. L. Cord became president of the Auburn Automobile Company, Auburn, Indiana. Like Stutz and Duesenberg, he believed in high-performance cars. This 1932 8-100 Boat-Tail Speedster was one of the classic Auburn cars. It was powered by a vee, twelve-cylinder engine that developed 160 hp. The car was built on a 133-inch wheelbase. The Lycoming-built engine had a 391-cubic-inch displacement. In July, 1932, a fully equipped Speedster covered the measured mile at Muroc Dry Lake at an average speed of 100.77 mph. It also completed 500 miles at an average speed of 89 mph. and covered 92.2 miles in one hour! Despite performance, good looks, and reliability, the cars stopped production in 1936.

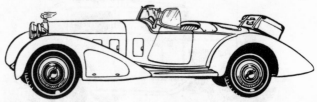

DELAGE D8.S TORPEDO Louis Delage began producing automobiles in 1906 and was well known for his racing cars. His later efforts were excellent touring and sports models, although he continued with his successful racers. This outstanding Delage D8.S Torpedo of 1932 was beautiful not only in appearance but also in performance. Like many quality car makers of the period, Delage made the engine and chassis only. This body was the work of Le Tourneur et Marchand. Mainly a two-seater, a portion of the deck was removable to reveal two more seats. Power was an eight-cylinder, inline, water-cooled, supercharged, 4,050-cc-displacement engine that could propel the car to 130 mph. The wheelbase was 11 feet 11 inches. A D8.S can be seen in the Musée de la Carrosserie Française, Puerto de Andraitx, Mallorca, Spain.

DELAGE D8.S CONVERTIBLE This Delage D8.S Cabriolet Décapotable (convertible) was produced in 1932 and 1933. The body was made by Henri Chapron and could seat four comfortably. The Delage eight-cylinder, supercharged engine was fitted. Bore was 77 mm. and stroke was 109 mm. It was water-cooled and had overhead valves. The wheelbase was 10 feet 10 inches. Four-speed transmission was provided. Despite the high quality of Delage automobiles, the firm went bankrupt in 1929 and was absorbed by Delahaye in 1935.

ROLLS-ROYCE SPORT TOWN SEDAN This 1932 Phantom II Sport Town Sedan combined elegance with a sporty-looking car. The chassis and engine were basically the same as the Phantom I, except for semi-elliptic rear springs, and a 5¼ to 1 compression ratio, which increased the engine output to about 60 hp. The gearbox was also built into the engine. The 150½-inch wheelbase and overall length of about 190 inches gave the car a very comfortable ride. A car of this type can be seen at the Classic Car Showcase, Houston, Texas.

PEERLESS SEDAN Pierce-Arrow, Packard, and Peerless were known as the "three P's" and considered the aristocracy of auto manufacturing in vintage U.S. motoring circles. The Peerless Motor Car Company, Cleveland, Ohio, produced this vee-type, twelve-cylinder-engine-powered, four-door sedan in 1932 as a last ditch effort to bolster lagging sales. The year proved to be the company's last. A 1932 Peerless Sedan can be seen in the Frederick C. Crawford Auto-Aviation Museum, Cleveland, Ohio.

RENAULT REINASTELLA   This Renault Reinastella Type RM2 four-door sedan of 1932 featured an aluminum body and fenders. It was powered by an eight-cylinder, inline, water-cooled, 41-hp., 7,125-cc-displacement engine. Bore was 90 mm. and stroke was 140 mm. Speed was about 90 mph. Renault had given up its distinctive sloping hood by this time and followed the straight-hood design used by most manufacturers.

NASH MODEL 971 CONVERTIBLE   This Nash Model 971 Convertible of 1932 was one of the first automobiles to be fitted with spotlights. The lights were made by the Lorraine Corporation of Chicago. One or two spotlights were fitted as desired by the purchaser. The car was powered by an eight-cylinder, overhead-valve, 5-liter-displacement engine that developed about 40 hp.

GRAHAM BLUE STREAK SEDAN   The Graham Brothers bought the Paige-Detroit firm, and after calling the cars Graham Paige for three years, the name was shortened to Graham in 1930. This 1932 Graham was truly distinctive because it was the first U.S. car to use front-fender skirts, and the chassis side-frame had banjo openings to provide greater strength and a better ride. Shock absorbers plus springs were installed. The powerplant was an eight-cylinder, inline, L-head made of aluminum, with a 245-cubic-inch displacement that developed 90 hp. at 3,400 rpm. A new design, straight-through muffler was used. The wheelbase was 123 inches. A Graham Blue Streak crossed the continent in 53 hours and 30 minutes in 1932 for a new record. Also in the same year, a Graham established a new record by climbing to the summit of Mount Washington, New Hampshire, in 13 minutes 26 seconds! Price of the car was $1,220.

WILLYS-KNIGHT SEDAN   The last Willys-Knight was introduced in 1932 and was kept in production for three years. The sleeve-valve, Knight-patented engine was apparently not considered a big enough attraction to potential customers. This last Willys-Knight engine developed 87 hp. The four-door sedan shown was priced at $1,395.

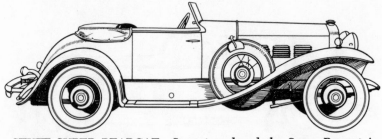

STUTZ SUPER BEARCAT Stutz introduced the Super Bearcat in 1932. This was a two-seater convertible built on a 116-inch wheelbase and was guaranteed to attain 100 mph. It was powered by the DV-32 eight-cylinder, double-overhead-camshaft, water-cooled, 322-cubic-inch-displacement, inline, 156-hp. at 3,900 rpm. engine that had four valves per cylinder. This engine was used in establishing a new Pikes Peak Hill-Climb record of 16 minutes, 47 seconds in 1932. The car could attain 32 mph. in 11 seconds in first gear, 64 mph. in 6 seconds in second gear, and 100 mph. in 4 seconds in third gear.

FORD V-8 After manufacturing more than forty-five million Model A cars between 1927 and 1931, the Ford Motor Company introduced the Ford V-8 in 1932. The change was caused by consumer demands for more luxury and power. Ford became the first company successfully to cast a one-piece V-8 engine block. The engine produced 65 hp. The body was well-made with more rounded corners. Price was $600. The design remained basically the same for ten years.

DUESENBERG SJ SPORTS PHAETON The Duesenberg SJ was built on a 153.5-inch wheelbase and was powered by basically the same engine as the "J," developing about 320 hp. This is the 1932 SJ Sports Phaeton, which was equipped with a supercharger. Duesenberg bodies were built by the Walter M. Murphy Company, Willoughby Company, Union City Body Company, Weymann American Company, Holbrook Company, Le Baron, and others in the U.S. and Europe. The average price of a completed Duesenberg was about $16,500. It was said that no one passed a Duesenberg. The big, beautiful, and powerful cars were magnificent. Fred Duesenberg died when the SJ he was driving crashed.

ALVIS SPEED TWENTY The T. G. John, Ltd., Company of Coventry, England, produced the Alvis Speed Twenty in 1932 and the car remained in production until 1934. Unlike previous Alvis models, the Speed Twenty was fitted with rear-wheel drive. The powerplant was a six-cylinder, inline, water-cooled, 2.5-liter-displacement, 85-hp. engine that drove the car to about 110 mph. An Alvis Speed Twenty can be seen at the Automuseum Nettelstedt, Lübeck, Germany.

LAGONDA M45 4½ LITERS   Lagonda, Ltd., of Staines, Middlesex, England, introduced this formidable sportster in 1933 and produced it until 1935 when it won the Le Mans 24-Hour Race. The wheelbase was 10 feet 9 inches and the overall length was 15 feet 6 inches. The powerplant was a six-cylinder, overhead-valve, pressure-lubricated, 115-hp., 4,453-cc-displacement, water-cooled engine. Four forward speeds plus reverse were fitted. Suspension was by means of semi-elliptic springs, front and rear.

NASH MODEL 1181 CABRIOLET   Nash produced this Model 1181 advanced eight Cabriolet in 1933. The automobile was intended to bolster Nash's sagging sales during the Depression. The four-seater weighed 3,750 pounds and sold for $1,395. The sporty car failed to take Nash out of its losing streak, because the company lost $1,188,863 in 1933!

INVICTA S   Invicta Cars, Cobham, England, first introduced their automobiles in England in 1924. Five years later the Type S was developed, and in this design the chassis swept up over the front axle. In 1930, the car won the Alpine Cup and made the fastest time in the Arlberg Hill-Climb. It also won the Glacier Cup and the International Alpine Trials during the same year. In 1931, the Invicta S captured the Monte Carlo Rallye and placed second in 1932. Designer Donald Healey won the 1933 Mont-des-Mules Hill-Climb. A six-cylinder, overhead-valve, water-cooled, 4,467-cc-displacement engine with two spark plugs per cylinder drove the car in excess of 100 mph. The engine was fitted with aluminum pistons and crankcase. The wheelbase was 9 feet 10 inches and the tread was 4 feet 8 inches. The 1933 Invicta Type S is shown. Invicta S cars were winning at Silverstone as late as 1966, despite the fact that Invicta ceased production in 1936! A car of this type can be seen at the Silver Springs Early American Museum, Silver Springs, Florida.

CHRYSLER CUSTOM IMPERIAL   Built on a 146-inch wheelbase, the Chrysler Custom Imperial for 1933 introduced an all-helical-gear transmission to the auto industry. The double-cowl phaeton body by Le Baron is shown. The car was powered by an eight-cylinder, L-head, 135-hp., water-cooled, inline, 385-cubic-inch-displacement engine. Also fitted was an accelerator-pedal starter.

TERRAPLANE CONVERTIBLE COUPÉ The Hudson Motor Car Company's low-priced line of Terraplanes helped the company through the Depression. This is the Terraplane Convertible Coupé of 1933, which featured an eight-cylinder, inline, water-cooled engine. During 1933, Hudson sold 40,982 automobiles, thanks to the Terraplane.

PIERCE-ARROW SILVER ARROW This elegant Pierce-Arrow Silver Arrow was made in 1933 and was years ahead in the superb styling still used by some manufacturers today. Power was a 175-hp., water-cooled, vee-type, twelve-cylinder engine. Price of the car was $10,000! In the previous year, a twelve-cylinder Pierce-Arrow was driven for 24 hours on the Utah Salt Flats at an average speed of 113 mph.! At this time Pierce-Arrow was a subsidiary of Studebaker, and, because of continued losses, Pierce-Arrow production ended in 1938. A car of this type can be seen at Harrah's Automobile Collection, Reno, Nevada.

CADILLAC ROADSTER Cadillac introduced a sixteen-cylinder engine, designed by Charles F. Kettering, in 1930 to combat the Marmon, Duesenberg, and Pierce-Arrow powerplants. This Cadillac Roadster of 1933 had the big new engine. Cadillac made the engine, chassis, and drive, while Fleetwood made the body. The wheelbase was 143 inches, and only 400 cars, all with custom bodies, were built that year. Price was about $5,000. The powerplant was a vee-type, sixteen-cylinder, water-cooled, 165-hp. engine of 453-cubic-inch displacement. The car was sporty with an elegant look. Note the skirted front fenders, externally mounted chrome horns, and long hood.

WILLYS MODEL 77 Willys felt the pains of the Depression and developed the Model 77 to sell for the very low price of $445, in an effort to bolster sales in 1933. It was powered by a four-cylinder, water-cooled, inline, 48-hp. engine.

BMW 315 ROADSTER This is the first BMW sports car: the 315 Roadster introduced in 1934. The company, Bavarian Motor Works (hence BMW), was formed early during World War I in Munich, Germany, to build engines for fighter planes of the Imperial Air Service. BMW began building motorcycles in 1919 and built its first car in 1928, which was an Austin Seven made under license. This "315" was also made as a closed family car. The roadster was powered by a six-cylinder, inline, water-cooled, 34-hp. engine of 1,490-cc displacement. The "315" captured the 1934 Austrian Alpine Trial. In 1935 the car won the Nürburgring Race. An assortment of lesser races were also won by the type. A 1936 BMW 315 Roadster can be seen at the Automuseum Nettelstedt, Lübeck, Germany.

LAFAYETTE 110 Nash Motors Company reintroduced the new low-priced Lafayette line in 1934, in an attempt to draw away buyers from Ford and Chevrolet. The wheelbase was 113 inches, and power was a six-cylinder, water-cooled, L-head, 75-hp. engine. The 1934 Model 110 Four-Door Sedan is shown. Lafayette prices ranged from $585 to $745.

MASERATI RACER The three Maserati brothers operated a race-car tuning shop in Bologna, Italy, in the early twenties. They specialized in the Diatto racers for which they also built engines. In 1926, the brothers started designing and building racing cars that became world-famous. This is the Maserati 8CM3000 of 1934 that was developed in the previous year. In 1933, the 8C cars won the French Grand Prix, Belgian Grand Prix, Nice Grand Prix, and the Coppa Ciano. The 8C cars were raced until 1939 with progressively enlarged engine installations, and won the Mille Miglia and Monaco Grand Prix in 1935. The 8C was powered by an eight-cylinder, water-cooled, inline engine of 2,992-cc displacement. This car was also fitted with hydraulic brakes, and later models had all-around independent suspension.

FORD V-8 TUDOR SEDAN This Ford V-8 Tudor Sedan was produced in 1934, the second year of the Ford V-8 engine. Henry Ford had jumped from the four-cylinder engine to the eight, because he hated six-cylinder engines due to the failure of his six-cylinder Model K in 1906. The V-8 was a great success and was Ford's answer to the Chevrolet sixes. It set the pace for the U.S. automobiles for decades. The word "vee-eight" was used in most automobile advertising for many years. This car can be seen at the Veteran Car Museum, Denver, Colorado.

TATRA 77   After working as designer with Gräf & Stift, with Nessel-dorfer, and as technical manager with Styr, Hans Ledwinka returned to Nesseldorfer. Nesseldorfer had been renamed Tatra, for the range of mountains in Czechoslovakia. The innovative designer made several sensational designs, and in 1934 produced this unusual Tatra 77 four-door sedan. The streamlined body was supported by a vertical back-bone frame on a 124-inch wheelbase. Power was an eight-cylinder, air-cooled, vee-type 3.4-liter-displacement engine. The engine was mounted in the rear and developed 70 hp., driving the car over 90 mph. Overhead camshafts were used. Four forward speeds were installed. The body was of monocoque construction and accommodated six passengers. Three headlights were used. Note the air scoops to cool the engine.

CHRYSLER AIRFLOW CUSTOM IMPERIAL   The Model CW shown here was the longest of the three Airflow Imperials with a 146½-inch wheelbase. The 1934 design featured a streamlined body with built-in headlights that was years ahead of its time, but failed to generate the expected sales. Other firsts were balanced-weight distribu-tion, synchronized front and rear springs, automatic overdrive, stabilizer bar, one-piece curved windshield on some models, and the use of high-strength, carbon-moly steel. Power was an eight-cylinder, inline, water-cooled, L-head, 150-hp. engine of 385-cubic-inch displacement. A CV Airflow Imperial, slightly smaller than the Model CW, established 72 stock car speed records during a one-day run at the Utah Salt Flats. The CV Airflow had a wheelbase of 128 inches.

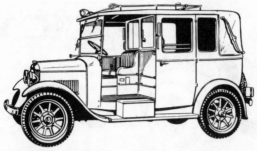

AUSTIN LONDON TAXICAB The Austin Motor Company, Birmingham, England, built this London taxicab to the rigid specifications of the London Passenger Transport Board. The body style of this 1934 auto is landaulet. In order to navigate through some of the narrow London streets, the car had a very small turning circle. It was powered by a four-cylinder, water-cooled, 1,661-cc displacement engine that developed 12 hp. Maximum road speed was 40 mph. The car accommodated four passengers, and luggage was stowed next to the driver. This London taxi can be seen at the Long Island Automotive Museum, Southampton, New York.

BREWSTER TOWN CAR The famous coachwork firm of Brewster designed and built this town car for Charlie Chaplin in 1934 and delivered it to the comedian in 1935. The car was built on a Ford V-8 chassis and was powered by an eight-cylinder, water-cooled, inline Continental engine because Brewster built neither chassis nor engines. The heart-shaped radiator frame was burnished aluminum alloy. The interior of this custom-built auto was most luxurious. The chassis cost $700 while the body sold for $15,000! Wealthy people did not want to be seen riding in an inexpensive Ford, so they bought the chassis and had Brewster custom-build the body. The car can be seen at the Forney Historic Transportation Museum, Denver, Colorado.

WILLYS MODEL 77   In an effort to improve the awkward appearance of the 1933 Model 77, in the following year Willys changed the louvered hood vents into five portholes on each side. The holes were trimmed in chrome to make the cheap car look more expensive. The Model 77 ended in 1935, when it was selling for $415!

NASH AMBASSADOR CONVERTIBLE   The one-millionth Nash automobile was produced in 1934. This 1934 Nash Ambassador Convertible was the top of the line model, built on a 142-inch wheelbase. The six-passenger car weighed about 4,500 pounds and was powered by an eight-cylinder, inline, water-cooled engine. The price was about $2,000.

M.G. TYPE NA MAGNETTE The M.G. Car Company, Ltd., Abingdon-on-Thames, England, introduced its Type NA Magnette in 1934. This two-seater was built on a 96-inch wheelbase and 45-inch tread. It was powered by a six-cylinder, water-cooled, 1,271-cc-displacement engine. A four-speed transmission was installed. The NA was the sports version, while the somewhat similar NE was designed for racing. The latter scored first prizes at Eifelrennen, the Empire Trophy Race, American A.C. Grand Prix, Bol d'Or 24-Hour Race, Circuit of Modena, Grand Prix de France, and others in 1934.

PLYMOUTH WESTCHESTER SUBURBAN Built on a 113-inch wheelbase, this four-door, six-passenger Plymouth Westchester Suburban was produced in 1935 and was one of the most luxurious wagons of the period. It was powered by a six-cylinder, inline, water-cooled, 85-hp., 201-cubic-inch-displacement engine. The water jacket extended the full length of the cylinder instead of only around the combustion chamber. "Chair height" seats were installed for comfort, as was a ride-stabilizer bar.

HUDSON SIX CONVERTIBLE COUPÉ In 1935, Hudson introduced several innovations in its line. One of these was the "Electric Hand" device that shifted gears by vacuum power. A small fingertip lever actuated solenoids which opened and closed the vacuum valves to perform the shifting. Another new item was "Axle-Flex," which improved riding on rough roads. An automatic choke was also featured. Despite losses in 1934, Hudson realized a half-million-dollar profit in 1935 and paid off its creditors. 1935 was the last year for the long, narrow hood. In 1936, the bulbous look was introduced, molding the fenders into the hood.

ASTON MARTIN MARK II This four-seat tourer was the Aston Martin Mark II and was the 1935 successor of the famous "International." The car is often referred to as the Ulster. In 1935, the type won the Mille Miglia, placed twelfth at Le Mans, and third in the Targa Abruzzo. The powerplant was a 1,500-cc-displacement, four-cylinder, water-cooled, inline engine with overhead camshaft and two carburetors.

SQUIRE SPORTSTER   Adrian Morgan Squire made only seven Sportsters in England between 1934 and 1939. His product, however, is considered to be a classic sports car. The car was very expensive, because Squire was aiming at the ideal sportster. Workmanship was excellent even if the design was conventional. The 1935 Squire Sportster with a Vanden Plas body is shown. It was powered by an Anzani R1, four-cylinder, water-cooled, overhead-camshaft, supercharged, 1,496-cc-displacement, 110-hp. engine. Two water pumps and an oil cooler were installed. The car could exceed 110 mph. and could reach 75 mph. in 15 seconds. Private owners raced the car, and one placed third in a Mountain Handicap in 1935.

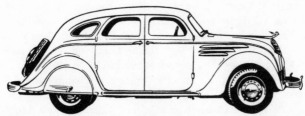

DeSOTO AIRFLOW SG   Production of this DeSoto Airflow began in November, 1934, and ended in September, 1935. It was a companion car to the Chrysler Airflow and was built on a 115½-inch wheelbase. A 100-hp., six-cylinder, water-cooled, inline engine of 241½-cubic-inch displacement was installed. An anti-sway stabilizer bar was fitted in the front of the car. A hypoid rear axle was used. In 1935, the DeSoto Airflow won the coveted Grand Prix Award for aerodynamic styling at the Concours d'Élégance at Monte Carlo.

AUTO UNION RACER   After Auto Union was formed in Zwickau, Germany, in 1932, by the fusion of Horch, Audi, DKW, and Wanderer, it decided to take up Grand Prix racing with the encouragement of the German government. They adopted a rear-engine design by Ferdinand Porsche, and this became the first make successfully to race a rear-engined Grand Prix car. In 1934, the car placed third in the AVUS Grand Prix, second in the Eifelrennen, and won the German Grand Prix, Czech Grand Prix, and Swiss Grand Prix. In 1935, the car won the Tunis G.P., Czech G.P., Italian G.P., and the Coppa Acerbo. The 1936 season saw the design win the Eifel, German, Swiss, Tripoli, Pescara and Italian G.P., and the European Championship! The results were similar in 1937. The Auto Union Type B Racer of 1935 is shown here. It had a wheelbase of 9 feet 2 inches and a 4-foot-8-inch tread. Power was a sixteen-cylinder, vee, water-cooled, 4.9-liter, 370-hp. engine fitted with a Roots supercharger. This car set a trend so strong that virtually every modern racing machine is rear-engine fitted!

BLUEBIRD RECORD RACER   One of the greatest milestones in man's attempt to achieve constantly increasing speed was the late Sir Malcolm Campbell's beautiful Bluebird record breaker. Campbell supervised the design and construction, which was accomplished by Sunbeam, Rolls-Royce, and Thompson and Taylor in England. The 2,500-hp. Rolls-Royce V-12 engine powered Bluebird to a record-breaking speed of 276.816 mph. on the sands of Daytona Beach in 1935. So great was the speed that the tires required replacement after each run. In August, 1935, Sir Malcolm Campbell broke his own record with 301.13 mph. at the Utah Salt Flats. Although this record was exceeded later, the Bluebird will always be remembered as the first land vehicle to exceed 300 mph. The car was 30 feet long and weighed five tons. The car can be seen at the Museum of Speed, Daytona Beach, Florida.

BUGATTI SURBAISSE The Bugatti Type 57 Surbaisse was designed in 1934 and remained in limited production until 1940; shown here is a 1936 model. During those six years 750 autos of this type were constructed, virtually by hand, with select variations for each customer. The total is less than a single week of Corvette production! Ettore Bugatti took great pride in every product of his Molsheim, France, works, and this sports car is one of his finest—a true classic in both appearance and operation. Among the owners of the Type 57 was Sir Malcolm Campbell, famous world speed record holder, who claimed that the Surbaisse was the "best all-around super sports car." The engine was a straight-eight-cylinder type of 3,257-cc displacement. Bore was 72 mm. and stroke 100 mm. Double overhead camshafts were gear-driven from the crankshaft. Dual-coil ignition was used. Pistons were made from aluminum. The engine developed 140 hp. at 4,800 rpm. The four-speed gearbox led to the rear axle via open shaft to a 4.16 to 1 final ratio. A competition version won the 1939 Le Mans. Jean Bugatti, Ettore's son, was testing this car on a reserved road for the Grand Prix at La Baule, when, at over 100 mph., he tried to avoid a drunkard on a bicycle and smashed into a tree. He was killed instantly. Ettore Bugatti died six years later and thus the Type 57 was the last of the production Bugattis, never to be forgotten.

SS JAGUAR TOURER   The partnership of William Lyons and William Walmesly in 1922 in Blackpool, England, started building sidecars for motorcycles, and within a few years established the Swallow Coachbuilding Company, Ltd. They built bodies on chassis supplied by Fiat, Wolseley, Standard, and Austin. In 1932, Lyons began production of long, sleek sports cars, and called them SS Jaguar. The SS meant Swallow Sports. Lyons moved to Coventry in the early thirties and produced this car in 1936. Power was a six-cylinder, inline, water-cooled, 90-hp., 2.5-liter engine that drove the car to a top speed of 94 mph. This car can be seen at the Automuseum Nettlestedt, Lübeck, Germany.

CHRYSLER LIMOUSINE   This Chrysler Limousine of 1936 was built on a 121-inch wheelbase. The side-fender-mounted spare tire was not standard, but used only on limousines in 1936. Power was an eight-cylinder, 110-hp., inline, water-cooled, 273.5-cubic-inch-displacement engine. This basic body design was called the Airstream to distinguish it from the Airflow.

LAFAYETTE MODEL 3612   After failing with the Lafayette in 1929, Nash revived the make in the early thirties as a low-priced car. This Lafayette Model 3612 three-passenger coupé was manufactured in 1936, and was the lowest-priced at $595 of all 1936 Lafayette models. The car was six-cylinder-engine-powered, and helped Nash to realize a profit of $1,020,708 for 1936.

NASH MODEL 3640   Nash introduced an unusual innovation in 1936. Shown is the 1936 Model 3640 Four-Door Sedan, which gave the purchaser the choice of a trunk or convertible beds! The rear seats of this four-seater were easily and quickly adaptable to a double bed simply by extending them into the trunk area. The idea caused a sensation.

GRAHAM CRUSADER   The Graham Crusader made its appearance in 1936, and the four-door sedan is shown here. Power was a six-cylinder, 218-cubic-inch-displacement engine with an optional centrifugal blower or supercharger. In the following year, an English body was mounted on the Graham chassis, and the British Lammas-Graham was built for a few years. A Graham won the last race at Brooklands in the summer of 1939.

ALVIS SPORTS SALOON   This Alvis two-door Sports Saloon is closely related to the Speed 25 Sports Tourer. It was developed in 1936 and featured independent front-wheel suspension. Power was a 4.3-liter, water-cooled, overhead-valve, eight-cylinder engine. All four forward gears were synchronized, and the car could attain over 100 mph.

CHEVROLET BUSINESS COUPÉ This two-seater Chevrolet Coupé of 1936 was welcomed by businessmen, because of its extra-large trunk that extended to the back of the seats. Power was a six-cylinder, overhead-valve, inline, water-cooled engine of 74 hp. at 3,200 rpm. Displacement was 206.8 cubic inches. Maximum speed was over 80 mph. Optional equipment included independent front suspension.

TOYOTA NO. 1 AB The Japanese Toyota firm began manufacturing motor vehicles in 1936. Their first products were a four-door sedan known as Model AA and a four-door touring car known as Model AB. The Touring Model AB is shown. Similar cars followed: the Model AE in 1939, and Models AC and BA in 1943. By 1953, Toyota was producing 16,500 units per year, and, by 1960, 154,000 Toyotas had been built. The figure jumped to 1,097,405 units and in 1969 to 1,200,000 vehicles.

PIERCE-ARROW LIMOUSINE The luxurious Pierce-Arrow Seven-Passenger Limousine of 1936 was built on a 147-inch wheelbase. It was the Model 1603, which was powered by the Pierce-Arrow V-12 engine that developed 185 hp. Note the one-piece flat windshield and headlights that fair into the fenders.

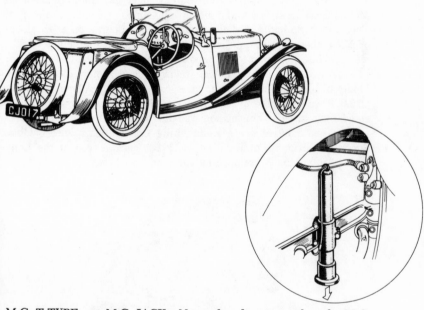

M.G. T TYPE AND M.G. JACK No car has done more than the M.G. T-Type Midget to make owning a sports car within the reach of people of all ages and of all incomes. This is the M.G.-TA of 1936, built on a 94-inch wheelbase with an overall length of 12 feet. Weight was 1,155 pounds. Power was a four-cylinder, inline, water-cooled, overhead-valve, twin-carburetor engine of 1,250-cc displacement. The basic T-Type design continued until the advent of the TF in 1953, with engine and chassis modifications. Also shown here is the M.G. optional hydraulic jack. One was fitted at each corner of the car and operated at the push of a button.

FIFTH AVENUE DOUBLE-DECK BUS The New York City Fifth Avenue double-deck bus was, for several decades, an attraction for tourists as well as an excellent mode of transportation in Manhattan. This is the 1937 Yellow Coach 83-Passenger Bus built by General Motors Coach and Truck Manufacturing Company, Pontiac, Michigan. The Model 735 had a loaded weight of 32,560 pounds on a wheelbase of 217 inches. The overall length was 33 feet, and the height was 13 feet 2 inches. Compressed air brakes were used. The bus had space for 71 seats and 12 standees. Power was a General Motors diesel engine Model 671, six-cylinder, inline, water-cooled, and developing 165 hp. at 2,000 rpm. Displacement was 671 cubic inches with a 5-inch bore and 6-inch stroke. Transmission was automatic hydraulic drive transmission made by Spicer Manufacturing Corporation, Toledo, Ohio. Speed was over 50 mph. This famous bus can be seen at the Long Island Automotive Museum, Southampton, New York.

FORD V-8 TUDOR Since its introduction in 1932, the Ford V-8 was the darling of performance-minded Americans, and this Tudor Sedan was one of the most popular models. Styling had been improved over previous years with a new grille and recessed headlights. The engine produced 65 hp.

MERCEDES TYPE 770K GROSSE   Two Type 770K Grosse (big) Mercedes were built for Adolf Hitler in 1937. They were the only cars personally owned by the dictator, and he used them for parades and for motoring to his retreat. The cars were built to his specifications and weighed five tons each on a 153-inch wheelbase! The seating for seven or eight was fitted with armor plating. Power was an eight-cylinder, supercharged, inline, water-cooled engine that could develop 230 hp. Four-wheel independent suspension, a one-shot lubricating system, and five-speed transmission were fitted. A platform was built into the right passenger compartment so the Führer would appear taller when standing in the car during parades or reviews! One of the cars was recently bought at auction for $153,000. A Mercedes 770K can be seen at the Museum of Transportation, Larz Anderson Park, Brookline, Massachusetts.

PACKARD-PIERCE   This car has a 1917 Pierce-Arrow body on a 1937 Packard chassis and is a one-of-a-kind combination. The original owner was satisfied with his 1917 Pierce-Arrow limousine until the chassis began to wear out after many years. Not pleased with the newer body styling, he had the body placed on a new Pierce-Arrow chassis. Many years later this chassis began to go, so the body was again removed and placed on a 1937 Packard chassis, with its Packard hood and fenders. It was driven this way for fourteen years. The Packard chassis has a 144-inch wheelbase and was powered by a twelve-cylinder, vee, water-cooled, 473-cubic-inch-displacement, 175-hp. engine. Independent front-wheel suspension was fitted. The car was driven by the same chauffeur throughout its life. It can be seen at The Museum of Automobiles, Morrilton, Arkansas.

KDF-WAGEN (Volkswagen Prototype)   In 1934, Chancellor Adolf Hitler of Germany announced that a people's automobile (*Volksauto*) would be made available so that the average German could afford a car. He invited Dr. Ferdinand Porsche to Berlin where the two men outlined their ideas in the Kaiserhof Hotel. The car was to seat four, have an air-cooled engine located in the rear, maintain 60 mph., and cost not more than $620. After much frustrating effort the first Volksauto appeared in 1937 and is illustrated here. Notice that rear windows were omitted and the door opened from the front, but this was remedied the next year. Because the German government had financed the design and the Strength through Joy or *Kraft durch Freude* (KdF) workers movement was to sponsor production, the first car was called the "KdF-Wagen." Only about 250 were built before World War II began. After the war the car was placed in production as the Volkswagen and enjoyed by millions.

BUICK ROADMASTER SEDAN   By 1937 Buicks had curved radiator grilles, shapely bodies, and built-in trunks. This is the 1937 Buick Roadmaster Four-Door Sedan Model 91. The six-passenger car was powered by the new Dynaflash eight-cylinder 320-cubic-inch-displacement engine that developed 38 hp. The wheelbase was 131 inches, and suspension featured coil springs on all wheels for a better ride.

TALBOT-LAGO T150SS The British Talbot Company of London was originally the Clement-Talbot Company in 1903. By 1908, Talbot was one of the leading exponents of the high-speed engine, and the make scored many racing successes. This beautiful Talbot-Lago T150SS featured a body by Figani-Falaschi and was made in 1937. It was fitted with a six-cylinder, inline, water-cooled, 3,377-cc-displacement, 123-hp., overhead-valve engine that gave the car a speed of over 150 mph. The wheelbase was 9 feet 6 inches and could seat two. The car was intended for competition at Le Mans, but there is no record of it racing in the classic.

CORD 812 PHAETON   With the original Cord production dropped in 1932 because of poor sales, the parent Auburn Company searched frantically for a new design. Gordon Buehrig, who had designed bodies for Peerless and Wills Sainte Claire as well as the Duesenberg "J" types, went to Auburn and designed the Cord 810, which soon developed into the Cord 812 of 1937. The style was breathtaking, with a long hood fitted with continuous horizontal louvers and retractable headlights. Power was an eight-cylinder, 289-cubic-inch-displacement, vee, water-cooled Lycoming engine that developed 125 hp. at 3,500 rpm. Bore was 3.5 inches and stroke was 3.75 inches. The car could accelerate from 0 to 60 mph. in 13 seconds. A supercharger was optional and gave the car a speed of over 100 mph. Front-wheel drive was used, and the car was fitted with an electrically preselected vacuum-operated gearshift. But 1937 was the last production year for Cord, because only 6,725 cars were sold in six years of production. A 1937 Cord can be seen at the Heritage Plantation of Sandwich, Sandwich, Massachusetts.

RENAULT JUVAQUATRE   This small, economy Renault Juvaquatre Type AEB-1 two-door, four-seater was produced between 1937 and 1939. It was powered by a four-cylinder, 1,003-cc-displacement, water-cooled, inline engine that developed about 12 hp. The car had a speed of about 75 mph., and fuel economy was 39 miles per gallon.

BENTLEY 3½ LITER ROADSTER This Bentley 3½ Liter Sport Roadster was introduced in 1933 and progressively refined up to World War II. This is the 1938 model with a body built by Park-Ward on a 10-foot-6-inch wheelbase. The overall length was 14 feet 6 inches. Power was a 3,669-cc-displacement, six-cylinder, water-cooled, inline, 110-hp. engine. The crankshaft had seven bearings and the compression ratio was 6.5 to 1. Twin carburetors and dual electric fuel pumps were fitted. The radiator shutters were thermostatically controlled by the temperature of the engine so that they closed when cold and opened when hot. The chassis weighed about 2,250 pounds.

HUDSON TERRAPLANE CONVERTIBLE The Terraplane began in 1932 as the Essex Terraplane but was soon called simply Terraplane. Sales were so good that the parent company, Hudson Motors, decided to add their name to the successful newcomer. This Hudson Terraplane was produced in 1938 on a 117-inch wheelbase. The six-cylinder, inline, water-cooled engine developed 101 hp. and had a 6.25 to 1 compression ratio. The car could seat five.

BMW 328 SPORTS ROADSTER The Bavarian Motor Works produced this model of the 328 Sports Roadster in 1938. It was developed from the BMW winner of the 1937 Eifelrennen at Nürburgring. Power was a six-cylinder, 1.9-liter, water-cooled, inline, 80-hp. engine fitted with overhead valves. Fritz Fielder designed the engine. The car could easily pass the 100-mph. mark. This design won the Tourist Trophy, Bucharest Grand Prix, German Grand Prix, Tobruk-Benghazi-Tripoli Race, Le Mans, and Mille Miglia in 1938–1939! The type is on display at the Briggs Cunningham Automotive Museum, Costa Mesa, California, and at the Automuseum Nettelstedt, Lübeck, Germany.

FRAZER-NASH BMW During the twenties and thirties Frazer-Nash manufactured sports cars that were well-made, good-looking, and functional. Attracted by the success of the 1938 BMW 328, Frazer-Nash obtained a licensing agreement with the Bavarian Motor Works to produce the car in Britain as a Frazer-Nash BMW. Although built in Britain, the car had a left-hand drive. All other features were the same as the BMW 328.

SS JAGUAR 100 The SS Jaguar 100 was developed from the SS Jaguar and was built from 1936 to 1939; shown here is a 1938 model. It is regarded as one of the truly classic sports cars. Power was a six-cylinder, water-cooled, overhead-valve, twin-carburetor, 3.5 liters displacement engine that developed 125 hp. at 4,250 rpm. The car weighed 2,575 pounds on a 104-inch wheelbase. Speed was over 100 mph. About three hundred SS 100 Jaguars were sold up to the beginning of World War II. A car of this type can be seen at the Danmarks Tekniske Museum, Helsingør, Denmark.

MAYBACH SW 38 Maybach produced this SW 38 four-door phaeton in 1938. As with most Maybach machines, it was large and powerful. Power was a six-cylinder, inline, water-cooled, 3.8-liter-displacement, 140-hp. engine. The car could exceed 100 mph. When World War II began in 1939, Maybach auto production stopped.

ALFA ROMEO SPYDER   This 8C 2900B Alfa Romeo Spyder two-seat sports car was made in 1938, and only forty-one were constructed. The body was built by Superleggera of Milan. A 2.9-liter, twin-supercharged, overhead-valve, eight-cylinder, inline, water-cooled, 300-hp. engine was fitted. Alfa Romeo was a consistent winner of such races as Le Mans, Targa Florio, Avusrennen, and Mille Miglia.

ALFA ROMEO LE MANS   Alfa Romeo started when, in 1911, Nicola Romeo became director of an Italian subsidiary of Darracq in Milan. After World War I he gained control of the firm and named it Alfa Romeo. This Alfa Romeo Le Mans was made in 1938 with an ultra-streamlined body by Superleggera Touring of Milan. The car was entered in the 1938 Le Mans 24-Hour Race and was well in the lead when a tire blew at 140 mph. Engine trouble later made the team retire from the Le Mans Race. Power was an eight-cylinder, overhead-valve, water-cooled, inline engine, of 2,991-cc displacement and 295 hp. at 6,000 rpm. Only one coupé of this type was constructed.

BUGATTI TYPE 57 This Bugatti Type 57 four-seat touring coupé was first developed in 1934 at Molsheim, France, and this is the 1938 Aravis-built body model. The car was fun to drive thanks to its good steering, excellent road holding ability, and speed. The type 57 engine was an eight-cylinder, water-cooled, 3,257-cc-displacement, 130-hp. powerplant with twin overhead camshafts that drove the car to over 105 mph. Type 57 cars were made from 1934 to the beginning of World War II.

DODGE SEDAN MODEL D-8 In 1938, Dodge introduced the Model D-8 Sedan. The five-passenger car was built on a 115-inch wheelbase and featured 11-inch brake drums and a pistol-grip parking brake under the instrument panel. Power was a six-cylinder, inline, water-cooled, 87-hp., 218-cubic-inch-displacement engine with bore of 3¼ inches and stroke of 4⅜ inches. Ten different body styles were offered that year with prices ranging from $808 to $1,275.

BUICK CONVERTIBLE   In 1938 this advanced Buick Convertible was shown to the public as a car of the future, and many of the features were incorporated into Buicks of later years. Although a two-seater, the car was produced in 1940 as the six-seat model 76C convertible with minor modifications on a 126-inch wheelbase. Power was an eight-cylinder, 320-cubic-inch-displacement engine that produced 38 hp. The design was also carried into the immediate post-World War II years.

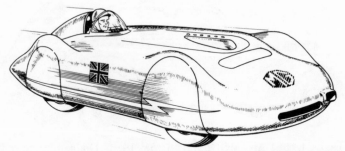

M.G. EX 135 RACER   Originally developed in 1934 as the Magic Magnette, two bodies were made for this car: one for competition racing and another to break speed records. The record racer 1938 version is shown. In 1934, the Class G speed record of 128.7 mph. was established, and in 1939 a flying-start mile was covered at a speed of 203.5 mph. Power was a six-cylinder, water-cooled, overhead-valve, 66-cubic-inch-displacement, inline engine.

CHEVROLET MASTER DE LUXE SEDAN Introduced in 1938, this Chevrolet Master De Luxe two-door sedan helped Chevrolet to maintain its sales leadership in the U.S. auto industry. Despite a severe recession, Chevrolet sales were 694,039 units, and the total Chevrolet production at the end of 1938 reached 15 million cars. New features at this time were the longer, vee-shaped grille with horizontal bars in lieu of vertical, headlights supported by the hood, and skirted fenders. A steel "box girder" frame and 16-inch wheels became standard, and wood was replaced by steel in the body structure.

WILLYS BANTAM In 1938, Willys produced the Willys Bantam, another bid for the low-price trade. The four-door, five-passenger car had all the current styling features of larger cars of the period, of which the hood-covered radiator was the most novel. It was powered by a four-cylinder, L-head, water-cooled, inline engine. The car became the prototype for the Willys Americar of 1942.

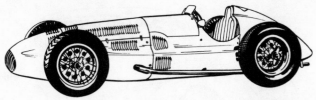

MERCEDES-BENZ GRAND PRIX RACER The Mercedes-Benz Type W-163 of 1939 won the Eifelrennen, Belgian Grand Prix, German Grand Prix, and in the Swiss race the type scored first, second, and third places. It placed second in the Yugoslavian Grand Prix. All of this took place in 1939. Power was a huge twelve-cylinder, vee, water-cooled, 480-hp., 2,962-cc-displacement engine that could be revved to 7,800 rpm. Bore was 67 mm. and stroke was 70 mm.

MASERATI 8CTF RACER The last pre-World War II Italian Maserati racer was the 8CTF of 1939. One of the cars, named "Boyle Special," was driven by Wilbur Shaw in the U.S. This car won the Indianapolis 500-Mile Race in 1939 and again in 1940. The car also placed third in the 1946 and 1947 Indianapolis 500-Mile Races! The car had a live rear axle and independent front-wheel suspension. Power was an eight-cylinder, inline, water-cooled, 2,990-cc-displacement, 355-hp. engine with twin overhead camshafts operating 32 valves. The crankshaft drove a Roots blower for supercharging.

PONTIAC FOUR-DOOR SEDAN   The Pontiac Four-Door Model 39-26 Sedan of 1939 was one of the first to include a built-in trunk in the body design. This six-seater was powered by a six-cylinder, inline, water-cooled, 223-cubic-inch-displacement, 85-hp. engine. By 1939 Pontiac had become the fifth largest auto maker in the U.S.

LINCOLN ZEPHYR TOWN CAR   The Lincoln Zephyr was introduced in late 1935 as a lower-priced member of the Lincoln family. It was considered the first successfully designed streamlined car in the U.S. Built on a 125-inch wheelbase, the design was powered by a twelve-cylinder, 75° vee, water-cooled, 292-cubic-inch-displacement engine. Vacuum-booster power brakes were fitted. Lincoln offered standard body styles, but the custom designs were completed by Le Baron, Brunn, Judkin, Dietrich, and Willoughby. This Lincoln Zephyr Town Car was made for Mrs. Edsel Ford in 1939. The body was handcrafted by Brunn coach builders.

PACKARD CABRIOLET   This luxurious Packard Cabriolet of 1939 featured a body built by Brunn. Power was a twelve-cylinder, vee, water-cooled, 473-cubic-inch-displacement engine that developed 175 hp. at 3,200 rpm. From 1933 to 1939 only 5,298 Packard Twelves were sold, and 1939 was the last year for the model. This car can be seen at the Long Island Automotive Museum, Southampton, New York.

PACKARD 12 CONVERTIBLE COUPÉ/ROADSTER   This sporty Packard 12 Convertible Coupé/Roadster of 1939 featured a body by Le Baron as well as the Packard Twelve engine. The 175-hp., V-12 engine had a bore of $3\frac{7}{16}$ inches and a stroke of $4\frac{1}{4}$ inches. This car body and the engine are true classics.

HUDSON CONVERTIBLE BROUGHAM   The Hudson Convertible Brougham of 1939 celebrated the 30th anniversary of the company. The wheelbase was 116 inches, and power was a six-cylinder, water-cooled, inline engine of about 100 hp. The car featured a gearshift on the steering column instead of on the floor. Hudson production was 82,161 cars in 1939. By May of that year, Hudson completed its car No. 2,614,165.

MERCURY NO. 1   The Ford Motor Company introduced the first Mercury car in 1939 as a medium-priced model between the Ford and Lincoln. The car had many features of the Lincoln Zephyr. The five-passenger 1939 four-door sedan is shown. Power was an eight-cylinder, vee, side-valve, water-cooled, 239-cubic-inch-displacement engine that developed 95 hp. at 3,800 rpm. Maximum speed was about 90 mph.

HORCH CABRIOLET Horch was the German Auto Union's answer to the Mercedes-Benz. This 1939 Horch Cabriolet Luxuswagen five-passenger, deluxe auto was powered by an eight-cylinder, inline, overhead-camshaft, water-cooled, 4,995-cc-displacement, 100-hp. engine. Speed was about 90 mph.

M.G.-VA Introduced in 1939, the M.G.-VA was the first four-seater sports car produced by the company, and was therefore classed as a touring car. It was also one of the few early M.G. cars to have skirted fenders. The engine was a four-cylinder, inline, water-cooled 1,250-cc-displacement engine that developed 55 hp. Bore was 66.5 mm. and stroke was 90 mm. A four-speed synchronized gearbox was fitted. The wheelbase was 7 feet 10 inches.

CADILLAC TOWN CAR The Cadillac Motor Car Company produced this town car in 1939 on a 141-inch wheelbase. The body was by Fleetwood. Power was a sixteen-cylinder, 135° vee, water-cooled, L-head, 431-cubic-inch-displacement engine that developed 185 hp. Two ignition distributors and two carburetors were installed. Bore was 3.25 inches, and stroke was 4.25 inches, with a compression ratio of 6.8 to 1. Speed of the car exceeded 100 mph. This was the epitome of American car pre-World War II elegance. Price was $8,000.

CHAPTER ELEVEN

Chariots of War, Then Peacetime—Varoom! 1940—1949

DURING LATE MAY and early June of 1940, German troops occupied northern France, Belgium, and the Netherlands. This twenty-six-day assault had worldwide repercussions, of course, but nowhere more than in Detroit. William S. Knudsen resigned as president of G.M. to head up the Council of National Defense.

Passenger car production during 1940 increased by almost a million units to 3,717, 385. Early in the year, on January 11, 1940, G.M. had turned out its 25-millionth car. Nash mass-produced the first "unitized" body. Olds appeared with what might be described as the first really reliable automatic transmission. Buick featured two dual downdraft carburetors. Sealed beam headlamps became the rule, rather than the exception.

Army Captain Robert G. Howie had designed a small, highly mobile four-wheel-drive, quarter-ton, jack-of-all-military-missions vehicle which would be known, in a refined and production form, as the ubiquitous "Jeep." American Bantam Car Company could not keep up with orders for it, so Willys-Overland and Ford were soon making it, too.

Packard started to make Rolls-Royce aircraft engines for the British after Henry Ford turned down the opportunity. Ford did get into the aircraft-engine business, helping turn out Pratt & Whitney radials. In the car field, Ford presented the 1940 Lincoln Zephyr Continentals, which used the 292-cubic-inch V-12 powerplants from the Zephyr.

430

Cadillac stopped production of its La Salle car. Walter Chrysler and C. Harold Wills died. In October, 1940, the first portion of the Pennsylvania Turnpike toll road opened between Pittsburgh and Harrisburg. It was constructed on a long-abandoned railroad route.

Despite many shortages in basic materials, and the necessity to utilize substitutes for numerous items, more autos and more trucks were turned out in 1941 than during the preceding year. Most cars appeared more massive. General Motors, for instance, announced the intention to run its front fenders back to become part of the front doors.

Chrysler experimented with a disappearing, all-steel convertible top; six such "Thunderbolt" cars were made. The 29-millionth Ford was assembled. On June 21, Ford signed a contract with the U.A.W. which required Ford workers to join that union. Louis Chevrolet died during 1941; Henry Ford suffered his second stroke.

Japanese forces bombed American military installations at Pearl Harbor in Hawaii, as well as Guam and in the Philippines early Sunday morning, December 7, 1941. The U.S. entered World War II by an Act of Congress the following day.

Before that declaration of war, Chrysler was already mass-producing Army tanks, and other auto concerns were equally involved in making various weapons and vehicles of war.

For the private car owner ordinary pleasure driving got really difficult during 1942. On January 5, auto tires became a rationed item. The production of passenger cars for civilians came to a halt on February 9; 222,862 1942-model private autos had been turned out prior to that date—then, no more. Nor were trucks made for civilian use after March 3. To conserve gasoline national speed limits were imposed, first to 40 mph., then to 35 mph. Finally, gasoline rationing via "stamps" went into effect on December 1, 1942.

Pontiac, making anti-aircraft guns, received the first Navy "E" Award (for excellence in production and quality). Shortly afterward, when this coveted designation was replaced by the combined Army-Navy "E," Chrysler was presented with the first in that series for its tank output.

During November the United States and Britain landed Army

units in French North Africa. Almost immediately many of the U.S. Army Signal Corps Dodge transmitter/receiver vans were destroyed by Luftwaffe fighters. Somebody stateside had forgotten to tell the American radio operators/truck drivers how to conceal their vehicles from the air. For a while American communications were pretty much dependent upon the more savvy British mobile radio units.

The year 1943, which saw a grand total of 139 passenger cars trickle off the U.S. "production" lines, and those mostly from parts-on-hand, opened with the O.P.A. (Office of Price Administration) banning all non-essential driving in seventeen eastern states. The year ended with the Automobile Council for War Production announcing that 1,038 automobile, auto-parts and auto-accessory plants were cooperating industry-wide and had already turned out $13 billion worth of war matériel.

On May 12, 1943, the war ended in Africa when the last Nazis were captured at Cape Bon. On September 8, Italy surrendered unconditionally.

On May 26, Edsel Bryant Ford, president of the Ford Motor Company, died. His ailments were attributed to stomach ulcers (which turned into cancer) accentuated by the drinking of unpasteurized milk from the family farm. Insiders felt the quite unprofessional diagnosis "broken heart" should have been appended. Edsel had been frustrated for years by his father's peculiar ideas and reactions. Old Henry reassumed the Ford presidency; his grandson Henry II serves at the Ford plants to increase operating efficiency.

During 1943 California shipbuilder and cement magnate Henry J. Kaiser announced he would be in the auto-making business come the end of World War II. William Bushnell Stout of metal transport plane fame (Ford Trimotor) had a "flying automobile" designed for postwar production.

During 1944 Joseph W. Frazer, an official of Graham-Paige Motors, let it be known he would return to auto-making, too, come peacetime. It had long been Frazer's ambition to have his own name on a car. Willys-Overland declared it would make a Jeep for civilians. Meantime, gas rationing was down to two gallons per week per car unless one could convince the local rationing body he or she qualified for more under various "essential" categories.

The government let it be known that Russia had already been provided with 345,000 vehicles. In November, the War Production Board okayed the manufacture of some light trucks for civilian work.

On June 6, 1944—"D-Day"—the Allies landed in Europe. The biggest naval action ever fought was the Battle for Leyte Gulf, October 22 to 27, which destroyed most of Japan's remaining naval power. Official passenger-car production in 1944 was 610—all other vehicles, 737,524.

During the early months of 1945 officials in Detroit and Washington were devoting considerable study to the best way of converting the auto industry to peacetime production.

V-E Day (Victory-in-Europe) came on May 8, 1945. The W.P.B. on May 22 lifted restrictions on much-needed replacement parts for non-military vehicles. The Board decided conversion to civilian auto/truck output could start on July 1.

President Roosevelt died April 12, 1945. Mussolini was executed on April 28. Hitler committed suicide April 29 or 30.

An atomic bomb was dropped on Hiroshima on August 6. Japan surrendered formally eight days later. Gasoline rationing across America ended on August 15.

On September 21, Henry Ford II became president of the Ford Motor Company; he had driven America's first civilian car from a Ford assembly line on July 3.

Creation of the Kaiser-Frazer Corporation was announced on July 26.

The vital part played by America's automotive industry during World War II not only deserves a book on its own, but many have been written devoted to that subject. One such compilation is *Freedom's Arsenal: The Story of the Automobile Council for War Production.*

Just fifty years after Selden had patented the design for an auto to be driven by a gasoline engine, the auto industry could look back with satisfaction on its role in World War II. Its output of $29 billion worth of military equipment included aircraft (fixed and rotary wing, gliders, bombers, fighters), ammunition, armored cars, bombs, carbines, engines of all types, guns, land and marine mines, machine guns, rifles, scout cars, steel helmets, submarine nets, tanks, torpedoes, trucks . . . and on and on. Chrysler, for instance, had produced 25,000 tanks, mostly Shermans; Willys-Overland had made 200,000 Jeeps. Ford rolled out 8,685 four-engined B-24 Librator bombers at Willow Run. More than $8 billion worth of items made by General Motors for the military (out of its $12-billion-plus World War II total) was matériel never before tackled by that firm. Transition to peacetime pursuits was not going to be easy for G.M., the automotive giant. A strike by U.A.W. members began at General Motors on November 21; it was to last until the following March. The union wanted, on the average, a 30-percent wage boost; final settlement would be for 15 percent.

Dead in 1945 was Vincent Bendix, who had developed the starter drive and four-wheel brakes.

Two, of many, new efforts during 1946 to crack the auto makers' market were those by Kaiser-Frazer and the Tucker Corporation of Chicago. Kaiser and Frazer autos got into series production. Preston T. Tucker got off to a much slower start with a more advanced design.

By August of 1946 a million postwar cars had been put together, the vast majority based on 1941/42 styling.

Because Charles Brady King had driven a motorcar along the streets of Detroit in 1896, the auto industry marked that event with a rip-snortin' twelve-day celebration starting May 29, 1946.

In Europe fuel was still rationed, so small cars with small engines were most popular; motor scooters, too! In some places a new temporary breed of cyclecars made an appearance. English M.G.'s invaded the U.S. starting with the Type TC and were favorably received by the sports-minded driver.

Automotive price and wage controls were completely removed by the order of President Truman on November 9, 1946. During 1946 the Indy 500 resumed for 3-liter-supercharged or 4.5-liter-unsupercharged cars. George Robson won at 114.82 mph. in a six-cylinder supercharged Thorne Engineering Sparks Special. This was the second and last six-cylinder car to win that 500-Mile Race—the first had been in the initial running back in 1911.

American passenger car production in 1947 (3,558,178) increased by almost 1,300,000 units over 1946. New assembly plants were springing up across the country.

During 1947 the Tucker rear-engined car was shown publicly; Packard turned out its one-millionth car; Kaiser-Frazer acquired the automotive assets of Graham-Paige. Goodrich began offering tubeless tires.

William C. ("Little Billy") Durant died in 1947, leaving little. James S. Couzens, Ford Motor Company's first business manager and later U.S. Senator, died wealthy and full of honors. Henry Ford, the first and the original, died on April 7, 1947, at age eighty-four. His career with its occasional capriciousness, demonstrated capabilities, and amazing credulousness is deserving of more attention than space permits here. Fortunately, there are many books on Henry and his indefatigable Model T, which make for some wonderful reading—even when they may be finding fault with some phase of his career. The truth of the matter is Ford was not only a master mechanic from his early days, but he was a masterly maneuverer of men with an uncanny ability for picking good men to do difficult jobs. The fact that he got harder to deal with in his older days just proves he was as human as the rest of the world. The fact that he was hard to reason with— sometimes, not always—in his younger, most productive period— can be attributed to the fact that he had a vision which he turned into the most successful single vehicle in history. Henry Ford, truly, did put America on wheels.

The 1947 Indy race was taken by Mauri Rose in the Blue Crown Spark Plug Special at 116.338 mph. John R. Cobb of Great Britain in his Railton set a land speed record of 369.70 mph. at the Bonneville Salt Flats in Utah.

During 1948 Mauri Rose repeated his previous year's win at Indianapolis, raising his speed about 3.5 mph. to 119.814 mph. In the first "escalator" clause, General Motors agreed to an 11-cent hourly raise for U.A.W. members with wages moving up or down depending on the "cost of living." A group allied with Walter Reuther took over the U.A.W. reins.

The year 1948 produced many "firsts" in automobiling: most cars and trucks since 1929; new marques such as the Playboy, Keller, and Davis. But the most long-lasting style item was the first tail fins on the Cadillacs, and under the Caddie's hood was a 160-hp. V-8 high-compression engine. Olds also offered a high-compression V-8. Buick introduced the first American hydraulic torque converter-type automatic transmission, Dynaflow, on its Roadmaster line.

In Australia, G.M. brought out that country's first mass-produced car, the FX-Type Holden. In the U.S., just under fifty Tuckers were on the roads. Willys-Overland was selling a six-cylinder Jeep station wagon and a rakish Jeepster convertible.

During 1948, when the 100-millionth American motor vehicle was produced, Charles W. Nash and William S. Knudsen died.

1949 was what the passenger car producers and salesmen would call "a very good year." For the first time sales of private vehicles would exceed five million cars, and this even though steel and coal strikes cut into auto production.

Plymouth offered a 1949 steel-bodied station wagon called the Suburban. The marketing staff decided for some strange reason that each should be the same color—a repulsive brown. Even Henry in his all-black period had done better! Enterprising Plymouth dealers who repainted these steel wagons in more attractive colors led the sales parade.

Hupp dropped out of the automotive field and Crosley tried to stay afloat with a 750-cc "Hotshot" two-seater sports car. It was a lively little thing, a bit ahead of its time. In Europe the Citroën 2CV with a 375-cc flat-twin featured front-wheel drive. It carried four in tight quarters and had a sloping, boxy appearance. But production could not keep up with sales.

"Hardtop convertibles"—that is, sedans with no center side supports or pillars—were offered on the more expensive Buicks, Oldsmobiles, and Cadillacs. Since the fixed roof "converted" only into a closed car when the windows were rolled up, wags termed these sporty-looking jobs the "unconvertible convertibles." But the idea caught the public fancy and pocketbook.

The winner at Indianapolis in 1949 was Bill Holland in an Offenhauser-powered car with chassis by Deidt bearing the Blue Crown Spark Plug Special designation. His winning speed was 121 plus mph.

But the "Furious Fifties" were ahead, with new race car designs being spawned on the opposite side of the Atlantic. These new designs and approaches both overseas and at home, with fresh racing techniques, engines, and components, would mean that 121 mph. would not qualify you for some races—it wouldn't even qualify you for room at the drivers' motel!

DODGE LUXURY LINER CONVERTIBLE   In 1940, Dodge introduced the Luxury Liner Deluxe D-14 Convertible built on a 119.5-inch wheelbase. The four-seater started the use of foam rubber in the seats. Power was a six-cylinder, inline, water-cooled, 87-hp., 217-cubic-inch-displacement engine with a bore of 3.25 inches and stroke of 4.30 inches. Dodge sold 189,643 cars in 1940, 26 percent of all Chrysler sales.

LANCIA CIANO   This Lancia was specially constructed in 1940 for the Italian Foreign Minister, Count Galeazzo Ciano, who was also Benito Mussolini's son-in-law. The body was designed and custom built by Pininfarina. The extremely long hood housed a 4.5-liter, vee-type, water-cooled, overhead-valve engine which Lancia pioneered in 1919. This car can be seen at the Colorado Car Museum, Manitou Springs, Colorado.

VW TYPE 82 KUBELWAGEN   After designing the Volkswagen in 1937, Dr. Ferdinand Porsche was asked to design a military version of the car in 1939. One thousand were built by the end of 1940. The car was flat-sided for ease of production and was called the *Kubelwagen,* which means "bucket car." Power was increased to 25 hp. and engine displacement to 1.13 liters. The German "Jeep" proved very successful, and the air-cooled engine operated as well in the Russian winter as in the North African heat. Further, the rear-mounted engine kept the car moving through mud, snow, and sand, while more conventional vehicles were stuck, spinning their wheels due to light rear ends. The chassis was produced in the government-owned Volkswagen plant, while the slab-sided bodies were made in Berlin.

LA SALLE CONVERTIBLE   This lower-priced companion to Cadillac was produced in 1940. The La Salle convertible of that year had its straight-eight engine replaced by a Cadillac vee-eight engine, thereby becoming the cheapest version of the Cadillac. In 1941, Cadillac's cheapest model under its own name sold for only $1,350. Since it was impossible to produce a La Salle for a lower price, the La Salle was dropped from production. The engine was a 303-cubic-inch-displacement, eight-cylinder, water-cooled, 75-hp. powerplant.

CROSLEY GARDEN WAGON   In 1939, Powel Crosley, Jr., introduced an American economy car that would be cheap to buy and operate. Power was a small two-cylinder engine of about 20-cubic-inch displacement. This 1940 Crosley Garden Wagon was intended for gardeners on large estates or just for transporting light loads. World War II interrupted complete development of the car until 1946.

NASH AMBASSADOR   This Nash Model 4088 Ambassador four-door sedan was produced in 1940 on a 125-inch wheelbase. Power was an eight-cylinder, inline, water-cooled, 128-hp engine. Price of this six-passenger auto was $1,195 F.O.B. Detroit.

AMERICAN BANTAM SUPER 4   This economy car was produced in 1941 and sold for $400. The car weighed 1,200 pounds on a 75-inch wheelbase. The water-cooled engine produced 22 hp. The car was called "America's Pioneer Economy Car."

LINCOLN CONTINENTAL SEDAN   Upon Henry Ford's resignation, his son Edsel became the Ford Motor Company president. In 1938, he ordered a special design to be built on the Lincoln Zephyr chassis for himself and his two sons. Two hundred orders for the car were submitted before the prototype was even completed, so Edsel Ford decided to place the car in production. Thus the Lincoln Continental was born. Production in 1941 was 1,250 cars, each on a 125-inch wheelbase with a weight of 3,890 pounds. Power was a twelve-cylinder, 75° vee, water-cooled engine with four main bearings. Displacement was 292 cubic inches, and the powerplant developed 120 hp. at 3,500 rpm. Bore was 2⅞ inches and stroke was 3¾ inches. The price in 1941 was $2,727. The 1941 two-door sedan is shown, and a car of this type can be seen at the Museum of Transportation, Larz Anderson Park, Brookline, Massachusetts.

HUDSON STATION WAGON Hudson produced this station wagon in 1941 on a 121-inch wheelbase. It seated eight and was powered by a six-cylinder, inline, water-cooled, 102-hp. engine. An eight-cylinder engine was also available. Hudson produced 79,529 cars in 1941 and realized a profit of $3,756,418.

WILLYS JEEP The famous Willys Jeep was built throughout World War II. It was developed to transport command and reconnaissance personnel as well as light cargo. The four-wheel drive allowed it to operate in mud, snow, and sand. Weight of this four-seater was 2,690 pounds on an 81-inch wheelbase. Overall length was 138 inches. Turning radius was 19 feet. It could climb a 69 percent grade fully loaded and, with special canvas sides and a snorkel, could cross streams over six feet deep! Power was a Willys four-cylinder, inline, water-cooled, F-head, 134-cubic-inch-displacement, 72-hp. engine. The Jeep, used by the U.S. Army, Navy, and Air Force, could carry 800 pounds over rough terrain and 1,200 pounds on highways. Production continued after the war.

CHEVROLET COUPÉ In 1941, the running board disappeared from the Chevrolet, and the wheelbase was increased to 116 inches. Removable hood sides were now replaced by a one-piece hood that opened from the front. The 1942 Chevrolet is shown here. The only change from 1941 models was the front fender that was extended to form part of the door. This set a trend that was followed for years. Power was a six-cylinder, water-cooled, inline-engine of 90 hp. The last 1942 Chevrolet rolled off the Flint assembly line on January 30, 1942, when the plant converted to the production of war matériel.

HUDSON SUPER-SIX MODEL 21 This Hudson Super-Six Model 21 four-door sedan was produced in the first two months of 1942, and then the firm converted to the production of war matériel, including guns and aircraft parts. This five-passenger car was built on a 121-inch wheelbase and was powered by the famous Super-Six engine.

PARIS TAXI—W.W. II Due to the extreme shortage of fuel and materials in German-occupied Paris, this lightweight three-wheel cyclecar was developed in 1942. It could seat two passengers plus the driver and was made mostly from non-strategic materials such as wood. A single-cylinder motorbike engine was used as power and drove the front wheel. The gas tank was on the handlebars, and the exhaust muffler attached to the side of the fender. The front of the car body was boat-shaped for strength and streamlining.

VW AMPHIBIOUS SCHWIMMWAGEN The success of the Kubelwagen prompted the German Weapons Bureau to have Dr. Porsche design an amphibious car for the German Army. The Volkswagen Schwimmwagen had a larger engine than the VW, with 30-hp. and 1,131-cc displacement. The sealed body was completely waterproof and featured a retractable propeller. The engine was fitted with an intake snorkel and top-mounted exhaust muffler. Production was in full swing by 1942 and continued into 1943.

STOUT SCARAB III   Inventor-designer William B. Stout, who designed the famous Ford Trimotor Plane, flying automobiles, and railroad cars, among other engineering achievements, designed this remarkable car in 1944. It was a development of two previous cars, also called the Scarab, designed and built by Stout ten years earlier. The body and bumpers as well as the floor pan were of reinforced fiberglass. The only non-plastic parts were the engine, drive train, headlights, door locks, seats, instruments, wheels, steering mechanism, and windows. The windshield was the first wraparound safety-glass windshield ever made. The huge interior was arranged like a small sitting room with a foldaway table! The wheelbase was 137 inches, overall length 195.5 inches, height 72.25 inches, and width 65 inches. Weight was about 3,300 pounds. A 221-cubic-inch-displacement, Ford V-8 engine of 95 hp. at 3,600 rpm. was located in the rear. Four-wheel independent oleo-strut suspension provided a remarkably steady ride. To prove the steadiness of the ride the car could be driven with a glass filled with water to the brim, and not one drop would spill! Despite the fact that Kaiser-Frazer was interested, the car was never placed in production. This car can be seen in the Detroit Historical Museum, Detroit, Michigan.

THE FLYING CAR   This has always captured the interest of both aeronautical and automotive engineers. After World War II, T. P. Hall designed and built this Flying Car in 1946, and, after he had logged 150 hours of flying time, he was grounded because of questionable safety by the authorities. Powered by a Franklin opposed-piston flat engine, it had an airspeed of 120 mph. and highway speed of 60 mph.

CHRYSLER TOWN AND COUNTRY This attractive Chrysler Town and Country of 1946 was a combination of station wagon and sports-coupé styling. It is also considered to be one of the first production hardtop designs. White ash and mahogany panels were attached to the steel body to form this most unusual appearance. This Chrysler C-38W had a 121.5-inch wheelbase and was powered by a six-cylinder, inline, water-cooled, 114-hp. engine with a displacement of 250.6 cubic inches. The car was manufactured from December, 1946, to February, 1949.

NASH AMBASSADOR This Nash Ambassador Suburban Model 4664 was produced in limited numbers in 1946. It was a standard four-door Nash Ambassador with ash and mahogany wood panels attached to the doors and body, to make the car a cross between a sedan and a station wagon. Power was a six-cylinder, inline, water-cooled, 112-hp. engine. In 1946, Nash Motors opened plants in Canada and California.

KAISER NO. 1 The Kaiser-Frazer Corporation was formed in 1945 by industrialist Henry J. Kaiser and auto company executive Joseph W. Frazer. Frazer had worked for Packard, Pierce-Arrow, Maxwell-Chalmers, and Chrysler. He then created the Jeep for Willys and went to Graham-Paige. Kaiser absorbed Graham-Paige, and then designer Howard "Dutch" Darrin was engaged to develop the first Kaiser car. Initially intended as a front-wheel-drive vehicle, it was produced as a conventional rear drive. This is the 1946 Kaiser Special that was built on a 123-inch wheelbase. The seats were 62 inches wide. A Continental six-cylinder, inline, water-cooled 226.5-cubic-inch-displacement, 100-hp. engine powered the automobile. The straight-line fender design was copied by many auto manufacturers. Despite good sales, the company lost over $19 million in 1946!

CHEVROLET FOUR-DOOR SEDAN Chevrolet resumed automobile production in 1945 on the 1946 models, one of which is this four-door sedan. It was virtually identical to the 1942 model which had been stopped in mid-production due to the U.S. involvement in World War II. Notice that the rear portion of the front fender forms part of the door, a styling feature pioneered by the more expensive General Motors cars.

CISITALIA COUPÉ Piero Dusio, an Italian textile manufacturer, began producing automobiles in 1946. This Cisitalia Coupé of 1946 was one of the eight cars of all time to be selected for excellence in modern car design by the Museum of Modern Art in New York. Pininfarina designed the car body, and Danti Giacosa and Carlo Abarth were among the engineers who worked on the design. Power was a four-cylinder, overhead-valve, inline, water-cooled engine of Fiat design. Displacement was 1,090 cc, and 60 hp. could be developed at 5,500 rpm. An inexpensive racing version which won some impressive victories was also produced.

MESSERSCHMITT (F.M.R.) The famous German fighter-plane designer turned to the manufacture of small automobiles in 1947. His Regensburg plant was converted to auto production and called F.M.R. or Fahrzeug und Machinenbau GMbh, Regensburg. This small car was called the F.M.R. Tiger and could attain 80 mph. on a two-cylinder, air-cooled engine of only 500 cc. Construction was a steel tubing chassis fitted with a floor pan. Many F.M.R.s were exported for use for business delivery of small parcels and for pleasure. This car is usually called the Messerschmitt Cabin Scooter.

TUCKER TORPEDO In early 1946, Preston Tucker started the development of a revolutionary rear-engine car that had many refinements and was to sell for only $1,000. The Tucker Torpedo made its appearance in 1947 amid considerable fanfare and applause. The car was powered by a six-cylinder, opposed-horizontal, air-cooled, 166-hp. engine. Three headlights were fitted, and engine cooling openings were cut into the rear fenders. The doors extended into the roof to facilitate getting in and out of the car. Safety features were also well ahead of their time and included a heavily padded instrument panel and a pop-out windshield that disintegrated without cutting edges! Advanced as it was, only forty-nine were made before the company went out of business.

BLUE CROWN SPECIAL The Blue Crown Specials were among the most successful racers in the Indianapolis 500-Mile Race during the post-World War II years. The cars were very well built and were designed by Lou Moore around the Offenhauser engine. Front-wheel drive, wishbone and torsion-bar independent suspension and inboard brakes were features of the design. With Mauri Rose at the wheel, the car won the 1947 and 1948 Indianapolis 500-Mile Races. It repeated the win in 1949!

NARDI DANESE   After World War II the Italians returned to the sport they love, motor racing. This Nardi Danese of 1947 was one of the many small speedsters that appeared in postwar Italy. The company was founded before the war, in Turin, by Enrico Nardi, who was a former racing driver and engineer. After the war he formed a partnership with Renato Danese, hence the name. The engine was a modified Fiat four-cylinder, water-cooled, inline, 1,100-cc displacement powerplant. Most of the Nardi cars were built to order and were successful in some minor races. Today, Nardi of Turin is famous for its speed equipment such as special manifolds, camshafts, crankshafts, and steering wheels.

VOLVO PV444   The Volvo PV444 was developed in 1944; however, the car was not publicly available until 1947 because of tooling problems. The four-seat, two-door fastback was powered by a four-cylinder, inline, water-cooled, 86.3-cubic-inch-displacement, overhead-valve engine that produced 44 hp. Overall length was 175.5 inches on a 111-inch wheelbase. Top speed was 91 mph. The car became popular abroad as well as in its native Sweden and was produced until 1965.

RENAULT 4CV This Renault 4CV Type R1060 economy car emerged from war-torn France in 1947. The four-door car could seat five, and, in a way, was a Volkswagen competitor. Power was a four-cylinder, water-cooled, inline, 760-cc-displacement engine that developed 22 hp. at 4,200 rpm. Bore was 55.5 mm. and stroke was 80 mm. The car could maintain 65 mph. on highways, and fuel consumption was 5.7 liters per 100 kilometers.

HUDSON CONVERTIBLE BROUGHAM In 1948, Hudson introduced a completely new line of cars featuring the "Step Down Design," which gave them the lowest center of gravity of all U.S. cars. This Hudson Convertible Brougham was built on a 124-inch wheelbase and was available with either a 123-hp., six-cylinder engine, or a 128-hp., eight-cylinder engine. Both engines were inline, water-cooled types.

HOLDEN 48/215 After World War II the Australian government was alarmed at the shortage of automobiles, because the war had cut off many imported items. It therefore asked auto manufacturers to submit proposals for an all-Australian-built car. General Motors-Holden, Ltd., won the contest with a car that General Motors Corp., U.S.A., had built as a prototype car in 1940. This saved much time, and by the end of 1948, 163 General Motors-Holden cars had been built. By 1951, production was 100 per day for this first all-Australian-built car. Power was a six-cylinder, inline, water-cooled, 132.5-cubic-inch-displacement engine. Bore was 3 inches and stroke was 3⅛ inches. The car featured unitized construction with no separate chassis and body. Suspension was rugged to fit the Australian roads of that period.

FERRARI "166" SPYDER CORSA The Ferrari "166" Spyder Corsa of 1948 was a refinement of the earlier 1947 Ferrari "125" and "159" designs. This was the first Ferrari to become famous, and the first to win important races. In 1948, the car won the Targa Florio and the Mille Miglia. Ferrari's company was called Societa Auto Avio Construzioni Ferrari at this time. The powerplant was a six-cylinder, water-cooled, inline, overhead-camshaft, 1,992-cc-displacement engine that had a bore of 60 mm. and a stroke of 58.8 mm. The car can be seen at the Long Island Automotive Museum, Southampton, New York.

WILLYS JEEPSTER   At the close of World War II, Willys, as the largest producer of the wartime Jeep, decided to produce a civilian version. The car made its appearance in 1948. It proved to be a disappointment and never caught the public's fancy, because the average buyer was looking for comfort and luxury. Until 1951, about 20,000 were made. High point in sales was 8,388 in 1949. The original Jeep four-cylinder engine was replaced with a six-cylinder, water-cooled, inline, 148-cubic-inch-displacement engine of 70 hp.

WILLYS STATION WAGON   This Willys Jeep 6-63 Station Wagon was developed from the wartime Jeep and made its appearance in 1948. The car had four-wheel drive, independent suspension, and room for six passengers. Power was a six-cylinder, side-valve, water-cooled, inline, 148.2-cubic-inch-displacement engine that produced 72 hp. at 4,000 rpm. Top speed was 70 mph. A three-speed transmission was fitted. An optional four-cylinder engine was also offered.

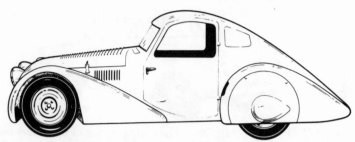

ZVEZDA RECORD RACERS   A series of Russian Zvezda (Star) record-breaking cars was designed by Alexander Pelzer in 1946, and the cars set world speed records for sixteen years. Powered by motorcycle engines, the teardrop bodies had front tracks that were wider than the rear tracks. In 1949 Andrei Ponisovkin set an International Class J (350 cc) record for the flying kilometer of 107.37 mph. and in 1953 Alexei Ambrosenkov covered 50 kilometers at 105.57 mph. in a 500-cc-powered Zvezda. In 1958 Édouard Lorent established a Class J record of 137.63 mph., and in 1961 he set a Class K record of 138.69 mph. in a 250-cc-powered Zvezda. The 1949 Zvezda is shown here.

BENTLEY MK. VI SEDAN   This Bentley Mark VI "E" Series four-door sedan was produced in 1949, although the Mark was introduced a few years earlier. The car had little of the sporting air of former Bentleys and was designed for comfortable and safe transportation. Power of this six-passenger car was a six-cylinder, F-head, inline, water-cooled engine with a displacement of 4,256 cc. that developed 140 hp. at 4,500 rpm. A four-speed transmission was fitted. Maximum speed was about 100 mph.

STUDEBAKER CHAMPION   The daring styling of this bullet-nosed 1949 Studebaker Champion was the work of industrial designer Raymond Loewy and was his second design series for Studebaker. Power was a six-cylinder, side-valve, inline, water-cooled, 226-cubic-inch-displacement engine that developed 94 hp. at 3,600 rpm. The maximum speed was about 90 mph. This car was produced until 1952.

TALBOT "GS26" CONVERTIBLE   This French Talbot "GS26" Cabriolet Décapotable Deux Portes (or two-door convertible) was made in 1949 as a high-performance sports car. The make won the Le Mans 24-Hour Race in 1950. Power was a six-cylinder, overhead-valve, inline, water-cooled engine of 4,482-cc displacement that developed 170 hp. at 4,200 rpm. A four-speed transmission was fitted, and speeds exceeded 110 mph. Talbot was absorbed by Simca in 1959. This car can be seen at the Musée de la Carrosserie Française, Puerto de Andraitx, Mallorca, Spain.

DELAHAYE CONVERTIBLE Émile Delahaye began building cars in France in 1893 and decided to build sports cars in 1934. He had entered many races in previous years with success. This is the 1949 Delahaye Sports Convertible Type 175. The type placed fifth at the 1949 Le Mans 24-Hour Race. Power was a seven-bearing, six-cylinder, water-cooled, inline, 4.5-liter engine.

PLYMOUTH STATION WAGON The Plymouth Special DeLuxe Station Wagon Model P-18 was produced in 1949 and built on a 118.5-inch wheelbase. This wagon was a two-door instead of four-door in order to seat three and still have plenty of stowage area in the rear. Power was a six-cylinder, L-head, inline, water-cooled, 97-hp. engine of 217-cubic-inch displacement.

HARTNETT L. Hartnett was the former General Motors-Holden managing director in 1948, when the G.M.-Holden was produced. He then decided that Australia needed a smaller, more economical car, and thus he founded the Hartnett Motor Company, Victoria, Australia. This is the 1949 Hartnett two-door sedan. Power was a two-cylinder, 600-cc-displacement engine that developed 19 hp. at 4,000 rpm. Only 135 Hartnett cars were built due to the poor response from the public.

BUICK HARDTOP COUPÉ This Series 50 six-passenger Buick Hardtop Coupé of 1949 was the first to feature the famous "portholes" in the fender sides. Power was an eight-cylinder, overhead-valve, in-line, water-cooled, 248-cubic-inch engine that developed 115 hp. at 3,600 rpm. Three-speed manual transmission was standard, however, Dynaflow automatic transmission was available if desired. This model started a refreshingly new styling for Buick.

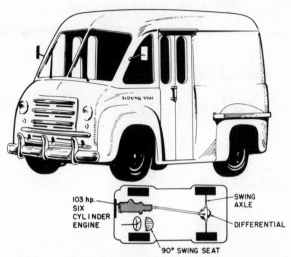

103 hp.
SIX
CYLINDER
ENGINE

SWING
AXLE

DIFFERENTIAL

90° SWING SEAT

DODGE ROUTE VAN   Dodge was one of the pioneers in the development of the Route Van. This type of truck was used for home and retail store deliveries of lightweight necessities of the kind requiring frequent stops. This Dodge Route Van of 1949 had a wheelbase of 115 inches. The engine was offset to the right, and the driver sat to the left of the engine instead of behind it. The door had a spring-closing and quick opening because of the many stops required. The driver's seat could rotate 90 degrees to face the door. Power was a six-cylinder, inline, water-cooled, 230.2-cubic-inch-displacement engine that developed 103 hp. at 3,600 rpm. The drive shaft was offset from the engine to the differential in the middle of the rear axle, which was of the swing type.

CHAPTER TWELVE

Fabulous Fifties' Production Records Forge Ahead 1950—1959

HOSTILITIES BEGAN in Korea on June 25, 1950. The U.S. Department of Defense reactivated the Ordnance Tank-Automotive Center in Detroit with the objective of mobilizing the automotive industry for war production. Despite the fact that almost all automobile companies received contracts for military hardware, a record figure of over 8 million civilian cars, trucks, and buses were produced in 1950, over 75 percent of all the motor vehicles made in the world. The United States imported 21,689 vehicles in 1950 and exported 304,000. During the year 3,234,000 old vehicles were scrapped.

REO began producing the 2.5-ton Eager Beaver truck for the military, Dodge introduced a 4-ton model, and White offered two truck models.

Automotive pioneer Ransom E. Olds died in 1950. He had experimented with steam-powered cars as early as 1894 and had organized the Oldsmobile Division of General Motors, as well as the REO Motor Car Company. Olds had made the first low-priced car in the United States, pioneered the mass production of automobiles, and manufactured the first practical powered lawn mower.

Chevrolet made its 25-millionth vehicle, and Oldsmobile made its 3-millionth vehicle during 1950. This was the year of Chrysler's silver anniversary and Mack's golden anniversary.

458

Several small cars were introduced in 1950. Kaiser-Frazer showed the Henry J compact four-seater, and Willys made a small engine for the car. Nash-Kelvinator showed the NXI in order to determine the public's reaction to a small, two-seat, personal car. This diminutive model eventually became known as the Metropolitan. Nash also introduced the Rambler on a 100-inch wheelbase and offered seat belts as optional equipment. Crosley introduced their Super Sports model which sold for less than $1,000. They also produced the Farm-o-Road, a farm and road vehicle with a 10-to-1 compression ratio!

Ford introduced automatic transmission for the Ford and Mercury cars and called them the Fordomatic and the Mercomatic. Crash pads were brought out by Kaiser, and Buick introduced a non-glare, tinted glass. Oldsmobile abandoned the six-cylinder engine in favor of an eight-cylinder powerplant named the Rocket V-8. The V-8 engine and automatic transmission were also found in the Studebaker. Nash developed a moisture-proof, plastic, insulated ignition system.

Styling changes for 1950 included larger radiator grilles, fenders integral with the body and hood, and increased window area with a one-piece, curved windshield. Wood began disappearing from station-wagon designs.

John Parsons won the 1950 Indianapolis 500-Mile Race with an average speed of 124 mph. in the Wynn Friction-Proof Special. The 1950 World Champion was Giuseppe Farina of Italy driving an Alfa Romeo. L. and C. Rosier, driving a Talbot, won the 1950 Le Mans 24-Hour Race.

In 1950 there were 34,763 deaths due to motor vehicle accidents. This amounted to 7.6 deaths for every 100 million vehicle miles traveled. Over 86 percent of United States travelers used the automobile for inter-city travel in 1950.

As the Korean War continued into 1951, with Chinese troops sent to aid the North Koreans, the use of strategic materials, such as zinc, tin, chromium and nickel, was restricted in non-defense industries. The shipment of spare tires for new vehicles was prohibited. Most of the auto companies were engaged in producing war matériel. Chrysler was making the T-43 heavy tank, and Cadillac built the T-41 light tank. General Motors Truck and

Coach Division made the new M-135 6x6 military truck for the United States Army.

For the first time in many years, Ford introduced a six-cylinder, overhead-valve engine, and Buick offered a V-8 engine on certain models. Continental Motors obtained production rights for the French Turbomeca gas-turbine engines for use in aircraft and automobiles. Oldsmobile featured the Rocket V-8 engine.

Lincoln introduced the plush Capri, and a hardtop model was included in the Nash Rambler line. Nash also had a two-passenger competition sports car, the Nash Healey, designed and built by the British firm of Donald Healey. Plymouth introduced the Belvedere hardtop, and Oldsmobile offered the Super 88. Ford introduced a hardtop, the Victoria, with an optional "Continental" external, rear-mounted spare tire. Willys-Overland introduced its first post-World War II six-cylinder passenger auto, the Aero Willys. Sears, Roebuck began marketing a modified Kaiser Henry J under the name of Allstate. Kaiser-Frazer stopped producing the higher-priced Frazer car. Crosley made a right-hand-drive light truck for the special delivery of mail and to service letterbox routes.

The radial-ply, steel-belted tire was patented on October 24, 1951, in France by Michelin, French Patent No. 1,001,585, thereby starting a tire revolution.

The 1951 World Champion Driver was Juan Mañuel Fangio of Argentina driving an Alfa Romeo. The Indianapolis 500-Mile Race was won by Lee Wallard driving the Belanger Special at an average speed of 126.24 mph. P. D. Walker and P. N. Whitehead, driving a Jaguar, won the Le Mans 24-Hour Race.

United States companies manufactured 6,765,263 vehicles in 1951, and by December the 100-millionth United States passenger car had been built. The average age of the United States passenger car in 1951 was 7.1 years and, in the same year, 3,774,000 vehicles were scrapped. There were 36,996 automobile traffic fatalities, which is about 7.6 deaths for every 100 million vehicle miles traveled.

War still raged on the Korean peninsula in 1952, but armistice talks began at Panmunjom. Fulgencio Batista seized power in Cuba, a dictatorship that lasted until 1959. The eyes of the world turned to Africa, where rising African nationalism achieved its first victory with the independence of Libya. In Kenya the Mau Mau, a secret terrorist organization, began a bloody campaign to oust white settlers. The British declared a state of emergency that lasted until 1960. Queen Elizabeth II of England began her reign.

The United States automobile manufacturers continued to produce military equipment such as cars, trucks, tanks, aircraft engines, marine engines, airplanes, and aircraft gun sights. United States civilian vehicle production dropped to 5,538,959 units in 1952. About 3,767,000 vehicles were scrapped during the year, and 6.6 years was the average age of passenger cars. Georgia became the twenty-first state to amend its constitution so that all state motor vehicle and gasoline taxes were earmarked for highway purposes. In the same year, 37,955 fatalities were caused by the automobile. This resulted in 7.4 deaths per 100 million vehicle miles traveled. About 85 percent of all U.S. local and long-distance travel was done by private automobile. The 120-mile New Jersey Turnpike opened.

Studebaker announced its 100th anniversary, and Cadillac celebrated its 25th year of existence. The operation of the Detroit Tank Arsenal was given to the Chrysler Corporation, and the company began construction of its 4,000-acre tank proving ground in Chelsea, Michigan. Buick introduced its Skylark luxury convertible in the $5,000 price range. Willys expanded its Aero series of passenger cars with the introduction of the Aero Eagle. DeSoto introduced the Firedome V-8 engine, and Plymouth offered automatic overdrive. Hudson introduced the Jet low-priced auto, and General Motors developed a 2.5-ton diesel-driven truck. General Tire bought Crosley and ended production of that automobile.

The 12-volt electrical system was introduced on the Chrysler Crown Imperial, and dual-range Hydra-Matic was offered on the Pontiac. Oldsmobile featured an automatic headlight dimmer, and a four-way adjustable seat was available on the Packard. The Lincoln introduced ball-joint front-wheel suspension, and suspended brake and clutch pedals became standard on all Ford Motor Company autos. Ford opened a new plant for assembling Lincoln and Mercury cars in Wayne, Michigan.

Alvin Macauley, former chairman of the board of Packard,

died. As its president, he had guided Packard during World War I and then led the company's development of aircraft, diesel, and tank engines.

In 1952 the World Championship Driver was Alberto Ascari of Italy, driving a Ferrari. The Indianapolis 500-Mile Race was won by Troy Ruttman at an average speed of 128.9 mph. H. Lang and F. Riess won the Le Mans 24-Hour Race in a Mercedes-Benz.

1953 was another eventful year with the death of Josef Stalin. Georgi Malenkov became the Soviet premier, and Nikita S. Khrushchev was elected the first secretary of the Soviet Communist Party's Central Committee. The Russians exploded their first hydrogen bomb. Workers in East Germany staged riots that were suppressed by Soviet troops. In Paraguay, General Alfredo Stroessner staged a coup and, in spite of opposition, remained in power. The Korean War ended in mid-1953, and this helped to spur the auto industry's civilian output to 7,323,214 peacetime vehicles for the year.

Tail fins were taking hold, and double-curvature windshields appeared. Grilles were becoming wider and window areas larger. Air conditioning was more common, and automatic transmission was available on all leading makes in the United States. Oil pressure and electrical system gauges were replaced with warning lights. The 12-volt electrical system, developed by Delco-Remy, was installed on Buicks, Oldsmobiles, and Cadillacs. Buick and Oldsmobile also offered power brakes. For the first time, Hydra-Matic automatic transmission became available on General Motors trucks.

In 1953 the eight-cylinder engine surpassed production of the six-cylinder engine in passenger cars for the first time, and Dodge offered its first V-8. Chevrolet began production of the Corvette plastic-laminated fiberglass body sports car. This was the first production plastic-body auto. Price was $3,250 with automatic transmission. Lincoln-Mercury introduced the Mercury "Sun Valley" Sports Coupé, featuring a transparent, green-tinted, Plexiglas panel which replaced the steel located over the driver's seat to admit sunlight. For a short while Pontiacs were fitted with Power Glide transmission. Cadillac and Oldsmobile used Dynaflow because a fire in the Hydra-Matic plant cut off the normal supply of automatic transmissions for the cars.

Several experimental cars were shown at auto shows: the Hudson Italia, DeSoto Adventurer (which eventually saw production), Packard Balboa, Dodge Firearrow, Buick Wildcat (which also saw production), and the Lincoln-Mercury fiberglass XI-500. Race driver Mauri Rose drove the experimental General Motors XP-21 gas-turbine 370-hp. Whirlfire. With a plastic body and a turbine-jet-powered engine the car weighed 2,500 pounds.

Kaiser-Frazer bought Willys-Overland and changed its name to Kaiser Motors Corporation. General Motors bought the Kaiser Motors' Willow Run plant. Ford Motor Company announced its intention to move its New Jersey assembly operations from Edgewater to a new plant on a 177-acre site in Mahwah. Ford and Buick celebrated their fiftieth anniversaries, and Plymouth announced its twenty-fifth year of production.

The 1953 Championship Driver was Alberto Ascari of Italy driving a Ferrari. A. R. R. Rolt and J. S. Hamilton won the Le Mans 24-Hour Race in a Jaguar. The 1953 Indianapolis 500-Mile Race was won by Bill Vukovich, whose average speed was 128.74 mph.

The average age of automobiles in the U.S. in 1953 was 6.5 years, and over 4 million vehicles were scrapped that year. The automobile was responsible for 37,955 fatalities, which is about 7 deaths for every 100 million vehicle miles traveled. According to the American Automobile Association, the average motorist drove 10,000 miles per year and spent between $900 and $1,000 on upkeep and maintenance.

In an atomic bomb test in Nevada, defense information for the future was developed by placing automobiles near ground zero to see what the effects of the explosion were.

1954 marked the Geneva settlement, which divided Vietnam into North and South Vietnam and recognized the independence of Cambodia and Laos. In the Far East there was the Battle of Dien Bien Phu, which effectively ended French rule and eventually led to the U.S. involvement in Vietnam. It also cut off a large part of the world's rubber supply. In Africa the Algerian nationalists began terrorist campaigns against the French, a struggle that ended with Algeria's independence in 1962.

In the less dramatic world of automobiles, the hardtop was still increasing in popularity, as were wraparound windshields. Safety padding on instrument panels was becoming more common. All Ford engines had overhead valves, and V-8 engines appeared in Chevrolets and Plymouths. Chrysler introduced the automatic transmission selector located on the instrument panel. Tubeless tires became standard equipment on all U.S. autos by the end of 1954.

Ford's answer to the Corvette was introduced in the fall of the year. It was the all-steel, two-seater Thunderbird. Ford also introduced a pushbutton chassis and suspension lubrication for the Mercury and the Lincoln. A reservoir of lubricant was attached to the chassis, and, at the push of a button, the lubricant was forced out of the reservoir and into the proper joints.

George Walter Mason died in 1954. He was the general works manager for Chrysler, president of Kelvinator Corporation, and then chairman of the board of Nash-Kelvinator. He was president and chairman of the board of American Motors until his death.

Chrysler Corporation developed an efficient gas turbine and installed it in a production Plymouth. The car was road tested and displayed throughout the U.S. It was exceptionally quiet-running and proved to be economical with a minimum of exhaust heat. General Motors introduced the Turbocruiser, the world's first gas-turbine-powered bus, and the XP-2, a jet-powered experimental speedster with aerodynamic styling that looked like a rocket plane with delta wings. Other experimental cars shown in 1954 were the Ford FX-Atmos dream car, Dodge Granada, Packard Panther fiberglass-body sports car, Plymouth Belmont and Explorer, DeSoto Adventurer MKII, and the Lincoln-Mercury Monterey XM-800.

The year saw the first of thirty General Motors training centers opened in Detroit. The first section of the New York Thruway also opened, as did a section of the Northern Ohio Turnpike, joining Youngstown with the Pennsylvania Turnpike, and West Virginia's 90-mile Turnpike. Wyoming amended its constitution in order to spend all state motor vehicle and gasoline taxes for highway purposes.

Auto racing was gaining in popularity, although the American Automobile Association planned to stop sanctioning races. The 1954 World Champion Driver was Juan Mañuel Fangio who drove a Maserati and also a Mercedes. Bill Vukovich again won the Indianapolis 500-Mile Race with an average speed of 130.84 mph. The 1954 Le Mans 24-Hour Race was won by J. F. Gonzalez and M. Trintignant driving a Ferrari.

U.S. auto firms produced 6,601,071 vehicles during 1954, and General Motors made its 50-millionth vehicle by November. General Motors, Ford, and Chrysler announced expansion programs. The average age of the U.S. passenger car in that year was 6.2 years, and over 4,350,000 vehicles were scrapped. Traffic fatalities dropped to 35,586, which is 6.3 deaths for every 100 million vehicle miles traveled. A President's Action Committee for Highway Safety was created by President Eisenhower.

In 1955 many European countries made history. The Warsaw Pact, a mutual defense treaty, was signed by the Soviet Union and other Iron Curtain countries. In the Far East, a U.S. military advisory group took over the training of the South Vietnamese Army. Premier Ngo Dinh Diem became president of South Vietnam.

By the end of the year U.S. automobile production broke all records with the manufacture of 9,169,292 vehicles. Total value was $14,473,844,000! The U.S. accounted for 67.5 percent of the world's automobile production, and it exported 447,000 vehicles and imported 59,548. A total of 4,392,000 vehicles were scrapped, and the average age of passenger cars was 5.9 years. Getting younger! Eighty-nine percent of U.S. inter-city travel was by automobile, and only 2½ percent was by bus. Automobile-caused fatalities in 1955 rose to 38,426, which resulted in 6.4 deaths for every 100 million vehicle miles driven.

Both Buick and Oldsmobile introduced the four-door hardtop. The idea caught on, and several other manufacturers began work in this direction. Ford Motor Company introduced the classic Continental Mark II to the public after hundreds of orders had already been received. The sporty Studebaker Hawk was also announced, and Chevrolet brought out the Nomad station wagon. A V-8 engine was offered in the Nash Ambassador and in the Packard. Packard developed a motor-controlled torsion-bar suspension. The Italian Pirelli rubber company announced a fabric-belted radial tire.

The "safety bug" was beginning to hit the U.S. auto manufacturers, and many firms supplied seat belts, while safety door latches became standard equipment on most major makes. The improved sealed-beam headlights became standard equipment also. Packard developed electrically actuated door locks as optional equipment. Seat-belt legislation, enacted in Illinois, required that holes be placed in the frame of all new cars for the attachment of seat belts.

Plymouth opened an automated engine plant in Detroit, and Chrysler bought the automotive component manufacturer Universal Products Company. Kaiser Motors Corporation discontinued the manufacture of Kaiser and Willys and concentrated on the production of Jeep-type vehicles. The company also reorganized as the Kaiser Industries Corporation with Willys as a subsidiary.

The 1955 World Champion Driver was again Juan Mañuel Fangio of Argentina driving a Mercedes. Stirling Moss won the Mille Miglia Race from Brescia, Italy, to Rome and return. Moss achieved this in a 300 SLR Mercedes in the record time of 10 hours, 7 minutes, 48 seconds. The Indianapolis 500-Mile Race was won by Bob Sweikert with an average speed of 128.209 mph.

Several experimental and dream vehicles were shown to the public: the Buick Wildcat MKIII, the Ford Mystère with a plastic body, Ford Futura, Chevrolet Biscayne, Oldsmobile Delta, Pontiac Strato-Star, Chrysler Flight Sweep cars, G.M. Firebird II gas-turbine, jet-powered car, General Motors Coach and Truck Division's Universelle truck, and the Cadillac Eldorado Brougham. A 15-inch, sun-powered car model was demonstrated at the General Motors Powerama in Chicago. Twelve photoelectric selenium cells were fitted. Over two million people attended the Powerama on the Chicago lakefront.

As the United States continued to progress in the auto industry, 1956 world history didn't stand still either. Premier Khrushchev denounced Stalin at the 20th Communist Party Congress in Moscow, which ushered in a period of de-Stalinization in the Soviet Union and Eastern Europe. Workers rioted in Poland. The Hungarian rebellion against the Communist régime was put down by Soviet troops and tanks. In Africa, Tunisia gained independence from France with Habib Bourguiba to become premier.

In the same year Louisiana and Montana amended their constitutions to earmark all state motor vehicle and gasoline taxes for highway purposes. The Federal government enacted the Highway Act of 1956. This provided for the construction of 40,000 plus miles of interstate highways, with the Federal government paying about 90 percent of the cost. Federal gasoline taxes were raised one cent per gallon to help finance the roads. A long section of the Indiana Turnpike was opened, linking Gary with the Ohio Turnpike. A motorist could now travel from New York to Chicago on high-speed highways.

Automobile pioneer Herbert H. Franklin died in 1956. He placed his car in production in 1902, and every Franklin automobile was fitted with an air-cooled engine until his company stopped auto production in 1930, by which time 15,000 vehicles had been sold. Franklin was also known for his aircraft engines that powered light airplanes.

Ford Motor Company stock held by the Ford Foundation was offered to the public for the first time in 1956. Over 10 million shares were placed on the market at $64 per share. Ford also announced a $600 million expansion program for 1956. Packard auto production moved from Detroit to the Studebaker-Packard plant in South Bend, Indiana. The General Motors Technical Center was dedicated.

A free-piston engine was demonstrated by General Motors. It could burn virtually any combustible liquid, from gasoline to vegetable oil. The exhaust from the free-piston cylinder was piped to a gas turbine which drove the wheels of a car. The experimental gas-turbine-powered car previously developed by Plymouth was driven from coast to coast to test the durability and economy of the design.

New automotive developments for 1956 included a new dual lighting system that replaced the single 7-inch, sealed-beam headlight on each side with two 5¾-inch lights on each side. They were arranged one above the other or side by side and had the advantage of aiming the high beam light and the regular light individually for efficiency and to prolong the life of the light. Although proposed for 1958, some 1957 models shown in 1956 featured the new lighting arrangement. Fourteen-inch wheels in lieu of 15- and 16-inch sizes were shown on the majority of 1957 models. Mercury introduced a retractable rear window controlled from the driver's seat, and Ford introduced a hardtop coupé in which the entire top could power-retract into the trunk. The idea was not new, but this was the first time it was placed into production. Fuel injection was an optional extra for Chevrolet, Pontiac, and Rambler. Plymouth introduced rear-facing seats in the third row of the nine-passenger station wagon. All Dodge, Plymouth, DeSoto, and Chrysler cars were fitted with torsion-bar suspension. Six-way power seats and electric door locks were made available on several high-priced cars. A special differential was offered that would not slip in mud or snow, and Turbo-glide automatic transmission was introduced for the Chevrolet.

The new Lincoln Premier received the only award ever given for excellence in design to an automobile by the Industrial Designers Institute.

U.S. auto production of motor vehicles dropped to 6,920,590 in 1956, and 4,948,000 trucks, buses, and passenger cars were scrapped. The average age of passenger automobiles in the U.S. was 5.6 years. Fatalities for the year attributed to motor vehicle accidents were 39,628, which was 6.3 deaths for every 100 million vehicle miles traveled.

Pat Flaherty won the 1956 Indianapolis 500-Mile Race in the John Zink Special at an average speed of 128.49 mph. The Le Mans 24-Hour Race was won by R. Flockhart and N. Sanderson in a Jaguar. Juan Mañuel Fangio of Argentina was once again the World Champion Driver in a Ferrari.

1957 was the year of Sputnik, the world's first artificial satellite, which initiated the Space Age. The International Geophysical Year of 1957–58 began, with many nations participating in studies in the Arctic and Antarctic. The Common Market was established in Europe, and Malaya gained its independence.

Milestones for the year in the world of automobiles: International Harvester's golden anniversary in truck production; Oldsmobile's sixtieth year of auto production; Pontiac's golden anniversary (including the Oakland years); and Plymouth's 10-millionth car. REO Motors, Inc., was sold to the White Motor Company.

Ford Motor Company introduced the Edsel automobile, named in honor of Edsel Ford. The car had self-adjusting brakes, a drum-type speedometer, and a pushbutton selector for the automatic transmission. Despite these and many other good qualities, it proved to be the wrong car at the wrong time, and the public spurned it, resulting in an enormous financial loss for Ford. A Studebaker economy car without frills, the Scotsman, was introduced to sell to low-income groups. Packard introduced the Clipper station wagon, which was the first Packard wagon in years. Mack Trucks introduced a forty-passenger, luxury-type, cross-country bus.

General Motors Truck and Coach Division developed an experimental gas-turbine-powered truck called the Turbo-Titan. Ford Motor Company also showed an experimental gas-turbine-powered truck. In addition, Ford revealed an experimental aluminum, high-speed, military vehicle that used unitized construction.

Refinements on U.S. cars were as follows: tail fins were enlarged, and most of them were fitted with taillights; wraparound windshields and rear windows were being used on most designs; and paper air cleaners were used by several manufacturers. Lincoln and Continental announced unitized body-frame construction. Buick offered aluminum brake drums with cooling fins, and Chrysler Corporation cars introduced a double-curvature windshield extending into the shape of the roof. Rear coil springs appeared on most Chrysler Corporation cars, and Lincoln, Continental, and Cadillac featured an exterior side mirror that was adjustable from within the car. Mercury offered air suspension as optional.

Lincoln, Continental, and Rambler used a method of priming the steel car body to prevent rust on exterior and interior surfaces of the steel; they dipped the entire finished body into a primer bath. Studebaker added a hardtop model to their President and Commander series, and Chevrolet inaugurated the luxury Impala series. Virtually all auto manufacturers adopted the dual-headlight system, and an off-center mounting for the rear spring on the Studebaker reduced diving during severe braking. Production of the two-seater Thunderbird was gradually phased out to be replaced by a four-seat version.

The U.S. automobile industry produced 7,220,520 vehicles in 1957, with a total value of over $13 billion. During the year there were 38,702 auto-related fatalities, which means that there were 5 deaths for every 100 million vehicle miles traveled.

Juan Mañuel Fangio of Argentina again became the World Champion Driver in 1957 driving a Maserati. The Indianapolis 500-Mile Race was won by Sam Hanks driving a Belond Exhaust Special at an average speed of 135.6 mph. The Le Mans 24-Hour Race was won by R. Flockhard and I. Bueb driving a Jaguar. Piero Taruffi of Italy won the Mille Miglia race in Italy driving a Ferrari at an average speed of 95 mph. The year 1957 marked the last running of this famous race.

The five-mile span of the Mackinac Bridge was opened to traffic in Michigan, and a long stretch of the Kansas Turnpike was included in the Interstate Highway System.

In 1958 the United States made a giant stride in space by successfully launching her first artificial satellite. *Nautilus,* the U.S. nuclear submarine, was the first ship to cross the North Pole under the ice pack. Nuclear test ban negotiations began in Geneva between the Western and Soviet blocs. De Gaulle was elected president of France, and the Russians provoked the Berlin crisis.

In this same year, General Motors Corporation marked its fiftieth anniversary with a Golden Milestone celebration lasting all year. Ford Motor Company made its 50-millionth vehicle, and Chrysler Corporation made its 25-millionth. Ford celebrated the fiftieth anniversary of the Model T by restoring one of the famous cars at the new Ford plant in Mahwah, New Jersey.

Edward Jordan died in 1958. He had organized the Jordan Motor Car Company in 1916 after working with the Thomas B. Jeffery Company. He kept production down to 5,000 cars per year and always made a profit until his company perished in the Depression.

Also dead in 1958 was Charles F. Kettering, organizer of the Delco Laboratories for ignition systems. Kettering developed the first self-starter for the 1911 Cadillac and became chief of General Motors Laboratories, where ethyl gasoline and quick-drying paints were perfected.

The third auto pioneer to die during the year was Lee Chadwick, who held over 150 patents. He made his first car in 1899 and one year later was general superintendent of the Searchmont

Company. Chadwick started his own company in 1903 and made the first car to use a supercharger in 1906. His cars were among the fastest of their time.

American Motors dropped the names of Nash and Hudson from their products and concentrated on Rambler. The 100-inch wheelbase Rambler American was introduced. Other newcomers were the Mercury Medalist, a bottom-of-the-line economy type; the four-passenger Thunderbird, featuring unitized construction; the Lark compact economy car introduced by Studebaker; the Ford Galaxie luxury series; and a high-priced, handmade car called Argonaut announced by Argonaut Motor Corporation. Checker Motors Corporation announced plans to produce the Superba automobile.

Lincoln introduced a new Lincoln Continental which was identical with the Lincoln, also new, except that the Continental was the more luxurious version and was called the Mark III. The wheelbase was 130 inches and the rear window opened electrically from the driver's seat. The convertible model was also fitted with a glass retractable rear window and a top that retracted into a steel-covered compartment.

Ford demonstrated an experimental operating model of an air-cushion vehicle, the Glidaire, which traveled on a thin cushion of air without wheels. General Motors displayed the Firebird III experimental vehicle that replaced the steering wheel, brake pedal, and accelerator pedal with single-stick control.

The White Motor Company bought the Diamond-T Motor Car Company, and Chrysler Corporation absorbed about one-quarter of the stock of the French Simca automobile firm. The end of Packard auto production was announced by Studebaker-Packard. Henceforth the firm would concentrate on economy types.

A double-chambered safety tire designed to prevent complete blowouts was introduced by Goodyear. Radial-belted tires began to enjoy popularity in Europe and the U.S.

Fins continued to get higher and windshields larger in 1958. Oldsmobile showed a flanged brake drum for more efficient cooling. Rambler made separately adjustable reclining seats available at extra cost, and Ford offered a trunk lid lock that released electrically from the driver's seat. Chrysler Corporation included swivel front seats as optional equipment and also offered an electronically controlled rear-view mirror. This mirror automatically changed to the night-driving, non-glare position whenever the headlight beam from a following car struck the mirror surface. Internally controlled external rear-view mirrors were offered by many manufacturers. Great progress was made in the development of new body paint that retained a new-car luster even without waxing. A lock for the right front seat back was offered by Buick on two-door models, and progress in metallurgy improved the life of exhaust pipes and mufflers.

In 1958 the World Champion Driver was J. Mike Hawthorn of Great Britain, who drove a Ferrari. Jimmy Bryan won the Indianapolis 500-Mile Race driving a Belond Special at an average speed of 133.79 mph. The Le Mans 24-Hour Race was won by P. Hill and O. Gendebien driving a Ferrari.

In the United States, 5,135,106 vehicles were produced, and a total of 430,808 automobiles, mostly Volkswagens and British sports cars, were imported into the U.S. Over four million vehicles were scrapped in the U.S. during the year. The average age of the U.S. passenger automobile was 5.6 years. Fatalities attributed to the motor vehicle totaled 36,981, which means that there were 5.4 deaths for every 100 million vehicle miles traveled.

The Connecticut Turnpike from the New York border to the Rhode Island border was opened to traffic, and additional funds were authorized by the Federal government to accelerate construction of the Interstate Highway System.

At the end of the decade, the 1959–1960 Treaty, accepted by twelve nations including the United States, provided for reserving Antarctica for scientific research and recognized no existing national claims to territory in the area. Fidel Castro came to power in Cuba, and he gradually linked Cuba with the Soviet bloc. The Communist Chinese suppressed an uprising in Tibet, and the Communist Pathet Lao forces began civil war in Laos.

In the U.S. the feeling against so-called "gas guzzlers" had grown to such proportions that five compact cars were introduced in 1959: Ford had the Falcon economy car, Dodge brought out the Dart, Plymouth revealed its Valiant, Chevrolet began producing its aluminum, air-cooled, rear-engine-powered Corvair, and Willys made the Maverick Special, a luxury Jeep-type station wagon.

Three companies planned to produce electric-powered vehicles for urban driving to reduce air pollution. Smog-producing hydrocarbon emissions from motor vehicles became a matter of concern in congested areas in California and elsewhere. The Automobile Manufacturers Association announced an emission control system that diverted vapors from the engine crankcase into the intake manifold to be burned by the engine, a system that would be offered in 1961.

Experimental vehicles in 1959 included air-cushion vehicles, the Air Car demonstrated by Curtiss Wright and the Levacar by Ford. Both vehicles traveled on a cushion of low-pressure air pumped downward by an engine-driven compressor in the vehicle. Chevrolet displayed an experimental gas-turbine-engine truck called the Turbo-Titan II. Chrysler showed the DeSoto Belle I, as well as an electrochemical system to power a car by converting fuel into electrical energy without the use of an engine/generator. Cadillac developed a radar device that would warn the driver with a loud buzzer and flashing lights when an object was detected in the path of the car. Curtiss Wright and the German NSU Werke auto manufacturer announced a license to produce a rotating internal-combustion engine that could be used for autos, planes, and boats. This became known as the Wankel engine, named after its German inventor.

Features for 1960 production cars were announced in late 1959. Unit body construction was becoming more popular, with Corvair, Valiant, Plymouth, Dodge, DeSoto, and Falcon employing the system. Pontiac announced a dual-chambered water pump to insure equal distribution into both cylinder banks on vee-type engines. Cadillac introduced an automatic parking-brake release which worked when the engine was started and the transmission placed in a drive position. Thunderbird hardtops featured a sliding metal roof panel operable from the driver's seat. Ford introduced an anti-theft ignition switch, and Chrysler announced an emergency flashing system of front and rear lights. This system is a standard item on every car today.

In 1959 U.S. auto companies produced 6,728,629 automobiles, trucks, and buses worth almost $13 billion. The U.S. imported 668,070 autos, or approximately 10 percent of U.S. production. A total of 5,096,000 vehicles were scrapped, which was a record at that time. The average age of the passenger car in the U.S. was 5.8 years, and there were 37,910 fatalities attributed to the motor vehicle, or 5.4 deaths for every 100 million vehicle miles traveled.

The Federal gasoline tax was increased by four cents per gallon at the pump in order to finance the Interstate Highway System. Pontiac produced its 7-millionth vehicle, and, at the end of the production year, the Edsel automobile was discontinued by Ford.

CADILLAC HARDTOP COUPÉ   The postwar Cadillacs pioneered styling features such as tail fins and wide grilles extending from headlight to headlight. This is the 1950 Cadillac Hardtop Coupé, powered by an eight-cylinder, vee-type, side-valve, water-cooled, 346-cubic-inch-displacement engine that developed 160 hp. at 3,500 rpm. Speed was about 100 mph. This luxurious six-seater was designed by Harley Earl.

CHEVROLET BEL AIR HARDTOP   In 1950, Chevrolet introduced Power Glide automatic transmission for all of its cars, and two million Chevrolets were made that year. This is the Chevrolet Bel Air Hardtop of 1950, which used the notch-back Styleline body. The Bel Air was the Chevy top of the line and included a long list of luxury features, such as carpets, clock, and high-quality upholstery. The hardtop style became very popular in the fifties. Power was a six-cylinder, inline, water-cooled, 235.5-cubic-inch engine. Bore was 3⅝ inches and stroke was 4 inches.

DAIMLER TOURING LIMOUSINE This four-door, eight-passenger British Daimler Touring Limousine of 1950 was fitted with an eight-cylinder engine instead of the twin-six that Daimler also had in production. The car was large, comfortable, and elegant. It was one of the last straight-eights in England. The eight-cylinder, inline, overhead-valve, water-cooled engine had a displacement of 5,460 cc and produced 150 hp. at 3,600 rpm. Four forward speeds were fitted.

SAAB NO. 1 Saab (Svenska Aeroplan AB) of Trollhättän, Sweden, made their first production automobile in 1950. Designs for the car began in 1944, when the firm feared a drop in aircraft production and decided to build a "people's car." This Saab 92 had a unitized body that held four passengers and was built on a 97.4-inch wheelbase. Overall length was 154.3 inches, and total width was 63.9 inches. Power was a two-cylinder, transverse-mounted, two-stroke, 25-hp., 466-cubic-inch-displacement engine driving the front wheels. Independent suspension was via torsion bars. Top speed was 67 mph. In 1954, power was increased to 28 hp., and a 33-hp. sports version was also produced. The car won awards in the Midnight Sun Rallye in 1953 and placed in the Coupe des Dames and the Tulip Rallye in 1955.

PLYMOUTH P-20   Plymouth cars were winners in 162 NASCAR Grand Nationals between 1949 and 1970. Shown is the 1950 Plymouth two-door sedan Model P-20 that was raced by Johnny Mantz. The street version of this car was a Plymouth DeLuxe with a wheelbase of 111 inches. A six-cylinder, inline, water-cooled, L-head, 97-hp., 217-cubic-inch-displacement engine was fitted.

NASH RAMBLER CONVERTIBLE SEDAN   The Nash Rambler made motoring history by becoming the first compact car when it was introduced in 1950. This is the Nash Rambler Model 5021 Convertible Sedan. This five-seater was built on a 100-inch wheelbase. Power was a six-cylinder, inline, water-cooled, 82-hp. engine that gave the car 25 to 30 miles per gallon of fuel. The car revived the original company name of Rambler. Nash produced 191,865 cars in 1950 for an all-time Nash record. The 2-millionth Nash rolled off the Kenosha, Wisconsin, assembly line in April, 1950.

M.G.-TD MIDGET This is the car that took the world by storm when it was introduced in 1950, because it combined reliability, performance, and a low price that almost anyone could afford. The M.G.-TD weighed 2,009 pounds on a 7-foot-10-inch wheelbase. Overall length was 12 feet 1 inch, and width was 4 feet 10⅞ inches. Power was a four-cylinder, overhead-valve, inline, water-cooled engine of 1,250-cc displacement that developed 54.4 hp. The turning circle was 31 feet. Acceleration from 10 to 30 mph. took 12.5 seconds, and from stop to 50 mph. took 15.2 seconds. The car was fitted with independent front-suspension and disc wheels instead of the spoked wheels as on previous models. This car is generally credited with awakening the U.S. to the world of sports cars. The TD finished in sixth place in the Sebring 12-Hour Race in 1952.

PONTIAC CHIEFTAIN The Pontiac Chieftain Model 27 of 1951 celebrated the company's silver anniversary with increased power and twenty-seven styling changes, plus sixteen mechanical improvements such as: timing chain, distributor, thermostat, starter, generator, carburetor, etc. This two-door sedan was powered by an eight-cylinder, inline, water-cooled, 116-hp. engine of 268.4-cubic-inch displacement. Either Hydra-Matic automatic transmission or Synchromesh hand-shifting was available. Bore was 3.375 inches and stroke was 3.75 inches.

HENRY J The Kaiser-Frazer Company produced the Henry J from 1951 to 1954, because they felt that Americans needed a small economy car during the slight recession in 1950. This was a compact car with dimensions almost identical to the more recent Ford Pinto. Power was a 134-cubic-inch-displacement, four-cylinder Willys engine. During 1952–1953, Sears, Roebuck & Company marketed a very slightly revised Henry J and called it the Allstate. Price of the Henry J was about $1,299. The car is generally considered to have been a failure and contributed to the company's decline.

CUNNINGHAM MODEL C-1 Racing personality Briggs S. Cunningham built this prototype sports car in 1951. He entered that year's Le Mans 24-Hour Race and finished in eighteenth place. In 1952, the car placed fourth. The engine was a Chrysler vee-type, eight-cylinder, 180-hp., 331-cubic-inch-displacement powerplant that Cunningham modified so he could draw from 220 to 310 hp. from the engine. Cunningham sports cars were produced through the fifties. This car can be seen at the Briggs Cunningham Automotive Museum, Costa Mesa, California.

HUDSON HORNET CONVERTIBLE The Hudson Hornet made its appearance in 1951 with a new high-compression engine that developed 145 hp. at 3,800 rpm. It was a six-cylinder, inline, water-cooled, L-head, 308-cubic-inch-displacement design, which was a 30 percent power increase over the existing Hudson eight-cylinder engine and improved the performance considerably. Hudsons stood third in the 1951 NASCAR list with twelve wins. In 1952, it placed first in twenty-seven out of thirty-four NASCAR Grand Nationals and was still champion in 1953 with twenty-two wins!

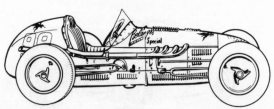

BELANGER SPECIAL This Frank Kurtis-designed and -built racer was Offenhauser-powered and with Lee Wallard at the wheel, it won the 1951 Indianapolis 500-Mile Race. It was quite small, little more than a stretched midget racer, and had no supercharger. After trading the lead with Jack McGrath for fifty miles, Wallard built up a safe lead as more and more cars were forced out by high speeds and high temperatures. The winning average speed was 126.24 mph.

POBIEDA SEDAN This Pobieda four-door sedan was made in the U.S.S.R. by the Gorkovski Avto Zavod (GAZ) and is the GAZ M-20 of 1952. It is one of the first Russian-designed cars. The five-passenger auto was powered by a four-cylinder, inline, water-cooled, side-valve, 2,120-cc-displacement engine that developed 49 hp. at 3,600 rpm. A three-speed transmission was fitted. Maximum speed was about 70 mph.

MERCEDES-BENZ 300 SL The famous Mercedes-Benz 300 SL gull-wing coupé was introduced in 1952. The car's powerplant was a six-cylinder, water-cooled, overhead-camshaft, inline, seven-bearing, 175-hp., 182-cubic-inch-displacement engine. Three carburetors were installed. The cars placed second and fourth in the 1952 Mille Miglia, and won the Le Mans at a speed of 96.7 mph. At Nürburgring they captured first, second, third, and fourth places! The 1952 prototype cars had aluminum bodies and weighed 1,900 pounds. A four-speed transmission was fitted. The 1952 prototype racer is illustrated. The gull-wing doors were used because a conventional door would interfere with the steel-tubing structure. The production models were revised so that the doors extended lower on the body sides in order to facilitate entering and exiting the car. The production models also featured some body sculpturing and minor vent grilles and used fuel injection.

RENAULT ROGUE   This 1952 Renault Rogue competition sports car scored many wins in its class. In 1952 it won the Coupe des Alpes, the Coupe des Dames in the Tour de France, and the Paris-St. Raphael Race. Successes continued in 1954 and 1955. In 1956, the car won in class at Monte Carlo and took eighth at the Acropolis. The car had a plastic body and weighed only 1,000 pounds. Power was a four-cylinder, inline, rear-mounted, water-cooled, 45-cubic-inch-displacement engine. Speed was about 107 mph.

H.R.G. SPORTS CAR   This tough, traditional British sports car was originally designed and built in 1948 by H. R. Godfrey with competition in mind. The H.R.G. won at Spa in 1948 and won the Team Prize in 1949. Also in 1949, the H.R.G. scored a class victory at Le Mans. The cars were victorious in class and team at the 1948 Alpine Rallye. The Coupe des Alpes was won in 1951 in the Production Touring Car Races at Silverstone. Shown here is the 1952 model. Power was a 1.5-liter-displacement, four-cylinder, water-cooled, inline, Singer-built engine. Speed was over 100 mph.

DeSOTO FIREDOME The DeSoto Firedome engine was introduced in early 1952 and was the first V-8 engine used by DeSoto. The Firedome Eight series of cars offered six body styles, and the four-door sedan Model S-17 of 1952 with a wheelbase of 125.5 inches is shown. The powerplant was an eight-cylinder, vee-type, water-cooled, 276.1-cubic-inch-displacement, 160-hp. engine. Bore was 3⅝ inches and stroke was $3^{11}/_{32}$ inches. A new automated plant was constructed for manufacturing the engine, and it could produce sixty complete V-8 Firedome engines per hour!

CUMMINS DIESEL SPECIAL The Cummins Diesel Company spent over half a million dollars to design and construct this diesel-engine-powered race car for the 1952 Indianapolis 500-Mile Race. During qualifications, driver Eddie Agabashian set a new track record of 138.01 mph. which gave him pole position. The car suffered a clogged supercharger and dropped out of the race in the seventy-first lap. This model was designed and built by Frank Kurtis, and the engine was a Cummins six-cylinder, inline, water-cooled diesel engine.

WILLYS AERO EAGLE The Willys Aero Eagle was built from 1952 to 1954. It was the first really new Willys design in almost a decade. This five-passenger, two-door model was powered by an efficient six-cylinder, water-cooled, inline, F-head engine that developed 90 hp. Kaiser absorbed Willys in 1953, and in 1954, the 226-cubic-inch-displacement Kaiser engine was offered as an optional powerplant. A hardtop coupé was also available.

COOPER-BRISTOL RACER   The British Cooper racing cars were first produced in 1946 by John Cooper and his father, Charles. In 1948 Cooper cars were fitted with Bristol engines and were known as Cooper-Bristol. The cars were made for F.I.A. Formula 2 competition and were much less expensive than the larger, more powerful Formula 1 cars. This placed the Cooper-Bristol within the reach of many private racing enthusiasts. Several hundred Coopers were built, and sold to and raced by private owners. The 1953 Cooper-Bristol shown here placed eighth in the Argentine Grand Prix, ninth at the Buenos Aires Autodrome, eleventh in the French Grand Prix, eighth in the British Grand Prix, ninth at Silverstone, sixth in the German Grand Prix, eleventh at Nürburgring, seventh in the Swiss Grand Prix, twelfth in the Italian Grand Prix, and thirteenth at Monza. The wheelbase was 7 feet 6 inches and track 3 feet 10 inches. Overall length was 11 feet 4 inches. The powerplant was a four-cylinder, inline, water-cooled, three-carburetor engine of 1,971-cc displacement that produced 150 hp. at 5,800 rpm. The body was steel tubing covered with sheet steel.

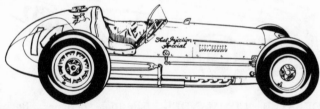

FUEL INJECTION SPECIAL   The Frank Kurtis-designed and -built Fuel Injection Special, with Bill Vukovich at the wheel, won the 1953 Indianapolis 500-Mile Race. The Offenhauser engine, with which the car was powered, was equipped with fuel injection instead of the more conventional carburetor. The car won the race and establishd a new track record of 138.392 mph. during qualifications.

DENZEL SPORTS CAR   From 1948 to 1960, Wolfgang Denzel of Vienna, Austria, built sports cars based on the Volkswagen. This is the 1953 model. Denzel rebored the Volkswagen engines to a displacement of 1,284 cc so the powerplant could develop 45 hp. Porsche engines were sometimes used, and the car styling followed that of the Porsche. Denzels competed successfully in many European and U.S. rallyes, among which was the International Alpine Rallye. In that event, Denzel won in 1954 and placed second in 1955. The modified Volkswagen engine was rear-mounted. The wide bench seat held three, and weight was 1,400 pounds. Four-wheel independent suspension used the torsion-bar system.

STUDEBAKER COMMANDER Industrial designer Raymond Loewy styled the series of post-World War II Studebakers and caused a styling revolution with the "notch-back" design. This 1953 Studebaker Commander started the third series of postwar designs by Loewy; the bullet nose gave way to a sloping hood. Power for this five-passenger car was an eight-cylinder, vee-type, overhead-valve, water-cooled, 232.6-cubic-inch-displacement engine that developed 120 hp. at 4,000 rpm. Speed was about 100 mph.

JAGUAR XK 120C The Jaguar XK series of sports cars was produced from 1948 to 1959. This is the Jaguar XK 120C of 1953 which was made from 1951 to 1954. In the 1953 Le Mans 24-Hour Race, Jaguars finished in first and second place. The type also won at Reims and Silverstone, plus the Acropolis and R.C.A. rallyes. A standard XK 120 was timed at over 172 mph. at Montlhéry! The XK referred to the engine, which was an eight-cylinder, inline, water-cooled, twin-overhead-camshaft, 180-hp. at 5,300 rpm. powerplant of 3,442-cc displacement. Two carburetors were fitted, and the compression ratio was 8 to 1. The wheelbase was 8 feet 6 inches and the overall length 14 feet 5 inches.

NASH-HEALEY SPORTS CAR Nash was the first U.S. car manufacturer to produce a true sports car: the Nash-Healey in 1951. Talented Donald Healey, British sports car racer and designer, developed this competition version for Nash in 1951. It had a Pininfarina-designed body, which led to its being dubbed the "three nation sports car." The car took fourth place in class in the 1951 Mille Miglia, and a coupé version placed sixth in that year's Le Mans Race. In 1952, the design placed third in the Le Mans. Power was a 3.8-liter Nash engine that was modified to produce 200 hp. The sleek 1953 model is shown.

HUDSON JET The Hudson Jet was Hudson Motors' long-awaited, light compact car and it made its appearance in 1953. The body design was by Murray and was fitted on a 105-inch wheelbase. The car was available with standard manual transmission, overdrive, or the General Motors Hydra-Matic drive. A six-cylinder, inline, water-cooled, 104-hp. economy engine powered the auto. The 1953 four-door sedan is shown.

OLDSMOBILE EXPERIMENTAL STARFIRE This experimental Oldsmobile "dream car" was revealed in 1953 and had many features that would become common in the later automobiles. The car was called the Starfire and was powered by a 200-hp., vee, eight-cylinder engine. The styling was used on many later models, and the experimental fiberglass body has become standard for many cars, both domestic and foreign. The one-piece, wraparound windshield was also an innovation that caught on.

PEGASO Z-102 The Pegaso was built in the former Hispano-Suiza factory in Barcelona, Spain. It was a complex and expensive sports car with prices ranging from $12,000 to $29,000. Only 125 vehicles were made between 1951 and 1957. This is the Pegaso Z-102 of 1953. The make was more of a G.T. or grand touring than a competition car, but it did take part in a number of events. It did well in hill-climbs, such as at Rabassada in Spain, where the record is still held by a Pegaso. In 1953, a Pegaso covered the flying mile at Jabbecke, Belgium, at a speed of 244.6 mph.! Power was an eight-cylinder, vee-type, four-overhead-camshaft, water-cooled, dry-sump engine. A five-speed transmission was fitted in the rear axle. Engine displacement was 2.5 liters, and 165 hp. could be developed.

NASH RAMBLER STATION WAGON The Nash Rambler Greenbrier two-door Station Wagon Model 5324 of 1953 was styled by Pininfarina, which accounted for its straight-line fender contour and enclosed front wheels. This station wagon helped to stimulate sales in 1953 which totaled $478,697,891.

CADILLAC LE MANS   This special Cadillac experimental and show car was made in 1953. It was fitted with the standard Cadillac engine with power augmented to 250 hp.! Styling refinements such as hooded headlights, wraparound windshield, and larger tail fins were all modern trends that were used in subsequent Cadillacs as well as other makes. The body was of reinforced, high-impact plastic, and power was an eight-cylinder, vee-type, water-cooled, overhead-valve, 331-cubic-inch-displacement engine. Maximum speed was 135 mph. Hydra-Matic automatic transmission was installed.

BUICK SKYLARK CONVERTIBLE   The sleek Buick Skylark Model 76X sporty convertible made its appearance in 1953 on a 121.5-inch wheelbase. This six-passenger car was powered with an eight-cylinder, vee-type, 322-cubic-inch-displacement, water-cooled engine that developed 51 hp.

CHEVROLET CORVETTE NO. 1   The new phenomenon from Europe, the sports car, was attracting more and more Americans. The Corvette was first introduced as a "dream car" in June of 1953 and became the first U.S. production sports car. Its body was made of reinforced fiberglass fitted on a conventional steel frame. The car seated two, and the six-cylinder, water-cooled, inline-engine of 150 hp. had three carburetors and an automatic transmission. Only 300 cars were made in 1953, but in 1969 a record 38,762 Corvettes were built. By that year the 250,000th Corvette had been completed.

MORGAN PLUS FOUR   From 1907 to the present, H. F. S. Morgan has built only sports cars in his shops in Malvern Link, England. The famous three-wheelers continued into 1939, and then the four-wheelers appeared after World War II. This is the Morgan Plus Four of 1954. The metal plates were formed around a wood frame. Previous four-wheelers had been powered by M.G. engines of various powers. Some highly tuned versions were fitted with British Ford Cortina engines which developed about 45 hp. at 5,000 rpm. and gave the car speeds over 85 mph. The Plus Four was fitted with a Triumph TR-3 four-cylinder engine. Note the resemblance to the M.G.-TF.

M.G.-TF MIDGET The basic M.G. sports car enjoyed popularity for about twenty years with only minor modifications resulting in models from the TA to the TF. The M.G.-TF was introduced in late 1953, and the car weighed 2,000 pounds on a 7-foot-10-inch wheelbase. Tread was 3 feet 11⅞ inches. Power was a four-cylinder, overhead-valve, water-cooled, inline, 1,250-cc-displacement engine producing 54 hp. at 5,200 rpm. The price was about $1,600. The car was a bit more streamlined than previous models with a vee radiator grille and headlights partially molded into the fenders. A 1,500-cc engine was available in 1955.

KAISER-DARRIN DKF-161 Early in 1952, famous auto designer Howard Darrin designed and built a dozen prototype sports cars in his shops in Santa Monica based on the 100-inch-wheelbase Henry J chassis. Kaiser decided to produce the beautiful car, and the Jackson, Michigan, plant made sixty-two advanced prototypes in 1953. In 1954, 435 production Darrin designs were completed. The body was made from Glaspar plastic, and power was the Willys F-head, six-cylinder, inline, water-cooled, overhead-valve, 90-hp. engine. The car was not extremely fast, but it handled beautifully. A three-speed transmission and overdrive were fitted. The Kaiser-Darrin DKF-161 created a sensation at auto shows around the U.S., but the collapse of the Kaiser Motors Corporation in 1955 spelled doom for the venture. Among the many innovations was a sliding door instead of the hinged type! Price was about $3,700.

ALFA ROMEO SPORT COUPÉ   This car was awarded the Grand Prize at the 1954 Salon de l'Automobile in Paris. Alfa Romeo, of Milan, powered the car with a six-cylinder, inline, double-overhead-camshaft, water-cooled engine of 3 liters displacement that produced almost 200 hp. at 6,000 rpm. A four-speed gearbox was fitted. Speed was about 135 mph. This car had a high-impact plastic body on a steel frame. Price was about $7,550.

DAIMLER EMPRESS SALOON   The stately British Daimler Empress Saloon of 1954 had a body designed and built by the famous Hooper coach builders. The five-passenger, four-door auto was powered by a six-cylinder, overhead-valve, inline, water-cooled, 3,468-cc-displacement engine that developed 139 hp. at 4,400 rpm. Bore was 83 mm. and stroke 108 mm. Speed was about 100 mph.

NASH RAMBLER STATION WAGON   The Nash Rambler Model 5428 Station Wagon of 1954 was built on a 108-inch wheelbase. This was the first year that the Rambler was produced in four-door models. In 1954, Nash was the first auto manufacturer to offer a complete air-conditioning system, with the entire unit located under the hood. Styling was by Pininfarina, with the protective chrome strip extending the full length of the car.

DORETTI-TRIUMPH   This British Doretti-Triumph sports roadster sounds Italian, but the car was named in honor of Dorothy Dean, a California foreign-car distributor who styled the body. The chassis was welded steel tubing, and the body was conventional sheet steel. The engine and transmission were the same as the Triumph TR-2. Price was $3,300. The car never attained full production status.

ALFA ROMEO-BERTONE B.A.T. The Carrozzeria Bertone designed the ultra-modern and functional body of this Alfa Romeo Sprint B.A.T. 5 in 1954. The cupola ended in a streamlined boat-tail, and the large slotted fins gave the car stability at high speeds. The headlights retracted into the inner surface of the front fenders. It was fitted with a complete bottom pan, therefore engine-cooling air outlets were located just forward of the doors. The car was made in limited quantity; price was $25,000.

FIAT-GHIA The Italian F.I.A.T. firm introduced this two-place G.T. sports car in 1954. The beautiful body was designed by Ghia of Turin and mounted on the Fiat chassis. The car weighed 2,100 pounds. Power was a Fiat vee-type, water-cooled, overhead-valve, 180-cubic-inch-displacement engine that developed 110 hp. at 6,000 rpm. Speed exceeded 100 mph.

JUSTICIALISTA   In 1954, Argentina's contribution to automotive design was this advanced Justicialista sports car. The body was made of high-impact plastic over a tubular steel frame. The top was removable so the auto could be driven as an open convertible. Notice the recessed headlights and slight fin on the rear fender. Power was a Porsche four-cylinder, opposed, air-cooled engine.

VAUGHAN SS WILDCAT   William Vaughan was the New York distributor for the British Singer automobiles. His burning desire to produce an outstanding G.T. sports car led him to have the car styled by the Italian coachwork master, Ghia of Turin. The body was plastic. Power was a Fiat eight-cylinder, vee-type, water-cooled engine of 1,497-cc displacement. A 1,297-cc or a 750-cc engine were also offered. Price of the car was to be about $3,500. However, it never got into production.

MULTIPLEX 186   The Multiplex 186 sport coupé was introduced in 1954 as one of the first independent U.S.-designed-and-built sports cars. The chassis was fabricated from square-section steel tubing, and the body was high-impact plastic. Independent front suspension was fitted. Power was a six-cylinder, inline, F-head, water-cooled engine of 124 hp. Curb weight was 1,700 pounds. This was another sports car that never got into volume production in a land that was just awakening to the sports-car craze.

M.G. MAGNETTE SALOON   Developed in 1953 and first produced in 1954, the M.G. Magnette four-passenger Saloon remained in production through 1956. The British Motor Corporation made the same car at the same time and called it the Wolseley 4/44. Power was a four-cylinder, overhead-valve, inline, water-cooled, 1,489-cc-displacement engine that produced 60 hp. at 4,600 rpm. A four-speed transmission was fitted, and maximum speed was 85 mph.

TRIUMPH TR-2   The British Triumph TR-2 was a rugged sports car developed by Sir John Black, managing director of the Standard Motor Company. The car had an 88-inch wheelbase and an overall length of 151 inches.Curb weight was 2,000 pounds. Power was a four-cylinder, inline, water-cooled, overhead-valve, 90-hp. engine of two liters displacement. Two carburetors were installed. The car did well at rallyes because of its maneuverability and independent suspension. It proved to be very popular in the United States.

NARDI DANESE   Introduced in 1954, this Nardi Danese competition sports car utilized a plastic body that was beautiful and simple. The two-seater was powered by a six-cylinder, vee-type, overhead-valve, water-cooled engine of 2,451-cc displacement that produced 190 hp. at 5,500 rpm. A four-speed transmission was fitted. Maximum speed was 130 mph. This car hoped to attract a large percentage of U.S. customers but never attained production status. Price was $5,250. Note the three headlights; the center light turned with the wheels for safe night driving.

NASH METROPOLITAN   After eleven years of research and planning, Nash introduced its long-awaited Metropolitan Model 541. The car was built in England by Austin and Fisher-Ludlow to Nash specifications and under their supervision. The two-seater had an 85-inch wheelbase; was 150 inches long, 61.5 inches wide, and 54.5 inches high. The body and frame were welded into a single unit. Power was a four-cylinder, inline, overhead-valve, water-cooled Austin A-40, 42-hp. engine. Up to 40 miles to a gallon of gasoline could be realized!

OLDSMOBILE SUPER-88   This Oldsmobile Super-88 Holiday Coupé Hardtop was made in 1954. Much of the styling was adopted from the experimental Starfire of 1953. This six-passenger car featured the famous Rocket V-8 engine with a displacement of 324 cubic inches. Maximum power was 185 hp. at 4,000 rpm., which propelled the sleek auto to 100 mph. Hydra-Matic automatic transmission was installed. Oldsmobile was the first car to use the Hydra-Matic automatic transmission.

CHEVROLET BEL AIR HARDTOP   Hardtops were very popular in the mid-fifties, and the Chevrolet Bel Air six-passenger hardtop was a big seller. Power was a six-cylinder, overhead-valve, inline, water-cooled, 235.5-cubic-inch-displacement engine that produced 108 hp. at 3,600 rpm. A three-speed transmission was installed, and the car could attain 90 mph.

FORD SKYLINER HARDTOP   A "new idea" from Ford in 1954 was the Skyliner roof in which a panel of slightly tinted Plexiglas to admit sunlight was inserted in the roof. The 1954 Crestline Skyliner Hardtop is shown. Power was an eight-cylinder, vee-type, water-cooled, side-valve engine of 239-cubic-inch displacement that produced 110 hp. at 3,800 rpm. Speed was about 90 mph.

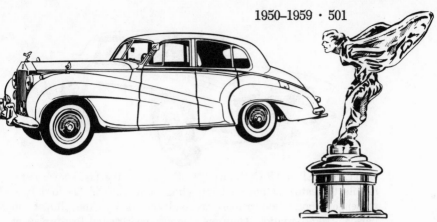

ROLLS-ROYCE SILVER SHADOW The Rolls-Royce Silver Shadow Saloon made its appearance in 1955. The five-passenger, four-door, luxurious auto was powered by a six-cylinder, inline, F-head, water-cooled, 4,887-cc-displacement engine that could propel the car to speeds in excess of 105 mph. Hydra-Matic automatic transmission was standard equipment. The type was joined by the Silver Cloud in 1956. The R-R radiator ornament is also shown.

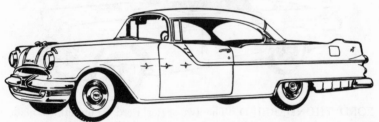

PONTIAC CATALINA HARDTOP This Pontiac Star Chief Custom Catalina Hardtop made its appearance in 1955, on a 124-inch wheelbase. Power was the new Strato-Streak engine that developed 180 hp. It was an eight-cylinder, vee-type, water-cooled, overhead-valve powerplant, with a displacement of 287.2 cubic inches. An unusual feature of this engine was that the right bank of cylinders was slightly forward of the left-hand bank. This was done in order to locate the distributor on the right so that the camshaft-drive gear force on the distributor was upward. It also enabled the fuel pump to be located to the left, in line with cooling blasts from the fan. This minimized the possibilities of vapor lock. Small details make good engines!

GAYLORD SPORTS CONVERTIBLE   This is the first-known auto-mobile to feature a powered retracting hardtop. The Gaylord two-passenger Sports Convertible was made in 1955 as the ultimate in personal transportation. Only one car was constructed for display at the Paris and New York Auto Shows. The design proved to be too expensive to produce, and the car never reached the market. The car can be seen at the Silver Springs Early American Museum, Silver Springs, Florida.

FORD THUNDERBIRD   The two-seater Ford Thunderbird made its appearance in late 1954 as either a personal or a sports car. The car was rugged with a steel body and was available as a hardtop or convertible. Power was an eight-cylinder, vee-type, overhead-valve, water-cooled, 292-cubic-inch-displacement engine that produced 192 hp. at 4,400 rpm. Fordomatic automatic transmission was installed. Maximum speed was about 110 mph. In recent years this two-seater has become a collector's item. Only 53,166 were built over a three-year period.

FERRARI SUPER SQUALO RACER   The Ferrari 555 Super Squalo Racer of 1955 placed third at Spa and Monza, first at Monaco, and first in the Tour of Sicily Race. Power was a four-cylinder, inline, water-cooled, 2,498-cc-displacement engine that developed 270 hp. and gave the car a speed of 165 mph. The car can be seen at the Gilltraps Auto Museum, Collangatta, Queensland, Australia.

DAIMLER CONQUEST   This sports drop-head coupé was produced by British Daimler in 1955. Power was an eight-cylinder, vee-type, water-cooled, 2,548-cc-displacement engine that developed 140 hp. at 5,800 rpm. Bore was 76 mm. and stroke was 70 mm. Four-speed transmission was standard. This was one of the first European short-stroke production engines. Speed was about 125 mph.

CHEVROLET NOMAD WAGON   This is the Chevrolet Nomad station wagon of 1955. Styling was considerably simplified from previous years by fairing the rear fender into the body. Note the Corvette-type taillight. Power was a six-cylinder, inline, water-cooled engine of 235-cubic-inch-displacement that developed about 136 hp. at 4,200 rpm. Maximum speed was about 90 mph. This two-door wagon could seat five and also had ample stowage space at the rear. The wheelbase was 115 inches, and overall length 197 inches, and shipping weight was 3,335 pounds. A 265-cubic-inch-displacement engine was also available. Price was about $2,600.

DODGE ROYAL SEDAN   Built on a 120-inch wheelbase, the 1955 Dodge Royal was the middle of the Dodge line. This is the four-door sedan, accommodating five passengers and powered by an eight-cylinder, vee-type, water-cooled, 270-cubic-inch-displacement engine, producing 175 hp. at 4,400 rpm. Note the one-piece, curved windshield, and lids over the headlights. The Royal was considered a reliable middle-priced car.

SAAB 93   The Saab 93 was introduced in 1956. It was similar to the 92 but had slight external modifications to the grille. Power was a three-cylinder, two-stroke, water-cooled, 456-cubic-inch-displacement engine that produced 33 hp. A coil-sprung chassis was fitted; length was 158 inches on a 97.7-inch wheelbase; width was 66.7 inches. A one-piece windshield was introduced in 1957, as well as more powerful brakes, and the designation was changed to 93B. Production continued into 1960. About 53,000 Model 93 Saabs were built.

HUDSON HORNET   This Hudson Hornet Model 35687-2 Hardtop was produced in 1956 and was fitted with a Packard V-8 engine. Despite the 1956 sales of $408 million, American Motors (Nash and Hudson) lost almost $20 million! Hardtops were in demand during the fifties. The next year was to be the last for Hudson, with the firm concentrating on the Rambler.

BENTLEY S1 SALOON   The Bentley Series S Saloon made its appearance in 1956. The Bentley S1 Saloon shown was a four-door, six-passenger machine with coachwork by Hooper. Power was a six-cylinder, F-head, water-cooled, inline 4,875-cc-displacement engine developing 170 hp. at 4,200 rpm. Automatic transmission, a Bentley-built Hydra-Matic system, was fitted.

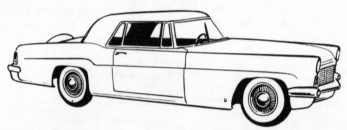

CONTINENTAL MARK II   The Continental Mark II was introduced by the Lincoln Division of the Ford Motor Company in late 1955, in an effort to revive the idea of the prewar Continental. The news that a new Continental was being developed was enough to encourage hundreds of advance orders, sight unseen, from the rich and famous, enclosing blank checks. The elegant body was designed by John M. Reinhardt. This five-passenger coupé was powered by an eight-cylinder, vee-type, overhead-valve, water-cooled, 368-cubic-inch-displacement engine that produced 300 hp. at 4,800 rpm. The speed was 112 mph. This classic was manufactured until 1968, after which the name Continental was used for full-size Lincoln cars, the top of the line. Price of this car was almost $10,000, and it was so well made that very few were traded in. About 3,000 were built. This is the 1956 model.

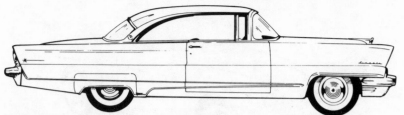

LINCOLN PREMIERE The 1956 Lincoln was selected by the professional judges of the Industrial Designers' Institute for the first award ever given to an automobile by the Institute. This sleek car was one of the best-selling Lincolns. The twin exhaust pipes exhaled through holes in the rear bumper. The wheelbase was 126 inches and the overall length was 223 inches. Width was 80 inches. The six-passenger car was powered by an eight-cylinder, vee-type, water-cooled, 368-cubic-inch-displacement engine that developed 285 hp. at 2,800 rpm. The compression ratio was 9 to 1. Aluminum alloy pistons were used. An automatic four-barrel carburetor was fitted. The 1956 Lincoln Premiere Hardtop Coupé is shown. Note the compatible hooded headlights and similarly sloping rear fenders.

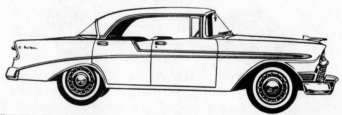

CHEVROLET HARDTOP This four-door Chevrolet Hardtop Bel Air Sedan was the Chevy top of the line in 1956. Power was an eight-cylinder, vee-type, overhead-valve, water-cooled engine that displaced 265 cubic inches and developed 205 hp. at 4,600 rpm. This five-seater had a speed of about 100 mph. and was offered with three-speed manual or Power Glide automatic transmission. Weight was about 3,400 pounds on a 115-inch wheelbase. The price was about $2,700.

VOLVO AMAZON   This four-door Swedish Volvo was introduced in 1957 as the Amazon and was powered by a 60-hp., 989-cubic-inch-displacement engine. Length was 175 inches on a 102.2-inch wheelbase. Width was 63.7 inches. Production continued into 1970. The later models were powered by a 1,213-cubic-inch-displacement engine that produced 82 hp. Speed was 94 mph.

FERRARI "315" SPYDER   This Ferrari "315" Spyder competition sports racer won the Mille Miglia–the 1,000-mile tour of Italy–in 1957, which was the last running of that race. Power was a twelve-cylinder, vee-type, water-cooled, 3,780-cc-displacement engine that produced 380 hp. Four overhead camshafts and a five-speed gearbox were fitted. Later in the same year the Venezuelan Grand Prix was won by the "315." This car can be seen at the Museum of Transportation, Larz Anderson Park, Brookline, Massachusetts.

FORD RANCH WAGON By 1957, station wagons were constructed without the familiar wood panels, as can be seen on this all-steel-bodied Ford Ranch Wagon. Power was an eight-cylinder, vee-type, overhead-valve, water-cooled, 292-cubic-inch-displacement engine that developed 206 hp. at 4,500 rpm. A three-speed manual or Fordomatic automatic transmission was available. Speed was over 100 mph.

VANWALL GRAND PRIX RACER Guy Anthony Vandervill was the manufacturer of Thinwall Bearings and began the development of racing cars in 1950. "Vanwall" was a combination of Vandervill and Thinwall. By 1956 he had engaged Colin Chapman of Lotus and Frank Costin to design a Grand Prix car. The design was remarkably clean and aerodynamically correct. In 1958 the British Vanwall won the Grand Prix races of Germany, Holland, Portugal, Italy, Belgium, and Morocco. These races gave Vanwall the honor of being the World Champion manufacturer for 1958. This 1958 Vanwall was powered with a 2,490-cc, four-cylinder, water-cooled, twin overhead-camshaft engine. A five-speed transmission was fitted. The body was aluminum, as were the fuel and oil tanks.

EDSEL CITATION This car, named in honor of Edsel Ford, who was eager to produce quality cars, failed to capture the public's admiration. The Ford Motor Company introduced the Edsel in 1957. The car shown is the 1958 Edsel Citation two-door hardtop, which was the top of the line. It cost between $3,535 and $3,801 as compared to the $2,519 price of the standard model. The Citation was powered by an eight-cylinder, vee-type, water-cooled, overhead-valve, 410-cubic-inch-displacement engine of 345 hp. The Edsel was a well-made product, similar to the Ford and the Mercury, but for some reason the car failed to score, and production ended in 1959.

RAMBLER AMBASSADOR This Rambler Ambassador Model 5883-2 station wagon was introduced in 1958 at a time when the names of Nash and Hudson were dropped by American Motors. The Rambler adopted many of the Hudson and Nash parts, which resulted in a larger car, like this Ambassador. This four-door, eight-passenger car was built on a 117-inch wheelbase, and power was an eight-cylinder, vee-type, water-cooled engine developing 270 hp.

FORD THUNDERBIRD This four-place Thunderbird was introduced in 1958 to replace the previous two-seater. The car was available in convertible and hardtop versions. Power was an eight-cylinder, vee-type, overhead-valve, water-cooled, 352-cubic-inch-displacement engine that produced 300 hp. at 4,600 rpm. A three-speed manual transmission or a Cruise-o-matic automatic transmission was offered. Speed was about 110 mph.

OLDSMOBILE DYNAMIC "88" The Oldsmobile Dynamic "88" Holiday Coupé of 1958 was fitted with the Oldsmobile Rocket engine. Heavy accent chrome-stripping and sculpturing were styling features. Power was an eight-cylinder, vee-type, overhead-valve, water-cooled, 394-cubic-inch-displacement engine that produced 315 hp. at 4,600 rpm. Either three-speed manual or Hydra-Matic automatic transmission was offered. Speed was over 110 mph.

AUSTIN-HEALEY SPRITE MK. I British automotive designer Donald Healey developed this small sports car for Austin in 1957. In 1958 the Austin-Healey Sprite Mk. I made its appearance. The arrangement of recessed headlights and oval grille gave the car the name "Bug-eye Sprite." The type finished in first, second, and third places in the 1959 Sebring 24-Hour Race and in 1960 Sterling Moss drove the Sprite to second place in that race. During the sixties "Bug-eyes" broke fifteen speed records in their class on the Utah Salt Flats with speeds of around 150 mph. The car still dominates present-day Sports Car Club of America Class H Races! The Sprite Mk. I weighed about 1,500 pounds on an 80-inch wheelbase. Power was a four-cylinder, inline, water-cooled, 58-cubic-inch-engine of 43 hp. The car was exceptionally well balanced and cornered beautifully. The styling was changed in 1962 and evolved into the present-day M.G. Midget sports cars. The Sprite Mk. I is still in demand today among sports car enthusiasts.

BUICK SUPER HARDTOP In 1958 Buick produced five series of passenger cars: the Special, Century, Super, Roadmaster, and Limited. This is the Buick Super Series 50 two-door hardtop coupé of 1958. The car was 219 inches long and 80 inches wide on a 127.5-inch wheelbase. Overall height was 59.4 inches. Power was an eight-cylinder, 90° vee-type, water-cooled, 364-cubic-inch-displacement engine that developed 300 hp. at 4,600 rpm. Automatic transmission was standard equipment.

CHEVROLET HARDTOP   The Chevrolet of 1959 did well in stock-car races in the U.S., and the two-door hardtop shown was one of the most successful racing machines. Power was an eight-cylinder, vee-type, overhead-valve, water-cooled 283-cubic-inch-displacement engine producing 185 hp. at 4,600 rpm. Speed was around 110 mph. Three- or four-speed manual transmission or Power Glide automatic transmission was offered. Note the large tail fins that were part of U.S. car design of the period.

FIAT "JOLLY" BEACH CAR   This five-seat, fringed-top, open, short-distance auto was built in 1959, and was called the Fiat "Jolly" Beach Car. The seats were wicker to endure wet bathing suits. The car was intended for those who could afford an extra car for going to the beach or to picnics over very short distances. Power was a four-cylinder, overhead-valve, inline, transverse, mounted-in-rear engine of 633-cc displacement that developed about 20 hp. at 4,600 rpm. A four-speed gearbox was fitted. Speed was about 50 mph. This vehicle was strictly for pleasure.

DODGE CUSTOM ROYAL Making its appearance in 1959, the Dodge Custom Royal MD3-H was built on a 122-inch wheelbase and featured a wide grille, tail fins, and plenty of chrome trim. Power of this six-passenger auto was an eight-cylinder, vee-type, 325-cubic-inch-displacement, water-cooled engine that produced 265 hp. at 4,600 rpm. Note the dual headlights. Optional equipment included: electronic fuel injection, tinted glass, automatic transmission, power steering, and power brakes. This was one of the first cars to use a compound curved windshield.

JAGUAR XK 150S COUPÉ The Jaguar XK 150 was a refinement of the previous XK 120 and XK 140. Some of the improvements were disc brakes, a lightened flywheel, twin fuel pumps, and a larger engine. The XK 150 was introduced in 1957 in a coupé version, and in the following year a convertible was offered. The 1959 XK 150S is shown. The car was 14 feet 9 inches long on an 8-foot-6-inch wheelbase. Track was 4 feet 3.5 inches and overall width was 5 feet 4.5 inches. Power was a six-cylinder, inline, twin overhead-camshaft, water-cooled, 3,781-cc-displacement engine that developed 265 hp. at 5,500 rpm. The compression ratio was 9 to 1. Three carburetors were installed. Independent front suspension was fitted with transverse wishbones and torsion bars plus telescopic dampers. Speed was over 130 mph., and it could go from zero to 100 mph. in 20 seconds.

CADILLAC COUPÉ Tail fins evolved in the fifties and reached their peak in 1959, as can be seen on this Cadillac Coupé Hardtop Series 75 designed by Harley Earl. This neatly designed, two-door, six-seater was powered with an eight-cylinder, vee-type, overhead-valve, water-cooled, 390-cubic-inch-displacement engine that produced 325 hp. at 4,800 rpm. Hydra-Matic automatic transmission was standard equipment. Speed was over 110 mph. This model had one of the longest wheelbases in Cadillac history.

PONTIAC STAR CHIEF SEDAN The 1959 Wide Track Pontiac Star Chief Sedan styling featured some sculpturing plus fluted fins over the taillights. This four-door, six-passenger auto was powered by an eight-cylinder, vee-type, overhead-valve, water-cooled, 389-cubic-inch-displacement engine developing 240 hp. at 4,000 rpm. Hydra-Matic or manual transmission was offered. Speed was about 115 mph. Wide Track means that the wheels were wider apart in order to give the car improved stability.

NASH METROPOLITAN The Nash Metropolitan was manufactured from 1954 to 1962. This Model 561 of 1959 was improved over previous models with the addition of window vents, a seat-adjusting mechanism, and larger tires. The externally mounted tire gave the car a decidedly foreign flavor. In this model a third person could sit behind the two front seats. A total of 94,986 Metropolitans were made.

AUSTIN 850 MINI-COOPER Known throughout the world as the Mini-Cooper, this Austin sedan made its appearance in 1959 as the British answer to the success of the German Volkswagen. The Austin 850 was fitted with a transverse, front-located, four-cylinder engine with front-wheel drive, which set the pace for many automotive designers over a decade later as well as for modern cars such as the VW Rabbit, Audi, and Fiat 128. Automotive designer John Cooper influenced the British Motor Corporation (parent company of Austin) to market a high-performance version which he had developed, hence the Mini-Cooper nickname by rallye and racing enthusiasts. The boxy looking subcompact was exceptionally maneuverable. It cornered flatly and was fitted with a Hydrolastic Suspension which offered a degree of automatic leveling. It was fun and safe to drive but the cramped quarters made long trips uncomfortable. With a speed in excess of 100 mph. the Mini-Cooper was very successful in races and rallyes including: first place at Monte Carlo in 1965; and first in the Geneva, Polish, Czechoslovak, and Finnish rallyes! About three million Austin 850 vehicles were made, and it spawned the BMC 1800, as well as the Austin America. Mini-Coopers are still in demand for competition purposes, and many are raced today.

FORD GALAXIE CUSTOM CLUB SEDAN This Ford Galaxie Custom Club four-door sedan was the top of the line of the Ford cars in 1959. Power was an eight-cylinder, vee-type, water-cooled, overhead valve, 292-cubic-inch-displacement engine that delivered about 210 hp. at 4,500 rpm. Speed was about 100 mph. A three-speed manual or the Fordomatic automatic transmission was available.

BUICK ELECTRA SEDAN The Electra Series was the Buick top of the line in 1959, the year the Electra was introduced. This is the 1959 Buick Electra Model 4700 four-door sedan. Note the panoramic rear window and angled fins. This six-passenger car was 220.6 inches long and 80.7 inches wide on a 126-inch wheelbase. Height was 57.3 inches. Power was an eight-cylinder, 90° vee-type, water-cooled, overhead-valve, 401-cubic-inch-displacement engine producing 325 hp. at 4,400 rpm. Automatic transmission was standard equipment.

CHAPTER THIRTEEN

Sporty Cars and Economy Types, Too 1960–1969

JOHN F. KENNEDY was elected President of the United States in 1960. Later he established the Peace Corps to serve in underdeveloped countries. Cyprus was now independent with Archbishop Makarios as president. The European Free Trade Association was established by the "Outer Seven": Austria, the United Kingdom, Denmark, Norway, Portugal, Sweden, and Switzerland. Finland joined later in 1961. In the Middle East, Egypt, with Russian aid, began construction of the Aswan Dam. Africa continued to make headlines. Immediately after the Republic of the Congo achieved independence, civil war broke out; political struggle within the central government developed between Patrice Lumumba, premier, and Joseph Kasavubu, the head of state. The United Nations' peace-keeping force entered the dispute. Moise Tshombe became premier in 1961. African nationalism reached its peak of success when sixteen nations gained freedom, and African nations made up one-third of the U.N. membership.

As the world revolved with its events of varying degrees of magnitude, United States auto manufacturers increased their production to 7,869,271 vehicles in 1960, 6,674,796 of which were passenger cars. The U.S. imported 468,312 vehicles and exported 322,561. The U.S. also accounted for 47.9 percent of world motor vehicle production. Over 90 percent of U.S. inter-city travel was via the private automobile in 1960.

The Lincoln and Continental warranties were extended to twenty-four months or 24,000 miles, the most generous in the industry.

About 4,783,000 motor vehicles were scrapped in 1960 in the U.S., and the average age of the U.S. passenger car in 1960 was 5.9 years.

Chrysler Corporation stated that 1960 would be the last year for the DeSoto.

In 1960, about $17.5 billion in consumer credit was used to purchase motor vehicles in the U.S.

Rebates are not new. Studebaker-Packard offered shareholders a refund of $100 if they bought a Studebaker. American Motors offered any purchaser of an A.M.C. car U.S. Savings Bonds as a refund or rebate.

Experimental ideas for 1960 included: the Chevrolet XP-700 Corvette, the General Motors nuclear-powered combat vehicle for the U.S. Army, the Plymouth NXR sports car, and the General Motors radar-type detector that warned the driver when the car was driven near the edge of the pavement.

Great strides were made in radiator coolant development to prevent freezing in winter and boil-overs in summer.

Several new small cars were announced in 1960: the Oldsmobile F-85 with aluminum V-8 engine, the Pontiac Tempest, with a four-cylinder engine and a V-8 as optional, Dodge Lancer, Buick Special with an aluminum V-8 engine, Lincoln Mercury Comet, International Harvester Scout, a rugged Jeep-type with a four-cylinder engine and unitized body, and of course, the Chevrolet Corvair. All were compact types to combat the ever-increasing wave of foreign car imports into the U.S.

New features for U.S. cars were revealed at the National Auto Show in Detroit: Lincoln Continental showed a four-door convertible; special grease installed at the factory in the chassis and suspension points that needed no replacement for 30,000 miles were added to Ford, Mercury, and Lincoln Continental cars; Cadillac demonstrated life-time chassis lubrication.

Thunderbird showed a swing-away steering wheel to facilitate entering and exiting the driver's seat. Studebaker Lark showed a sliding softtop. Rambler introduced a ceramic-coated muffler and tail pipe and also showed an aluminum six-cylinder inline engine. Ford introduced the Econoline series of panel trucks and announced self-adjusting brakes and aluminized mufflers. All U.S. cars had reinforced areas on the floor making it possible for dealers to install seat belts with safety.

U.S. automobile manufacturers continued to expand: Chrysler opened a new plant at St. Louis, Missouri; Mack trucks began a new plant at Hagerstown, Maryland; and American Motors expanded its Kenosha and Milwaukee, Wisconsin, operations. Ford bought Sherman Products, makers of Ford Tractor parts, and opened a glass research center in Lincoln Park, Michigan. General Motors enlarged its plants at Warren, Willow Run, and Tarrytown.

Almost 10 percent of the 41,000-mile Interstate Highway System was completed with another 5,000 miles under construction in 1960.

Mickey Thompson of El Monte, California, attempted to break the speed record in the Challenger I. He sped across the Bonneville Salt Flats in Utah at 406 mph. This, however, was not recognized as a record, because mechanical troubles prevented the car from making another pass in front of the officials.

The 1960 World Champion Driver was Jack Brabham of Australia driving a Cooper. Jim Rathmann won the Indianapolis 500-Mile Race driving the Ken-Paul Special at an average speed of 138.77 mph. Driving a Ferrari, P. Frere and O. Gendebien won the Le Mans 24-Hour Race. The U.S. National Auto Champion was A. J. Foyt, Jr.

Fatalities due to the motor vehicle in 1960 were 37,137, which was 5.3 deaths for every 100 million vehicle miles traveled.

In 1961 the Charter of the Alliance for Progress was signed in Punta del Este, Uruguay. Its aim was to increase economic and social development in Latin America with U.S. aid. The United States severed diplomatic relations with Cuba, and this was the year of the Bay of Pigs incident. In Europe, the East Germans erected the wall between East and West Berlin. Yuri A. Gagarin, Russian astronaut, was the first man to orbit the earth. In the Middle East, Kuwait achieved independence, and in the Far East, India annexed Portuguese Goa, Damáo, and Diu. The United States sent guerrilla warfare specialists to train South Vietnamese soldiers. Dag Hammarskjöld, U.N. secretary-general, was killed in a plane crash on a mission to the Congo. The Union of South Africa became a republic and later left the British Commonwealth.

U.S. motor vehicle production in 1961 dropped to 6,676,511 units, and the number of motor vehicles imported into the U.S. dropped to 288,741 units. The U.S. exported 258,975 motor vehicles that year. The average age of passenger cars was 6.0 years, and 4,979,000 motor vehicles were scrapped in the U.S. By the end of 1961, Chevrolet had produced its 44-millionth motor vehicle.

Lawrence Fisher, one of the five Fisher brothers, died in 1961 and was the third of the brothers to pass away. The brothers learned their skills from their father, who was a master carriage maker. The Fisher Body Company was founded by the brothers in 1908, and they pioneered closed bodies for automobiles. In 1926 they sold the company to General Motors for over $200 million. Lawrence Fisher later became president of Cadillac.

Also dead in 1961 was Abner Doble, who at sixteen made his first steam car. When he attended M.I.T., he built several more. Four years later almost one hundred had been built and sold. He founded Doble Steam Motors in 1920 and also acted as a consultant to locomotive manufacturers in Europe and Asia.

Goodyear Tire and Rubber Company demonstrated a new synthetic rubber that would increase the life of rubber tires. Two-ply instead of four-ply tires were being produced for compact cars in 1961.

Chevrolet introduced its new Chevy II series of compact cars, and Pontiac showed the Gran Prix sporty and luxurious personal car. Studebaker-Packard revealed a top-of-the-line model in its sporty Hawk series, the Gran Turismo. Chrysler's powerful 300-H high-performance sporty car stirred plenty of attention, and orders were received from state police for patrol work on high-speed highways. Ford introduced the sporty Futura model in its Falcon line, and Buick showed the Skylark as a sporty top-of-the-line model in its Special series. Dodge introduced the 770 Lancer Sport Coupé in the compact series. Oldsmobile showed its Starfire sporty convertible, and Cadillac demonstrated the new Town Sedan in the Calais series. American Motors introduced the Custom 400 series in its Rambler American, Rambler Classic, and Rambler Ambassador V-8 powered cars.

General Motors began production on a new inter-city bus that was powered by a V-8 diesel engine. Willys revealed its new Jeep Fleetvan walk-in delivery vehicle that weighed just over 1,000 pounds. International Harvester introduced multiple variations for their Scout, from an enclosed runabout small pickup or a panel truck to an open model without roof, windows, or doors.

Also in 1961 several innovations made the news. American Motors offered factory-installed seat belts and a dual-brake system. They also introduced the E-stick automatic clutch transmission that permitted the driver to shift gears manually, but the system automatically engaged and disengaged the clutch. Ford introduced a clutch Interlock for its manual transmission that prevented inadvertent shifting into low gear or reverse gear. Ford also developed an engine winter/summer antifreeze that would last for 30,000 miles or two years of driving. Buick introduced the first U.S. passenger car V-6 cylinder engine. PCV (pollution control valves) for reducing automotive emissions were installed in cars in California.

Studebaker bought Chemical Compound, Inc., the manufacturers of STP oil and gasoline additives. Philco Corporation and Autolite Products were purchased by the Ford Motor Company. Studebaker bought the Curtiss Wright South Bend, Indiana, plant, and American Motors and Oldsmobile opened new engineering centers.

Sculptured styling and vestigial fins dominated the U.S. car, and the wraparound window had disappeared because of the annoying "dog-leg" that impaired complete freedom for entering and exiting the front seats. Vent panes returned with some operated by hand crank and some by pushing out the window. Others were electrically operated.

Some manufacturers used stainless steel instead of rust-prone chrome for trim. Dual headlights began appearing in the better European cars.

The 1961 World Champion Driver was Phil Hill of the U.S. driving a Ferrari. A. J. Foyt, Jr., won the Indianapolis 500-Mile Race in the Bowes Seal Fast Special at an average speed of 139.13 mph. The Le Mans 24-Hour Race was won by Phil Hill (U.S.) and O. Gendebien (Belgium) driving a Ferrari. The U.S. NASCAR Champion for 1961 was Johnny Roberts of Baltimore, Maryland. Innis Ireland of England won the U.S. Grand Prix at

Watkins Glen driving a Lotus at an average speed of 103.22 mph.

The National Driver Register Service was established for the purpose of cross-indexing information on drivers of motor vehicles whose licenses had been revoked due to intoxicated driving causing death, or repeated speeding or reckless driving. This information was exchanged among the states.

Auto traffic fatalities were 38,091 in 1961, which is 5.2 deaths for each 100 million vehicle miles traveled.

1962 was the year the United States and the Soviet Union appeared to be on the brink of war when Soviet missiles were discovered in Cuba. President Kennedy forced Khrushchev to have them dismantled. John Glenn was the first American astronaut to orbit the earth. Kurdish tribes in northern Iraq rebelled, demanding an independent state. Adolf Eichmann, chief administrator of the Nazi program for exterminating Jews, was tried and executed by Israel. Civil war broke out between Yemeni republicans, who were supported by Egyptians, and Yemeni royalists, backed by Saudi Arabia. In the end, the monarchy was overthrown. A Neutralist government was set up in Laos under Prince Souvanna Phouma, but Pathet Lao continued sporadic fighting in the North.

The number of motor vehicles made by U.S. auto manufacturers in 1962 was 8,173,408 units, worth over $15.5 billion. The U.S. imported 387,204 motor vehicles in 1962 and exported 231,977 units.

In 1962, 5,454,000 motor vehicles were scrapped, and the average age of passenger cars in the U.S. was 6.0 years.

General Motors produced its 75-millionth motor vehicle, and the number of General Motors shareholders passed the one million mark. Ford Motor Company was the first manufacturer to produce 30 million V-8 engines.

Dead in 1962 was Rollin H. White, who, with his brothers Walter C. and Windsor T., began working for the White Sewing Machine Company, which was owned by their father. The brothers produced their first automobile in 1900, and in 1906 the White Company was formed. The first White car was made in 1910, and the company expanded to become a leader in truck manufacturing.

The 1963 cars being developed in 1962 had many innovations. Virtually all cars had self-adjusting brakes. Pontiac offered a fully-transistorized ignition system. The positive crankcase ventilation system (PCV) was adopted by the U.S. auto industry. Front-wheel disc brakes were offered as optional by Studebaker and as standard on the Avanti. Seat-belt anchors for the front seat became common.

New vehicles introduced in 1962 ranged from sports models to mobile homes. Ford showed its Galaxie 500 XL luxury series and the Fairlane Sports Coupé. Buick brought out the Skylark convertible and the Wildcat hardtop sports types. Oldsmobile produced the Jetfire Sports Coupé that was fitted with a turbocharger. The sensational Shelby Cobra high-performance sports car, introduced by Shelby American, Inc., of Los Angeles, was powered by a Ford V-8 engine, and had an aluminum body and steel chassis. All were made in England. Chevrolet produced their Corvair Monza convertible and Monza Spyder sports models. Plymouth brought out their Sports Fury model. Ford produced the Falcon Sports Futura, and Lincoln Mercury made a compact Comet station wagon called the Villager. Studebaker began producing its fiberglass body sports coupé called the Avanti and introduced the Lark Standard no frills series. This was aimed at the large corporations, i.e., fleet buyers. Studebaker also offered. an all-purpose camper called the Champ. Traville Corporation of Detroit produced the Traville, a deluxe travel home, mounted on a Chevrolet chassis. Ford offered a travel home unit that could be mounted on a Ford truck chassis, called the Condor. Pontiac introduced the Tempest Le Mans model, and Buick brought out the Riviera sports type. Checker Motor Corporation introduced two station wagons: the Aerobus, available in nine- or twelve-passenger models, and the Texan. Chrysler revealed its two-door 300-J hardtop sporty model.

Following the growing European practice, the U.S. auto industry adopted amber lights for front turn signals, because the color is more readily visible than white in day or night. Simultaneously, auto supply stores offered amber-colored tinting-paint for drivers who wanted to color the signal lenses of their older cars.

European-made radial-ply belted tires appeared on U.S. cars more and more, especially the Michelin. Goodyear introduced a new tire cord made of polyester fiber. General Tire developed a tire claimed to last 50,000 miles, and U.S. Rubber developed an improved method of bonding the ply and thread on tires.

The 1962 World Champion Driver was Graham Hill of Great Britain driving a BRM racer. Rodger Ward won the Indianapolis 500-Mile Race driving the Leader Card Special at an average speed of 140.29 mph. The Le Mans 24-Hour Race was won by Phil Hill of the U.S. and Olivier Gendebien of Belgium driving a Ferrari at an average speed of 115.4 mph.

There were 40,804 U.S. traffic fatalities attributed to the automobile in 1962, which was the highest toll since records were first kept. This came to 5.3 deaths for every 100 million vehicle miles traveled that year.

In 1963 President John F. Kennedy was assassinated in Dallas, Texas, on November 22, and Lyndon Baines Johnson was sworn in as President. Pope John XXIII died, and Cardinal Montini was elected as Pope Paul VI. The United States, the Soviet Union, and Great Britain signed a treaty banning nuclear tests above ground and under water. Fighting broke out between Greek and Turkish Cypriots and a U.N. force to maintain order was on the island. Aden joined the British protectorate of the Federation of South Arabia. Terrorist groups worked for unification with Yemen, and the area later achieved independence in 1968 as Southern Yemen. In the Far East, the Federation of Malaysia was created by union of the Federation of Malaya, Singapore, Sarawak, and North Borneo. The Diem regime in South Vietnam was overthrown. Jomo Kenyatta became Kenya's first prime minister, which marked continued progress in Africa.

U.S. auto makers produced 9,199,436 motor vehicles in 1963. Value quoted was $17,517,422,000. The U.S. imported 426,658 vehicles and exported 267,781 units during the same year.

Motor vehicles scrapped in the U.S. in 1963 totaled 5,909,000, and the average age of the U.S. passenger car was 6.0 years.

The Ford Motor Company produced its 60-millionth vehicle.

Production began on several new U.S. cars: the Buick Riviera two-door hardtop, a sporty-type full-size personal car; Studebaker's Super Lark economy car and Super Hawk sporty car; Lincoln Mercury's Comet sportster compact car and Marauder full-size car; and the Chrysler New Yorker Salon luxury car.

Mobile homes and campers had aroused the public's interest, causing continued increased production. The Cortez mobile home for four people was introduced by the Clark Equipment Company, and International Harvester featured a Scout adaptation to a family camper.

New models introduced by U.S. manufacturers were: the Oldsmobile Jetstar 88 and the sports-type Jetstar No. 1, the Studebaker Challenger, and the Lincoln Mercury Comet Caliente in the compact line. Chevrolet introduced a new van, the Chevelle medium-size line, and Studebaker showed the first truck bodies made from fiberglass.

Prototype cars exhibited by U.S. manufacturers included the Chevrolet Monza GT and Monza SS, Ford Mustang II, Lincoln Mercury Cougar II and Super Cyclone, and Oldsmobile's J-TR sporty four-place convertible. Pontiac introduced their X-400.

Studebaker moved from the U.S. to Hamilton, Ontario, Canada, but continued to sell cars in the U.S. Lincoln Mercury stopped production on its medium-priced Meteor series.

Ford, Chevrolet, American Motors, and Fisher Body all expanded their plants for increased production.

Gross weight of trucks permitted on U.S. highways was increased to 90,000 pounds, width increased to 102 inches, height increased to 13.5 feet, and length increased to 40 feet for trailers.

U.S. car body styling in 1963 was restrained and sleek with angular accents in lieu of chrome. Fins were gone.

Utah became the twenty-eighth state to amend its laws to dedicate all state motor vehicle and gasoline taxes for highway purposes.

The 1963 Indianapolis 500-Mile Race was won by Parnelli Jones driving the Agajanian Special at an average speed of 143.137 mph. A. Scarfiotti and L. Banini won the Le Mans 24-Hour Race in a Ferrari. The World Championship Driver was Jim Clark of Scotland driving a Lotus-Climax.

Traffic fatalities reached record proportions in the U.S. with 43,564 deaths attributed to the automobile in 1963. This was 5.4 deaths for every 100 million vehicle miles driven that year.

In 1964 the Panamanians staged anti-U.S. riots. France established diplomatic relations with Communist China. The Soviet Presidium ousted Khrushchev and made Aleksei N. Kosygin premier and Leonid I. Brezhnev the first secretary of the Communist Party. China exploded her first atomic bomb, and France recognized Communist China. Nehru died in India and was succeeded by Lal Bahadur Shastri. Africa was much in the news as Tanzania was formed by the unification of Tanganyika and Zanzibar with Julius K. Nyerere as the first president. Nyasaland became the independent state of Malawi, and Northern Rhodesia gained independence as Zambia.

Car interest in the U.S. was reflected by the fact that almost 16 million visitors attended the General Motors Futurama at the New York World's Fair in 1964. General Motors produced over 4 million vehicles during the year.

U.S. manufacturers produced a record 9,292,275 motor vehicles in 1964. The value exceeded $18 billion, which represented 42.8 percent of the world's total motor vehicle production. The U.S. imported 553,189 motor vehicles and exported 320,169 units. New car registrations in the U.S. exceeded 8 million during the year.

Seven million seven thousand motor vehicles were scrapped in the U.S., and the average age of passenger cars was 6.0 years.

Dodge celebrated its golden anniversary in the auto industry and introduced a new Camper Wagon.

A $2-billion two-year capital expenditure program for plants and equipment was announced by General Motors Corporation.

A double-lining tire was introduced by Goodyear enabling the car to ride on the inner lining following a blowout. Several U.S. tire manufacturers announced interest in the belted radial designs.

Sporty cars were still on the upswing with the production of Ford's Mustang, Plymouth's Barracuda, and American Motors' Marlin. Buick also introduced the Gran Sports models of the Riviera and Skylark series.

Some new experimental vehicles and show cars revealed in 1964 were: the General Motors turbine-powered Firebird IV and GM-X, the Buick Silver Arrow, Dodge Charger II, Chevrolet Chevy II Super Nova compact sporty car, Oldsmobile front-wheel-drive Toronado, American Motors Rambler Tarpon, and the Ford Aurora station wagon and gas-turbine, 600-hp. truck tractor.

Dodge introduced the intermediate Coronet series and the two-door hardtop Monaco. Ford announced the top-of-the-line LTD in its Galaxie series.

The 1964 World Champion Driver was John Surtees of England driving a Ferrari. J. Guichet and N. Vacarella won the Le Mans 24-Hour Race driving a Ferrari, and A. J. Foyt, Jr., won the Indianapolis 500-Mile Race in a Sheraton-Offenhauser at an average speed of 147.35 mph.

A record 47,700 auto-related fatalities were experienced in 1964, which is 5.6 deaths for every 100 million vehicle miles traveled during that year.

In 1965 the U.S. marines landed in the Dominican Republic. President Johnson signed Medicare and the war on poverty legislation. West Germany established diplomatic relations with Israel, causing most Arab nations to sever ties with West Germany. In the Far East, the United States began bombing North Vietnam. India and Pakistan fought over Kashmir, and though the fighting ceased, the dispute was never settled. Ahmed Ben Bella, the Algerian premier, was overthrown by Colonel Houari Boumédienne. Rhodesia unilaterally declared independence from Great Britain.

U.S. automobile manufacturers produced 11,057,366 motor vehicles during 1965, which was a record. Total value was over $22 billion. The U.S. exported 167,724 motor vehicles and imported 590,323 units. Consumer credit for the purchase of motor vehicles in the U.S. rose to $28.619 billion. The U.S. produced 45.9 percent of the world's vehicles in 1965. More than three million Chevrolet motor vehicles were produced, which was a record for a single make.

The Automotive Products Trade Act of 1965 between the United States and Canada went into effect. This Act eliminated all tariffs on new motor vehicles or new automobile parts to be used for production.

Five tire manufacturers produced belted radial designs for the U.S. market: the Michelin X, Dunlop SP-41, Continental, Pirelli Cinturato S, and Goodyear F-800. All were made in Europe, and had tread that continued around the shoulders of the tire.

Experimental and show cars exhibited during the year included many sporty types: the Chevrolet Mako Shark II, Ford

Bordinet Cobra, Mercer Cobra, the GT Mark I, Lincoln Mercury Comet Cyclone, Comet Escapade, Dodge Charger II, American Motors St. Moritz and Tahiti, and the Plymouth XP-VIP, among others.

Oldsmobile began producing the front-wheel-drive Toronado, and American Motors began work on the DPL, Rebel, and Rogue. Ford introduced the four-wheel-drive Jeep-type Bronco, the Fairlane 500 XL and Fairlane GT for 1966. Lincoln Mercury announced it would add the foreign-made Capri to the Comet series. Shelby American started work on a high-performance version of the Mustang called the Shelby GT 350. Chevrolet began producing the top-of-the-line Caprice and the Sportsvan camper, and Dodge brought out the Charger sports fastback.

The 1965 World Champion Driver was Jim Clark of Scotland driving a Lotus-Ford. He also won the Indianapolis 500-Mile Race in the Lotus-Ford at an average speed of 150.686 mph. The Le Mans 24-Hour Race was won by M. Gregory and J. Rindt in a Ferrari.

A total of 7,070,000 motor vehicles were scrapped in the U.S., and the average age of passenger cars was 5.9 years old.

Fatalities involving the motor vehicle reached 49,163, 5.5 deaths for every 100 million vehicle miles traveled that year.

In the Americas in 1966, Guyana, formerly British Guiana, became independent. In Europe, De Gaulle requested NATO troop removal from France. While in the Far East, Sukarno was forced to yield power to Suharto, who had outlawed the Communist Party and restored Indonesia to the United Nations. After Shastri's death, Indira Gandhi, Nehru's daughter, became the prime minister of India. Africa was much in the news with Kwame Nkrumah's government in Ghana toppled by a military coup forcing him into exile. The United Nations terminated South Africa's mandate over Southwest Africa and proclaimed U.N. administration over the country.

In 1966 the United States Federal government created the Department of Transportation to insure fast, safe, convenient and efficient transportation for the economic stability and general welfare of the country. In addition, the National Traffic and Motor Vehicle Safety Act was passed to coordinate and establish national safety standards for motor vehicles driven on U.S. roads.

Air pollution problems in urban areas caused a renewed interest in electric vehicles. Ford revealed a sealed sodium-sulphur battery that would power a light vehicle, and despite charging, would last the life of the vehicle. General Motors demonstrated an electric-powered Corvair, powered by a fuel cell.

Over 88 percent of all inter-city travel in 1966 was by passenger automobile. United States auto manufacturers produced 8,598,326 motor vehicles with a value of over $21.5 billion, which represented 41.8 percent of the world's motor vehicle production. The U.S. exported 256,529 motor vehicles and imported 970,625.

A total of 870,000 motor vehicles were scrapped in the United States, and the average age of passenger cars was 5.7 years old.

Safety items became increasingly important, and an energy-absorbing collapsible steering column was offered by General Motors, American Motors, and Chrysler Corporation cars. Ford cars offered an energy-absorbing steering wheel with a padded hub. Many makes included safety belts as standard equipment, and others offered them as optional.

Three more sports types appeared: Chevrolet brought out its Camaro, Lincoln Mercury introduced the Cougar, and Shelby American began producing the Shelby GT500.

Cadillac introduced the front-wheel-drive Eldorado, and Lincoln Mercury showed the Mercury Marquis and Mercury Brougham. Kaiser revealed the Jeep Super Wagoneer four-wheel-drive deluxe station wagon, Chevrolet added the Chevelle Concourse, and Dodge added the Coronet R/T and SE models.

Ford, General Motors, Chrysler, and American Motors offered a 50,000-mile warranty on the engine, axles, transmission, and differential.

Dream cars of the year included the Pontiac Banshee, American Motors' sporty AMX, and the Vixen and Cavalier, which were shown to the public.

Studebaker ended automobile production after sixty-four years. However, the Avanti II was continued by the Avanti Motor Corporation of South Bend, Indiana, and was powered with a Chevrolet engine.

American Motors Corporation, using single unit construction, produced its 5-millionth automobile.

The 1966 World Champion Driver was Jack Brabham of Australia driving a Brabham-Repco. B. McLaren and C. Amon won the Le Mans 24-Hour Race driving a Ford GT40, and the Indianapolis 500-Mile Race was won by Graham Hill driving a Lola-Ford at an average speed of 144.317 mph.

A record total of 53,041 traffic fatalities involving motor vehicles was reported for 1966, resulting in 5.7 deaths for every 100 million vehicle miles traveled.

In 1967, NATO established new headquarters at Casteau, Belgium. Britain devalued the pound and instituted an austerity program. Communist China exploded her first hydrogen bomb. South Vietnam held its first national election with Nguyen Van Thieu as president and Nguyen Cao Ky as vice-president. In Africa, the Republic of Biafra was proclaimed when the eastern province of Nigeria seceded. Antarctica made news when Peter J. Barrett and geologists from New Zealand discovered bone fragment and plant fossils embedded beneath icy surfaces of Antarctica, which indicated that Antarctica formerly had a warmer climate.

General Motors produced its 100-millionth U.S.-made vehicle, and Ford made its 70-millionth vehicle. U.S. auto manufacturers produced 8,976,226 motor vehicles worth $19,245,485,000. The United States exported 363,165 motor vehicles and imported 1,109,095. This was the first year that motor vehicle imports reached the one-million mark. The U.S. percentage of world motor vehicle production dropped to 37.6 percent.

Over 800,000 U.S. businesses depended on motor vehicle use in 1967, and 13,300,000 persons were employed in the highway transport industries who used buses and trucks. Over $13 billion worth of auto parts were produced for the automobile industry by other industries. Over 625,000 mobile homes, campers, etc., were manufactured.

During the year 7,331,000 motor vehicles were scrapped, and the average age of passenger cars in the United States was 5.6 years old. Recorded was a total of 52,924 traffic fatalities. This amounted to 5.5 deaths per 100 million vehicle miles traveled.

Frank Matheson died in 1967. Frank and his brother Charles built the Matheson cars from 1903 to 1913. Also dead in 1967 was Frank J. Duryea. The brothers Frank and Charles Duryea built the first marketable gasoline-powered automobile in 1893.

Sporty cars were still in demand and the U.S. manufacturers introduced several models. Shelby American showed the Shelby Cobra, a high-performance convertible with a padded roll-over bar. Plymouth introduced the Road Runner and American Motors had the four-seat Javelin. Ford showed its fastback intermediate Montego. Pontiac introduced the Firebird sporty compact type.

Safety and air pollution controls were here to stay for the 1968 production cars. All had emission control systems and seat belts for all passengers. Emphasis was placed on the elimination of protruding items on the interior and the exterior of the car. Spinner-type wheel hubs were gone as were most figureheads over the radiators. Lincoln retained its four-pointed star figurehead but had it spring-mounted to avoid injury. Padded interiors were common, and many firms recessed the interior door handles into the door or armrests. Pontiac featured energy-absorbing bumpers. Ford introduced a front end that was constructed to crush gradually in order to reduce the impact of a high-speed collision. Disc brakes were more popular, at least for the front wheels. Chrysler offered a windshield washer and wiper for the rear window on its station wagon, and Oldsmobile recessed the horn ring inside the steering wheel. Lincoln Continental offered double-chambered safety tires as original equipment, and General Motors introduced high-strength steel beams welded into the doors for collision protection.

Almost 40 percent of U.S. 1967 automobiles had air-conditioning equipment, and convertible production was generally reduced.

Electric-powered vehicles, which reduced pollution in urban areas, were still in demand. Westinghouse revealed their two-passenger electric-powered city vehicle. The U.S. Department of Commerce held a seminar on electric-powered vehicles with eight papers presented on electric cars at the Society of Automotive Engineers (S.A.E.) annual meeting. Ford introduced the Comuta electric car developed in cooperation with British Ford. General Motors introduced the Electrovair II electric car. G.M. also worked in conjunction with the University of Pennsylvania to develop a small, emission-free automobile. Ford worked with Mobil Oil to develop a gasoline-powered, emission-free vehicle.

Lincoln Continental offered dual-chambered tires as original equipment, and the Pontiac Firebird was fitted with a deflated spare tire and a charge of Freon to inflate it when necessary.

Buick began importing the German-made Opel Rallye Kadett for the United States market. Diamond and REO joined White and thus became the Diamond REO Truck Division, White Motor Corporation.

By 1967, twenty-six states had enacted compulsory annual motor vehicle inspection laws to assure good mechanical condition for all cars.

The 1967 World Champion Driver was Denis Hulme of New Zealand driving a Brabham-Repco. A. J. Foyt, Jr., won the Indianapolis 500-Mile Race in a Coyote-Ford at an average speed of 151.207 mph. The Le Mans 24-Hour Race was won by A. J. Foyt, Jr., and D. Gurney in a Ford GT40.

1968 placed the United States in the news again as Frank Borman, William A. Anders, and James A. Lovell, Jr., were the first men to orbit the moon. Dr. Martin Luther King, Jr., and Senator Robert Kennedy, the Democratic presidential candidate, were assassinated. Richard M. Nixon won the U.S. presidential contest. A military coup deposed Peruvian President Fernando Belaúnde Terry. In Europe, international monetary crises developed because of the faltering British pound and French franc. Soviet troops invaded Czechoslovakia; President Ludvík Svoboda and Alexander Dubček were allowed to retain their posts; but the Czechs had to accept Soviet troop occupation for an indefinite time. In the Middle East, President Abdul Rahman Arif of Iraq was ousted in a bloodless coup that was led by the former premier Ahmed Hassan al-Bakr, who later assumed premiership. Israel attacked the Lebanese airport in Beirut, and the United Nations Security Council censured Israel. North Korea seized the *Pueblo*, a U.S. Navy intelligence ship, holding its officers and crew for eleven months. Peace talks for the Vietnam cease-fire began in Paris among representatives of Hanoi, the National Liberation Front, Saigon, and Washington. President Johnson ordered a halt to the bombing of North Vietnam. In the Arctic, the first overland crossing of the North Pole by foot and dogsled took place. The Royal Geographic Society of Britain's 3,600-mile expedition, encompassing more than fifteen months, reached the Pole the following year in April.

Automobile and auto accessory advertising represented about

30 percent of all newspaper advertising in 1968. The United Auto Workers left the A.F.L.-C.I.O. and joined the Teamsters Union in the Alliance for Labor Action (A.L.A.). A new fifty-story General Motors Building opened in New York, and Delco Electronics Division supplied the guidance and navigation systems that steered the *Apollo 8* spacecraft to the moon and back to earth.

During 1968 U.S. automobile manufacturers produced 10,718,236 motor vehicles, worth over $24 billion. The United States exported 422,629 motor vehicles and imported 1,749,591. Mobile homes, travel trailers, truck campers, etc., in the U.S. totaled 818,230. The 250-millionth U.S.-produced motor vehicle appeared. New car registrations in the United States reached 9,403,862.

The average age of passenger cars in the United States was 5.6 years, and the U.S. made 38.1 percent of the world's motor vehicles in 1968. The United States Post Office ordered 24,000 postal delivery vehicles, weighing about 800 pounds each, to be used for the delivery of mail in suburban areas.

Clessie L. Cummins, founder of the Cummins Engine Company, died in 1968. He was a pioneer in the development of the high-speed, lightweight diesel engine which led to diesel application in trucks, buses, and automobiles.

Traffic deaths involving motor vehicles reached 55,200, which means that there were 5.4 deaths for every 100 million vehicle miles traveled.

The trend toward highway safety accelerated. General Motors dedicated a safety research laboratory and a large vehicle dynamics test area. Considerable experimentation was conducted with inflatable plastic bags that were stored and not readily visible. They were instantly inflated upon car impact and were located so as to keep the passengers from being thrown forward. Plymouth experimented with a periscope that gave the driver unrestricted side and rear vision. Skid-control braking that was actuated by a mini-computer was made available on the Lincoln Continental and Thunderbird. An energy-absorbing S-shaped frame was developed by Ford to absorb the impact of a collision, and Pontiac developed an engine-driven, tire-inflating pump to prevent motorists from being stranded on busy highways. Chevrolet Corvette offered headlight washers; Chrysler station wagons featured air deflectors above the rear window to help keep the rear windows clear; and Chevrolet developed a system to spray a solution on the tires for better traction on ice and snow.

Electric power was still of interest. American Motors, working with Gulton Industries, developed an electric compact called the Amitron that was powered with lithium nickel fluoride batteries. Rowan Controller Corporation showed an electric-powered car at the New York Auto Show. Autolite's battery-powered racer Lead Wedge set an electric-powered speed record of 138.9 mph.

Checker Motors diesel-powered taxicabs were announced. The Lincoln Continental Mark III was introduced, and the American Motors AMX sporty car was revealed in 1968. International Harvester made a gas-turbine-powered truck in prototype form.

Mercury and Chrysler offered a wood-grain covering on selected hardtops and convertibles as was previously done only on station wagons. General Motors and Chrysler experimented with pneumatic and hydraulic operation of accessories to replace the electrical devices.

Wings were being used on Formula 1 racing machines to keep the rear of the car pressing against the road to improve traction. The World Champion Driver was Graham Hill of England driving a Lotus-Ford. The Le Mans 24-Hour Race was won by Rodriguez and Bianchi in a Ford GT40. Bobby Unser won the Indianapolis 500-Mile Race driving an Eagle-Offenhauser at an average speed of 152.882 mph.

1969 highlighted the United States' progress in space as U.S. astronaut Neil A. Armstrong became the first man to walk on the Moon. The president of France, Charles de Gaulle, resigned and was replaced by Georges Pompidou. Despite world condemnation, the Iraqi Revolutionary Court executed some forty persons accused of spying for Israel, the United States, and Iran. In the Far East, however, the Soviet and Chinese forces fought on the Manchurian border over a disputed island in the Ussuri River. The Nixon administration withdrew 25,000 troops from Vietnam. Pope Paul VI became the first pope to visit Africa when he flew to Kampala, Uganda, to attend an African episcopal symposium. Portugal utilized 40 percent of her national budget and 120,000 troops to quell rebels in its territories of Angola, Mozambique, and Portuguese Guinea.

In the United States, there were 3,710,000 miles of paved roads and streets in 1969. Guidance and navigation systems manufactured by Delco Electronics Division of General Motors guided the *Apollo 11* and *Apollo 12* spaceships to the moon and back.

U.S. manufacturers produced 10,142,820 motor vehicles, worth $23.7 billion. Exports totaled 437,802 and imports jumped to 2,017,885. Imported cars were mostly economy types and sports cars. The U.S. produced about one-third of all the motor vehicles built in the world.

Americans spent over $21 billion on gasoline and lubricating oil and spent over $35 billion on new and used cars! Car thefts increased 12 percent over the 1968 rate. The average U.S. production worker worked about twenty-five weeks to earn enough for the purchase of a new eight-cylinder, four-door, automatic transmission sedan. This meant working approximately nine weeks to earn money for the purchase of a four-year-old used car.

General Motors Institute, accredited as a bachelor's-degree-granting institution, marked its golden anniversary in 1969. Over 105 million driver's licenses were issued in the United States, and Pontiac celebrated the production of its 13-millionth car in 1969. International Harvester announced its one-millionth tractor.

The United States Department of Transportation declared that it would accept proposals for the construction of Experimental Safety Vehicles (ESV's). Safety features continued on the upswing. Roll-over structures were fitted into the roof of the Plymouth Barracuda and the Dodge Challenger. A new type of windshield that crumbled into blunt-edged granules upon impact was introduced by American Motors. Rear window defrosters and disc brakes were added to many models. Belted radial tires made an impression of U.S. buyers, and the Tire Industry Safety Council was formed.

About half of the U.S.-produced automobiles had bias ply-belted tires as original equipment. Advantages of the radial-ply tire were not yet impressed upon the U.S. industry.

New features introduced in 1969 were: odometers that could not be turned back, plastic grilles, hidden windshield wipers and radio antennae, and larger turn and braking lights. During 1969, over a half million pickup truck-campers were on the road as the recreational vehicle reached a peak in popularity. The pickup truck-campers were especially popular because the vehicles could be used for both recreation and business.

The Taylor Aerocar, announced in Longview, Washington, was the only flying car of its type to be certified by the F.A.A. U.S. manufacturers turned more and more to the production of small sporty cars, compact and subcompact cars due to the avalanche of small imported cars. Ford introduced the 103-inch wheelbase Maverick, and American Motors announced the Hornet and the SC/Rambler sporty high-performance car. Pontiac introduced a high-performance Firebird with an airfoil/air deflector across the rear. Mercury brought out the sporty Cyclone Spoiler. Dodge showed its Charger Daytona sporty car equipped with hidden headlights and a more powerful engine. Chevrolet produced the sporty Monte Carlo intermediate luxury car.

Auto emissions were a growing problem. The U.S. Senate Commerce Committee proposed the development of steam-powered cars, and the Post Office Department commissioned Electric Fuel Propulsion, Inc., to construct four experimental electric postal vehicles for testing. Auto thefts constituted a problem, and in order to combat them, some foreign and all U.S. car manufacturers included steering column locks on new vehicles.

The average age of the U.S. passenger car in 1969 was 5.5 years old. A record 56,400 fatalities involving motor vehicles were recorded in the U.S., which amounted to 5.3 deaths for every 100 million vehicle miles traveled.

The 1969 World Champion Driver was Jackie Stewart of Scotland driving a Matra-Ford. Mario Andretti won the Indianapolis 500-Mile Race driving a Hawk-Ford at an average speed of 156.867 mph. The Le Mans 24-Hour Race was won by J. Ickx and J. Oliver driving a Ford GT40.

Certainly the sixties were not lacking in new car models or in new features. Many U.S. manufacturers developed small economy cars and sporty types in order to combat the ever-increasing number of imported cars. Safety was a 1960s keynote that was carried into the seventies.

PLYMOUTH FURY   The Plymouth Fury PP1-H hardtop for 1960 featured a unitized body and was built on a 118-inch wheelbase. In April, 1960, Plymouth for the fourth straight year won the Mobilgas Economy Run. Power was a six-cylinder, inline, water-cooled, overhead-valve engine of 225-cubic-inch displacement, and 145 hp. at 4,000 rpm.

PLYMOUTH VALIANT V-200   The Plymouth Valiant V-200 compact car made its appearance in 1960. It featured unitized construction, the replacement of the generator with an alternator, and a new inline-slanted engine. The car, built on a 106.5-inch wheelbase, was powered with a six-cylinder, inline-slanted, overhead-valve, water-cooled, 170-cubic-inch-displacement engine developing 148 hp. at 5,200 rpm. Note the racing-type oval grille and sculptured body accents.

DODGE DART   The Dodge Dart was introduced in 1960 as a contender in the lower-priced field. Three models were offered: the Seneca, Pioneer, and Phoenix. The Dodge Dart Phoenix two-door hardtop is shown. Built on a 118-inch wheelbase, the cars were powered with a six-cylinder, inline, water-cooled engine that produced 145 hp. at 4,000 rpm. Displacement was 225 cubic inches, and the compression ratio was 9 to 1. Note the big-car styling with wide grille, dual headlamps, and tail fins.

FORD FAIRLANE   This four-door Ford Fairlane was produced in 1960. Note the sculptured styling that carried a wedge-shaped fin from headlights to the end of the rear fender. Power was an eight-cylinder, vee-type, overhead-valve, water-cooled, 312-cubic-inch-displacement engine that delivered 205 hp. at 4,000 rpm. Either three-speed manual or Fordomatic automatic transmission was available. Speed was about 100 mph.

MERCEDES-BENZ LIMOUSINE The Mercedes-Benz Hardtop 300 Limousine made in 1960 was a comfortable car, combining classic and modern features. The rear springs were adjustable, allowing the car to ride level regardless of the load. Power was a six-cylinder, overhead-cam, inline, water-cooled, fuel-injection engine of 2,996-cc displacement that produced 160 hp. at 5,300 rpm. A Borg-Warner automatic transmission was installed. Speed was just over 100 mph.

OLDSMOBILE F-85 The Oldsmobile F-85 Cutlass was introduced in 1960 and was the first Oldsmobile compact car. The 1961 F-85 Cutlass Four-Door Deluxe Sedan is shown. This car was powered with an eight-cylinder, vee-type, overhead-valve, water-cooled, 215-cubic-inch-displacement engine of 155 hp. at 4,800 rpm. Hydra-Matic automatic or three-speed manual transmission was offered. A higher-powered engine was available with optional turbocharger. Speed was about 100 mph.

DeSOTO ADVENTURER The DeSoto Adventurer was introduced in 1958 as a customized model. This is the 1961 DeSoto Adventurer PS3-M with a wheelbase of 122 inches, a two-door hardtop that seated five. Power was an eight-cylinder, vee-type, water-cooled, 383-cubic-inch-displacement engine producing 305 hp. at 4,600 rpm. The year 1961 was the last for DeSoto passenger cars, with production ending in December of 1960. Starting in 1928, total DeSoto production was 2,056,000 vehicles.

FORD THUNDERBIRD The third generation of Ford Thunderbirds appeared in 1961. The '61 Thunderbird was much more luxuriously appointed than previous designs and was no longer in the sports car class, although the vehicle was a sporty car. Power for this four-seater was an eight-cylinder, vee-type, water-cooled, overhead-valve, 390-cubic-inch-displacement engine that produced 300 hp. at 4,600 rpm. Automatic transmission was standard and speed was approximately 130 mph.

DODGE LANCER WAGON The Dodge Lancer compact car was built on a 106.5-inch wheelbase and made use of unitized construction. This is the Dodge Lancer Station Wagon of 1961 that was powered by a six-cylinder, inline, overhead-valve, water-cooled, 225-cubic-inch-displacement engine that developed 145 hp. at 4,000 rpm. The year 1962 was the last year that the name "Lancer" was used for the cars.

VOLVO P-1800 SPORTS COUPÉ The Volvo P-1800 Sports Coupé was developed in 1960 as a two plus two sportster using standard Volvo mechanical components. This is the 1961 model that was 171.5 inches long on a 96.5-inch wheelbase. Total width was 67 inches. Power was a four-cylinder, inline, water-cooled, 122-cubic-inch-displacement engine that developed 135 hp. Electronic fuel-injection was fitted. Speed was about 115 mph.

RAMBLER AMERICAN   The Rambler American series was introduced by American Motors in 1958. The car was fitted to the 100-inch wheelbase that was used by the original Rambler. At first only a two-door sedan was offered, but the line increased the body styles until, in 1961, a four-door sedan and a convertible were added. This is the 1961 Rambler American Model 6107-2 convertible that was powered by a six-cylinder, overhead-valve, inline, water-cooled, 125-hp. engine. Economy was the keynote.

CHRYSLER NEWPORT   Large tail fins were still part of U.S. auto styling in 1961 as can be seen on this stylish Chrysler Newport RC1-L that was introduced in 1961. This is the 1961 sedan. The Newport was a luxury car built on a 122-inch wheelbase. Power was an eight-cylinder, vee-type, overhead-valve, water-cooled engine of 413-cubic-inch displacement producing 350 hp. at 4,600 rpm. Note the trapezoidal grille in front of the radiator that gave the nose a sports car appearance. Speed was over 110 mph. A swivel driver's seat was optional.

FORD FALCON   The Ford Falcon was Ford's first compact car and was introduced in 1960. The Falcon two-door sedan of 1961 is shown. Power was a six-cylinder, inline, overhead-valve, water-cooled, 144-cubic-inch-displacement engine that developed 90 hp. at 4,200 rpm. Either a manual three-speed transmission or Fordomatic automatic transmission was available. Speed was about 85 mph.

CHEVROLET CHEVY II   Chevrolet's Chevy II compact car made its appearance in 1961. This is the 1962 four-door Chevy II Model 300 Sedan that was available with four- or six-cylinder engines. The standard powerplant was a four-cylinder, overhead-valve, water-cooled, inline, 153-cubic-inch-displacement engine that produced 90 hp. at 4,000 rpm. Either a three-speed manual or Power Glide automatic transmission was available. Speed was about 85 mph. Single-leaf tapered plate rear springs were used.

MERCEDES 300 SL ROADSTER   The Mercedes 300 SL sports car was one of the best performing sports types in the recent past. First produced in 1952 as a gull-wing-door coupé, it was later produced as a convertible roadster as well. Shown is the 1962 roadster. In 1957 the 300 SL placed third in the Tour de France and second in the Rome-Liège-Rome Rallye. In 1958 it won the Snow and Ice Rallye. This 3,000-pound car was built on a 94.5-inch wheelbase. Overall length was 180 inches and width was 70.5 inches. Power was a six-cylinder, overhead-cam, water-cooled, inline-slanted, 183-cubic-inch-displacement, fuel-injected engine that developed 240 hp. at 6,100 rpm. The compression ratio was 8.5 to 1. Speed was about 140 mph.

STUDEBAKER AVANTI   After concentrating on the low-priced Lark, Studebaker decided to build an elegant sports car. Industrial designer Raymond Loewy was commissioned to design the body, and the result was outstanding. This fiberglass-body 1962 Avanti Sports Coupé was powered with an eight-cylinder, vee-type, overhead-valve, water-cooled, supercharged, 289-cubic-inch-displacement engine that developed 280 hp. at 4,800 rpm. It was fitted with either a four-speed manual or automatic transmission. Speed was about 145 mph.

BUICK RIVIERA This luxurious Buick Riviera personal car was produced in 1963. David Holls designed the body, combining elegance with sporty styling. This two-door four-seater was powered with an eight-cylinder, vee-type, overhead-valve, water-cooled, 401-cubic-inch-displacement engine producing 325 hp. at 4,400 rpm. Automatic transmission was standard. Speed was 125 mph.

CHEVROLET IMPALA Introduced in 1962, the Impala was Chevrolet's top of the line. This is the 1963 Chevrolet Impala two-door hardtop that did so well at the stock car Grand National events. Driven by Junior Johnson, the car won at Atlanta and Charlotte as well as at five other Grand National events. During the 1963 season, this car was the fastest qualifier at ten events in which Johnson set nine track records! It was the best performing stock car of 1963.

RAMBLER CLASSIC The restyled Rambler Classic for 1963 was built on a 112-inch wheelbase and featured a one-piece galvanized outer side that was welded to a one-piece galvanized inner side called the Advanced Single Unit Construction. This is the 1963 four-door, five-passenger Rambler Classic sedan. Optional power was a new 198-hp. V-8 engine. *Motor Trend* magazine selected Rambler as the "Car of the Year" for "engineering excellence and outstanding design achievement."

FORD NASCAR In 1963 Fireball Roberts drove this Ford Fairlane to his second Southern 500 Race Victory at a record speed of 129.784 mph. This was considered to be an unbreakable record at that time. The production Ford was fitted with a six-cylinder, inline, overhead-valve, water-cooled, 170-cubic-inch-displacement engine developing about 101 hp. at 4,400 rpm. Maximum speed of the production model was about 90 mph. Racing mechanics rework and tune engines so they can deliver much more power than the street versions.

MERCURY   The 1964 Mercury was 215 inches long on a 120-inch wheelbase. Power was an eight-cylinder, vee-type, overhead-valve, water-cooled, 250- to 425-hp. engine. The Mercury was quite successful in U.S. stock car racing, and the two-door Mercury shown was raced by Joe Weatherly in many NASCAR (National Association for Stock Car Auto Racing) races. Note the non-production engine exhaust outlet located behind the door at the bottom of the car.

CHRYSLER TURBINE CAR   After spending about ten years developing a gas-turbine automobile engine, Chrysler Corporation made fifty test automobiles powered by gas turbines in 1964. The test cars were lent to over two hundred people, each for a period of three months, to test their reactions to the new powerplant and to test the mechanical performance of the engine under normal use. When the program ended in 1966, a total of over one million miles had been driven. The turbine engine developed 130 hp., which is really equal to a 200-hp. piston engine. The turbine weighed only 410 pounds and had 80 percent fewer moving parts than a piston engine. The car never entered production despite the fact that the tests proved favorable.

PLYMOUTH BARRACUDA The Plymouth Model VV2-P Barracuda was introduced in 1964 as a high-performance, sports-type automobile. This "fastback" design had the largest rear window ever used in a production automobile, with over 14 square feet of tinted glass. The rear seats folded forward to form a large utility area similar to those found in station wagons. This is the Plymouth Barracuda VV2-P29, powered by an eight-cylinder, vee-type, overhead-valve, water-cooled, 273-cubic-inch-displacement engine that produced 180 hp. at 4,200 rpm. A six-cylinder 145-hp. engine was also available.

CHEVROLET CHEVELLE Chevrolet first produced the medium-size Chevelle in 1964. The car was available in two- and four-door sedans, hardtops, station wagons, and convertibles. The 1964 two-door Malibu hardtop coupé is shown. Overall length was 194 inches on a 115-inch wheelbase. Width was 75 inches. Power was either a six- or an eight-cylinder engine. The eight-cylinder powerplant was a vee-type, overhead-valve, water-cooled, 283-cubic-inch-displacement engine that developed 195 hp. at 4,800 rpm. Price was about $2,800.

FACEL VEGA II   The French Facel Vega elegant five-passenger sports touring cars were built for a dozen years after World War II. The basic body design was by Jean Daninos. This is the Facel Vega II of 1964, which was the last year of production. Power was a Chrysler eight-cylinder, vee-type, water-cooled, 413-cubic-inch-displacement engine that delivered 390 hp. at 4,800 rpm. Speed was approximately 140 mph. A four-speed Pont-à-Mouson gearbox was fitted. Chrysler automatic transmissions were optional. Some Facel Vegas were fitted with Volvo or Austin-Healey engines.

PORSCHE 904-GTS CARRERA   This 1964 fiberglass-bodied Porsche 904-GTS Carrera first made its appearance late in 1963 with a minimum production of one hundred. The car was used extensively on the circuits by private owners. Power was a 1,966-cc-displacement, four-cylinder, horizontal, opposed, air-cooled engine that developed 180 hp. at 7,000 rpm. The engine was mounted just ahead of the rear axle. In 1964 the car won at Daytona and Sebring as well as the Targa Florio. Class victories in other European events secured the championship for Porsche. The Porsche won the Tour de France and placed second at Monte Carlo in 1965. The car was later powered by a six-cylinder engine and redesignated 906.

FORD MUSTANG   The sporty Ford Mustang was first produced in 1964, and the car became so popular that over one million were sold in two years. The fastback four-seater Ford Mustang of 1965 shown here was built on a 108-inch wheelbase. Overall length was 182 inches and the width 68 inches. The Mustang was available with either a six- or an eight-cylinder engine. The eight-cylinder powerplant was a vee-type, overhead-valve, water-cooled, 289-cubic-inch-displacement engine that developed 271 hp. at 6,000 rpm. Either three- or four-speed manual transmission or automatic transmission was available. Speed was about 120 mph.

CADILLAC ELDORADO CONVERTIBLE   The sleek Cadillac Eldorado Convertible was the epitome of glamour in 1965. The two-door four-seater was built on a 129.5-inch wheelbase. Overall length was 224 inches, and width was 80 inches. Power was an eight-cylinder, vee-type, water-cooled, overhead-valve engine that developed 340 hp. Price was about $7,000.

RAMBLER MARLIN The American Motors sporty Marlin Model 6559-7 was first produced in 1965. The six-passenger fastback hardtop was built on a 112-inch wheelbase. Overall length was 195 inches and height only 54 inches. Width was about 74.5 inches. Power was an eight-cylinder, vee-type, water-cooled, 327-cubic-inch-displacement engine that developed 270 hp. Price was approximately $3,000.

MFI-13 (SONETT PROTOTYPE) The Swedish Malmö Flygindustri made this MFI-13 design that first appeared in 1965 as a two-seat sports car after two years of development. Power was the three-cylinder Saab Monte Carlo two-cycle, water-cooled engine that was equipped with three carburetors. The chassis was of box-frame and tray construction and the body was steel. Coil-spring suspension was used on all four wheels. The car was considered too expensive for the small firm to produce. Thus it was sold to Saab and became the prototype for the well-known Saab Sonett sports cars.

FORD GT40 RACER The Ford Motor Company introduced this mid-engine GT coupé in 1964. The Ford GT40 was refined during the year, and in 1965 the car won the Daytona 2,000-kilometer race at an average speed of 99.94 mph. In 1966 the cars placed first, second, and third in the Le Mans 24-Hour Race. The 1966 Ford GT40 Racer is shown here. Variations of the car won the 1968 and 1969 Le Mans and won the International Championship of Makes in 1969. Power was a 289-cubic-inch displacement, eight-cylinder, vee-type, water-cooled, overhead-valve engine that produced 390 hp. at 7,000 rpm. Many of the cars were lightweight with a bonded and riveted aluminum honeycomb body construction that was a single unit.

DODGE CHARGER The Dodge Charger was first produced in 1966 as an advanced styling fastback. Features included retractable headlights in the grille and a one-piece taillight running from side to side across the rear. The 1966 Dodge Charger Model BW2-P was built on a 117-inch wheelbase. Length was 203 inches, and width was 75 inches. Power was an eight-cylinder, vee-type, water-cooled, overhead-valve, 426-cubic-inch-displacement engine that developed 425 hp. at 5,000 rpm. Price was over $3,000.

FORD GALAXIE 500   The Galaxie 500 was Ford's top-of-the-line series, and this is the 1966 four-door Galaxie 500 Sedan. Overall length was 210 inches, and width was 79 inches on a wheelbase of 119 inches. Power was an eight-cylinder, vee-type, overhead-valve, water-cooled engine that developed 425 hp. Price was $3,500 for this five-seater.

OLDSMOBILE TORONADO   The front-wheel-drive Oldsmobile Toronado was first produced in 1966 as a two-door, five-passenger hardtop coupé. The 211-inch-long auto was built on a 119-inch wheelbase and was 79 inches wide. An Oldsmobile Super Rocket engine was used with an eight-cylinder, vee-type, water-cooled, overhead-valve, 425-cubic-inch-displacement powerplant that produced 385 hp. at 4,800 rpm. Automatic transmission was standard. Note the sporty styling with flared fenders over the wheels and fastback rear. Speed was about 130 mph.

RAMBLER CLASSIC REBEL   The Rambler Classic Rebel hardtop Model 6619-7 was first produced in 1966 and featured a thin roof and straight-line design. Built on a 112-inch wheelbase, the overall length was 195 inches and width was 74.5 inches. Power was an eight-cylinder, vee-type, water-cooled, 270-hp. engine. A six-cylinder engine was also available. Price was about $2,600.

RENAULT ALPINE   The Société des Automobiles Alpine, founded in 1955 by Jean Redélé, always had a close association with Renault and used Renault engines in most Alpine cars. This is the A210 Renault Alpine sports car of 1966. The cars placed ninth, tenth, eleventh, twelfth, and thirteenth in the 1967 Le Mans, taking the 1.3- and 1.5-liter group 6 classes. In 1968 the cars finished in eighth, ninth, tenth, and eleventh places and took the Index of Performance and Thermal Efficiency honors. The cars were very much underpowered for competition. However, the aerodynamic body shape helped to compensate for this shortcoming. Power varied from 998-cc to 1,150-cc and 1,300-cc Renault engines. The largest developed about 125 hp. The little two-seaters were extremely attractive and set the style for many future sports types.

VOLVO 144   The Volvo 144 four-door, five-passenger sedan was introduced in 1966 and remained in production for about five years. Overall length was 182.5 inches on a 103-inch wheelbase. Width was 68.3 inches. Power was a four-cylinder, inline, overhead-valve, water-cooled, 122-cubic-inch-displacement engine that developed 90 hp. The auto was also available with a 110-hp. or a 145-hp. engine. A two-door version was also made and designated as the Volvo 142. Speeds were from 90 to 100 mph.

CHEVROLET CAMARO   The four-seat Chevrolet Camaro made its appearance in 1967 as a two-door hardtop, compact, sporty car and enjoyed considerable popularity. Power was an eight-cylinder, vee-type, water-cooled, overhead-valve, 327-cubic-inch-displacement engine that produced 210 hp. at 4,600 rpm. and gave the car a speed of over 120 mph. Either manual four-speed or automatic transmission was offered.

SAAB SONETT II   Saab revised the MFI-13 prototype of 1965 to accept standard Saab 96 tooling and changed the body from steel to a four-piece fiberglass body in 1967. The two-cycle engine was replaced with a Ford V-4 engine in 1968 in order to make the car more attractive to American buyers. The 1967 model is shown here.

FERRARI 275 GT BERLINETTA   This Ferrari sports/gran tourismo car placed eighth in the 1967 Le Mans 24-Hour Race. The 275 GT Berlinetta was 171 inches long and 67 inches wide on a 94.5-inch wheelbase. Power was a twelve-cylinder, vee-type, water-cooled, overhead-valve, 200-cubic-inch-displacement engine that produced 280 hp. at 7,500 rpm. Three two-barrel carburetors were fitted. A five-speed transmission was used. Weight was 2,550 pounds.

SAAB 96   The Saab 96 was introduced in 1960 as an outgrowth of the earlier Saab 93. The original two-cycle, three-cylinder powerplant was replaced with constantly improved types until, in 1966, a Ford four-cylinder, water-cooled, vee-type, 91-cubic-inch displacement, four-cycle engine that developed 65 hp. was installed. This made the car more acceptable to foreign buyers and ended the Saab two-cycle engine production which had reached a total of 320,000 engines from 1950 to 1968. Shown is a 1968 Saab 96.

BUICK GS 400   The Buick GS 400 of 1968 was a sporty high-performance automobile built on a 112-inch wheelbase. Overall length was 200 inches, and width was 75.6 inches. Power for the five-passenger car was an eight-cylinder, vee-type, water-cooled, four-barrel-carburetor, 400-cubic-inch-displacement engine that produced 340 hp. at 5,000 rpm. The compression ratio was 10.25 to 1. Aluminum alloy pistons were used. Manual three- or four-speed transmission was offered.

AMX SPORTSTER   American Motors introduced the AMX Sportster in 1968, and it caused widespread interest among performance-minded enthusiasts. The two-seater was built on a 97-inch wheelbase and was 179 inches long. All-welded, single-unit construction was used. Front suspension consisted of twin ball joints and coil springs plus a sway bar. Rear suspension was semi-elliptic leaf springs. Power was an eight-cylinder, vee-type, four-barrel-carburetor, water-cooled, 360-cubic-inch-displacement engine that produced 290 hp. at 4,800 rpm. Either four-speed manual or automatic transmission was available. Acceleration was from 0 to 60 mph. in 6.1 seconds and to 80 mph. in 10 seconds. More than 11,000 AMX models were made in 1968, and the car set 106 national and international speed records.

PLYMOUTH VALIANT   The Plymouth Valiant 100 Model DV-L for 1968 was built on a 108-inch wheelbase and offered a six- or eight-cylinder engine. Also featured were safety items such as a stronger door-latch mechanism, double-jointed inside rear-view mirror mounts, and recessed interior door handles. Power was an eight-cylinder, vee-type, water-cooled, 273-cubic-inch-displacement engine that developed 190 hp. at 4,400 rpm.

FORD THUNDERBIRD   The fourth generation of Ford Thunder-birds emerged in 1968 as luxurious five-seaters. This is the 1968 two-door hardtop Ford Thunderbird Landau. Power was an eight-cylinder, vee-type, overhead-valve, water-cooled, 428-cubic-inch-displacement engine that produced 365 hp. at 4,600 rpm. Speed was over 130 mph. Automatic transmission was standard.

LAMBORGHINI MIURA   Italian auto maker Ferruccio Lambor-ghini introduced his Miura GT car in 1968. Top speed was approxi-mately 170 mph. Power was a twelve-cylinder, double-overhead-cam, water-cooled, 240-cubic-inch engine mounted transversely behind the two seats and driving the rear wheels. The engine developed 430 hp. at 7,350 rpm. The car could accelerate from 0 to 50 mph. in 4.1 seconds and to 100 mph. in 12.3 seconds! Overall length was 171.6 inches and width was 69.3 inches on a 98.4-inch wheelbase. Weight was 2,905 pounds, and the price was less than $20,000.

JAVELIN SPORTSTER The American Motors four-place Javelin Model 6879-5 was a sporty car credited with helping the company's financial position. This is the 1968 Javelin built on a 109-inch wheelbase. The car was 191 inches long and 72 inches wide. Standard power was a six-cylinder, inline, water-cooled, 232-cubic-inch-displacement engine that produced 145 hp. at 4,300 rpm. A 390-cubic-inch-displacement V-8 engine was optional. Three- or four-speed manual or automatic transmission was offered. A total of 56,462 Javelins were constructed during the 1968 model year.

OLDSMOBILE 98 HOLIDAY The Oldsmobile 98 Holiday was the top of the line for Oldsmobile. This is the four-door 98 Holiday Luxury Sedan for 1968. The wheelbase was 127 inches, and power was an eight-cylinder, vee-type, water-cooled, 455-cubic-inch-displacement engine. Power brakes, power steering, automatic transmission, and power windows were standard equipment on this luxurious vehicle.

AMBASSADOR SST   American Motors Ambassador SST was the top of the line and was built on a 122-inch wheelbase and 208-inch overall length. The 1969 four-door Ambassador SST is shown. Exhaust emission control and seat and shoulder belts were standard. Power was an eight-cylinder, vee-type, water-cooled, 304-cubic-inch-displacement engine that developed 210 hp. at 4,400 rpm. and was fitted with a two-barrel carburetor. The SST was available in the two-door sedan, two-door hardtop, coupé, and station wagon models in addition to the four-door sedan.

SAAB 99   The Swedish Saab 99 five-passenger auto was introduced in 1969 after eleven years of planning and design. The car was made in two- and four-door models, and the 1969 two-door is shown. The powerplant was a specially designed Triumph four-cylinder, water-cooled, overhead-valve, inline, 104-cubic-inch-displacement engine that was built in England for Saab. The engine developed 80 hp. and drove the front wheels via a four-speed gearbox. The wheelbase was 97.4 inches, and overall length was 171.3 inches, with a width of 66.2 inches. Speed was about 95 mph. The car was also available with automatic transmission, and therefore required a higher-powered engine that was achieved with fuel injection.

FIAT 128   The Italian Fiat 128 joined the ever-increasing number of European front-wheel-drive economy cars in 1969. The four-door, five-seater was powered with a four-cylinder, water-cooled, overhead-valve, inline, transversely mounted, 1,116-cc-displacement engine that developed 55 hp. at 6,000 rpm. Speed was about 82 mph.

FORD CUSTOM 500   This Ford Custom 500 two-door sedan made its appearance in 1969 and was built on a 119-inch wheelbase. Overall length was 213.3 inches, the width was 78 inches. Weight was 3,525 pounds. Power was a six-cylinder, inline, water-cooled, 240-cubic-inch-displacement engine that produced 150 hp. The car was designed for value-seeking families and stressed economy combined with luxury.

CHAPTER FOURTEEN

Wheels on the Moon and ESV's 1970 and Beyond

IN THE AMERICAS during 1970, the United States saw student protests against the Vietnam War. In Canada, Prime Minister Pierre Elliott Trudeau invoked the War Measures Act after the murder of the Quebec Labor Minister Pierre Laporte by the Quebec Liberation Front. While in Chile, Salvador Allende, a Marxist, was elected president. Europe made numerous headlines as West Germany and the U.S.S.R. signed a non-aggression pact, and in England, conservative leader Edward Heath became prime minister. Violent food price riots in Poland led to Wladyslav Gomulka's resignation, and he was replaced by Edward Gierek as the first secretary of the Communist Party. France's Charles de Gaulle died. In the Middle East, Nasser died in Cairo and was succeeded by Anwar Sadat. Civil war broke out between the Jordanian Army and the Palestinian guerrilla groups. In the Far East, Prince Sihanouk was deposed as chief of state in Cambodia and was replaced by General Lon Nol. U.S. and Vietnamese troops invaded Cambodia. Africa and the world took note of the surrender of secessionist Biafra on January 12, which ended the thirty-one-month civil war in Nigeria.

In 1970 United States automobile manufacturers were operating many plants in foreign countries: 50 in South America, 60 in Europe, 17 in Africa, 40 in Asia, and 27 in Oceania.

The production from U.S.-based plants was down to 8,239,257 vehicles, worth about $19.5 billion. The U.S. exported 379,089 vehicles in 1970, but imported vehicles jumped to 2,167,091. This

563

caused concern in the U.S. automotive industry. German, Japanese, and British cars were favored in that order.

The boom in imported cars began for the U.S. in the late 1960s, and by 1967 one out of fifteen U.S. new car purchasers chose a foreign-made vehicle. By 1970 about one out of four buyers selected a foreign-made vehicle. Three considerations caused this switch: economy in purchase price and in operation, performance in sports types not requiring a huge V-8 engine to achieve it, and quality, which placed Mercedes-Benz among the top ten imports. U.S. manufacturers, having deserted the small car market, equated price with size and power in the late sixties and 1970. The Europeans did not. Further, with multi-car families on the upswing, an inexpensive but reliable small car became a necessity by 1970. Existing U.S. compacts all exceeded 100 hp. by 1970 and lost their economy. U.S. manufacturers promised to produce cars equal to the imports in the economy, performance, and luxury classes.

Chrysler Motors made arrangements with Mitsubishi to construct the subcompact Dodge Colt economy car in Japan in accordance with Chrysler specifications. Other U.S. auto manufacturers soon followed this idea, and the cars were known as captive imports.

In 1970, with 6.7 percent of the area on earth and 5.7 percent of the earth's population, the U.S. owned 36.2 percent of the world's trucks and 46.1 percent of the world's cars.

U.S. automobile production accounted for the following approximate percentages of U.S. consumption of raw materials: steel 15.9; aluminum 8.2; copper 7.8; cotton 1.9; malleable iron 41.2; nickel 11.3; rubber 69.2; and zinc 29.0.

Also in 1970, U.S. manufacturers made a total of 351 models. Consumer credit for automobiles in the U.S. was more than $36 billion, and the average age of U.S. passenger cars was 5.5 years.

The most popular U.S. passenger car body style in 1970 was the two-door hardtop, with four-door sedans second choice and four-door hardtops in third position. Convertibles dropped in sales from over 200,000 in 1969 to 91,863 in 1970.

General Motors announced the Chevrolet Vega 2300 as their first U.S.-built small economy car, and announced that its 1971 products would operate on low-leaded or no-lead gasoline at about 91 octane.

The United Automobile Workers went on strike against General Motors for fifty-eight days, which reduced the U.S. Gross National Product by $9 billion. Walter Reuther, U.A.W. president, was killed in a plane crash on May 9, 1970.

There were 54,800 deaths attributed to accidents involving motor vehicles in the U.S., which is about 4.9 deaths for every 100 million miles driven.

The 1970 World Championship Driver was Jochen Rindt of Austria driving a Lotus-Ford. Al Unser won the 1970 Indianapolis 500-Mile Race in a Colt-Ford with an average speed of 155.75 mph. The Le Mans 24-Hour Race was won by R. Attwood and H. Hermann in a Porsche. Gary Gabelich drove the Blue Flame Speedster to a world record speed of 622.41 mph. The jet-powered car used natural gas as a fuel, hence the name Blue Flame. It established the record on the Bonneville Salt Flats.

During 1970, the U.S. Department of Transportation awarded contracts to A.M.F. Incorporated, Fairchild Industries, General Motors, and Advanced Systems Laboratory to design and construct an Experimental Safety Vehicle, or ESV, which would be developed more in 1971.

1971 ushered in a wage-price freeze enacted by the Nixon administration. As the United States labored through the freeze, the Middle East witnessed a coup d'etat attempt against King Hassan II of Morocco, but to no avail. In the Far East, Communist China was admitted to the United Nations, and Nationalist China (Taiwan) was ousted.

U.S. automobile production climbed to 10,637,738 vehicles, worth over $27 billion. The U.S. exported 486,780 vehicles and imported 2,826,421.

The two-door hardtop style was the biggest seller of U.S. cars with the four-door sedan in second place, and the four-door hardtop was the third most popular in the U.S. in 1971.

More U.S. automobile manufacturers introduced captive imports in 1971. Buick sold German-made Opel cars in its many showrooms. Plymouth sold the Cricket subcompact, which was a modified British Hillman Avenger, and Lincoln-Mercury dealers began selling the German-built Ford Capri. Captive imports were intended to stem the tide of imported cars entering the U.S.

Two front-wheel-drive foreign cars appeared in the U.S. in

1971 to threaten Volkswagen's position as the best-selling import. The subcompacts Fiat 128 and Subaru FF-1 both featured water-cooled engines, front-located, with front-wheel drive. VW engineers were beginning to consider a successor to the aging Beetle.

General Motors announced that the Oldsmobile 98, Buick Electra, and Cadillac deVille would no longer be produced in convertible models.

The shock in the automotive world in 1971 was the collapse of Rolls-Royce. This was caused by the expense of developing a jet engine for Lockheed's 1011 TriStar Airliner. At the time of the bankruptcy the British government nationalized the Rolls-Royce aero engine, and other defense-related assets were used to save the auto division from bankruptcy. The company reorganized as Rolls-Royce Motors Holding, Ltd., and issued stock in order to continue the production of those marvelous motor vehicles.

The Experimental Safety Vehicles began to take shape in late 1971. The stringent requirements of the U.S. Department of Transportation stated that the cars must be so constructed that passengers would survive a head-on impact into a wall at 50 mph. at angles up to 50 degrees to left or right. Also, so passengers could withstand side impacts at 30 mph. and rear-end collisions at 75 mph., plus two complete roll-overs at 60 to 70 mph. The car should not exceed a weight of 4,000 pounds. The ESV cars must stop from 60 mph. in 155 feet on a dry surface, maintain 0.6g lateral acceleration on a 100-foot-radius turning circle, and make an abrupt 180-degree U-turn at 70 mph. entry speed without rolling over. Moreover, the car must accelerate from 30 mph. to 70 mph. with a 60 percent load in less than 12 seconds. All the test vehicles were overweight and tipped the scale from 4,600 to 4,900 pounds. The A.M.F. ESV had a vault-strong body structure with thick windshield posts. An enormous aluminum front bumper was hydraulically mounted to move three feet upon impact, while the rear bumper was a sponge cell. A rear-view periscope was cut into the roof. Fairchild reworked a Plymouth Fury with extensive reinforcement and fitted a front bumper that automatically extended one foot at speeds over 30 mph. The rear bumper was a sponge cell, and a rear-view periscope was fitted into the roof. The General Motors ESV had a cantilevered roof with massive supports, plus enormous side-guard beams running through the doors. The front end was designed to collapse in sections in the event of severe impact, and this energy-absorbing feature would stop short of the passenger compartment. Many of the body panels were aluminum. Cross-car padded structures protected all passengers. Germany, Japan, Great Britain, Italy, France, and Sweden began their own research into Experimental Safety Vehicles.

Students and faculty members of the Industrial Design Department of Pratt Institute, Brooklyn, New York, developed and built a prototype functional urban taxi called the Prattaxi in 1971. The Prattaxi was boxlike in appearance and featured easy entry and exit, plenty of room for luggage and passengers, and air conditioning under the passenger's control. The school applied for and is waiting for funding by the U.S. Department of Transportation.

The age group most involved in accidents in 1971 was the twenty-five-to-forty-four-year-old span, and approximately 40 percent of the licensed teenage drivers were involved in accidents. In 1971 there were 54,700 fatalities involving motor vehicles, which came to 4.7 deaths for every 100 million miles traveled. About one-third of those killed in car crashes were between the ages of fifteen and twenty-four.

Moulton P. Taylor of Longview, Washington, completed and test flew his Aerocar flying automobile in 1971. The aluminum wings and tail were detachable from the fiberglass auto body. This vehicle was the only convertible airplane-automobile to be certified by the Federal Aeronautics Administration for sale to the public.

The *Apollo 15* spacecraft took an electrically driven vehicle to the moon in 1971. Astronauts James Irwin and David Scott drove the Lunar Roving Vehicle (LRV) for several miles during their exploratory excursions on the moon's surface. The vehicle was folded into three sections to facilitate storage on the spacecraft.

The Indianapolis 500-Mile Race was won by two-time winner Al Unser with an average speed of 157.735 mph.

1972 marked the first U.S. trade deficit since 1888. Governor George C. Wallace was seriously injured in an attempted assassination while campaigning in Maryland. The Watergate burglars were apprehended in the Democratic National Headquarters, and Richard M. Nixon was re-elected as the President in a near-record landslide. In Europe, Great Britain, Ireland, and Denmark joined the E.E.C. (European Economic Community). Arab commandos disrupted the XXth Olympic games at Munich by taking thirteen Israeli athletes as hostages. Terrorism rocked Northern Ireland in the continued Protestant-Catholic conflict. Israel launched further raids into Arab territories as a retaliation for continued Palestinian terrorist activities. East Pakistan became the independent state of Bangladesh after a civil war. President Nixon made historic visits to Peking and Moscow.

U.S. automobile manufacturers produced 11,857,686 motor vehicles, and U.S. auto production passed the 300-million mark. The top producer in 1972 was Chevrolet with 2,299,771 vehicles manufactured during the year. Its nearest competitor was Ford with 1,868,010 units. The U.S. produced about one-third of the motor vehicles made in the entire world, and the production of motor vehicles in the U.S. created about 13 million jobs in many industries. The U.S. imported 2,736,050 motor vehicles and exported 531,009.

General Motors Corporation announced that it would produce the Wankel rotary engine in limited quantities for possible use in either the Vega or the Corvette.

Recreational vehicles rolled into high gear in 1972. Mobile homes, camper trailers, truck campers, travel trailers, and pickup covers increased in popularity. A rise in pickup-truck sales was caused by this surge in recreational vehicles. They were used to haul trailers and hold camper bodies. The average RV family, composed of four persons and headed by a white collar worker, spent 10 percent of its time in the recreational vehicle.

Several new imported cars appeared in the U.S. in 1972: the Alfa-Romeo, long-remembered for sports and racing types, entered the economy car race with the Alfasud front-wheel-drive car that featured controlled front-end collapsibility. The German-built Buick Opel 1900 captive import appeared in Buick showrooms. The Volvo 164 and Volvo 1800 ES were compact and subcompact cars that tried to stem the tide of the Japanese car imports to the U.S.

F.I.A.T., S.p.A., Italy's largest auto producer, completed an automobile factory in the Soviet Union in 1972 to be owned and operated by the U.S.S.R. Their first auto was a copy of the Fiat

124 called the Zhiguli. The factory cost $800 million and brought $50 million in fees to F.I.A.T.

Several European and Japanese automobile manufacturers constructed Experimental Safety Vehicles. Volkswagen made a 2,600-pound, 180-inch-long car made in "three-ply construction" with an inner shell around the passengers and an outer "crumple zone" plus the bumpers. Mercedes-Benz added special bumpers and reinforcement to a 250 that enabled it to take a roof load of 22,000 pounds without collapse of the roof or doorposts. Volvo made its own ESV without regard to D.O.T. (Department of Transportation) requirements. The car weighed 3,200 pounds, was fitted with a crumple front end and special engine mounts that deflected the engine downward and under the car rather than into the passenger compartment. F.I.A.T. worked on two ESV concepts, one based on the 850 and another based on the 124. In addition to following the D.O.T. requirements, they added fire protection features for driving safely in fogs, and vehicle/pedestrian safety. Japanese Toyota and Honda planned ESV mini-cars for the future.

The Insurance Institute for Highway Safety stated in 1972 that bumpers claimed by manufacturers as "improved" provided little protection against costly damage in low-speed impacts. The average cost of repair after striking a barrier at 5 mph. with the front of the car was $231.

A total of 56,600 fatalities were associated with the motor vehicle in 1972, which amounts to 4.53 deaths for every 100 million motor vehicle miles traveled. This was the lowest rate ever recorded thus far in any nation.

A hand-held radar gun was developed by Jack Fritzlen and manufactured by C.M.I., Inc., Minturn, Colorado. A policeman needs only to point the gun at the passing motorist, and the speed of the vehicle appears on the scope at the back of the gun called the Digital Doppler.

Belted radial tires were receiving worldwide attention by 1972, and the secret Michelin process made the company so powerful that it could afford to become part owner of the French Citroën Company. Despite the clamor for belted radials, Pirelli Tires joined forces with British Dunlop to avoid bankruptcy due to Italy's severe labor strife.

The United Automobile Workers called a strike against General Motors that lasted 174 days in 1972. The workers lost over $19 million in wages, and the U.A.W. paid $3.5 million in strike benefits. General Motors lost the production of 39,000 Chevrolet Vegas and Camaros and Pontiac Firebirds.

In the interest of protecting the environment, steam-driven vehicles again made the news in 1972. The Du Pont Company developed a synthetic steam engine that used a special fluid instead of water to flash into steam and drive a turbine that developed 200 hp. In Oakland, California, the first steam-powered bus in more than forty years in the United States began carrying passengers. Three of the 51-passenger vehicles were ordered by the California State Legislature for testing the steam engine's ability to reduce air pollution. Noise level was lower, and there were no diesel exhaust fumes, although this fuel was used in the steam boiler.

New Jersey became the first state to test automobiles for exhaust pollution. At the yearly inspection a device was placed inside the exhaust pipe for measuring carbon monoxide and hydrocarbons, the two main pollutants from auto engines. If the car failed the test, the owner was given fourteen days to remedy the problem or the car was banished from the road, and the driver subject to arrest.

Regulations requiring auto manufacturers to recall and remedy faulty car components caused Ford Motor Company to recall 900,000 vehicles because of steering defects on some of its 1972 models. General Motors recalled 3.7 million cars to fit shields around the steering system in order to prevent gravel or small stones from jamming the mechanism. The Center for Auto Safety accused General Motors of concealing a defect in Cadillac steering mechanisms. General Motors was also accused of hiding the fact that Chevrolet Corvair heaters were defective and dangerous to health. A month later 756,000 Corvairs were recalled.

Used car sales increased in the United States in 1972 because three- and four-car families were on the upswing.

Auto racing seemed to be more popular than ever in 1972 with many amateurs entering the sport, driving Three-Quarter Midgets and Formula V cars. The Indianapolis 500-Mile Race was won by Mark Donohue driving a McLaren-Offenhauser at an average speed of 162.962 mph. By winning the Los Angeles

Grand Prix at Riverside, California, in a Porsche at an average speed of 122.585 mph. for the 200-Mile Race, George Follmer also won the Canadian-American Challenge Cup Series (Can-Am). Ove Anderson of Sweden led a trio of French Alpine Renaults to win the Monte Carlo Rallye after a night of blizzards and accidents wrecked the chances of the German Porsches. Emerson Fittipaldi of Brazil was the 1972 World Champion Driver.

Lunar Rovers were used by the astronauts of the *Apollo 16* and *Apollo 17* spacecrafts in 1972. In fact, the crew of *Apollo 17* repaired a fender with maps while on the moon!

National leaders made the 1973 headlines in the United States as Vice-President Spiro T. Agnew pleaded *nolo contendere* to a charge of income tax evasion and later resigned. Gerald R. Ford was named to replace Agnew. "Watergate" dominated the American political scene. Salvador Allende Gossens, the Marxist president of Chile, was overthrown and reportedly committed suicide. Juan Perón returned from exile to become Argentina's president. East and West Germany established diplomatic relations and formally acknowledged their post-World War II separation. Greece formally abolished the monarchy. Western Europe was plunged into an energy crisis when the Arabs embargoed oil shipments to Europe, the United States, and Japan. Large-scale fighting once again broke out between Israel and the Arab nations. The war ended in an inconclusive cease-fire. The Arabs embargoed the shipment of oil to the United States, Western Europe, and Japan, and boosted their prices. The U.S. and the South Vietnamese signed a cease-fire agreement with the North Vietnamese and the Vietcong, but fighting continued elsewhere in Indochina. The People's Republic of China held its 10th Party Congress and declared the U.S.S.R. a greater enemy than the U.S. Africa suffered through a drought-induced famine which crippled much of western Africa.

In 1973, U.S. auto manufacturers in U.S. plants made an all-time record of 12,637,335 motor vehicles, valued at over $35 billion. There were 95 U.S. auto assembly plants in 74 cities in 28 states in the U.S., plus 20 plants in Africa, 59 in Asia, 66 in Europe, 27 in Oceania, and 31 in South America. The U.S. imported 2,626,929 motor vehicles in 1973 and exported 661,006.

Several new automobiles were introduced throughout the world in 1973. One of the most unusual was an electrically powered two-seater developed in Amsterdam, Holland, strictly for city shopping or commuting. Looking more like a telephone booth than a car, the vehicle was painted white to symbolize purity (freedom from pollution). Matra-Simca introduced, in France only, their three-seats-across Bagheera sports/G.T. car for sale. The Toyota Corolla SR/5 subcompact car made its appearance and was widely exported. The Lotus Europa Special super-sports car was offered to the public in 1973. Volkswagen introduced the VW Sports Bug, a flashy version of the Beetle. Advanced vehicle engineering produced a flying Pinto automobile by adding detachable wings, engine, and tail. Triumph increased the power of the Spitfire. General Motors introduced a motor home with six wheels. Renault presented its 17 subcompact front-wheel-drive car, and Saab brought out its front-wheel-drive EMS subcompact.

In 1973, Brazil found itself with the largest auto industry in South America. Volkswagen, F.I.A.T., Ford, General Motors, Chrysler, Mercedes-Benz, Toyota, and Saab-Scania produced cars for domestic and export use. Total production was over a half-million units, with Saab-Scania as the leading producer of heavy trucks. Mercedes-Benz led in medium trucks, and Toyota produced mostly small trucks and pickups. The only pure Brazilian automobile was the Puma sports car, with Volkswagen or Chevrolet engines, of which only thirty-five were produced each month.

General Motors announced that a G.M.-specification radial tire would be standard equipment on some 1974 models and as an option on others. Goodyear Tire and Rubber Company predicted that radial tires would account for more than half the replacement auto tires sold in 1980 as compared to 12 percent in 1972.

Many manufacturers were phasing out convertible models in 1973. General Motors announced that it would begin to phase out hardtop models in the big Chevrolet, Buick, Oldsmobile, Pontiac, and Cadillac automobiles in a drive for safer designs.

An experimental Chevrolet Vega, fitted with an electric motor, ran at 60 mph. for over 100 miles. It could go from 0 to 40 mph. in 10 seconds. The car weighed 4,200 pounds because of the motor and batteries.

A computerized braking system to prevent wheel-lock for trucks was introduced; it could stop trucks in less time with no skids. About ten companies offered this system.

Chrysler Corporation received a patent in 1973 for its electronic ignition controller. The system eliminated the usual distributor points and condenser. No ignition tune-ups were necessary, except when the spark plugs were changed—about every 18,000 miles.

To reduce air pollution, a Gremlin was run on hydrogen gas because it packs more energy per pound than any fuel known and is the cleanest fuel available. The operation of the vehicle was successful in this 1973 experiment.

Government regulations, insurance, and the inflated dollar rang the death knell for the "hot" cars such as the Shelby GT 350 Mustang, Buick GS, Oldsmobile 4-4-2, Ford Boss 302, Plymouth Hemi-Cuda, Dodge Challenger, etc. It appeared that this type of car had vanished forever in the name of safety and ecology.

The Franklin Institute Research Labs developed a porous, water-absorbing asphalt that would eliminate flooded roads and streets that tie up traffic, damage automobiles, and cause serious accidents. The use of this asphalt would mean relief from flash flooding and ensure safer roads and the preservation of vegetation.

In 1973 U.S. motor vehicle deaths reached a new low in fatalities per mile: 4.2 deaths for every 100 million miles traveled, with 55,600 fatalities recorded.

Auto racing was even more popular for both professional and amateur drivers in 1973. Go-carts became very sophisticated and faster with spoilers and wings. Some even sported streamlined bodies. The 1973 Indianapolis 500-Mile Race was won by Gordon Johncock with an average speed of 159.014 mph. driving an Eagle-Offenhauser. The World Champion Driver was Jackie Stewart of Scotland. Emerson Fittipaldi of Brazil won the Argentina Grand Prix driving a Lotus-Ford. British race driver Roger Williamson was killed while racing his March racer in the Dutch Grand Prix when the car struck a guardrail, flipped over, and burst into flames.

While the Western World was struggling to rid itself of pollution, congestion, and noise from its early adoption of the automobile, the Soviet Union was just beginning to enjoy the motor vehicle. Shunned for decades as a symbol of bourgeois decadence, the private car suddenly became the main symbol of the Kremlin's new attentiveness to the Soviet consumer. Auto production more than doubled between 1967 and 1973, and plans were made to increase production even further. In 1973 no other industry enjoyed the attention paid to the auto industry by the Soviet government. The infant industry had no time payment arrangements, as payment for a new car was in cash. Only one auto sales office per city was provided, and no cars were on display. Virtually all gas stations were self-service, with a charge to wipe the windshield. Many repair centers, short of mechanics, rented a stall to the car owner who desired to make his own repairs. In 1973, the Soviet Union stood where the U.S. was fifty years before, but it planned on moving fast.

By contrast to the U.S.S.R., the U.S. car buyer could virtually "custom build" his car in the showroom with a wide selection of colors, materials, and options at his disposal.

Major U.S. news developments for 1974 were: The U.S. Congress' move toward impeachment of President Nixon and his resignation. Gerald R. Ford's oath of office as the thirty-eighth U.S. President before Chief Justice Warren Burger on Friday, August 9, 1974. Later President Ford granted former President Nixon a "full, free and absolute pardon" for any criminal acts he may have committed during his term of office. Nelson A. Rockefeller was selected as the Vice-President on August 20, beginning a four-month process before Rockefeller was sworn in. Conditional amnesty was granted for Vietnam War resisters. The economy worsened with rising prices. Former Chief Justice Earl Warren and the Lone Eagle Charles Lindbergh died. Hank Aaron broke Babe Ruth's home run record, and Muhammad Ali regained the world heavyweight boxing title. The world witnessed the joint U.S.-Soviet Apollo-Soyuz Space Project and the comet Kohoutek. President Ford put a cap on the atomic arms race. The economic crisis in Britain, the Arab-Israeli truce, the war on Cyprus, the world population and food crises, and the World Food Conference in Rome added to the headlines. There was violence in Angola with a coalition delayed, and the United Nations suspended South Africa. The Palestine Liberation Organization leader, Yasir Arafat, addressed the United Nations General Assembly. Premier Constantine Caramanlis and his New Democracy Party swept the first free election held in Greece since 1964. Japanese Prime Minister Kakuei Tanaka officially told leaders of his Liberal-Democratic Party that he would resign but would remain in office until the party had picked a successor.

Trouble in the Middle East created an oil embargo that caused a serious shortage of gasoline in the U.S. and other Western nations. Lines of cars leading to gasoline stations became a common sight in the U.S. The shift of many buyers to smaller cars in an effort to stretch their gasoline caused the biggest change in the auto industry since it switched over to war production during World War II. Gasoline shortages affected business in the many shopping malls throughout the nation because consumers would not use their cars for shopping any distance from home. Many gas pumps went dry due to lack of deliveries. Gasoline prices rose in the U.S. but nothing like the $1.84 a gallon in Portugal. Because most of its production was on larger cars, General Motors was forced to permanently discharge 120,000 employees due to a production cutback. Another fuel problem was the motorist's dilemma in finding unleaded gasoline for some of the newer cars.

In 1974 U.S. auto factories produced a total of 10,058,569 motor vehicles, with a value of almost $32 billion. The U.S. imported 2,719,316 motor vehicles and exported 815,507. The two-door hardtop accounted for 35 percent of the U.S. passenger cars made, and convertibles were only 6 percent of U.S. auto sales.

Ford Motor Company announced that the company's new luxury compacts, the 1975 Granada and 1975 Monarch, would be built at the Wayne, Michigan, and Mahwah, New Jersey, plants which were building big Fords in 1974.

General Motors stated that it would convert its South Gate, California, plant to the production of subcompact cars for 1975.

Some new cars that appeared in 1974 were the following: Japan's Nissan Motors introduced its Excellent to the firm's Sunny line for the domestic market only. Nissan also introduced the Datsun B-210 subcompact car that appeared in the U.S. with many luxury features at a modest cost, and Mercedes-Benz produced the 450 SL Coupé as the top of the line, with many ESV features. The Mazda RX500 sports car prototype was shown but no production dates given. A Wankel-engine-powered Chevrolet Corvette prototype received acclaim at the 1974 Frankfurt Auto Show, but no production information was available. The British subcompact Reliant Robin three-wheeler was introduced for the European market only.

One-third of the new U.S. cars purchased in the U.S. in 1974 were equipped with steel-belted radial tires, two-thirds had power disc brakes, one-fifth had rear-window defoggers, two-thirds had remote-controlled side-view mirrors, 90 percent had automatic transmission, and half were fitted with V-8 engines.

The Environmental Protection Agency tested a hybrid gasoline-electric car in an effort to find the answer to reduced emissions. The car was started with the electric motor, and when it reached speed, the gasoline engine took over. It was found that more pollution is produced when a gasoline engine accelerates. With the engine running at a near constant speed, the pollutants are at a minimum. A much modified Buick Skylark was used with an engine half the size of the standard Skylark engine, a Mazda rotary. Test results were not released.

General Motors recalled 1.2 million passenger cars and trucks because of a defective brake part. Chevrolets, Buicks, Pontiacs, and Oldsmobiles were involved. Chrysler was ordered by the Environmental Protection Agency to recall 825,000 automobiles and trucks because of a defective pollution control system. This proved to be the first major recall ordered for environmental reasons.

Mainly due to the oil crisis, Japan suffered its worst auto production slump since World War II, with production down about 15 percent. Volkswagen lost money in 1974 for the first time in its twenty-nine-year history and laid off 126,000 workers. France's Citroën and Peugeot auto firms talked about merging financially because production was down in 1974. However, Ford Motor Company offered to aid Citroën. General Motors sales fell 35.7 percent. Ford sales fell 20.5 percent, and Chrysler sales dropped 18.5 percent. In contrast, American Motors, specializing in smaller cars, enjoyed a sales increase of 18.1 percent in 1974. Car prices were also increased by all U.S. manufacturers.

Many auto races were cancelled, such as the Sebring 12-Hour

Race, due to the shortage of fuel. However, some big races ran on schedule in 1974. The 1974 Le Mans 24-Hour Race was won by Henri Pescarolo and Gerald Larousse driving a Matra. Carlos Reutemann of Argentina won the South African Grand Prix in a Brabham with an average speed of 116.20 and dedicated the victory to Peter Revson, who died in a crash during the race. Richard Petty won the Daytona 500 with an average speed of 140.894 mph. driving a Dodge, and he also won the Carolina 500 Race. The Belgian Grand Prix was won by Emerson Fittipaldi of Brazil driving a McLaren and completing the 197-mile course in one hour and forty-four minutes. David Pearson won the Atlanta 500 Race in a Mercury with an average speed of 139.391 mph., and he also won the Rebel 500 Race in Darlington, South Carolina. Mark Donohue won the International Race of Champions at the Daytona Speedway and announced his retirement from auto racing.

More than 92 million passenger cars were in use in the U.S. in 1974, with the average age about 5.7 years old. Over 8 million cars were scrapped in the U.S., but four out of every five junked cars were totally recycled.

A total of 46,200 fatalities were associated with motor vehicles for the year. This represented 3.64 deaths for every 100 million vehicle miles and was a record low for the U.S.

Some major events and trends in 1975 arousing worldwide interest were: The intense struggle between the Portuguese Communists and the moderates for control of their country. After twenty-eight years as the world's largest democracy, India moved toward a dictatorship as Prime Minister Indira Gandhi declared a national emergency. The thirty-year war in Indochina came to a rapid conclusion in April and May as the pro-American governments of South Vietnam, Cambodia, and Laos succumbed to Communist forces, and U.S. personnel were evacuated. Almost 150,000 Vietnamese refugees fled to the United States. Only seventeen days separated two bungled assassination attempts against President Ford in September in northern California. Patty Hearst and her Symbionese Liberation Army companions were objects of intense public interest after her capture by the F.B.I. in September, 1975. Lower inflation rates accompanied the sharpest economic downturn in a generation as the unemployment rate exceeded 9 percent and the Gross National Product turned steeply negative. New York City's politicians and people prepared for what appeared to be almost certain default on a $12 billion plus debt.

Motor vehicle production in the U.S. for 1975, however, was 8,989,185 units. U.S. exports were about 900,000 vehicles, and the U.S. imported 2,650,000 vehicles, which was one-third of the total domestic production. Overall, imports captured a record 18.5 percent of the U.S. buying market, and in California imports took close to 40 percent. Japanese cars were the biggest factor—about 800,000 Japanese vehicles were sold in the U.S. in 1975.

The year 1975 marked the fiftieth anniversary of M.G. and seventy-fifth anniversary of Mack Trucks. In honor of the coming Bicentennial Year, the Middletown, New Jersey, police cars were painted to resemble a draped U.S. flag.

Ford Motor Company engaged fashion designers Bill Blass, Hubert de Givenchy, Pucci, and Cartier to develop the interior and exterior décor of the 1976 Lincoln Continentals. The signature of each individual designer was to appear on the instrument panel and the grille.

In view of the energy shortage and the general tendency to conserve gasoline, a survey was made to see what kind of cars were being driven by members of the U.S. Senate. Information on ninety-five U.S. Senator-owned cars was gathered, and it was found that sixty-five were large cars, twenty-three were medium size, and only seven were compact or small. It only proved that the government officials did not practice what they preached.

Several new cars were introduced in 1975. Volkswagen made an abrupt about-face. It introduced the Rabbit, which sported a front-located, water-cooled engine with front-wheel drive as compared with the rear-located, air-cooled engine with rear-wheel drive of the Beetle. Rolls-Royce announced its magnificent Camargue with a price of $70,000 to $80,000, making it the most expensive car of 1975. Chevrolet introduced the Monza Town Coupé luxury subcompact car. British Triumph deserted their standard sports car pattern and brought out the TR-7 wedge-shaped hardtop sportster. Cadillac introduced the Seville, and Ford brought out the Granada and Monarch "European size" luxury automobiles, all of them designed to resemble the Mercedes and to compete with it. The Italian Lamborghini Countach sports/G.T. car proved to be the fastest production car of 1975 with a top speed in excess of 185 mph. The Bricklin Vehicle Corporation produced the only production safety vehicle of 1975. It featured energy-absorbing bumpers that were 200 percent more effective than the U.S. requirements, a steel-plate-shielded tank, roll-cage, and aerodynamic shape. Nissan Motors introduced the Cedric and Gloria luxury cars for Japanese consumption only. Alfa-Romeo began producing the Alfetta sports sedan in 1975. Ford introduced its F-150 pickup truck. Buick offered the new Skyhawk V-6-powered economy model that was the smallest Buick built in sixty years. The Bavarian Motor Works introduced the BMW 530i that looked like a sedan but had the handling qualities of a sports car.

Chrysler Corporation announced plans to eliminate all of its full-size automobiles by the fall of 1977. General Motors and Ford Motor Company began massive programs to scale down the size of their full-size cars during the next five years.

In general, new cars in 1975 featured safety bumpers and steering columns. Chrome was used sparingly. Plastic body side striping was designed to protect against dents made by careless door opening by adjoining cars in parking lots. The opera window was another way to make a non-two-door hardtop look fashionable and still retain the pillar.

The British government announced that it would commit up to $25 million to bail out the British subsidiary of Chrysler Motors and recommended that the firm lay off one-third of its work force. A House of Commons Advisory Panel report stated that British car assembly workers produced only half as much in a shift as their European counterparts. The panel also condemned poor quality, bad labor relations, and unsatisfactory delivery records despite too much manpower.

The results of a study on how the Japanese have been so successful in the competitive automobile market showed that the Japanese auto industry strives to perfect rather than to innovate new designs. They add many extras as standard equipment and sell for less.

The 1975 World Champion Driver was Niki Lauda of Switzerland driving a Ferrari 312T. He won the U.S. Grand Prix in the same car at an average speed of 116.10 mph. Lauda also won the Monaco Grand Prix in the Ferrari 312T at an average speed of 75.53 mph. The Belgian Grand Prix was also won by Lauda in the same car at an average speed of 107.06 mph., and he also won the Swedish Grand Prix in his Ferrari at an average speed of 100.41 mph. Jody Scheckter won the South African Grand Prix in a Tyrrell 007-Ford with an average speed of 115.51 mph. The Dutch Grand Prix was won by James Hunt driving a Hesketh 308-Ford with an average speed of 109.86 mph. Vittorio Brambilla won the Grand Prix Molson Trois Rivières in Quebec driving a March 75B at an average speed of 59.59 mph. He also won the Austrian Grand Prix in the same car at an average speed of 107.67 mph. The British Grand Prix was won by Emerson Fittipaldi driving a McLaren at an average speed of 120.01 mph. In this race, sixteen of the twenty-six starting cars crashed without fatalities.

Motor vehicle fatalities dropped to 46,050 in 1975. This was attributed to new safety features, shoulder and lap belts, improved roads and road signs, plus reduced speed limits.

In 1976, Prime Minister Harold Wilson of Great Britain announced his resignation effective when the Labor members of the House of Commons elected a successor. Italy faced a political crisis in April which precipitated a national election in June. Black Africa was visited in early May by Henry Kissinger, and he enunciated the new American policy for the active support of the black nationalists in their campaign for a majority rule in southern Africa. China witnessed its worst violence in a decade as crowds went to Peking's T'ien An Men Square to honor the late Premier Chou En-lai, and later a new premier was named. In the United States, an analysis cited the prospect of less than 7 percent unemployment and 2 to 3 percent inflation. The presidential campaign was finalized in the November 2 elections with Jimmy Carter elected as the thirty-ninth President of the United States. On the lighter side, 1976 was a record year for kite sales of 75 million, four times the 1950 sales of 15 million. "Kiting," said one member of the American Kite Flyers' Association, "is a tranquilizer in today's chaotic world."

Several new automobiles made their appearance in 1976. Chevrolet introduced its Chevette mini-car in four-seat or two-seat models with a 40 mpg. mileage. Renault presented its front-wheel-drive Renault 5 four-seater mini-car to the U.S. market. Porsche introduced two new cars in 1976: the 924, which, contrary to previous Porsche designs, featured a water-cooled, front-mounted engine, and the 911 Turbo Carrera, which was the fastest street car in the U.S., with a supercharged, fuel-injected engine. British Leyland revealed its long-awaited Jaguar XJ-S luxury two-plus-two G.T. automobile. Chrysler Motors introduced the Plymouth Arrow Japanese-built mini-compact car. General Motors Buick Division introduced an Opel made by Isuzu in Japan and stopped importation of the car from Germany because of rising costs. Lancia introduced the Lancia Beta in the U.S. after sixty-eight years of production in Europe. Plymouth released the Volare and Dodge the Aspen "European size" cars. A.M.C. offered the four-wheel-drive Jeep CJ-7 in hardtop or soft-top. Cadillac featured the Eldorado Convertible, and 1976 was its last year.

Once the dream of every American boy, the convertible reached the end of the line because of the discomfort of high-speed highway driving plus the noise and air pollution of urban areas. Auto air conditioning also helped to bring on the convertible's demise. American Motors dropped the manufacture of convertibles in 1968, Chrysler followed in 1971, Ford in 1973, and most General Motors cars in 1975. In 1976, the Cadillac Eldorado was the last convertible to be manufactured in the United States.

General Motors announced that the 1977 Fleetwood Eldorado would be the same size as the 1976, but that the other models would be reduced to a size closer to the "European size" Seville. The four years following 1976 would see smaller cars from Detroit. The U.S. auto industry had been forced into a multi-billion-dollar program by more efficient small imports, higher gasoline prices, and the possibility of 28-mpg. fuel-economy legislation from the Federal government. Tomorrow's standard-size sedan could be the size of the 1976 Ford Granada with big car comfort. U.S. auto makers suggested that future cars would be mechanically simpler with cleaner lines. There would be less chrome and much more glass with thin-line roof pillars and a lower belt line. Fronts would be soft urethane foam with a cellular energy-absorbing bumper backing. Wheelbases would get shorter and shorter in gradual steps. Shortening the wheelbase nine inches automatically shortened the overall length of the average full-size car by a foot or more, not from the passenger compartment, but from the trunk and engine area. Most firms began work on a "world" car design that would be a mini-size car or subcompact. Ford expected to introduce its German- and Spanish-produced Bobcat or Fiesta mini-car in 1977 to combat the Chevette and to compete for world sales. The trend was certain to lead toward front-wheel drive. It was believed to be quite possible to have an American diesel-engine-powered car in the near future. Electronic ignition and fuel injection for all cars seem to be just over the horizon, as are fixed seats with adjustable brake, accelerator, and clutch pedals and steering wheel.

Vehicles for the distant future have occupied U.S. designers' attention for years. Some of the concepts appear as strange as did the first horseless carriages to non-believers. Among some of the amazing ideas from Ford Motor Company designers are ducted-fan flying cars, nuclear-powered vehicles, two-wheeled gyroscopically stabilized cars, steering wheels without steering columns in front of the driver, and wheelless vehicles that ride on a cushion of air.

Perhaps we will see the ideas and plans develop into reality. Only time will tell. One thing is certain, however, civilized man's romance with the motorcar may continue to take many forms. Whether it's the sporty car or family sedan, large or small, it is a love affair that will last forever.

PININFARINA MODULO   The legendary Giovanni Battista Pininfarina died in 1966. The famous Italian auto-body-designing and building firm continued under the leadership of Sergio Pininfarina and Renzo Carli. Pininfarina-designed bodies have been sported by Alfa-Romeo, Fiat, Peugeot, Lancia, Nash, and others. In 1970 the designers developed a true milestone in automobile design, the Modulo. The name means "modular"—built up from identical units. The upper and lower halves were identical except for various necessary openings for wheels, lights, windows, etc. The basic body could accommodate high or low power and two or four seats in the ultra-streamlined shape depending upon the requirements of the buyer. Space utilization was most realistic. The front end needed only space for the occupant's feet and controls. The Modulo could be ultra slim resulting in a superb air entry form and excellent visibility. Maximum volume was reached at the seats, where it belongs, and the enormous window and windshield areas were superb. It was also a roomy car, though only 37 inches high. Access was afforded by sliding the entire windshield-window area forward. The engine was located behind the seats. The amount of room left for luggage was determined by the size of the engine. Holes in the roof took advantage of the partial vacuum created by fastback types, drawing in air from slots behind the windows. The air cooled the radiators and exited through the holes. The car was not a production model but intended to show manufacturers what could be done to advance the art of auto design.

PUMA GTE The Puma GTE sports car is the only Brazilian-designed and built automobile. Designed by Rino Malzoni, the car was more than a match for the European designs. The wheelbase was 84.6 inches and the overall length 156.1 inches. Weight was 1,540 pounds. Acceleration from zero to 60 mph. required 9.9 seconds, and top speed was 110 mph. This 1970 car was powered with a 90-hp., four-cylinder, flat, opposed, air-cooled engine of 96.6-cubic-inch displacement. Two carburetors were fitted. The engine was rear-mounted. The body was reinforced fiberglass, and four-speed transmission was fitted. The Puma was manufactured by Veicules e Motores, Ltda.

CHEVROLET CORVETTE STINGRAY In 1970 Chevrolet made improvements on the sporty Corvette that was initially introduced in 1953. The car was made in the convertible and the semi-convertible coupé with removable roof panels and a rear window. The convertible is shown. The wheelbase remained at 98 inches, and the 350-cubic-inch-displacement engine was standard. An optional 454-cubic-inch-displacement engine that produced 460 hp. was available and was fitted with aluminum pistons. A manual four-speed fully Synchromesh transmission and self-adjusting disc brakes on all wheels were some of the improvements.

BLUE FLAME RECORD RACER Reaction Dynamics designed and built this unusual speedster in 1970 for the Institute of Gas Technology in an attempt to break the then existing automobile speed record of 600.6 mph. The car was powered by liquefied natural gas (LNG) as fuel with hydrogen peroxide for the oxidizer. The LNG was heated from its extreme cryogenic state of minus 258 degrees Fahrenheit to allow it to vaporize prior to burning. The LNG and hydrogen peroxide mixed. As the flame began, the hydrogen peroxide broke down into water, causing clouds of white steam to be expelled with the flame. This jet-powered car had the capability of developing 20,000 pounds of thrust, but the controls were limited not to exceed 13,000 pounds of thrust. The car sped on the Bonneville Salt Flats, with Gary Gabelich at the controls, for the two required runs past the officials and established a new automobile world speed record of 622.41 mph. in 1970. All accomplished by cooking and heating gas! Although it appeared to be a three-wheeler, it was actually a four-wheeler, with the two front wheels very close together in order to meet the rules requiring four wheels.

FERRARI 512S RACER The Ferrari 512S Group 5 endurance racer was completed despite a metalworkers' strike in Italy. It placed third in the 1970 Daytona 500 despite the fact that its chassis broke twice. With Mario Andretti at the wheel, the design won the Sebring Race. Fourth place at the Le Mans Race also went to the 512S. Power was a twelve-cylinder, 60° vee-type, rear-mounted, 4,994-cc-displacement engine with four overhead camshafts operating 48 valves, producing 560 hp. at 8,500 rpm. The chassis was steel tubing that was stiffened with sheet aluminum plates.

SAAB SONETT III The Swedish Saab Sonett III of 1970 was primarily designed for the U.S. market. In fact, it was not even sold in Sweden. The styling was the work of Italian designer Sergio Coggiola. Power was a German-built Ford V-4, overhead-valve, water-cooled, 91.4-cubic-inch-displacement engine that produced 73 hp. at 5,000 rpm. A four-speed manual transmission and single carburetor were standard. It had a weight of 1,760 pounds on an 84.6-inch wheelbase; the overall length was 153 inches. Coil springs and tubular shocks were provided all around. Front-wheel drive was featured, as were dual exhausts and front disc brakes, plus retractable headlights.

OLDSMOBILE VISTA CRUISER The Vista Cruiser was the middle of the line for Oldsmobile station wagons. An interesting feature of this 1970 model was the slanted window in the roof located just forward of the luggage rack, designed especially for the benefit of the rear passengers. The car featured 105 cubic feet of cargo space on a 121-inch wheelbase. The lower body was wood-grain paneled. A 350-cubic-inch, eight-cylinder, vee-type Rocket engine was used for power. It was Oldsmobile's most popular station wagon.

DODGE COLT The Japanese-made Dodge Colt subcompact appeared in the United States in 1970, and the four-door sedan is shown. The $2,100 car weighed 2,025 pounds on a 95.7-inch wheelbase. Length was 160.6 inches, and width was 61.4 inches. Power of the four-passenger car was a four-cylinder, inline, water-cooled, 97.5-cubic-inch-displacement engine developing 83 hp. at 5,600 rpm. A four-speed manual Synchromesh transmission was standard. Front disc brakes were fitted.

CHEVROLET CAMARO The Chevrolet Camaro was the first serious effort to produce an American G.T. car since the 1963 Corvette and featured superb cornering plus luxurious appointments. This four-seater weighed 3,670 pounds on a 108-inch wheelbase. Overall length was 188 inches, width 74.4 inches, and height 50.5 inches. Power was an eight-cylinder, vee-type, water-cooled, overhead-valve, 350-cubic-inch-displacement engine that developed 300 hp. at 4,800 rpm. A four-barrel carburetor was fitted. Automatic transmission was standard. From zero to 60 mph. took about 8.8 seconds.

DATSUN 240Z Japanese Nissan Motors introduced the Datsun 240Z in 1970, and the car became an immediate success, especially in the United States. The two-seater fastback G.T. car weighed 2,355 pounds on a 90.7-inch wheelbase. Overall length was 162.8 inches. Power was a six-cylinder, inline, overhead-cam, water-cooled, 146-cubic-inch-displacement engine that produced 150 hp. at 6,000 rpm. Two carburetors were fitted. A four-speed manual transmission was installed. The car could reach 80 mph. from zero in 15.2 seconds. It is understood that Datsun studied every successful sports G.T. car before it designed this $3,526 car.

BRABHAM BT-34 RACER This Formula 1 race car was designed by Ron Tauranac of Brabham's and constructed by Jack Brabham's Motor Racing Developments, Ltd., Europe's largest builder of formula racing cars. This Brabham BT-34 Formula 1 racer was the most unusual design of 1971 and nicknamed "Lobster Claw." The two rectangular boxes at each side of the front housed the radiators. The radiators could be smaller if placed in undisturbed air. The engine was a 3,000-cc-displacement, Ford Cosworth, eight-cylinder, vee type, with four overhead camshafts and a hemi-head. The wheelbase was 95 inches.

PLYMOUTH ROAD RUNNER Plymouth's sporty intermediate Road Runner made an impact on young drivers. This is the 1971 model. This high-performance car was driven in many NASCAR events, and, in 1970, Plymouth won the N.H.R.A. (National Hot Rod Association) Manufacturers' Cup. Standard power was an eight-cylinder, vee-type, water-cooled, 383-cubic-inch-displacement engine with a four-barrel carburetor. A 440-cubic-inch-displacement engine with a six-barrel carburetor and a 426-cubic-inch-displacement hemi-engine with a six-barrel carburetor were offered as optional.

AMERICAN MOTORS GREMLIN The unique styling of the American Motors Gremlin subcompact car has influenced many other designers. This is the 1971 Gremlin that was built on a 96-inch wheelbase. Power was a 232-cubic-inch-displacement, six-cylinder, in-line, water-cooled engine. Column or floor-mounted three-speed manual transmission was standard. Note the air deflector above the rear window which forced air down against the window by destroying the negative pressure normally formed by bobtail/hatchback designs.

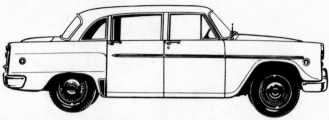

CHECKER MARATHON Checker Motors Corporation, Kalamazoo, Michigan, introduced the Checker Marathon Deluxe nine-passenger, four-door sedan in 1971 to celebrate the firm's golden anniversary. The 129-inch wheelbase provided a very smooth ride. Three folding seats, placed against the back of the front seats, made those passengers face the rear. Chair-height seats added to the riding comfort, and door openings were high and wide. The car was available with either an economy six-cylinder, 250-cubic-inch-displacement, 145-hp. engine or an eight-cylinder, vee-type, 350-cubic-inch-displacement, 245-hp. engine. Automatic transmission, electric windshield wipers, an impact-absorbing steering column, and an anti-pollution emission control system were standard.

TAYLOR AEROCAR III After twenty years of development, Moulton P. Taylor built this flying automobile in his Longview, Washington, shop in 1971. His Aerocar was certified by the F.A.A. for sale to the public and was the only machine of this type so certified. The two-seat auto body was fiberglass, and the wings and tail were aluminum. The transformation from car to plane required ten minutes. Empty weight was 1,500 pounds, and the car/cockpit accounted for 1,100 pounds of this. Power was a Lycoming air-cooled, four-cylinder engine of 143 hp. Air speed was 135 mph., and ground speed was 60 mph. The wing area was 190 square feet. Baggage capacity was 100 pounds.

ANYCAR or ForChevAmChrysWagen Manufacturers Hanover Trust Company used this composite automobile to advertise the bank as the place to go for an auto loan, any auto loan. The car was seen on television, in newspapers, and it made a tour of dealer showrooms. The vehicle was composed of parts of twenty-two cars and designed by Gene Winfield. The car weighed 3,300 pounds on a 114-inch wheelbase. A Mercury 289 engine was used for power. The Comet, VW, Chrysler 300, Chevrolet Caprice, Mustang, Dodge, Falcon, Pontiac, Oldsmobile, Rolls-Royce, Buick, Triumph, Mercedes, Firebird, Ford Fairlane, and an assortment of tires were used. Can you identify any of the parts?

PLYMOUTH DUSTER Plymouth offered four models of their Valiant compact car in 1971. The high-performance Plymouth Duster was the most popular Valiant model and boosted Valiant sales to its most successful year. The sporty Duster was powered by a 340-cubic-inch-displacement engine.

PONTIAC GRAND PRIX   The 1971 Pontiac Grand Prix luxury personal car featured the "European Look" with a long, tapered hood and a boat-tail shape at the rear. The wheelbase was 121 inches, and power steering and power front disc brakes were standard. Power was a 400-cubic-inch-displacement, eight-cylinder, vee-type, water-cooled engine. A larger 455-cubic-inch-displacement engine was also available.

GENERAL MOTORS ESV   General Motors built this Experimental Safety Vehicle in 1971 to U.S. Department of Transportation specifications for the contract price of one dollar, when the car cost was closer to $3 million. The 4,700-pound vehicle had no windshield pillars, thereby improving visibility and eliminating a point of impact in a crash. The car concentrated on occupant safety, with deep padding and inflatable air bags. The aluminum body saved weight. The seats were fixed, but the pedals were adjustable. Taillights were near the roof line for visibility. High strength vanadium alloy steel was used for the frame and body side pillars, which extended to the roof and formed a roll-over cage. The trunk opened from the side. Instruments were grouped in the order of their importance, with operating instruments clustered in front of the driver. The car underwent a series of crash tests.

PRATTAXI This remarkable 1971 taxi was the result of a three-year Industrial Design Department student and faculty study at the Pratt Institute, Brooklyn, New York. It was the first practical approach in decades to create a specifically designed city taxicab. Advantages were: easy entry and exit, plenty of leg, knee, hip, and shoulder room, luggage within sight of both passengers and driver, air conditioning under passenger control, flat floor and padded passenger compartment. In addition there were these features: a short wheelbase for easy maneuvering, it was easy to park, it had a fully enclosed driver's compartment, long life, lower operating cost, lower initial cost due to flat sides, front, top, etc., light weight for lower emissions, and large windows for driver and passenger visibility. The height made this taxi easy to hail from a distance, and built-in ramps at the doors facilitated entry of wheelchairs. The wheelbase was 108 inches and overall length was 156 inches. Width was 71 inches and height was 75 inches. The door height was 60 inches, and door width was 32 inches.

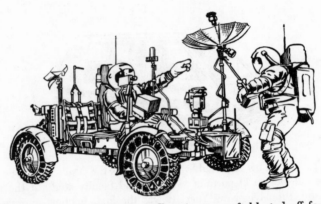

LUNAR ROVER   When the *Apollo 15* spacecraft blasted off for the moon in 1971, it contained a Lunar Roving Vehicle (LRV) that was folded into three segments for stowage. It could be assembled by one astronaut on the moon. The Boeing Company was the prime contractor and was chosen to build a trainer, three LRV's, and six test vehicles at a cost of $38 million. The wheels were wire mesh woven into a single ply. Each wheel was driven by a ¼-hp. electric motor; these were powered by two 41-volt silver-zinc batteries. The vehicle weighed 1,370 pounds on earth but only 230 pounds on the moon due to the one-sixth gravity of the moon. It was designed to cross a 28-inch crevasse, climb a 25-degree slope, and travel 25 miles on the moon. The vehicle was left on the moon when the astronauts returned to earth.

FAIRCHILD ESV The Republic Aviation Division of Fairchild Hiller Corporation developed this Experimental Safety Vehicle in 1971 for the U.S. Department of Transportation. The design combined aerospace structural technology with conventional manufacturing practices. The front bumper was attached by means of variable orifice hydraulic cylinders which automatically extended the bumper about 12 inches at speeds over 30 mph., thereby providing added cushioning in high-speed impacts. On top of the roof was a rear-view periscope. The interior was fully padded, and instantly inflatable air bags were provided. The roof structure included a roll cage secured to the platform frame; the engine was mounted so that it would not enter the passenger compartment in high-velocity crashes, and the doors were reinforced to endure broadside crashes. The car cost approximately $2 million to develop and was used in actual test crashes.

VOLVO 164 This Swedish four-door, five-passenger compact car made its appearance in 1972. The Volvo 164 of 1972 was powered by a four-cylinder, inline, water-cooled, 121-cubic-inch-displacement engine that produced 118 hp. at 5,800 rpm. A four-speed manual or automatic transmission was offered. Two single-barrel carburetors were fitted. The 2,600-pound car was built on a 103.2-inch wheelbase and was 182.7 inches long. Track was 53.2 inches.

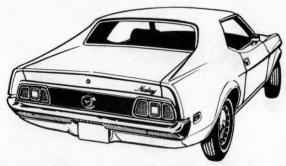

FORD MUSTANG The Ford Mustang of 1972 was available in either straight-six or V-8 engines. The eight-cylinder powerplant of this sporty car had a displacement of 302 cubic inches and produced 141 hp. at 4,000 rpm. A three-speed manual or automatic transmission was offered. One two-barrel carburetor was installed. The 3,300-pound car was built on a 109-inch wheelbase. Overall length was 189.5 inches, width 74.1 inches, and track was about 61 inches. The Mustang in its many variations has been one of the most popular U.S. sporty or pony cars.

FORD PINTO This Ford Pinto runabout subcompact was made in 1972 on a 94-inch wheelbase. The four-passenger, two-door automobile weighed 2,220 pounds, was 163 inches long, and 69.4 inches wide. Power was a four-cylinder, inline, water-cooled, 122-cubic-inch-displacement engine that produced 86 hp. at 5,400 rpm. A single two-barrel carburetor was installed. Four-speed Synchromesh manual transmission was standard, and automatic transmission was optional. Rack-and-pinion steering and front disc brakes were fitted. The Runabout was a handy hatchback design. Price was about $2,200.

MERCEDES-BENZ 280 SEL The Mercedes-Benz 280 SEL was powered by a V-8 engine as standard equipment for the first time in 1972. This 3,900-pound German auto was built on a 112.2-inch wheelbase. Overall length was 196.9 inches, and width was 71.3 inches. The powerplant was an eight-cylinder, vee-type, fuel-injected, water-cooled, 276-cubic-inch-displacement engine that produced 230 hp. at 5,000 rpm. Automatic transmission was standard. In 1972, Mercedes-Benz sold over 35,000 cars in the United States.

BUICK RIVIERA The luxurious Buick Riviera of 1972 revealed very innovative styling in the boat-tail trunk and rear window lines. Built on a 122-inch wheelbase, the overall length was 217.3 inches, width 79.5 inches, and the car was 54 inches high. Power was an eight-cylinder, vee-type, water-cooled, 455-cubic-inch-displacement engine that produced 250 hp. at 4,000 rpm. A four-barrel carburetor was standard, as was automatic transmission. The Riviera was considered a personal luxury car and could seat five passengers. The exhaust gases were recirculated for emission control.

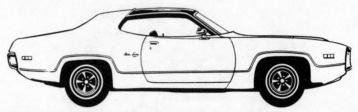

PLYMOUTH SATELLITE The Plymouth mid-size economy Satellite line for 1972 featured four hardtops: the Satellite Coupé, Sebring, Sebring Plus and the Road Runner. The sporty Sebring Plus is shown. The wheelbase was 115 inches, overall length 210.8 inches, track 62 inches, and width 79.1 inches. The five-seater was powered with either a six-cylinder, 225-cubic-inch-displacement engine or optional V-8 engines of 318- or 400-cubic-inch displacement for those who wanted high performance.

CHEVROLET VEGA GT KAMMBACK WAGON For 1972, Chevrolet introduced the Vega GT Kammback Wagon. The GT package included a larger engine, instruments instead of lights for warning signals, a padded steering wheel, anti-roll bars, and mag wheels. The car was a delight to handle, and the special design roof produced less drag than a fastback design. Power was a four-cylinder, inline, water-cooled, 140-cubic-inch-displacement engine that produced 90 hp. A single two-barrel carburetor was fitted. Three-speed manual transmission was standard. Optional was a four-speed manual or automatic transmission. The 2,200-pound car was built on a 97-inch wheelbase and was 169.7 inches long.

MERCEDES-BENZ 350SL In 1972 the Mercedes 280SL Coupé was replaced by the 350SL Sport Coupé and Convertible. The 3,700-pound car was built on a 96.9-inch wheelbase. Overall length was 172 inches, width 70.5 inches, and tread or track was 57 inches. Power for this two-seater was an eight-cylinder, vee-type, fuel-injection, water-cooled, 276-cubic-inch-displacement engine that developed 230 hp. at 5,000 rpm. Automatic transmission was standard. The 350SL was judged to be one of the ten best cars in the world by *Road & Track* magazine.

AMERIGO GARDNER TRUCK CAMPER Amerigo Gardner, a subsidiary of Kampgrounds of America, introduced this truck camper in 1972. Some of the features were: two exits, one overhead and one at the rear; low weight (2,284 pounds) and low center of gravity; and an automatic power converter that changed 110 volts to 12 volts. The unit could be attached to virtually any standard-size pickup truck. The price was about $3,000.

VOLVO 1800ES   Introduced in late 1971, the 1972 Volvo 1800ES was a two-door station-wagon-like subcompact car. It was produced through 1972 and into early 1973. This 2,500-pound car was built on a 96.5-inch wheelbase and was 67 inches wide. Tread was 51.7 inches, and overall length was 171.4 inches. Power was a four-cylinder, inline, water-cooled, fuel-injected, 121-cubic-inch-displacement engine that produced 125 hp. at 6,000 rpm.

PONTIAC FIREBIRD FORMULA   The Firebird Formula was the performance car of the Pontiac line in 1972. The four-seater had a 108-inch wheelbase and weighed 3,500 pounds. Length was 191.6 inches, width 73.4 inches, and track was about 60 inches. The Formula had a choice of three V-8 engines: a 350-cubic-inch-displacement, 160-hp. at 4,400 rpm., a 400-cubic-inch-displacement, 200-hp. at 4,000 rpm., and a 455-cubic-inch-displacement, 300-hp. at 4,000 rpm. engine. A choice of either a four-speed manual or automatic transmission was offered. The entire front was protected by an all-encompassing, energy-absorbing Endura plastic that was color-matched to the car.

FORD TORINO The Ford Torino intermediate size car for 1972 combined comfort with a sporty appearance and good performance. The five-passenger, two-door Torino hardtop shown was built on a 114-inch wheelbase. Overall length was 208 inches, and width was 79 inches. Power was an eight-cylinder, vee-type, water-cooled, overhead-valve, 351-cubic-inch-displacement engine fitted with a double-barrel carburetor. Either a four-speed manual transmission or Cruise-o-matic automatic could be installed.

FORD MAVERICK The 1972 Ford Maverick compact car was offered in a four-door sedan, two-door sedan, and the sporty Grabber. The four-door sedan family car is shown. This five-passenger model was built on a 103-inch wheelbase and weighed 2,700 pounds. Overall length was 179.4 inches. Power was an economy six-cylinder, inline, water-cooled, 250-cubic-inch-displacement engine that produced 98 hp. at 3,600 rpm. A choice of a three-speed manual or automatic transmission was offered.

FORD THUNDERBIRD By 1972 the Ford Thunderbird had evolved into a luxurious, full-size automobile. The five-passenger, two-door sport coupé of 1972 is shown. This 4,600-pound car was built on a 120.4-inch wheelbase. Overall length was 216 inches, width 79.3 inches, and track was about 63 inches. Power was an eight-cylinder, vee-type, water-cooled, overhead-valve, 460-cubic-inch-displacement engine that produced 212 hp. at 4,400 rpm. A single four-barrel carburetor was fitted. Automatic transmission and front disc brakes were standard.

JEEP WAGONEER The four-wheel-drive American Motors Jeep Wagoneer station wagon for 1972 had a gross weight of 5,400 pounds on a 110-inch wheelbase. Overall length was 183.7 inches, and width was 75.6 inches. The standard engine for this four-door, six-passenger vehicle was a 258-cubic-inch-displacement, six-cylinder, inline, 110-hp. at 3,500 rpm. powerplant. The 304-cubic-inch- and 360-cubic-inch-displacement, eight-cylinder, vee-type engines were optional. They developed 150 and 175 hp. respectively. This car had an attractively decorated interior, and a wood-grain side exterior accent stripe was fitted.

JEEP CJ-6 American Motors acquired the rights to the Jeep vehicles in 1969 and developed the rugged car into a recreational vehicle as well as a utility vehicle. The wheelbase for the 1972 Jeep CJ-6 was increased to 104 inches, length to 162 inches, and width to 60 inches. The front tread was widened 3 inches to 51.5 inches for increased stability. Power was a choice of a 232-cubic-inch- or 258-cubic-inch-displacement, six-cylinder or a 304-cubic-inch-displacement, eight-cylinder, vee-type engine. Three-speed manual transmission was fitted to the three large engines, and a four-speed manual transmission was standard on the 232-cubic-inch engine. The car featured four-wheel drive, and gross weight was 3,900 pounds.

OPEL 1900 The German-built Buick Opel 1900 made its appearance in 1972. This 2,125-pound subcompact four-passenger auto was built on a 95.7-inch wheelbase. Length was 171 inches, and width was 64.3 inches. Price was about $2,500. Power was a four-cylinder, inline, water-cooled, 115.8-cubic-inch-displacement engine developing 75 hp. at 4,800 rpm. Manual four-speed all Synchromesh transmission was standard. Front disc brakes were fitted as was a single two-barrel carburetor. The four-door sedan is shown.

OLDSMOBILE 98 COUPÉ   The top of the line for Oldsmobile was the luxurious 98. The 1972 Oldsmobile 98 Coupé two-door hardtop is shown. This 4,725-pound auto was built on a 127-inch wheelbase and was 226 inches long. Tread was 64 inches and width 79 inches. Power of this five-seater was an eight-cylinder, overhead-valve, 90° vee-type, water-cooled, 455-cubic-inch-displacement engine that produced 320 hp. at 4,400 rpm. A four-barrel carburetor was fitted. Acceleration from zero to 60 mph. took 8.7 seconds, and braking from 60 mph. to stop required 146 feet. The price of $5,000 included automatic transmission, power windows, power steering, and a remote-operated outside mirror.

FORD PINTO SQUIRE WAGON The subcompact Ford Pinto Squire station wagon of 1972 had the same wheelbase, engine, and power train as the sedan and runabout. However, it was 10 inches longer than the sedan. The cargo area was a big 60.5 cubic feet, and a spare tire was installed under the cargo floor. The cargo capacity was 900 pounds, and the small car could tow an 800-pound trailer. The Squire was sold with wood-grained side body panels, but the roof rack was optional. The price was about $2,400.

FORD COURIER MINI-PICKUP This Ford Mini-Pickup of 1972, made by Toyo Kogyo of Japan, was based on the Toyo Kogyo Mazda Pickup. Modifications according to Ford specifications allowed the pickup to stand up to U.S. road and driving conditions. The Ford Courier had separate body and frame construction with rubber bushings between them. The cab was also made as a separate unit. Power was a four-cylinder, inline, water-cooled, 74-hp. engine fitted with a two-barrel carburetor. A four-speed manual transmission was standard. Gross weight was 3,910 pounds, and the payload was 1,400 pounds. The pickup box, 74 x 62 inches, was larger than those of the Courier's competitors.

ALFASUD   Alfa-Romeo decided to enter the economy car race in 1972 and to challenge Germany and Japan for the U.S. market. The Alfasud was the result and was built in the Naples Alfa-Romeo plant. Hence the name Alfasud (Alfasouth). The basic design was the work of Giorgio Guigiaro, which resulted in a front engine and front-wheel drive. Power was a four-cylinder, flat, opposed, double-overhead-camshaft, 67-cubic-inch-displacement, water-cooled engine that developed 73 hp. at 6,000 rpm. The unitized body had been designed with controlled collapsibility in mind, and fuel tank was located in front of the rear axle. A four-speed manual transmission was standard.

DODGE DIAMANTE   Designed by Dodge engineers and built by Ron Mandrush of Synthetex, Inc., Dearborn, Michigan, the Diamante was a Dodge dream car presented at auto shows in 1972. Unlike many dream cars, the Diamante was operable, as it was built on a Challenger 110-inch-wheelbase chassis and powered with a 426-cubic-inch-displacement hemi-engine. The car combined aerodynamic styling with safety features such as the integral roll-over cage roof. Diamante means diamond in some Romance languages.

HORNET RALLYE X The American Motors Hornet Rallye X compact car of 1972 was built on a 108-inch wheelbase. Weight was about 2,800 pounds, and overall length was 179.3 inches. The Rallye X, a high-performance Hornet, had a choice of the standard 232-cubic-inch-displacement engine or the 258-cubic-inch-, 304-cubic-inch- and 360-cubic-inch-displacement engines.

HONDA COUPÉ The Honda 600 Coupé was introduced in 1972 as a subcompact economy car. Power was a two-cylinder, overhead-camshaft, air-cooled, 37-cubic-inch-displacement engine that developed 36 hp. at 6,000 rpm. Front-wheel drive was used. A four-speed manual transmission was standard as were power-assisted, front-wheel disc brakes, front bucket seats, radial tires, and tachometer. The 1,300-pound car was built on a 78.7-inch wheelbase. Overall length was 123 inches, and width 51 inches. This five-passenger mini-car was priced at $1,610.

FORD CAPRI 2600 R.S. When it was discovered that the Ford Mustang pony car sales continued to be strong in the United States, Ford decided to introduce a European pony car in 1969. The result was the Capri, developed jointly by Ford Great Britain and Ford Germany. The only difference in the cars was that those made in Germany had German engines, while the British-built cars had British powerplants. As a European Economic Community member, Germany sold the cars throughout Europe. In competition the Capri placed second in the European Hill-Climb of 1970, and second in the South Africa Springbok Series. In 1972 the Capri won the Monza Four-Hour Race. A 1972 competition car is shown. Power was a six-cylinder, vee-type, water-cooled, 2,900-cc-displacement engine that produced 290 hp. Four-wheel disc brakes were fitted. A top speed of 165 mph. could be attained with competition versions.

CHRYSLER IMPERIAL LE BARON The luxurious 1972 Chrysler Imperial Le Baron, the pride of Chrysler, emphasized safety and riding comfort. The wheelbase was 127 inches, length 229.5 inches, width 79.6 inches, and track was about 63 inches. Power was an eight-cylinder, vee-type, water-cooled, 440-cubic-inch-displacement engine that produced 225 hp. at 4,400 rpm. A single four-barrel carburetor was fitted. Automatic transmission, power steering, and power brakes were standard equipment.

ALFA-ROMEO 2000 GT VELOCE   The 1972 Alfa-Romeo 2000 GT Veloce was a five-passenger gran turismo automobile with excellent handling for those who desired rapid cornering and sports car performance. The wheelbase of this 2,335-pound car was 92.5 inches, and overall length was 161.4 inches. Power was a four-cylinder, inline, water-cooled, 84-cubic-inch-displacement engine with aluminum block and cylinder heads that developed 129 hp. at 5,800 rpm. Four-wheel, power-assisted disc brakes were fitted. The car could accelerate from zero to 60 mph. in nine seconds, and top speed was about 118 mph. The price was approximately $5,500.

G.M. URBAN CAR   This two-seater experimental urban car was developed in 1972 in gasoline engine and electric motor versions. The tiny vehicle was designed for city driving and to minimize the pollutants exhausted to the atmosphere. The electric motor was powered by an 84-volt battery pack. A separate 12-volt battery was used to power auxiliaries such as windshield wipers, headlights, horn, etc.

MATRA LE MANS WINNER Two of these Matra MS670 sports racers placed first and second in the 1972 Le Mans 24-Hour Race. Henri Pescarolo and Graham Hill brought their Matra across the finish line about forty miles ahead of the second-place Matra driven by Howden Ganley and François Cevert. The winning car is shown. The wheelbase was 8 feet 2.5 inches, front track 4 feet 8 inches, and rear track 4 feet 7 inches. The all-enveloping body was monocoque aluminum. The powerplant was a twelve-cylinder, vee type, developing about 420 hp. and mounted in the rear. Notice the rear wing between the two vertical fins that produced negative lift and forced the rear of the car downward for better traction and braking. Endurance as well as high speed is a requirement of Le Mans racers.

BRUBAKER BOX In 1972, Brubaker Industries, a Los Angeles industrial-design group, developed this useful fun car that combined the best features of a van and dune buggy. The Brubaker Box was built on a standard Volkswagen Beetle chassis and met all U.S. Federal safety standards. It was 1 inch shorter, 1 inch lower, and 8 inches wider than the Beetle. Inside it was a full 2 feet wider at elbow height! One large 4-foot door slid open on the curb side. An L-shaped contour couch was fitted at the rear. Wooden bumpers were positioned well away from the fiberglass body. Mag wheels and wide-belted tires were standard. The driver and his passenger sat well behind the front wheels, but instruments were located at the windshield so the angular difference from eyes to road and eyes to instruments was minimal.

ROLLIN ARMOR WOODEN CAR Rollin Armor of Kensington, California, constructed this battery-powered wooden car in his spare time for $1,800 in 1972. The car was 12 feet 8 inches long and 53 inches high. Weight was 1,600 pounds, including 600 pounds of batteries. The batteries were located under the hood and behind the two seats for balance, and the motor was placed between the seats. It could travel about sixty miles on a single battery charge and could exceed 50 mph. In stopping or going downhill, decreased pressure on the accelerator made the motor act like a generator. The batteries could be charged up to 100 amps in this way, thereby extending the vehicle's range. The wheels, brakes, rear axle, and torsion bars were scavenged from a junked Morris Minor. The chassis and body were of wood.

PLYMOUTH CRICKET The British-made Plymouth Cricket subcompact car of 1972 was built on a 98-inch wheelbase, and overall length was 161.4 inches. Power was a four-cylinder, inline, water-cooled, 91.4-cubic-inch-displacement engine that produced 55 hp. at 5,000 rpm. The same engine was available with two carburetors which increased the horsepower to 70 at 5,400 rpm. A four-speed manual transmission was standard, and automatic transmission was optional. The Cricket was available in two-door, four-door, and station wagon models. The four-door sedan is shown.

PORSCHE 911T The German Porsche 911 was the first six-cylinder car to bear the Porsche nameplate and was introduced in 1964. In 1968, suffix letters were added to the 911: T for touring, L for luxury, and S for super. The Porsche 911T for 1972 is shown. This 2,200-pound car was built on an 89.4-inch wheelbase. Overall length was 163.9 inches, and width was 63.4 inches. Power was a six-cylinder, flat, air-cooled, rear-mounted, fuel-injected, 143-cubic-inch-displacement engine that produced 157 hp. at 5,600 rpm. Four-speed manual transmission was standard, but a five-speed manual or automatic transmission was optional. The Porsche 911 won the 1967, 1968, and 1969 under-2-liters Trans Am Championships.

CADILLAC FLEETWOOD ELDORADO COUPÉ The classically elegant Cadillac Fleetwood Eldorado Coupé appeared in 1972. Power of this two-door, five-passenger automobile was an eight-cylinder, vee-type, water-cooled, 500-cubic-inch-displacement engine that produced 235 hp. at 3,800 rpm. Automatic transmission and a four-barrel carburetor were standard. The wheelbase was 126.5 inches, and overall length was 223.2 inches. Track was 63 inches.

FERRARI DINO 246 GT   Enzo Ferrari named his Dino GT cars after his deceased son. The Ferrari Dino 246 GT appeared at the 1967 Turin Auto Show and was introduced in the U.S. in 1972. The 1972 Dino is shown. The car's disadvantage was its loud engine roar that could be heard both inside the car and out, but its great advantage was its handling capability that was more than the average driver would need, even on rough roads. Power was a six-cylinder, transversely mounted, midship, water-cooled, double-overhead-cam, 145-cubic-inch-displacement engine producing 175 hp. at 7,000 rpm. The 2,770-pound car was built on a 92.1-inch wheelbase, length was 165.4 inches, and width 67 inches. Acceleration from zero to 60 mph. required 7.9 seconds and to 80 mph. 13.1 seconds. A five-speed manual transmission was fitted.

CHEVROLET CAPRICE COUPÉ   The Caprice was the Chevrolet top-of-the-line vehicle in 1972. The Caprice Coupé is shown. This luxurious car was built on a 121.5-inch wheelbase and overall length was 219.9 inches. Track was 64 inches. Power of this five-seater was an eight-cylinder, vee-type, water-cooled, 402-cubic-inch-displacement engine that produced 210 hp. Weight was 4,100 pounds.

CHEVROLET EL CAMINO   The Chevrolet El Camino was a luxuriously appointed pickup freight vehicle. This 1972 El Camino is shown fitted with a highly styled, low-profile camper shell that could accommodate two persons with sleeping space and room for supplies, etc. The El Camino was powered with Chevrolet's six-cylinder, inline, water-cooled, 250-cubic-inch-displacement engine that produced 110 hp. The 1972 El Camino featured chamfered pistons to reduce exhaust emissions, an improved automatic choke, and special spark-plug cables that attached more securely. This glamorous vehicle was popular on large estates and ranches.

AMERICAN MOTORS JAVELIN SST and AMX   The American Motors Javelin SST and AMX sporty, high-performance cars for 1972 were powered by American Motors' largest engine, the 401-cubic-inch-displacement, eight-cylinder, vee-type, water-cooled powerplant that produced 255 hp. at 4,600 rpm. The compression ratio was lowered to 8.5 to 1 that year so the engine could operate on regular grade gasoline. Bore was 4.17 inches, and stroke was 3.68 inches. A four-barrel carburetor was fitted on the cars. The wheelbase was 110 inches, overall length was 191.8 inches, and curb weight was about 3,000 pounds.

LUNAR ROVER The second Lunar Rover was taken to the moon on board the *Apollo 16* spacecraft. The design of this LRV with minor modifications was virtually identical to that used in 1971. The prime contractor was Boeing Company, and the driving motors were made by the Airesearch Manufacturing Division of the Garrett Corporation. Speed of the vehicle was about 10 mph. Airesearch also made the steering motors. Either front or rear wheels could be steered, and both could be steered if desired.

CHEVROLET VEGA This subcompact Chevrolet Vega 2300 four-passenger, two-door sedan of 1972 was priced at about $2,100. Weight was 2,210 pounds on a 97-inch wheelbase. Length was 169.7 inches, and width was 65.4 inches. Power was a four-cylinder, inline, water-cooled, 140-cubic-inch-displacement engine that developed 80 hp. at 4,400 rpm. A single-barrel carburetor was fitted. Manual three-speed Synchromesh transmission was standard. The car was designed to compete with the ever-increasing small car imports to the United States.

TOYOTA HI-LUX MINI-PICKUP   This Toyota Hi-Lux Mini-Pickup truck was introduced in 1973. Built on a 101.6-inch wheelbase, the overall length was 168.5 inches. The cargo bed length and width were 62 and 73 inches respectively, and the vehicle weighed 2,480 pounds. Power was a four-cylinder, inline, water-cooled, overhead-cam, 120-cubic-inch-displacement engine that produced 97 hp. at 5,500 rpm. A two-barrel carburetor and four-speed manual transmission were standard. The mini-pickup had become very popular because of the low price. The Hi-Lux listed for $2,350.

TRIUMPH TR-6   This product of British Leyland held a respected position in the sports car world for over six years. It was virtually unchanged in basic appearance with only minor mechanical improvements. A direct descendant of the TR-4, TR-4A, and TR-250, with minor styling and mechanical modifications, the TR-6 followed the appearance and performance of a sports car. The vertical, inline, six-cylinder engine of 152 cubic inches was fitted with two carburetors. The bore was 2.94 inches, stroke 3.74 inches, overall length 12 feet 11 inches, wheelbase 7 feet 4 inches, and the curb weight was 2,960 pounds. Transmission was four-speed with Synchromesh. The car was exceptionally maneuverable, with good speed, making it a popular entrant at sports car rallyes and speed events, where it earned its share of prizes. Because of its ruggedness and rough-riding qualities it was often called a "man's car."

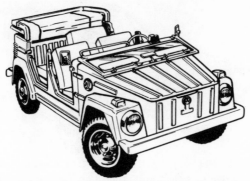

VW THING   When Volkswagen introduced the Thing in 1973, the appearance brought to mind the Kubelwagen or German Jeep of World War II. Built on a modified VW Beetle chassis, the Jeep-like vehicle featured a convertible top, folding windshield, and tough business-like styling. In addition, the doors were removable. A VW Thing placed third in its class in the Mexican 1,000-Mile Baja Race in November, 1972. Price was $2,750.

BMW 2002 Tii   Initially shown at the 1969 Frankfurt Auto Show, the German BMW 2002 Tii Touring Sedan handled like a sports car. The 1973 version of this subcompact car is shown. It was built on a 98.4-inch wheelbase, weighed 3,065 pounds, and was 166.5 inches long and 62.6 inches wide. The four-seater was powered with a four-cylinder, inline, water-cooled, overhead-camshaft, 121.3-cubic-inch-displacement engine producing 140 hp. at 5,800 rpm. A four-speed manual transmission was standard. Acceleration from zero to 60 mph. took only 9.9 seconds. Gas mileage was about 25 miles per gallon.

RENAULT 17 SPORTS COUPÉ In 1973 Renault produced more front-wheel-drive cars than any other manufacturer. During that year, the Renault 17 subcompact was introduced, and the Sports Coupé is shown. The car was equipped with four-wheel disc brakes, a 10-to-1 compression ratio, and fuel injection, plus excellent roadability and quick steering. The 2,315-pound car was built on a 96-inch wheelbase, and overall length was 167.7 inches. Width was 64 inches with a 53-inch tread. Power was a four-cylinder, inline, fuel-injected, over-head-valve, water-cooled, 95.5-cubic-inch-displacement engine that produced 106 hp. at 6,000 rpm. A four-speed manual Synchromesh transmission was standard. The louvered rear side windows eliminated the glare and also allowed the driver to see out. Zero to 60 mph. took but 11.3 seconds.

PORSCHE TARGA The Porsche Targa made its appearance in 1967. It had a built-in roll-bar covered by a wide chrome band. The Targa had an optional removable rear window that, when combined with the removable top, gave the Targa four open/closed variations. The 1973 Targa is shown with the top removed, and the rear window in place. The Porsche Targa was basically a 911 and was available in the 911T, 911E, and 911S.

SAAB 99 EMS   In 1973 the Swedish Saab firm produced the Saab 99 EMS that could meet the U.S. 5 mph. forward and 2½ mph. rear-barrier collision requirements. Because of this, some insurance firms reduced the premiums for Saab owners in the United States. This 1973 2,500-pound subcompact was built on a 97.4-inch wheelbase and was 174 inches long. Width was 66.5 inches and track about 55 inches. Power was a four-cylinder, inline, overhead-camshaft, water-cooled, fuel-injected, 121-cubic-inch-displacement engine that produced 110 hp. at 5,500 rpm. A four-speed manual transmission was standard. Front-wheel drive was fitted. The rear seats could fold flat to increase trunk space.

AUSTIN MARINA   Following the agile Mini-Cooper and Morris Minor, British Leyland presented their Austin Marina in 1973. With a wheelbase of 96 inches and overall length of 166.1 inches, this subcompact weighed 2,170 pounds. Track was 52 inches, and width was 64.8 inches. The five-passenger car used the M.G. engine, which was a four-cylinder, inline, water-cooled, 109.7-cubic-inch-displacement powerplant that produced 68.5 hp. at 5,000 rpm. A four-speed Synchromesh manual transmission was standard. The car was based on simple, time-proven ideas and therefore was not innovative. The car was offered in two- and four-door models and was priced in the $2,850 range.

PONTIAC GRAND PRIX   The Grand Prix was Pontiac's personal luxury automobile. The 1973 model was available only in a two-door hardtop. With a wheelbase of 116 inches and overall length of 216.6 inches, the tread was about 61 inches. Power was an eight-cylinder, vee-type, water-cooled, 455-cubic-inch-displacement engine that produced 220 hp. at 3,600 rpm. A four-barrel carburetor was fitted. Automatic transmission was standard. The energy-absorbing bumper system could compress up to three inches and return to normal with the use of pressurized gas and hydraulic fluid.

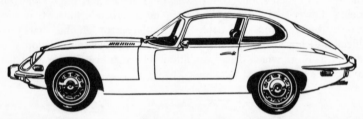

JAGUAR XKE 2-plus-2   The Jaguar XKE made its appearance in 1960 and is acknowledged to be one of the most attractive sports/G.T. cars ever built. It placed fourth in the 1962 Le Mans Race. The 1973 XKE 2-plus-2 version is shown. This had the standard two front seats, and in addition two more seats were placed in the rear. Power was a twelve-cylinder, vee-type, water-cooled, overhead-camshaft, 326-cubic-inch-displacement engine that produced 241 hp. at 6,000 rpm. Four one-barrel carburetors were installed, and four-speed manual transmission was standard, with automatic as an option. The wheelbase was 105 inches, overall length 184.4 inches, track approximately 54 inches, and width was 66.1 inches. Four-wheel disc brakes were fitted.

MASERATI BORA GT One of the finest sports/G.T. cars of 1973 was the Italian Maserati Bora. The frame was welded rectangular steel tubing. For those who love to drive, this car was superb. The wheelbase was 102.3 inches, length 170 inches, width 69.5 inches, and the height was only 44.7 inches. Curb weight was 3,500 pounds. Power was an eight-cylinder, water-cooled, vee-type, 288-cubic-inch-displacement engine with aluminum block and heads. Four two-barrel carburetors were fitted. Double overhead camshafts operated the valves. The car could attain 70 mph. in 7.8 seconds, and had an approximate top speed of 154 mph. Price of this quality car was $24,800.

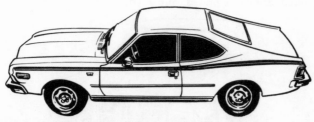

AMERICAN MOTORS HORNET HATCHBACK American Motors introduced the Hornet Hatchback compact car in 1973. When the rear seats were folded flat, the entire sloping rear hinged open and increased the luggage volume from 9.5 cubic feet to 23 cubic feet. The four-passenger, two-door vehicle also had energy-absorbing bumper systems. The 2,800-pound car was built on a 108-inch wheelbase. Power of the 185-inch-long car was a six-cylinder, inline, water-cooled, 232-cubic-inch-displacement engine that produced 100 hp. at 3,600 rpm. Price was about $2,500.

DATSUN 610   The Datsun 610 subcompact car appeared in 1973 and the two-door hardtop, four-door sedan, and five-door station wagon were available. The two-door hardtop of 1973 is shown. The Datsun 610 aimed to offer cars that were both sporty and luxurious in appearance and still economical. Standard on all models were reclining seats and an electric rear-window defroster. Power was a four-cylinder, inline, overhead-camshaft, water-cooled, 108-cubic-inch engine that produced 105 hp. at 6,000 rpm. A new design engine mounting reduced the noise level in the car. A manual four-speed Synchromesh transmission was standard, but automatic transmission was offered. Front disc brakes were fitted.

MERCEDES-BENZ 280   In 1973 the Mercedes-Benz 280 replaced the former 250. The car handled very much like a sports car despite the fact that it was a five-passenger sedan. Four-wheel power disc brakes stopped the car safely in a short distance. The four-door U.S. version is shown. Power was a six-cylinder, inline, double-overhead-camshaft, water-cooled, 167-cubic-inch-displacement engine that produced 132 hp. at 6,500 rpm. Automatic transmission was standard. Four-wheel independent suspension was fitted. The wheelbase was 108.3 inches, overall length 184.5 inches, width 70.5, and track 57 inches. Price was about $9,000 in the U.S. where the Mercedes had made a dent in Lincoln and Cadillac sales.

PLYMOUTH SEBRING PLUS The 1973 Plymouth Sebring Plus intermediate size sporty five-passenger car was a comfortable, quiet-riding automobile in the Satellite series. The car was fitted with a large engine that gave it more than average performance. The eight-cylinder, vee-type, water-cooled, 400-cubic-inch-displacement engine produced 255 hp. at 4,800 rpm. A three-speed manual or automatic transmission was offered. The wheelbase was 115 inches, overall length 203.2 inches, width 79.1 inches, and the tread was about 61 inches.

CHEVROLET MONTE CARLO S The 1973 Chevrolet Monte Carlo S was a luxurious personal car built on a 116-inch wheelbase. The styling followed the classic European luxury cars with a long hood and opera window. The car had excellent road feel, and roll angle was very low. The S was the specially equipped Monte Carlo with automatic transmission, rear anti-sway bars, and radial tires. The five-passenger coupé was powered by an eight-cylinder, vee-type, water-cooled, five-bearing, 350-cubic-inch-displacement engine that produced 145 hp. at 4,000 rpm. A two-barrel carburetor was fitted. A larger 454-cubic-inch-displacement, four-barrel-carburetor engine was also available. The car was 210.4 inches long and 77.6 inches wide.

AVANTI II   In 1964 when the tottering Studebaker Corporation decided to drop the Avanti, Nate Altman, a former South Bend, Indiana, Studebaker dealer, made an all-out attempt to save the car. He did this by buying two old Studebaker buildings and collecting former Studebaker craftsmen. Thus, Avanti Motors was born. The cars, handmade to order, were sold directly from the factory. No dealers were involved. About 300 units were sold each year at prices ranging from $8,600 to $10,000. The 1973 Avanti II shown was powered with a 400-cubic-inch-displacement Chevrolet V-8 engine. A choice of four-speed manual or automatic transmission was offered. The Avanti could be called the American Rolls-Royce.

SUZUKI MINI-BRUTE   The Japanese Suzuki Mini-Brute four-wheel-drive wagon of 1973 was light, nimble, and performed well in the Mexican 1,000-Mile Baja Race. The two-seater had a wheelbase of only 75 inches and was powered by a 360-cc-displacement, two-cycle engine (about one-fourth the size of a VW engine) that produced 33 hp. at 6,000 rpm. Curb weight was 1,320 pounds, and the price was $2,800. Four-speed manual transmission was standard. The car could climb mountains in the rough and attain a speed of 65 mph. on roads. The turning circle was only 28 feet in diameter.

SCHIMMELPENNICK ELECTRIC   After considering the fate of the world's big cities due to the traffic congestion and automobile pollution, Ludd Schimmelpennick, a mechanical engineer from Amsterdam, Holland, developed this two-seat, electrically driven urban vehicle in 1972. The white polyester runabout was less than six feet long, over six feet tall, and about four feet wide. It could run at a speed of 19 mph. The Amsterdam City Council provided funds in 1973 for an experimental "White Car Station." A fleet of seven cars were parked, along with battery-charging equipment, at the city border. People entering the city to shop or work could park their "gasoline eaters" at one of the White Car Stations and rent a White Car to enter the city. White was selected to symbolize purity (freedom from pollution). To construct a car cost approximately $1,875.

TRIUMPH SPITFIRE 1500   The British Triumph Spitfire has won its share of prizes at rallyes and races. In 1973 the engine size was increased to make the car a more formidable contestant. This 1,680-pound sports car had a wheelbase of 83 inches and was 147 inches long. Power was a four-cylinder, inline, overhead-valve, 1,500-cc-displacement, water-cooled engine that produced about 90 hp. at 5,500 rpm. A four-speed manual transmission was fitted. From zero to 60 mph. took 13.6 seconds, and top speed was over 100 mph.

MGB SPORTS CAR   Introduced in 1962, the B series of M.G. sports cars is the heir to the famous M.G. cars of the past. Shown is the MGB MKII of 1973. The unit-type chassis was built on a 91-inch wheelbase, and overall length was 153.3 inches. This 1,900-pound car was 59.9 inches wide with a 49.3-inch track. Power was a four-cylinder, inline, overhead-valve, water-cooled, 110-cubic-inch-displacement engine that produced 94 hp. at 5,400 rpm. A four-speed manual transmission was fitted. Top speed was approximately 105 mph. From zero to 60 mph. took about 12.1 seconds.

AVE MIZAR PINTO FLYING CAR   AVE (Advanced Vehicle Engineering) of Van Nuys, California, worked for five years to develop this flying car in 1973. It was called the Mizar. The group successfully mated the wings and tail of a Cessna Skymaster to a Ford Pinto automobile with quick-release pins. The 300-hp. Lycoming engine produced a flying speed of 171 mph. and a range of over 1,000 miles. The price was about $28,000. The conversion from auto to plane took only a few minutes. On the ground the Pinto used its own engine, and the aircraft engine, the wing and tail were left behind.

G.M. MOTOR HOME General Motors introduced this Motor Home in 1973. The body was constructed of bonded fiberglass and aluminum panels, with an interior of thick polyurethane foam for noise supression and thermal insulation. The center of gravity was only 37 inches above the ground. The vehicle was available in 23- and 26-foot lengths and included a double sink, refrigerator, bath, range with exhaust hood, and plenty of cabinet space. Power was a 455-cubic-inch-displacement V-8 engine with automatic transmission and front-wheel drive. Six-wheel brakes were fitted, and the parking brake worked on all four rear wheels. Air springs connected each pair of rear wheels to soften the ride.

CORVORADO This unusual car combination was produced by Dunham Coach, Boonton, New Jersey, in 1973. It consisted of a Chevrolet Corvette engine installed in a highly modified Cadillac Eldorado body. Price was about $16,000.

LOTUS EUROPA SPECIAL Famous British racing car designer and team owner Colin Chapman had been producing his successful Lotus Grand Prix Racers for years, when he decided to introduce in 1966 a street legal automobile known as the Lotus MK46 Europa. The 1973 Lotus Europa Special is shown. During prior years, a Renault engine and transaxles were fitted, but, in 1973, a 1,600-cc English Ford twin-overhead-camshaft, four-cylinder engine was used with the Renault transaxle. In 1968 this prototype won the 1,600-cc Special G.T. Championships. The car weight was 1,900 pounds, construction was a steel backbone with independent front and rear suspension. The body was fiberglass and the 113-hp. engine was located in a compartment between the two seats and the rear axle. Numerous sports car and racing authorities agreed that this vehicle was the closest to a race car that a street legal car could come.

VW SPORTS BUG Volkswagen introduced a sporty version of the VW Beetle in 1973. The car was fitted with oversize radial tires on mag-type wheels, a padded steering wheel, bucket seats, a short-throw Synchromesh gearshift lever, a cast aluminum-magnesium alloy engine, four-wheel independent suspension, and a double-jointed rear axle with trailing arms. It had a special high-gloss paint job in either yellow or silver and jet black trimming. The Sports Bug was a limited production edition.

DE TOMASO PANTERA Alejandro De Tomaso came to Italy from his native Argentina in the fifties and then became a race car driver. Soon he began designing and building cars which received acclaim. In 1973, the De Tomaso Pantera (Italian for Panther) appeared with an all-steel unit construction body engineered and made by the famous Ghia in Turin. Lincoln-Mercury imported the car for the U.S. market. Both De Tomaso and Ghia are tied to Ford. The car had superb handling qualities and was comfortable and luxurious for a G.T. car. The wheelbase was 98.4 inches and overall length was 167 inches, with a width of 67 inches. A Ford engine powered this beauty and was an eight-cylinder, vee-type, water-cooled, overhead-valve, 351-cubic-inch-displacement engine that produced 273 hp. at 5,400 rpm. A five-speed manual transmission and four-barrel carburetor were fitted. Top speed was 130 mph., and the car could go from zero to 100 mph. in 14 seconds. The price was about $10,000.

TOYOTA CELICA ST The Japanese subcompact Toyota Celica ST of 1973 was the sporty car of the Toyota line. Built on a 95.5-inch wheelbase, the 2,300-pound auto was 168.2 inches long and 63 inches wide. Power was a four-cylinder, inline, water-cooled engine of 120-cubic-inch displacement that produced 97 hp. at 5,500 rpm. A two-barrel carburetor was fitted. Four-speed manual transmission was standard, and automatic transmission was optional.

FIAT 128 STATION WAGON The Italian Fiat 128 subcompact economy station wagon of 1973 was built on a 96.4-inch wheelbase. Length and width were 157.8 inches and 63.9 inches respectively, and height was 56.9. Power was a four-cylinder, inline, water-cooled, 79-cubic-inch-displacement engine that produced 66 hp. at 6,200 rpm. A two-barrel carburetor was fitted. Four-speed manual transmission was standard.

TOYOTA COROLLA SR/5 This Japanese import made its appearance in 1973 as a four-passenger, two-door coupé. The Toyota Corolla SR/5 was equipped with wide, low-profile tires that gave it a sports car look but not a sports car performance. This economy car weighed 2,069 pounds on a 91.9-inch wheelbase. Overall length was 157.9 inches and width 62.8 inches. Power was a four-cylinder, inline, water-cooled, 96.9-cubic-inch-displacement, cast-iron block engine that produced 88 hp. at 6,000 rpm. A five-speed Synchromesh manual transmission was fitted. To accelerate from zero to 60 mph. required about 12 seconds, and top speed was about 96 mph.

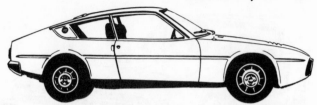

MATRA-SIMCA BAGHEERA When a leading French guided-missile manufacturer, Matra, joined a well-known automobile producer, Simca, to produce racing cars, the results were very successful. In 1973, the Matra-Simca combination turned to sports production cars with the Matra-Simca Bagheera, named after the sleek panther in Kipling's *Jungle Books*. This 150-mph. sports/G.T. car was arranged with three bucket seats across. Power was a four-cylinder, transversely mounted, 15-degree slant, overhead-valve, water-cooled engine with a bore and stroke of 76.7 mm. and 70 mm. The mid-engine design put the powerplant just behind the seats. Aluminum alloy cylinder heads were fitted, as were two double-barreled carburetors. A four-speed manual transmission was standard, as were the four-wheel hydraulic disc brakes. Unit body construction was used, with a pressed-steel frame and a fiberglass shell. Upon its introduction, the car was available only in France for a price of about $6,000.

CHEVROLET IMPALA This Chevrolet two-door hardtop Impala was one of the most popular cars of 1973. The 4,400-pound car was built on a 121.5-inch wheelbase. Overall length and width were 222.6 inches and 79.5 inches respectively, and height was 53.7. Power was an eight-cylinder, vee-type, water-cooled engine of 400-cubic-inch displacement that produced 150 hp. at 3,200 rpm. A two-barrel carburetor was fitted. The five-passenger auto was equipped with automatic transmission.

SAAB SONETT III The 1973 Saab Sonett III was mechanically the same as the 1970 model, but the appearance of its fiberglass body was changed. In addition to styling, the 1973 Sonett featured dual built-in roll-over bars and impact-absorbing bumpers. The fiberglass body was aerodynamically designed for streamlining and balance. Price was about $4,000.

ANYCAR II As a follow-up on the 1971 Anycar, Manufacturers Hanover Trust Company had a second composite automobile made to advertise their auto loan department. This was an entirely different design from the earlier car and included parts from Cadillac, Dodge, Mercedes, Catalina, Mustang, Imperial, Pontiac, Volvo, Toyota, Triumph, Hudson, Continental, Mach 1, Corvette, Valiant, Ford, Volkswagen, Plymouth, Toronado, and Chrysler. Again, how many can you identify?

CORTEZ MOTOR HOME The Cortez Motor Home of 1973 was made by the Cortez Corporation, Kent, Ohio. The motor home accommodated four for sleeping and was fitted with a toilet, shower, refrigerator, dinette, stove, and sink. The 8,500-pound vehicle was 21.3 feet long and was powered by a 455-cubic-inch-displacement Oldsmobile Toronado V-8 engine that drove the front wheels. Power brakes and power steering were standard. Because of the front-wheel drive, the Cortez Motor Home did not have the usual drive shaft to the rear wheels and therefore had a low profile for a vehicle of this type. The low center of gravity made it a pleasure to drive. Optional luxuries included a waste disposal unit, air conditioner, water purifier, and six-way power seat.

DODGE COLT STATION WAGON The two-passenger Dodge Colt subcompact station wagon for 1973 was built on the standard Colt wheelbase. Power and power train also remained the same. New wheel covers and a new bumper system were fitted. Emission controls on this Japanese-made car met United States standards.

HONDA CIVIC   The Japanese Honda Civic economy mini-car was introduced in 1972 and made its appearance in the United States in 1973. This 134-inch-long car was built on a 90-inch wheelbase and was priced at about $2,200. Power was a four-cylinder, overhead-camshaft, water-cooled, inline, 1,169-cc-displacement engine that produced 69 hp. at 5,500 rpm. Weight was 1,400 pounds. A four-speed manual transmission was standard, as were rack-and-pinion steering and front-wheel drive.

JEEP POSTAL VEHICLE   A.M. General Corporation, a subsidiary of American Motors, made over 40,000 of these quarter-ton 1973 postal delivery vehicles for the U.S. Postal Service in the A.M. General South Bend, Indiana, plant. The vehicles were based on the Jeep and were powered by the American Motors six-cylinder, water-cooled, in-line, 232-cubic-inch-displacement engine that produced 100 hp. at 3,600 rpm. Notice the right-hand drive, which allowed the driver to enter and exit from the vehicle directly to the sidewalk. Doors were of the sliding type.

MERCEDES-BENZ ESV-22 Based upon the 450 SE luxury sedan, this Mercedes-Benz ESV-22 of 1973 was an outgrowth of the firm's several experimental safety vehicles. Some of the safety features were: anti-locking brakes, fully padded passenger compartment, hydraulic suspension, energy-absorbing bumpers, washer/wiper system for the headlights, rubber rain moldings to prevent pedestrian injury, deep foam front of car, and no protruding door handles, insignia, etc. Even the outside rear-view mirror was soft plastic that would bend on impact.

G.M.-BTV General Motors developed this simple BTV (Basic Transportation Vehicle) in 1973 so it could be manufactured in the less industrialized nations of the world. The body had no curved metal surfaces and could be cut from a flat sheet with metal shears much the way a dress is cut from a pattern. A BTV plant can be as small as a large barn, and a BTV is often cheaper than a good horse in some countries. The Basic Transportation Vehicle is being constructed in Ecuador, Portugal, the Philippines, Africa, Malaysia, and in the Middle East. The engine and drive train are supplied from a G.M. plant in England.

UAZ-469 This was the first Russian automobile to be marketed worldwide and was called the Lada. It was first exported to Scandinavia and Britain, and then was offered in France and West Germany. The all-purpose utility model is shown. The Lada, assembled at the Volzhsky auto plant on the Volga River, was manufactured under an agreement with the Italian F.I.A.T. company, which has provided considerable technical guidance to the Soviet Union's automobile industry.

AUDI FOX The Porsche-Audi Division of Volkswagen introduced the Audi 80 Fox subcompact car in 1973. This four-seater weighed about 2,400 pounds with a wheelbase of 97.2 inches. The overall length was 171.9 inches and width was 63 inches. The front-located engine was offset to the right side of the car, and the radiator alongside it on the left side of the car. The powerplant was canted or tilted to the side to lower the hood for better visibility. Front-wheel drive was featured. Power was a four-cylinder, inline, water-cooled, single-overhead-cam engine producing 75 hp. at 5,800 rpm. A four-speed manual transmission was fitted. Unit body frame construction was used. Audi is the former Auto Union firm.

DODGE COLT GT HARDTOP The captive import Dodge Colt was made expressly for Chrysler Motors by Mitsubishi in Japan. The Colt for 1974 was all new, and this subcompact line included a coupé, hardtop, station wagon, and a sedan. The 1974 Dodge Colt GT two-door hardtop shown was powered with a 2,000-cc, single-overhead-camshaft, 94-hp. engine. The G.T. had a tachometer included in its instrument cluster. The car had no safety bumpers, because pillarless cars with less than a 115-inch wheelbase were exempt from this ruling. Styling was exceptionally clean on this five-passenger car.

JENSEN-HEALEY SPORTS CAR This British sports car was designed by Donald Healey and constructed by Jensen Motors. The Jensen-Healey with its simple and pleasing lines made its appearance in 1973. The 1974 model is shown here. The two-seater weighed 2,155 pounds on a 92-inch wheelbase. Overall length was 162 inches. The powerplant was a Lotus four-cylinder, water-cooled, double-over-head-camshaft, inline, inclined, 121-cubic-inch-displacement engine that produced 140 hp. at 6,500 rpm. Four valves were fitted on each cylinder. Two carburetors were standard, as was a four-speed manual transmission. The car could reach 60 mph. from zero in 9.7 seconds, and cornering was excellent. A relatively smooth ride was possible thanks to a coil spring suspension. Price in the United States was about $4,500.

VOLKSWAGEN PASSAT The 1974 Volkswagen Passat was designed for the European market and eventually replaced the VW 1600. Passat is the name of a Brazilian wind. The design was developed from the Audi 80 and was prepared by the Italian stylist Georgio Guigiaro of Turin. The car was an attempt by VW chief Rudolf Leiding to rid Volkswagen of its ancient designs. The front-located engine and front-wheel drive most likely spawned the Rabbit.

CHRYSLER IMPERIAL LE BARON The Chrysler top of the line, the luxurious Imperial Le Baron for 1974 was equipped with four-wheel disc brakes and offered the ultimate in road transportation. The 5,184-pound car was built on a 124-inch wheelbase, and overall length was 231.1 inches. Width was 79.7 inches, and track was 64 inches. Power was an eight-cylinder, vee-type, overhead-valve, water-cooled, 440-cubic-inch-displacement engine producing 230 hp. at 4,000 rpm. Automatic transmission, power steering, and power brakes were standard. Acceleration from zero to 60 mph. took 11.3 seconds, and top speed was over 120 mph.

PLYMOUTH FURY GRAN SEDAN The Plymouth top-of-the-line models were the two-door Fury Gran Coupé and the four-door Fury Gran Sedan hardtop models. The Gran Sedan of 1974 was built on a 120-inch wheelbase. The standard powerplant was the 318-cubic-inch-displacement V-8. However, optional engines were the two-barrel 360-cubic-inch-displacement or the four-barrel 400-cubic-inch- or 440-cubic-inch displacement. Automatic transmission, power steering, and power brakes were standard.

JEEP CJ-5 RENEGADE The 1974 American Motors Jeep CJ-5 Renegade provided Jeep performance, and had safety features such as a roll-bar structure and passenger safety rail. The rugged four-wheel-drive vehicle was at home off the road as well as on it. Finish was available in yellow, orange, or plum with black trim. Forged aluminum wheels and heavy-duty cooling were also included. Power was an eight-cylinder, vee-type, water-cooled, 304-cubic-inch-displacement engine. Power brakes and power steering were optional, but three-speed manual transmission was standard. The Renegade was developed for the Jeep enthusiast who liked custom touches and safety.

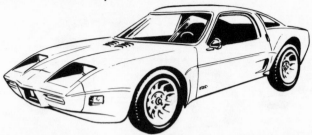

CORVETTE WANKEL   America took the spotlight at the 1974 Frankfurt Auto Show with this Chevrolet Corvette Wankel prototype automobile. The aluminum body of this two-rotor-engine-powered sports car was built in Italy. This non-production auto weighed 2,600 pounds and was built on a 90-inch wheelbase. The two-seater was fitted with an energy-absorbing bumper system and roll-over cage protection. The two-rotor Wankel engine was mid-mounted and had a displacement of 266 cubic inches. Side scoops drew in carburetor air and also cooled the engine compartment. The fuel tank was located between the passenger and engine compartments and was protected with structural walls. Considerable aerodynamic experimentation went into the body design. Four-wheel disc brakes were fitted.

MERCEDES-BENZ 450 SL COUPÉ   Introduced in 1974, the Mercedes-Benz 450 SL Coupé was the limited-production flagship of the company. Only 150 vehicles were available each month in the United States. The car met 72 of the 134 Department of Transportation requirements for Experimental Safety Vehicles. The four-seater weighed 3,995 pounds and was built on a 112.8-inch wheelbase. Overall length was 195.3 inches, and width was 73.6 inches. Power was an eight-cylinder, vee-type, single-overhead-camshaft, water-cooled, electronic-fuel-injected and electronic ignition, 275.8-cubic-inch-displacement engine that produced 190 hp. at 4,750 rpm. Automatic transmission was standard. The price was about $15,000.

TOYOTA CORONA MARK II   The Japanese Toyota Corona Mark II of 1974 was offered in a variety of 31 sedans, 36 hardtops, 7 wagons, and 3 light vans. The Mark II L two-door hardtop is shown. The wheelbase of this 2,300-pound car was 95.7 inches, overall length 170.7 inches, width 61.8 inches, and track 51 inches. The standard powerplant was a 120-cubic-inch-displacement, 97-hp. engine. However, several optional engines were offered: a six-cylinder, overhead-camshaft engine with ratings from 115 hp. to 135 hp.; a four-cylinder, single-carburetor engine of 110 hp.; a four-cylinder, twin-carburetor engine of 125 hp.; and a fuel-injected, four-cylinder engine of 130 hp. Toyota produced 20,000 units each month.

CADILLAC FLEETWOOD ELDORADO   The luxurious 1974 Cadillac Fleetwood Eldorado personal car, built on a 126-inch wheelbase, was four inches shorter than the Calais and deVille series. The Eldorado was available as a coupé or convertible. This 224.1-inch-long car was 79.8 inches wide, and its track was about 63 inches. The front-wheel-drive auto was powered with an eight-cylinder, vee-type, water-cooled, 500-cubic-inch-displacement engine that produced 210 hp. at 3,600 rpm. A four-barrel carburetor was fitted, and automatic transmission was standard.

MATADOR BROUGHAM COUPÉ This 1974 American Motors Matador Brougham Coupé was the elegant top of the Matador line. The 4,000-pound car, built on a 114-inch wheelbase, was 209.3 inches long. Power was an economy six-cylinder engine or an eight-cylinder, vee-type, water-cooled, 360-cubic-inch engine that produced 195 hp. at 4,400 rpm. Either three-speed manual or automatic transmission was available. The brougham offered the opera window, vinyl top, and power front disc brakes.

AMERICAN MOTORS SPORTY-X MATADOR The intermediate size A.M.C. Matador was styled with the assistance of Oleg Cassini, Pierre Cardin, and Emilio Pucci. Thus its appearance was different from all other U.S. cars when it was introduced in 1973. The 1974 version, lower and longer than the previous year, had a 114-inch wheelbase and a 209.3-inch overall length. Height was 51.8 inches, and track was 60 inches. The curb weight was 4,049 pounds. The Sporty-X Matador was the sporty, high-powered version that won the Winston Western 500 at Riverside, California, at an average speed of 104.55 mph. The Matador X powerplant was an eight-cylinder, overhead-valve, water-cooled, vee-type, 401-cubic-inch-displacement engine producing 235 hp. at 4,600 rpm. A choice of manual or automatic transmission was offered. The car could reach 60 mph. in 8.3 seconds.

DATSUN 260Z   The Japanese Datsun 260Z G.T./sports car of 1974 was an improved version of the earlier 240Z. The latter was the SCCA C-Production National Champion and winner of the East African Safari. Built on a 90.7-inch wheelbase, the car was 169.1 inches long, 64.1 inches wide, and its tread was about 53 inches. The powerplant was a six-cylinder, inline, single-overhead-cam, water-cooled, 156-cubic-inch-displacement engine. Two carburetors were fitted. A four-speed manual Synchromesh transmission was standard, and automatic transmission was optional. The two-seater weighed 2,590 pounds.

RELIANT ROBIN   The British subcompact Reliant Robin made its appearance in 1974. The three-wheeled car had a steel chassis with a fiberglass sedan body that seated four comfortably. The single front wheel made steering effortless, and cornering was controlled by the one wheel lifting off the road. Fuel economy was between 40 and 50 miles per gallon. Power was a 45.6-cubic-inch-displacement engine of 32 hp. at 5,500 rpm. The transmission was an aluminum-cased Synchromesh four-gear manual system. The rear seats could fold down to increase the luggage capacity. Designed primarily for European conditions, the car was not intended for the North American market.

CITROËN SM MASERATI   The revolutionary French Citroën SM luxury G.T. car was called Maserati, because it used their engine. The car made its appearance in 1970. The 1974 Citroën SM is shown. The entire car was steel except for the hood and front fenders, which were aluminum. The shape was aerodynamically designed, with the headlights and license plate enclosed in a streamlined glass form. Among the many safety features was a plastic fuel tank located between the rear wheels. This was for maximum impact shielding. Many controls were mounted on the steering column. A hydro-pneumatic suspension system was fitted, and the car automatically leveled itself regardless of load. The 3,200-pound car, built on a 116-inch wheelbase, was 192.6 inches long and 72.3 inches wide. The engine was a six-cylinder, vee-type, double-overhead-camshaft, water-cooled, 163-cubic-inch-displacement powerplant that developed 180 hp. at 6,250 rpm. Aluminum block and cylinders were used. This front-wheel drive five-seater was fitted with a five-speed manual transmission.

MERCURY COUGAR   The 1974 Mercury Cougar emerged as a mid-sized luxury automobile much like the Thunderbird. The 4,275-pound car was built on a 114-inch wheelbase. Overall length was 215.5 inches, and width was 78.6 inches. Power was an eight-cylinder, overhead-valve, water-cooled, 351-cubic-inch-displacement engine that produced 160 hp. Automatic transmission was standard. This five-passenger automobile provided an extremely quiet ride and handled well.

MAZDA RX-4 The Japanese Mazda RX-4 of 1974, a larger version of the earlier RX-3, was available in a coupé, sedan, and station wagon. The four-passenger, two-door coupé shown weighed 2,700 pounds on a 99-inch wheelbase. Overall length was 179 inches, and track was 54 inches. The two-rotor Wankel engine with a displacement of 80 cubic inches produced 110 hp. at 6,000 rpm. A four-speed manual transmission was standard, but automatic transmission was available. The car had many luxury features such as: tinted glass, reclining bucket seats, a rear-window defroster, and a built-in windshield radio antenna.

DODGE CHALLENGER The Dodge Challenger high-performance, sporty compact car was built on a 110-inch wheelbase and was 198.6 inches long. Width was 77.4 inches and track about 60 inches. The standard engine was a 318-cubic-inch displacement, but the optional rallye package offered the eight-cylinder, vee-type, water-cooled, 360-cubic-inch-displacement engine that produced 245 hp. at 4,800 rpm. Three-speed manual transmission was standard, and four-speed manual or automatic transmission was optional. The two-door hardtop presented a very sporty appearance.

NISSAN EXCELLENT The Japanese Nissan Excellent was added to the firm's Sunny line in 1974. The sporty-looking hatchback was intended only for the Japanese domestic market and not for export. A four-cylinder, water-cooled, inline, 1,200-cc-displacement engine that produced 85 hp. powered the car. A 1,428-cc-displacement engine was also available. A five-speed manual transmission was used. Front disc brakes were fitted.

DATSUN B-210 In 1974, Japanese Nissan Motors introduced the Datsun B-210 subcompact car to replace its 1200 series. The line offered a two-door, four-door, and a hatchback selling from $2,400 to $2,600. The 1974 hatchback is shown. The 1,960-pound car was built on a 92.1-inch wheelbase. Overall length was 160 inches and width 60.8 inches. Power was a four-cylinder, inline, overhead-valve, water-cooled, 78.5-cubic-inch-displacement engine. A four-speed manual transmission was standard. Acceleration from zero to 60 mph. required 15.9 seconds. Reclining bucket seats, an electric rear-window defogger, and tinted glass were standard.

FORD CORTINA SERIES 4   The Cortina was made by British Ford and was intended for domestic use as well as export to many countries, including the United States. This is the Ford Cortina Series 4 four-door sedan of 1974, weighing 2,013 pounds, built on a 98-inch wheelbase and with an overall length of 168 inches. Power of this compact car was a four-cylinder, overhead-valve, water-cooled, 97.5-cubic-inch-displacement engine that developed 67 hp. at 5,000 rpm. A single-barrel carburetor and three-speed transmission were fitted. Safety features included an energy-absorbing steering column and armrests, double-thick laminated glass, and a safety-designed front-end structure. The Cortina engine was used in many Formula race cars.

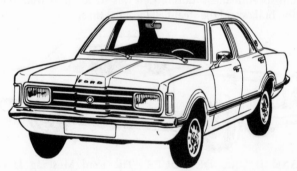

FORD TAUNUS GXL   The Taunus compact car was a product of German Ford in Frankfurt and was intended primarily for domestic sales. The Ford Taunus GXL four-door sedan of 1974 is shown. Power was a 2,000-cc-displacement, overhead-cam, water-cooled, four-cylinder engine. Overall length was 168 inches, front track was 52.5 inches, and rear track was 51 inches. Curb weight was 2,000 pounds, and overall length was about 168 inches.

MUSTANG II MACH 1 Since the original Mustang pony car appeared in 1964, the car had increased considerably in size and luxury. The Ford Motor Company introduced the new Mustang II in 1974 to revive the old concept of a compact, sporty-looking, and reasonably priced car. Body types offered were the fastback, notch-back, two-seater, two-plus-two, Mach 1 (shown), and the luxurious Grande. This 3,200-pound auto was built on a wheelbase of 96.2 inches and was 175 inches long. Width was 70.2 inches with track of 55.5 inches. Power was a six-cylinder, vee-type, overhead-valve, water-cooled, 171-cubic-inch-displacement engine which produced 119 hp. at 5,200 rpm. Four-speed manual transmission was standard as were the front-wheel disc brakes and the steel-belted radial tires.

MUSTANG II GRANDE COUPÉ The Ford Mustang II Grande Coupé was the luxurious version of the Mustang II and was available only in the notch-back body style. The Grande was fitted with a softer suspension and well-padded seats. The standard Mustang II power-plant was a four-cylinder, inline, single-overhead-camshaft, 2.3-liter-displacement engine that produced 95 hp. The compression ratio was 8.4 to 1. Unit steel body construction was used, and the car weighed 2,680 pounds.

FIAT X-1/9 SPORTS CAR   Italy's F.I.A.T. company introduced their X-1/9 mid-engine sports car in 1974 to replace the Fiat 850. This was the first Fiat specifically designed for the U.S. market. The Fiat X-1/9 had retractable headlights, and the roof was removable and could be stored in the front compartment. The unit chassis and body construction included a roof roll-bar structure. The 1,935-pound two-seater was built on an 86.7-inch wheelbase with a 150.5-inch length. Width was 61.7 inches and track 53 inches. Power was a four-cylinder, inline, transversely mounted, water-cooled, 78.7-cubic-inch-displacement engine that produced 51 hp. at 5,600 rpm. A single carburetor was fitted. Four-speed manual transmission was standard as were the four-wheel disc brakes. Despite the rear location of the engine, the radiator was placed forward on this Bertone-styled sports car.

MAZDA RX500 PROTOTYPE   The Mazda RX500 sports car prototype of 1974 was aimed at the Datsun 240Z market, although it looked like a full-fledged racing type. Powered by a two-rotor Wankel engine located between the seat backs and rear axle, the car was estimated to have a top speed of 145 mph. The 1,870-pound two-seater was built on a 96.5-inch wheelbase and was 170 inches long. Power was a 60-cubic-inch-displacement rotary engine that developed 180 hp. at 8,500 rpm. Transmission was four-speed manual Synchromesh.

SUBARU GL COUPÉ   The Japanese Subaru GL Coupé subcompact car appeared in the U.S. in 1973 and offered good value for the list price of $2,598. The 1974 Subaru GL Coupé is shown. Made by Fuji Heavy Industries of Tokyo, the car was built on a 96.6-inch wheelbase and weighed 2,000 pounds. Overall length was 164.4 inches, and width was 59.2 inches. Power was a four-cylinder, flat, opposed, water-cooled, 83-cubic-inch-displacement engine that produced 61 hp. at 5,000 rpm. A four-speed manual transmission was fitted, as was a two-barrel carburetor. This front-wheel-drive car had rack-and-pinion steering and fully independent suspension. The bucket seats could be adjusted to seventeen different positions, and a tachometer and rear-window defogger were standard. Twenty-five miles to the gallon of gas was claimed.

GLASSIC MODEL A   In 1974 the Glassic Motor Car Company of Palm Beach, Florida, began producing replicas of famous old-time cars. This is the Glassic Model A. The body was carefully reproduced, line for line, in fiberglass with colors molded in. The powerplant was a modern V-8 engine fitted with automatic transmission. This five-passenger full-size Model A replica sold for $7,595.

SAAB 99 COMBI-COUPÉ The Saab Combi-Coupé made its appearance in 1973 as a new version of the 99 model. In the United States the car was known as the Saab 99 LE Hatchback. The 1974 model is shown. This front-wheel-drive subcompact car was fitted with dual diagonal brakes, roll-cage construction, and folding rear seats. This 2,720-pound auto was built on a 97.4-inch wheelbase and was 178 inches long. Width was 66.5 inches with a 54-inch track. Four-wheel disc brakes were fitted. Power was a four-cylinder, inline, fuel-injected, water-cooled, 121-cubic-inch-displacement engine producing 110 hp. at 5,500 rpm.

TRIUMPH TR-7 This wedge-shaped sports car was developed in 1975 to offer sedan comfort in a sports vehicle. The direct opposite of the previous TR-6, which was a noisy, powerful six-cylinder convertible with a brute shape, the TR-7 had a fixed hardtop with a four-cylinder engine. The wheelbase was 85 inches and the total length was 164.5 inches, while the track or tread was just over 55 inches. Curb weight was 2,241 pounds. The inline engine was inclined 45 degrees in order to achieve the low hood contour. Transmission was manual four-speed with Synchromesh on all speeds. Rack-and-pinion steering was fitted, and suspension was front independent, while rear was live action and coil springs.

VOLKSWAGEN RABBIT The familiar Volkswagen Beetle proved to be a popular automobile for four decades, and in 1975 the company introduced another inexpensive car, the VW Rabbit. The newcomer was radically different from the Beetle with a water-cooled, four-cylinder, transverse, front-mounted engine, tilted back, with front-wheel-drive as compared to the rear-mounted, rear-wheel-drive, air-cooled engine of the Beetle. The Rabbit also boasted improved performance plus superior mileage. Speeds of over 90 mph. were possible while gasoline consumption could be as good as 38 miles to the gallon. This VW could reach 50 mph. in just over 8 seconds. The wheelbase was 94.5 inches and the overall length 155 inches. The interior was more spacious than that of the Beetle. As can be seen, the body styling was contemporary and much different from the Beetle, which was conceived in 1934.

MERCURY COMET The Mercury Comet for 1975 was redesigned to be more luxurious inside as well as in overall appearance. This compact car was styled to resemble a big car so that it could accommodate the average family. Comet options included a fuel economy reminder light and other items.

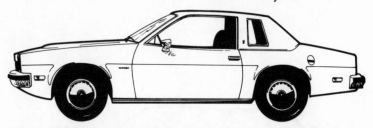

MONZA TOWNE COUPÉ With the smaller-size cars in demand in 1975, due to savings in initial cost and maintenance, the Chevrolet Division of General Motors introduced a luxury version of their subcompact Monza, the Towne Coupé. Vinyl-covered roof, deep bucket seats, and real leather interior were some of the luxury items. A three- or four-speed stick shift transmission was offered, coupled with the 2.3-liter, 78- or 87-hp. engine with a one- or two-barrel carburetor plus a 3.42 axle ratio. The Towne Coupé was rated by the Environmental Protection Agency as 21 mpg. in city driving and 30 mpg. on the highway test. The automatic transmission version used a 4.3-liter, 110-hp. engine. The car weighed 2,733 pounds and had a wheelbase of 97 inches, length of 177.8 inches, width of 65.4 inches, and a height of 49.8 inches.

FORD GRANADA The Granada was a brand-new Ford luxury automobile introduced in 1975. It was about 1,000 pounds lighter and 2 feet shorter than most U.S. standard-size cars. The Granada was specially developed to compete with the Mercedes 280, which had enjoyed ever-increasing sales in the U.S. luxury car market for several years. It was a bit longer and slightly lighter than the Mercedes; 197.7 inches vs. 195.5 inches, and 3,408 pounds vs. 3,440 pounds. Interior dimensions were virtually identical. The styling of the Granada strongly resembled that of the Mercedes, and the Granada was called a European-size luxury car. Price of the five-place Granada was about $3,700. Standard equipment was a 200-cubic-inch engine with three-speed manual transmission and a 19-gallon tank for an extended driving range.

ROLLS-ROYCE CAMARGUE   Without question the most expensive automobile of 1975 at $70,000 to $80,000 was the elegant Rolls-Royce Camargue. It reflected the accumulated experience of this fine car builder. The auto was a two-door saloon of stressed-steel construction except for the trunk lid, doors, and engine hood, which were of aluminum alloy. The body was designed by the Italian Pininfarina group and hand-built by the craftsmen at Mulliner Park Ward. A 6,750-cc, 90° V-8, overhead-valve engine had cylinder blocks of high silicone content aluminum and a crankshaft of chrome moly steel. Two automatic air-conditioning and heating systems were designed: one for the upper areas and the other for the lower areas of the passenger compartment. They not only maintained the selected temperature but also controlled humidity. The car automatically adjusted itself to proper height, depending upon the load. Electrically operated gear selection and automatic transmission, with three forward speeds and reverse, made it almost impossible to detect the shifting of gears. Four-wheel independent suspension with front anti-dive and rear anti-lift features aided in the superb riding qualities in this 120-inch-wheelbase and 207-inch-long quality automobile.

FIAT 124 SPORT COUPÉ   Sports cars were once considered rich men's playthings, but during the quarter century ending in 1975 prices had dropped, and now anyone could afford a sports car. Italy's largest automobile manufacturer introduced the medium-priced Fiat 124 Sport Coupé for 1975 as a companion to the 124 Sport Spider convertible. The car combined the handling of a sports car with the comfort of a sedan. The wheelbase was 95.5 inches with front track 53 inches and rear track 51.8 inches. The body/frame was unitized as one unit. The engine was an overhead-cam, inline, four-cylinder, front-mounted, water-cooled type of 107.13-cubic-inch displacement. A five-speed manual transmission was standard. Front suspension was by means of wishbone control arms, coil spring, hydraulic shock absorbers, and an anti-roll bar. Rear suspension consisted of trailing arms, a transverse Panhard rod, coil springs, and hydraulic shock absorbers. Disc brakes were installed on all wheels.

BUICK SKYHAWK   With the interest in smaller cars growing due to high fuel prices and initial costs, Buick introduced the Skyhawk. It was the smallest Buick automobile to be built in sixty years. The car had a 97-inch wheelbase and an overall length of 179.3 inches. It weighed 3,000 pounds. Power was by a new vee-type, six-cylinder engine that developed 110 hp. A telescoping steering column and energy-absorbing bumpers were among the safety features. The car could use unleaded gasoline and was equipped with the General Motors exhaust pipe catalytic converter to reduce engine exhaust emissions into the atmosphere.

LAMBORGHINI COUNTACH In 1975 this product of the outstanding Italian firm of Automobili Ferrucio Lamborghini was the fastest production car in the world with a speed well over the 185-mph. mark! The appearance alone suggested speed even when the car was at rest. The Countach had a tubular space frame chassis and a Bertone-designed aluminum body. Suspension was independent at all four wheels, using double transverse A-arms with coil springs, shock absorbers, and double anti-roll bars. Dry weight was 2,343 pounds. Tires were low profile on magnesium wheels. The engine was longitudinally located behind the two bucket seats with the transmission located between them, yet the rear wheels drove via a shaft that ran back through the engine sump. The Lamborghini engine was a vee twelve-cylinder type of 3,929-cc displacement with a bore and stroke of 82 mm. and 62 mm., developing 375 hp. Six carburetors were fitted as was an electric fuel pump. The radiators were in the engine compartment and cooled by the N.A.S.A. flush-type ducts in each side of the body and door. An electric fan supplemented cooling during low speed. Price of the Lamborghini Countach in 1975 was $42,500.

FORD F-150 PICKUP/CAMPER Pickup trucks as well as campers were ever increasing in popularity. This F-150 half-ton pickup was introduced in 1975 and had a load rating of 2,275 pounds on a 133-inch wheelbase. An inline six-cylinder engine of 300-cubic-inch displacement was installed. Solid state ignition was fitted. The gross vehicle weight was almost 6,000 pounds. It became extremely popular to fit on the cargo area a camper module which had sleeping, cooking, storage, and heating facilities for up to four adults. This module was removable to enable the cargo area to be used for its original purpose. The camper model is shown.

BMW 530i   The BMW 530i appearance was not that of a sports car but rather that of a sedate sedan. Introduced in 1975 by the Bavarian Motor Works, it replaced the earlier BMW Bavaria. The 530i was a luxury sedan priced at $9,200, with the handling qualities of a sports/G.T. The car seated five, weighed 3,630 pounds on a 104-inch wheelbase, and had a 190-inch overall length. A six-cylinder, inline, overhead-valve engine of 182 cubic inches, fitted with electronic fuel injection, drove the car at speeds up to 120 mph. A four-speed manual transmission was standard. Both front and rear suspension included coil springs, tube shocks, anti-roll bars, and trailing arms. The car could reach 60 mph. in 10 seconds from a standing start, and could speed through a 700-foot slalom at 52 mph! The exhaust emission control equipment included: exhaust gas recirculation, and thermal reactor and air injection because the company rejected the use of a catalytic converter type.

NISSAN (DATSUN) CEDRIC/GLORIA   Despite the fact that the United States is a lucrative Japanese car market, the 1975 Cedric and Gloria series made by Nissan Motor Company (Datsun) were not exported to the United States. The cars were large and luxurious and made in sedan, two- and four-door hardtop, and station wagon models. A new emission control system was fitted, combining engine modifications and the use of a catalytic converter. Power was a six-cylinder engine of either 2,000-cc or 2,800-cc displacement. The 1975 2,800-cc Gloria is shown.

SUPER VEE RACER For many years, racing car enthusiasts were forced to satisfy their interests with reading about racing and attending only the big professional races. But in 1975 the enthusiasts could buy a smaller version of the big racers and enter amateur races sponsored by the Sports Car Club of America and similar organizations. Three popular amateur Formula classes were available: Formula Vee Racer with a 1,200-cc Volkswagen engine, Formula F Racer with a 1,600-cc Cortina engine, and the Formula Super Vee with a 1,600-cc Volkswagen engine. These were gentlemen's Formula race cars and not to be confused with stock cars or road dragsters. They were not permitted to drive on public roads and had to be taken by trailer to the race courses. The amateur Formula cars could attain speeds of over 150 mph. in the straightaway and had such stability that they could carry through the esses and hairpin turns at speeds that nearly equaled the professional racers. The Formula Super Vee Racer shown here is a Lola T 340.

OLDSMOBILE TORONADO The principal modifications to the 1975 Oldsmobile Toronado were styling changes. The car had a front-engine, front-wheel drive which operated via a wide chain belt. Automatic transmission was standard. Front-wheel drive had traction advantages in mud and snow, as well as ease in taking curves. The 1975 Toronado was 228 inches long on a 122-inch wheelbase. Curb weight was 4,787 pounds. The power was a V-8, 215-hp. at 3,600 rpm., 455-cubic-inch-displacement engine. A four-barrel carburetor was fitted, and an exhaust catalytic converter reduced the exhaust pollution.

CADILLAC SEVILLE Even the Cadillac Motor Car Division of G.M. produced, in 1975, a restyled and resized version to compete with the "European-size" imported luxury automobile that had been biting into U.S. luxury car sales. With a wheelbase of 114.3 inches, overall length of 204 inches, width of 71.8 inches, height of 54.7 inches, and a weight of 4,340 pounds, the Seville was 27 inches shorter, 8 inches narrower, nearly 1,000 pounds lighter, and virtually identical in height to the conventional full-size 1975 Cadillac but otherwise very close to the Mercedes-Benz sedan. The Seville had a dignified, classic appearance. Power was by a V-8, 350-cubic-inch-displacement engine that featured electronic fuel injection designed to eliminate stalling and surging whether the engine was hot or cold. The standard 80-ampere generator more than compensated for the two electric fuel pumps, and the new design battery never needed water replenishment. Interior luxury items included a quartz digital clock, automatic climate control, an A.M./F.M. signal-seeking radio, and numerous courtesy and reading lights.

ALFA-ROMEO ALFETTA The Italian firm of Alfa-Romeo, long remembered for their racing and super sports cars, introduced this Alfetta four-door sports sedan in 1975. It was powered with a four-cylinder, water-cooled, fuel-injected, aluminum engine. Five-speed manual transmission was standard as were four-wheel disc brakes. The car was, in effect, a sports car with sedan coachwork. The price was over $6,000, and a sportier G.T. model was over $8,000.

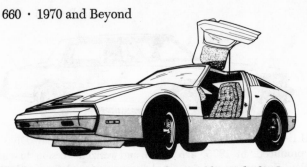

BRICKLIN SAFETY VEHICLE   The Bricklin Vehicle Corporation, Scottsdale, Arizona, made the only production safety vehicle in 1975. The two-seater was styled like an imported sports type and contained the following safety features: an energy-absorbing bumper system that absorbed impacts 200 percent more than required by the U.S. government, a fuel tank shielded on five sides by steel plate, a steel roll-over cage surrounding the passenger compartment, a deeply padded instrument panel, and weight distribution and aerodynamic shape designed for ease of control at any speed! The body was made from space-age acrylics reinforced by fiberglass, which made it stronger than steel or ordinary fiberglass. The acrylic was the car color, and scratches could merely be buffed out. The car never needed painting because of this and the fact that the body could not rust. The doors were gull-wing and required only 12 inches at the side of the car to open. They opened and locked closed automatically. The Bricklin had a 96-inch wheelbase and was 179 inches overall. Power was a V-8 Ford 351W engine of 351-cubic-inch displacement developing 175 hp. at 3,800 rpm. The curb weight was 3,470 pounds. Some insurance companies offered Bricklin owners a 20 percent discount on premiums!

PORSCHE TURBO CARRERA   This was the fastest production car in the U.S., and maybe in the world, for 1976. The vehicle was designed as the ultimate G.T. car, and price was in the $26,000 range. The turbocharged, air-cooled, rear-mounted engine displaced 2,993 cc and developed 234 hp. at 5,500 rpm. Fuel injection was featured. In basic appearance the car resembled the 911 except for the whale tail spoiler to prevent oversteering at high speeds. Interior appointments were very luxurious.

PORSCHE 924 Germany's Porsche abandoned their long-used air-cooled, rear engine concept in 1976 by introducing a front-located, water-cooled engine in the 924. The powerplant was an inline, four-cylinder, fuel-injected, 121-cubic-inch-displacement, single-overhead-camshaft engine developing 125 hp. at 5,800 rpm. The wheelbase was 94.5 inches, front track 55.9 inches, and rear track 53.9 inches. Overall length was 170 inches, and width was 66.3 inches. The car was developed because the price of the 911 became prohibitive, and the 914 lost sales in Europe. The 2,480-pound, rear-wheel-drive, two-plus-two G.T. could reach 60 mph. in 11.5 seconds.

RENAULT 5 The French Renault 5GTL was one of the biggest-selling cars in Europe and in 1976 was revised for the U.S. market. This four-seater featured a unitized body/chassis monocoque structure with independent front suspension. The wheelbase was 95.2 inches with an overall length of 141.5 inches. Width was 60 inches, and weight was 1,819 pounds. The four-cylinder, inline, slanted, water-cooled, transverse engine displaced 78.66 cubic inches and developed 58 hp. at 6,000 rpm. Front-wheel drive was featured as were the Michelin belted radial tires. Top speed was 87 mph. on regular fuel, and 40 miles per gallon could be expected on highway travel.

JAGUAR XJ-S In direct contrast to their discontinued XK series, the 1976 British Jaguar XJ-S was intended to be the quietest, most comfortable and luxurious high-performance car on the market. The four-seater was powered with a twelve-cylinder, vee-type, single-overhead-camshaft, water-cooled, fuel-injected engine of 326 cubic inches that produced 244 hp. at 5,250 rpm. The 4,190-pound auto had a 102-inch wheelbase and was 191.7 inches long. Width was 70.6 inches and height only 49.7 inches. The car could go from zero to 60 mph. in 8.6 seconds. Automatic transmission was standard. Price was about $19,000.

CHEVETTE Chevrolet introduced the Chevette four-passenger subcompact car in 1976 and claimed it was "international in design" because it copied and improved upon the best features of imported subcompacts. The car had a 94.3-inch wheelbase and was 158.7 inches long. Width was 61.8 inches, tread 51.2 inches, and weight was 1,998 pounds. Power was a four-cylinder, overhead-cam, water-cooled, 1.4-liter-displacement, inline engine. Aluminum pistons were used. Either four-speed manual or automatic transmission was offered. The hatchback is shown here, but a sportier two-seater Scooter was also available. Exceptional care had been given to anti-corrosion such as: galvanizing, enameling, spray-coating, zinc priming, etc. The turning circle was very small, and the car was rated at 40 miles per gallon on the highway.

LANCIA BETA   This Italian luxury compact car of 1976, featuring a four-wheel independent suspension and unitized or monocoque construction, was pioneered by Vincenzo Lancia a half-century ago. The passenger compartment also featured controlled crushability of front and rear bodywork sections. The wheelbase was 100 inches and front track 55.35 inches with a rear track of 54.8 inches. Power was a four-cylinder, inline, transversely mounted, tilted to the rear, water-cooled, two-barrel-carburetor engine with a displacement of 107.13 cubic inches. A fully synchronized five-speed manual transmission was standard. Drive was via the front wheels. Four-wheel disc brakes were fitted. Weight was 2,640 pounds.

GYRON TWO-WHEELER   This delta-shaped car of the future is based on ideas from the engineering and styling sections of the Ford Motor Company design team. The car has four wheels, two large wheels arranged bicycle fashion and two smaller wheels which serve as outriggers when the car slows or stops. In operation the two small wheels retract and a gyroscope stabilizes the car in such a manner that the car can be operated from either of its two contoured seats. A steering dial takes the place of the conventional wheel. A two-wheeler has advantages over the conventional four-wheeler: the ease of turning and less expenditure of effort from the engine. We may see two-wheelers before we expect them.

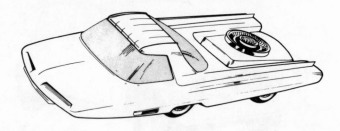

NUCLEON   Many automotive designers are preparing for the day when nuclear reactors will be reduced considerably in weight and bulk. This advanced nuclear-powered design by Ford Motor Company engineers is ready for that day. The power capsule would contain a radioactive core and would include the drive train utilizing an electronic torque converter. The Nucleon should be able to travel at least 5,000 miles between rechargings of the atomic fuel.

SEATTLE-ITE   Considerable thought is being given to the car of the future by automotive engineers and stylists all over the world. We may see these ideas materialize as a single unit or as a part of future cars. This sleek auto of the future was developed by the designers at the Ford Motor Company. The unique six-wheeler is called Seattle-ite XXI and features front-wheel drive on all four front wheels. Ford designers feel that the four driving and steering wheels will greatly improve tracking, traction, and braking efficiency. The car has a variable-density glass windshield and top, and fingertip steering.

VOLANTE FLYING CAR This Ford Motor Company car of the distant future would operate in the air as well as on the ground, but without wings! Called the Volante, the car uses the ultra-sophisticated ducted fan principle called triathodyne. The front rotors have two sets of contra-rotating blades and the two rear rotors consist of opposite-rotating multi-bladed fans. When in the air, the Volante would be controlled by a system of adjustable lateral and longitudinal vanes which would allow the car to maneuver in all directions. The system cancels out any propeller torque characteristics, and therefore no aerodynamic tail surfaces are necessary.

TOYOTA F101 FUTURE MINI-CAR This Toyota mini-car was developed for possible production in the future. The streamlining aids in increasing the mileage and reduces the size of the engine needed. Retractable headlights and an energy-absorbing front are features.

FORD FUTURE MINI-CAR With most of the auto makers beginning to "think small," many have begun to design smaller cars for the future. Ford designers developed this test car for possible production in the future. It would be either a two-seater subcompact or a mini-car intended for urban driving. The car is mid-engine powered with a droop snoot for streamlining. Maybe we will see it in showrooms soon.

Automobile Museums of the World

THIS LISTING of worldwide museums, which includes interesting and historic automotive exhibits, has been compiled from the best information available at the time of printing. It must be remembered that many vehicles are not the property of the museum but belong to private collectors and therefore are frequently moved from museum to museum. In fact, even museum-owned vehicles are often sold or exchanged. It is suggested that before the reader travels many miles to a museum, he or she should telephone or write the establishment to learn the visiting hours, the days of the week, and the months of the year that the museum is open. Many are closed for short unseasonal periods. A list of the cars presently on exhibition can also be requested. The vast majority of auto museums have photographs and/or postcards of each car for sale. It is also a good idea to check before the trip to learn if cameras are allowed in each museum.

UNITED STATES OF AMERICA

Arkansas

The Museum of Automobiles, Petit Jean Mountain, Morrilton. (Includes 1899 Winton, 1901 De Dion Bouton, Panhard-Levassor, Duryea 1903 Cadillac, 1906 Buick, 1907 Stanley Steamer, Rolls-Royce Silver Ghost, Cretor Popcorn Wagon, and many, many more interesting cars.)

California

Briggs Cunningham Automotive Museum, 250 E. Baker Street, Costa Mesa. (Includes Rauch and Lang, Mercer, American, Duesenberg, Peugeot Grand Prix Racer, Mercedes-Benz SSK, Talbot, Lago Grand Prix Racer, and many more.)

Cars from the Stars' Museum, 6920 Orangethorpe Avenue, Buena Park. (Includes Al Jolson's Mercedes, $35,000 Volkswagen, Quarter-Million-Dollar Maybach, "Ironsides" Ford Police Wagon, Dr. Porsche's Hanomag, Norma Talmadge's Rolls-Royce, General Dwight D. Eisenhower's 1942 Buick, and many more.)

Museum of Natural History Los Angeles County, Exposition Park, 900 Exposition Boulevard, Los Angeles. (Includes Baker Electric, Chalmers-Detroit, Franklin, Little Roadster, M.G.-TC, Welch, Woods, Pierce Great-Arrow, and many more.)

Colorado

Buckskin Joe's Antique Museum, Fremont County Road-3A, Canon City.

Colorado Car Museum, 1377 Manitou Avenue, Highway 24, Manitou Springs. (Includes John F. Kennedy's Lincoln Continental, Count Ciano's Lancia, Queen Elizabeth's Daimler, 1914 Hupmobile, 1909 Maxwell, and many more.)

Forney Transportation Museum, 1416 Platte Street, near jct. Valley Highway and Speer Boulevard, Denver. (Includes Amelia Earhart's Gold Bug Kissel, Prince Aly Khan's Rolls-Royce, Teddy Roosevelt's 25-foot W.B. Hispano-Suiza, and many others.)

Ray Dougherty Car Collection (south of Longmont), R2 Box 253A, Longmont. (Includes International Auto Buggy, REO, 1908 Waverley Electric, Mobile Steamer, Fuller, Lozier, Case 40, E.M.F. Touring, Metz, and many more. Shown by appointment only.)

Veteran Car Museum, 2030 South Cherokee, Denver. (Includes great collection of interesting vehicles.)

Delaware

The Magic Age of Steam, Route 82, Yorklyn. (Includes White, Doble, Toledo, many Stanley Steam cars and rides on a Stanley Steamer Mountain Wagon.)

District of Columbia

Vehicle Hall, Smithsonian Institution National Museum of History and Technology, Constitution Avenue, between 14th and 12th, N.W., Washington, D.C. (Includes Roper, Selden, Long, Duryea, Winton, Cleveland, Sears, Pierce, Autocar, Kelsey & Tilney, and many, many more.)

Florida

Bellm's Cars and Music of Yesterday, 5500 N. Tamiami Trail (U.S. 41), Sarasota. (Includes Mercer, Pierce-Arrow, Packard, Model T, Model A Ford, Tucker, Indianapolis racers, and over one hundred more.)

Elliott Museum, Hutchinson Island, Martin County (four miles east of Stuart). (Includes Pierce Stanhope, Stutz Special Bearcat, Lincoln Brunn Body Town Car, Empire Speedster, Hupmobile, 1902 Cadillac, and others.)

Museum of Speed, Route U.S. 1, South Daytona. (Includes Malcolm Campbell's Bluebird, dragster champion, stock car racers, motorcycle speed record holder, famous Osiecki Mad Dog Racer, The Green Monster, and many, many more.)

Silver Springs Early American Museum, on Florida 40, Silver Springs. (Antique and classic cars and carriages.)

Illinois

Chicago Historical Antique Auto Museum, 3200 Skokie Valley Road, Highland Park. (Includes Cord Phaeton, Mercedes 300 SL Gullwing, Auburn Convertible Sedan, Duesenberg, and many others.)

Museum of Science and Industry, East 57th Street and South Lake Shore Drive (in Jackson Park), Chicago. (Includes 1896 Benz, Bernardi, Simplex, Duesenberg, Stevens-Duryea, and many more.)

Time Was Village Museum, 1325 Burlington Street, 4 miles south on U.S. 51, Mendota. (Includes Roamer Sports Touring, 1910 Locomobile, Stanley Steamer, Packard, and others.)

Indiana

Goodwin Museum, 200 South Main Street, Frankfort. (Includes 1901 Frisbie, 1904 Gatts, Stutz Bulldog, Grand Prix Bugatti, and others.)

Indianapolis Motor Speedway and Museum, 4790 W. 16th Street, 6 miles N.W., Speedway. (Features famous racing cars, including eleven Indy-500 winners, among which are the 1914 Delage, Miller Special, Belanger Special, Belond Special and more, plus 1903 Premier Racer, 1912 Fiat Racer, Cooper Climax, and many more.)

Kansas

King's Antique Car Museum, P.O. Box 522, Hesston. (Includes 1902 Holsman, Overland Touring, Stanley Steamer, 1926 Rolls-Royce, and many more cars and trucks.)

Kansas State Historical Society, Memorial Building, 120 West 10th at Jackson Street, Topeka. (Includes Great Smith and others.)

Kentucky

Calvert Auto Museum, P.O. Box 245, Calvert City. (Includes Cord Phaeton, 1914 Ford Touring, Baby Overland Touring, and others.)

Maine

Boothbay Railway Museum, P.O. Box 123, 1 mile north of Boothbay Center on Me. 27, Boothbay. (Includes 1911 Ford and a score more.)

Seal Cove Automobile Museum, Seal Cove, Mount Desert Island.

Maryland

Fire Museum of Maryland, 1301 York Road, Lutherville. (Includes considerable fire-fighting memorabilia plus 1906 Christie Tractor with La France Steamer, Ahrens-Fox Pumper, Mack Pumper, and others.)

U.S. Army Ordnance Museum, c/o U.S. Army Ordnance School, Aberdeen Proving Ground, Aberdeen Boulevard, Aberdeen. (Includes mostly tanks and guns but has Pershing's Locomobile and Patton's Dodge cars.)

Massachusetts

Edaville Railroad and Museum, P.O. Box 7, 3 miles west off Mass. 58, South Carver. (Includes Detroit Electric, Oakland, LaSalle Lancia, and others.)

Heritage Plantation of Sandwich, P.O. Box 566, Grove and Pine Streets, Sandwich. (Includes Duesenberg J, Knox, Mercer, Packard Victoria, and others.)

Museum of Transportation, Larz Anderson Park, 15 Newton Street, Brookline. (Includes Grand Prix Ferrari, Pierce Motorette, Stutz Bearcat, Ford Model K, plus state cars of Franklin Delano Roosevelt, Adolf Hitler, and many others.)

Sturbridge Auto Museum, Old Sturbridge Village, 2 miles west on U.S. 20, Sturbridge. (Includes steam, gas, and electric cars from 1897 to 1939.)

Michigan

Detroit Historical Museum, 5401 Woodward Avenue at Kirby, Detroit. (Includes Scripps Booth Cycle Car, 1909 Buick, Bi-Auto-Go, Stout Scarab, Chrysler Turbine Car, plus others.)

Gilmore Car Museum, 5272 Sheffield Road, Hickory Corners. (Includes Lozier, Pierce-Arrow, Stevens-Duryea, White Steamer, Bugatti, Daimler, and others.)

Greenfield Village and Henry Ford Museum, ½ mile south of U.S. 12 between Southfield Road and Oakwood Boulevard, Dearborn. (Includes historic Ford vehicles and 1888 Benz Velociped, Duryea Trap, Edison Electric, Riker Truck, Sears Motor Buggy, and many more.)

Poll Museum, U.S. 31 and New Holland Street, 5 miles north on U.S. 31, Holland. (Classic and antique autos plus fire trucks, including President William H. Taft's White Steamer.)

Minnesota

Hemp Old Vehicle Museum, P.O. Box 851, Hemp Farm on Country Club Road, Highway 34, Rochester. (Includes Detroit Electric, 1908 Sears, 1908 Brush, 1905 Ford, and others.)

Missouri

Autos of Yesteryear Museum, Highway 63 North at jct. 1–44, Rolla. (Includes Franklin, Kissel White Eagle, Stanley Steamer, and others.)

Kelsey's Antique Cars, Highway 54, P.O. Box 564, Camdenton. (Includes 1899 Mobile, 1906 Stanley Steamer, 1909 Velie, Auburn Boat-tail Speedster, and others.)

National Museum of Transport, 3015 Barrett Station Road (at Dougherty Ferry Road near Kirkwood), St. Louis. (Includes vast collection of autos, buses, and railroad items.)

Montana

Montana Historical Museum, Veterans-Pioneers Memorial Bldg., 225 N. Roberts Street, Helena. (Collection of Ford automobiles from the 1903 to 1930 era.)

Nebraska

Harold Warp Pioneer Village, Minden (on U.S. 6, 34, 12 miles south of Route 80, Minden exit). (Very large and interesting collection of antique and classic cars, including Milwaukee Steamer, 1898 Duryea, Mobile Steamer, 1902 Cadillac, 1907 Regal, etc.)

Sawyer's Sandhills Museum, 440 Valentine Street (on U.S. 20), Valentine. (Includes Austro-Daimler, Flanders, and others.)

Stuhr Museum of the Prairie Pioneer Auto Collection, U.S. 281–34 Junction, Grand Island. (Includes Hupmobile, Maxwell, Pullman, 1909 Model T, and others.)

Nevada

Harrah's Automobile Collection, 3½ miles east on 2nd Street, Reno. (Includes Mercedes-Benz SSK, Crane Simplex, Lozier, Marmon, Doble, Pope-Hartford, Frayer-Miller, and over 1,000 more, plus airplanes and boats.)

New Hampshire

Meredith Auto Museum, Route 3, Meredith. (Includes Orient Buckboard, Baker Electric, Stutz, Pathfinder, and others.)

New Jersey

Roaring 20 Autos, Inc., R.D. 1, Box 178-G, State Highway 34 and Ridgewood Road, Wall (1 mile south of Garden State Parkway, exit 96). (Includes U.S.-built cars from 1910, mostly in the late 1920s and early 1930s.)

New York

Golden Age Auto Museum, W. Grand Street, 1 mile north on N.Y. 5– Palatine Bridge, Canajoharie.

Resnick Motor Museum, 46 Canal Street, Ellenville. (Includes 1888 De Dion Bouton, Mercedes Racer, 1905 Rolls-Royce, Minerva, and others.)

Long Island Automotive Museum, Route 27 (1 mile N.W. on N.Y. 27), Southampton. (Includes Ferrari Corsa Spyder, Simplex Speed Car, Type 35 Bugatti, Mercer Runabout, White Opera Coupé, Autocar Rear-Entrance Tonneau, Isotta Fraschini Roadster, Léon Bollée Tricar, and many, many more historic vehicles.)

Old Rhinebeck Aerodrome Museum, P.O. Box 57 (3 miles N.E. via U.S. 9, on Stone Church Road), Rhinebeck. (Includes Maxwell Truck, Scripps Booth, Sears Auto Buggy, 1909 Renault and others, plus World War I airplanes in flying condition.)

North Carolina

Estes-Winn Memorial Antique Automobile Museum, Grovewood Road (near Innsbrook Road, 2 miles N.E.), Asheville (near Biltmore Homespun Shop and Grove Park Inn). Includes LaSalle Phaeton, Maxwell, 1906 Cadillac, and more.)

North Dakota

Beck's Great Plains Museum, P.O. Box 3, St. Anthony Route, Mandan (on North Dakota Highway 1806 between Mandan and Ft. Lincoln State Park). (Includes 1914 Model T Ford Speedster, Seagrave Fire Truck, 1916 Dodge Touring, Model A Ford, plus others.)

Ohio

Allen County Museum, 620 West Market Street, Lima. (Includes Milburn, LaSalle Hearse, Ahrens-Fox Fire Engine, and others.)

Frederick C. Crawford Auto-Aviation Museum, 10825 East Boulevard (at University Circle), Cleveland. (Includes White Steamer, Elmore, Peerless, Mercedes, Thomas Flyer, 1906 Cadillac, and many more interesting automobiles plus airplanes.)

Oklahoma

Antiques Inc., Car Museum, P.O. Box 1887, Muskogee. (Includes Duesenberg Model J, Isotta Fraschini, Mercedes-Benz 540K, Rolls-Royce Silver Ghost, and more.)

Pennsylvania

Automobilorama, P.O. Box 1855, Mechanicsburg, U.S. Route 15 at Gettysburg exit of Pennsylvania Turnpike. (Includes Malden Steamer, Dolson, Peerless, Knox, Mercer, Thomas Flyer, Maxwell, Zimmerman, Wisconsin Racer, and many others.)

Boyertown Museum of Historic Vehicles, P.O. Box 30, Boyertown at Rtes. 73 and 100, Warwick. (Includes SGV, Duryea, Dile Sport and others, plus fire pumpers, etc.)

Magee Transportation Museum, P.O. Box 150, Bloomsburg. (Includes Paige, Thomas Flyer, 1903 Orient, Duesenburg Victoria Convertible, and others.)

Swigart Museum Antique Autos, Route 22 East (in Museum Park), Huntingdon. (Includes 1910 Packard, Scripps Booth, Black, Grant, Du Pont, and others.)

South Carolina

Joe Weatherly Stock Car Museum, Darlington Raceway (3 miles west on S.C. 34), Darlington. (Includes the largest collection of stock racing cars in the world.)

South Dakota

Horseless Carriage Museum, U.S. 16 (10 miles south of Rapid City). (Includes Stutz, 1918 Chevrolet, three- and five-wheeled cars, Russian auto, and others.)

Pioneer Auto Museum, U.S. Highways 16 and 83, Murdo. (Includes Fuller, Argo, Jewel, Sears-Roebuck, Velie, 1902 Olds, Cunningham, Marmon, and many others.)

Tennessee

Cox's Car Museum, P.O. Box 253 (on Parkway), Gatlinburg. (Includes 1903 Ford, Jordan, 1912 Cadillac, and others.)

Old Car Museum, Dixie Gun Works, Inc., Highway 51 South, Union City. (Includes Waverley Electric, Pierce-Arrow, Packard, and others.)

Smoky Mountain Car Museum, Highway 441, Pigeon Forge. (Includes Brush, Hupmobile, Marathon, Overland, Cord, and others.)

Texas

Classic Car Showcase, Greenway Plaza, Houston. (Includes many classic automobile, such as Delage, Isotta Fraschini, Duesenberg, etc.)

Pate Museum of Transportation, Highway 377 (just north of Cresson), P.O. Box 711, Fort Worth. (Includes Premier, American La France Fire Truck, Paige, Alvis, Schacht, Franklin, and others.)

Witte Confluence Museum, HemisFair Plaza, San Antonio. (Includes Moon, Stutz, Auburn, Horch, Woods, Columbia, and others.)

Virginia

Car and Carriage Caravan, Luray Caverns. (Includes Metz, Westcott, Franklin, Packard, Stanley Steamer, Morgan Super Sports, and others.)

FOREIGN COUNTRIES

Argentina

Museo Automovil Club Argentino, Lujan. (Includes Holsman, Daimler, Schacht, 1908 Fiat, 1904 Cadillac, 1904 Panhard-Levassor, and many more.)

Australia

Bronks Motor Museum and Book Shop, 17 Military Road, Watson's Bay, New South Wales. (Includes Holsman, De Dion Bouton, Bedelia, Talbot Darracq, Kubelwagen, and many more.)

Gilltraps Auto Museum, Collangatta, Queensland. (Includes Albion, Panhard-Levassor, Russell, Clément-Bayard, Daimler, Unic, and many more.)

Lakes Entrance Antique Car and Folk Museum, 20–24 Princes Highway, Lakes Entrance, Victoria. (Includes Opel Tourer, Minerva, Morris Cowley, and motorcycles.)

Science Museum of Victoria, 304-328 Swanston Street, Melbourne, Victoria.

Austria

Heeresgeschichtliches Museum, The Arsenal, Vienna. (Sarajevo assassination Gräf & Stift is only car.)

Technisches Museum Für Industrie Und Gewerbe, Mariahilfer Strasse 212, Vienna. (Markus, Benz, Daimler, Serpollet, and more.)

Belgium

Mahy Collection, St. Pietersnieuwstraat 11, Ghent. (Includes one of the finest collections of antique and classic cars.)

Provinciaal Automobielmuseum Houthalen, Domaine de Kelchterhoef, Houthalen, Limbourg. (Includes Vivinus, De Dion Bouton, Imperia, Fondu, Nagant, Renault, Panhard, Lanz, Horch, Wanderer, Bimbo, Dennis, and hundreds more.)

Brazil

Museu Paulista de Antiguidades Mecanicas, Cacapava, São Paulo. (Includes Hispano-Suiza Alfonso XIII, Alfa-Romeo, Rolls-Royce, and others.)

Canada

Canadian Automotive Museum, 99 Simcoe Street South, Oshawa, Ontario. (Includes 1898 Redpath, Oakland, Durant, Gray-Dart, Star, and more.)

Cars of Yesterday Museum, Trans-Canada Highway, St. Jacques, New Brunswick.

Classic Car Museum, 813 Douglas Street, Victoria, British Columbia. (Includes classic cars used by famous personalities: Lincoln Limousine, Royal Tour Packard, Clark Gable's 1941 Packard, and others.)

Gateway Gallery of Antiques, Box 12, Amherst, Nova Scotia. (Includes Metz, Brush, Orient, and others.)

Jean-Marie Paradis Auto Museum, St. Augustin, Portneuf, Quebec. (Includes Franklin, American Austin, Autocar, and others.)

The Manitoba Automobile Museum, Elkhorn, Manitoba. (Includes McLaughlin, Flanders, Russell-Knight, E.M.F., Case, Briscoe, Overland, Saxon, and many others.)

North Battleford Western Development Museum, Box 183, North Battleford, Saskatchewan. (Includes Jewett, Franklin, Avery Truck, and others.)

The Prairie Pioneer Village & Museum, Highway No. 2, Moose Jaw, Saskatchewan. (Includes Model T, Maxwell, and others.)

Spokewheel Car Museum, Route 2 East, Dunstaffnage, Prince Edward Island. (Includes Durant, Model T, Essex, REO, and others.)

Western Canadian Pioneer Museum, Highway 2A, Wetaskiwin, Alberta. (Includes Menard, Locomobile, Maxwell, Innes, Tudhope McIntyre, Cord, Winton, and hundreds more.)

Yorkton Western Development Museum, Yorkton, Saskatchewan. (Includes Maxwell, E.M.F., Flanders, Essex, Henny, and others.)

Czechoslovakia

Národní Technické Muzeum V Praze, Kostelni 42, Prague. (Includes Decauville, De Dion Bouton, Koprivnice, Laurin & Klement, Renault, Bugatti, and others.)

Tatra Technical Museum, Koprivnice. (Includes cars and trucks from 1901 Nesselsdorf to 1950 Tatra Racer.)

Denmark

Danmarks Tekniske Museum, Ole Romers Vej, Helsingør. (Includes Christiansen, Swift, Delaunay Belleville, Humber, Austin 7, Hammelvognen, and others.)

Egeskovmuseet, Egeskov near Odense. (Includes 1905 Renault, Wanderer, Mack Truck, Rovin, and more.)

Jysk Automobilmuseum, Gjern. (Includes Vivinus, Adler, Fiat Torpedo, Swallow, Auburn, Oakland, and others.)

The Raben Car Collection at Aalholm Castle, Nysted. (Includes La-Croix de Laville, Unic, Delahaye, Brasier, Berliet, Lorraine Dietrich, Hispano-Suiza, Holsman, Benz, Lancia Lambda, Lagonda, and many others.)

Trafik-Historisk-Museum, Petershvile near Helsingør. (Includes 1907 Cyclonette, Cord, Type 40 Bugatti, and others.)

England

Birmingham Museum of Science and Industry, Newhall Street, Birmingham, Warwickshire. (Includes Singer, Bean, Star Benz, Wolseley, BSA, and others.)

Caister Castle Motor Museum, Caister Castle, Norfolk.

Cheddar Motor Museum, The Cliffs, Cheddar, Somerset. (Includes Swift Cycle Car, White Steamer, Aston Martin, Lutzmann, Garrard-Speke, plus others and motorcycles.)

City Museum Bristol, Queen's Road, Bristol. (Includes Grenville Steam Carriage, Daimler, Bristol Tourer, and others.)

Manx Motor Museum, Crosby, Isle of Man. (Includes Sunbeam-Mabley, Napier, Daimler, Lancia Lambda, Leyland Fire Engine, and others.)

Montagu Motor Museum, Palace House, Beaulieu, Hampshire. (Includes Rolls-Royce Silver Ghost, Alfa-Romeo, Alldays, Auburn, Bentley, Austro-Daimler, Burrel, Cannstadt-Daimler, Georges-Richard, Jowett, Talbot Phoenix, and hundreds more.)

Murray's Veteran & Vintage Motor Cycle Museum, Bungalow Corner, Isle of Man. (Includes Kerry, Minerva, Coventry Eagle, Triumph, Douglas, Indian, O.K. Bradshaw, Velocette KSS, Sunbeam, and many other motorcycles.)

Science Museum, South Kensington, London. (Includes Serpollet Steam Carriage, Parkyns-Batman Steam Tricycle and many other models.)

The Shuttleworth Collection, The Aerodrome, Old Warden, Biggleswade, Bedfordshire. (Includes Arrol-Johnston, Locomobile, Baby Peugeot, DeDietrich, Crossley, Morris Oxford, and others.)

Transport Museum, High Street, Kingston-upon-Hull, Yorkshire. (Includes Bollée Tricar, Gardner-Serpollet Steamer, and others.)

France

Conservatoire National des Arts et Métiers, 292 rue Saint-Martin, Paris.

Musée Automobile de Lourdes, Esplanade du Paradis, Lourdes. (Includes 1882 DeMontais Steamer, Turcat-Mery, 1929 Record Panhard, Le Mans Simca-Gordini, and others.)

Musée Berliet-Automobiles M. Berliet, Vénissieux, Rhône. (Most complete collection of Berliet cars from 1894 to 1959.)

Musée d'Automobiles de Normandie, Clères, Normandy. (Includes Bolide, Goessant, Grégoire, and others.)

Musée d'Automobiles du Forez, 42 Sury-le-Comtal, Loire. (Includes Delahaye, Lagonda, Germain, Délage, Amilcar, Salmson, Hotchkiss, Mase Torpedo, and many more historic cars.)

Musée de Briare, RN7, Briare, Loiret. (Includes Rochet-Schneider, Sphinx, Panhard-Levassor, and others.)

Musée de l'Abbatiale, LeBec-Hellouin 27, Eure, Normandy. (Includes Simca-Gordini, Délage, De Dion Tricar, Amilcar Compound, and others.)

Musée de l'Automobile du Mans, Circuit Permanent de la Sarthe, Le Mans, Sarthe. (Includes 1888 Benz, 1899 Renault, Delaugère-Clayette, Francon, Alma Six, and many, many more.)

Musée des Techniques, 292 Rue Saint-Martin, Paris.

Musée Française de l'Automobile, Château de Rochetaillée-sur-Saône, Rhône. (Includes Hitler's Mercedes 770, Brasier, Ferrari Racer, Lancia Astura, Rolland Pilain Racer, Le Aebre, Bugatti Racer, Voisin, and many more interesting cars.)

Musée National de la Voiture et du Tourisme, Château de Compiègne, Oise. (Includes Amédée Bollée La Mancelle, Léon Bollée Tricycle, Jenatzy's "La Jamais Contente," Panhard Voiture, De Dion Dog Cart, and many other historic vehicles.)

Musée Renault des Champs-Elysées, 53 Avenue des Champs-Elysées, Paris. (Includes a beautiful collection of historic Renault automobiles from 1898 through 1966 including old and new racers.)

Muséon di Rodo, 3 Bis Route de Nîmes, Uzès, Gard. (Includes 1904 Le Métais, Amilcar, 1897 Peugeot, De Dion Bouton, and more.)

German Democratic Republic

Verkehrsmuseum, Augustusstrasse 1, Dresden. (Includes Benz three-wheeler, Mercedes Knight, Wanderer, AWE Racer, and others.)
Zweitakt-Motorrad-Museum, Augustusburg/Erzgebirge. (All two-cycle motorcycles including 1894 Hildebrand und Wolfmuller, Golem, DKW, Stock, Puch und Zundapp, BMW, and more.)

German Federal Republic

Auto museum L. L. Hillers, Tremsbuttel bei Bargteheide. (Includes Piccolo, Hanomag, Colibri, Wanderer, Adler, NSU, and more.)
Automuseum Nettelstedt, Nettelstedt, über Lübeck. (Includes Maybach W5, Benz Comfortable, Renault Cl, Dürkopp, Daimler Phoenix, De Dion, Wanderer, Veritas, Talbot, Simson Supra, Alvis, and many more.)
Daimler-Benz Aktiengesellschaft, Stuttgart-Untertürkheim. (Collection of Daimler, Benz, and Mercedes.)
Deutsches Museum von Meisterwerken der Naturwissenschaft und Technik, Museumsinsel 1, Munich. (Includes first Benz Auto [1886], Daimler Stahlradwagen, Lohner Porsche, Léon Bollée Trike, Mors Kettenwagen, Piccolo, Rumpler, and many more.)

Holland

Het National Automobielmuseum, Veursestraatweg 280, Leidschendam. (Includes A.C. Racer, Austin Taxi, Rikkers, Franklin, Grégoire, Hedag, Holsman, Humber, Isotta Fraschini, and many others.)
Lips Automuseum, Grotestraat 63, Drunen. (Includes A.C. Sociable, Alvis, Brasier, Brush, Brennabor, Darracq, Delahaye, Durant, Jordan, Knox, Praga Piccolo, Lagonda, Messerschmitt, Minerva, Rover, and many other outstanding cars.)

Hungary

Haris Testverek Auto Müzeuma, Mòricz Zeigmond Körtér 12, Budapest. (Includes Phoenix, Raba, Martin Frigyes, Hora, Benz, and many Hungarian cars.)

Italy

Museo dell'Automobile Carlo Biscaretti di Ruffia, Corso Unita d'Italia 40, Turin. (Includes Nardi Monaco, Nibbio, Maserati, Grand Prix Italia, and others.)

Museo Nazionale della Scienza e della Tecnica, Leonardo da Vinci, Via San Vittore 21, Milan. (Includes Grand Prix Alfa-Romeo, San Giusto, Fiat Gas Turbine Car, and others.)

New Zealand

Museum of Transport and Technology, Western Springs, Auckland. (Includes International Auto Bug, Duo Cyclecar, Renault, and others.)

Yaldhurst Transport Museum, School Road, Yaldhurst, Christchurch. (Includes 1903 Milwaukee, Orient Buckboard, Daimler, Siddley-Deasy, Unic, and more.)

Northern Ireland

The Transport Museum, Witham Street, Belfast. (Contains motorcycles, fire trucks and automobiles, many of Irish origin such as the 1908 Chambers.)

Norway

Norsk Teknisk Museum, Fyrstikkalleen 1, Oslo. (Includes Bjering, Benz Phaeton, Minerva Landau, Daniels, N.S.U., and others.)

Portugal

Museu do Automóvel, Caramulo. (Includes Darracq, Abadel, Graham-Paige, Hurtu, Maserati, Hotchkiss, Pegaso, Wolseley, and others.)

Scotland

Doune Motor Museum, Doune Park, Perthshire. (Includes Nardi Danese, Riley Nine Lincock, Lagonda, Aston Martin Le Mans, and others.)

Museum of Transport, 25 Albert Drive, Glasgow. (Includes early Scottish cars such as the Albion, Argyll, Arrol-Johnston, Galloway, Beardmore, Drummond, Clyde, and many others.)

Myreton Motor Museum, near Aberlady, East Lothian. (Includes Alvis, Speed-Six, Darracq, Galloway, Lagonda, Citroën Half-Track, and many others.)

Royal Scottish Museum, Chambers Street, Edinburgh. (Includes Cugnot's Traction Engine, Murdock's Road Locomotive, Albion, Arnold-Benz, Bollée Trike, and others plus motorcycles.)

Spain

Colección de Automóviles de Salvador Claret, Sils, Gerona. (Includes Jewett, Marmon, Pegaso, Le Zèbre, Lancia, Apulia, and others.)
Musée de la Carrosserie Française, Puerto de Andraitx, Mallorca. (Includes Delage, Hispano, Renault, Panhard, and others.)

Sweden

Industrimuseet, Göteborg. (Includes 1903 Regal, 1912 Minerva, Opel, Wolseley, and others.)
Landskrona Museum, Slottsgaten, Landskrona.
Svedinos Bilmuseum, Ugglarp. (Includes Marquette, Volvo, Adler, Allard, Tatra, Morris, Horch, and others.)
Tekniska Museet, Museivägen 7, Stockholm. (Includes Scania, Norden, Helios, Milburn, Vabis, Kalmar, and many other cars and motorcycles.)

Switzerland

Musée de l'Automobile, 1392 Château de Grandson VD, Lac de Neuchâtel, Vaud. (Includes Cooper Racer, Delage, Stanley Steamer, Delahaye, Clément, De Riancy, and many others.)
Verkehrshaus der Schweiz, Lidostrasse 5, Lucerne. (Includes Popp, Weber, Adler, Martini, Berna, Pic-Pic, Austin-Seven, Dufaus, Alvis, and many others.)

Union of Soviet Socialist Republics

Polytechnical Museum, Novaya Ploshad 3-4, Moscow. (Includes 1911 Russo-Baltique, 1898 Stoewer, 1901 De Dion Bouton, and many others.)

Wales

Pembrokeshire Motor Museum, Garrison Theatre, Pembroke Dock, Pembrokeshire. (Includes Graham-Paige, A.C. Sociable, Lagonda, Benz Ideal, Alldays, Radco, and others.)

Glossary of Automotive Terminology

In an attempt to clarify any questions in the reader's mind regarding some of the terms used in this volume, a Glossary of Automotive Terminology has been prepared. It also includes automotive terms not mentioned in this book but that are a normal part of automotive jargon. Conversion factors between metric and U.S. measurements are also offered for those who are not familiar with this relationship.

A-ARM   A chassis component in competition cars that aids in suspension linkage and engine support; shaped like an "A."

ABBREVIATIONS   bhp.—brake horsepower
hp.—horsepower
kph.—kilometers per hour
mph.—miles per hour
cc—cubic centimeter
mm.—millimeter
OHC—overhead camshaft
OHV—overhead valve
rpm.—revolutions per minute
cu. in.—cubic inch

AERODYNAMICS   The study of the behavior of the airflow as it passes around a moving object and the forces exerted by the air on the object. In car design the positive and negative lift of the airflow is studied in wind tunnels. Negative lift is preferred to press the vehicle closer to the ground. Car air resistance is also studied.

AIR-COOLED ENGINE   An engine cooled directly by the flow of air moving over it rather than by an indirect radiator-water system.

AIR INTAKE   An opening at the front or side of the car designed to admit air with minimum resistance for water, brake, or oil cooling.

ANTI-ROLL BAR   A torsion bar mounted transversely at the front or

683

rear and connected to the suspension links. The effect is to limit the body roll during cornering. Can correct oversteer and understeer when properly installed.

ASSEMBLY LINE   A moving conveyor used in the manufacture of automobiles. The car is assembled as it moves from department to department where specialized workers add parts.

ATMOSPHERIC ENGINE   A very early form of steam engine in which the vacuum from condensation of the spent steam causes atmospheric pressure to drive the piston.

AUTOCROSS   A competition in which drivers must maneuver the car through a clearly marked, twisting course. Each driver's run is timed separately. Also known as slalom or gymkhana.

AUTOMATIC INLET VALVES   An early system whereby the engine inlet valves opened atmospherically when the piston returned from top dead center for the inlet stroke. Soon replaced by mechanically actuated valves.

AUTOMATIC TRANSMISSION   A transmission that shifts its own gears according to the prevailing speed, load, and road conditions. Also called automatic gearbox. Operation can be electrical or hydraulic.

AUTOMATION   A means of controlling production processes via electronic instead of human means.

AVANT TRAIN   A very early two-wheeled power unit that consisted of an engine, gearbox, steering wheel, and controls. It could be attached to the front of any powerless vehicle, such as a horse-drawn wagon or carriage, to convert it to an automobile. Not used after circa 1900.

AXLE   A spindle or rod on which a wheel revolves or which revolves with a wheel.

BALL JOINT   Replaced the front-wheel kingpin suspension/steering system in the mid-fifties. A ball joint is fixed to each end of a vertical, one-piece support arm, with the distance between the ball joints greater than the distance between the kingpin bearings, thereby reducing bearing loads and making steering easier. The ball joints are spring-loaded so they compensate automatically for any wear and produce the correct amount of friction. See Kingpin.

BATTERY   A device for storing electrical energy. Primary use is for starting internal-combustion engines. Also used for electrical devices when engine is stopped.

BEARING   A lubricated support for a revolving shaft, made of material softer than the shaft.

BELT DRIVE   A system where the final drive from gearbox to wheels is by leather or rubber belts that are contained on pulleys. Today many of the engine-driven auxiliaries use belt drive.

BERLINA   From World War I, it described a closed luxury car with small windows, which allowed the occupants to see out but to be barely seen from the outside.

BLANKING DIE   A production tool, fitted in a press, that cuts a predetermined shape from flat sheet metal like a cookie cutter.

BLOWN ENGINE   An engine that is supercharged. See Supercharger.

BODY   That portion of the vehicle that carries and/or encloses the passengers or the freight.

BOILER   A device in which water is heated and vaporized into steam for the operation of a steam engine.

BONNET   British for hood.

BOOT   British term for trunk compartment.

BORE   The diameter of a gasoline or steam reciprocating engine cylinder. The displacement can be increased by increasing the diameter (reboring).

BRAKE   An apparatus fitted to the wheels for stopping and/or holding a motor vehicle. This is done by pressing a wad of friction material against a steel drum on the wheel or by squeezing a disc on the wheel with two friction pads. Early brakes often worked on the drive shaft or gearbox.

BRAKE FADE   When brakes overheat because of constant use, they sometimes lose their effectiveness. This is brake fade.

BRAKE HORSEPOWER (bhp.)   The measure of an engine's horsepower without the loss in power caused by the gearbox, generator, differential, water pump and other auxiliaries. The actual horsepower delivered to the driving wheels is less.

BUCKET SEAT   An individual seat, usually one of a pair in front, that is severely contoured to provide lateral support and lateral restraint in cornering.

BULKHEAD   A transverse partition usually separating the engine compartment from the driver or passengers. Any transverse partition. Also called scuttle or firewall or dashboard.

BUMPER   Strong protective transverse bar at the front and rear of a vehicle and attached to the chassis. It prevents damage to the body in the event of very low-speed contact with objects. British term is fender.

BUS   A self-propelled motor vehicle designed to transport ten or more passengers. Contraction of omnibus.

C-POST   The rear or back window structural pillars that support the rear window and rear portion of a car's roof. Also called C-pillar.

CABRIOLET   An obsolete description of an auto with collapsible top (convertible) and seating two or four passengers. Also called a drophead coupé.

CALIPER   A clamp that straddles the disc and clamps onto the disc when the brakes are applied in a disc brake system.

CAM   An eccentric (off-center) lobe or projection on a rotating shaft; used to transmit a motion at a predetermined time during the rotation of the shaft.

CAMBER   When viewed from the front or rear, this is the inward or outward tilting of the wheels from the vertical.

CAMSHAFT   A rotating shaft with a number of cams or eccentric lobes used to operate the engine valves, usually via pushrods and rocker arms.

CANTED ENGINE   See Lay-down Engine.

CARBURETOR   A device through which air and fuel are atomized and drawn into the engine. It meters the proper proportions of fuel and air to form a combustible mixture and varies the ratio according to the engine operation.

CARDAN JOINT   A universal joint with the two yokes at right angles to each other. Invented by Geronimo Cardano of Italy in the sixteenth century. Modified examples are used on cars today.

CASTER   The angle between the steering axis and the vertical when viewed from the side.

CASTING   Making a part by pouring molten metal into a cavity of the part's desired shape and letting it solidify by cooling. The part made by this process.

CATALYTIC CONVERTER   A muffler-shaped, anti-pollution device located in the auto exhaust system that changes the unburned hydrocarbons into carbon dioxide and water vapor which are harmless in the atmosphere.

CENTER OF GRAVITY   The point at which a body will balance in all three axes—longitudinal, lateral, and vertical. Generally the point at which the weight of a body is concentrated. Very important in designing a car.

CHAIN DRIVE   The driving of one shaft by another by means of a toothed wheel on each shaft, with the wheels connected by an endless chain with special links engaging the teeth.

CHASSIS   The basic-strength auto frame including the engine, suspension, wheels, brakes and drive train. A car without its body or coachwork. In monocoque or unit construction it is integral with the body.

CHOKE   A temporary restriction in a carburetor throat that reduces the flow of air and enriches the fuel-air mixture to aid in starting the engine.

CLINCHER TIRE   Obsolete tire with flanged beads on each side of the inner surface that are fitted into turned-over edges of the wheel rim.

CLUTCH   A friction device used to connect the engine to the drive train. Used when changing gear ratios during acceleration. Can connect or disconnect the engine and the drive train at driver's will.

COACHWORK   The automobile body: especially the comfort and luxury appointments as distinguished from the operational chassis.

COIL   A pulsating transformer that converts the 12 volts from the battery to about 20,000 volts during the closing and opening of the contact points in order to jump the spark-plug gap. It is made of an iron core and wound about by two series of wire, called the primary and secondary windings. The former is heavy wire with a few hundred turns, and the latter is fine wire with many thousand turns.

COMBUSTION   In an internal-combustion engine, the exploding or rapid burning of the air-fuel mixture in the combustion chamber of the cylinder. The resultant pressure from gases forces the piston down and thereby produces power.

COMBUSTION CHAMBER   The space remaining at the top of the cylinder when the piston is at the top dead center position. Where the fuel-air mixture begins to burn.

COMPACT CAR   A passenger auto with a wheelbase between 100 and 111 inches. Can be luxurious or austere.

COMPRESSION   In internal-combustion reciprocating engines, the squeezing of the fuel-air mixture in the cylinder of a spark-ignition engine or the squeezing of the air in a diesel engine. Compression makes combustion more effective and increases engine efficiency.

COMPRESSION RATIO   The ratio of the cylinder volume with the piston at bottom dead center to the cylinder volume with the piston at top dead center.

CONNECTING ROD   The arm that connects the piston to the crankshaft and converts the reciprocating motion into rotary motion.

CONVERTIBLE   Any car with a folding roof. Term used in U.S. since the 1930s. In the 1950s, the "hardtop convertible" was developed to look like a convertible but had a fixed roof that did not fold. Also called a drophead coupé.

CORNERING   Rounding a corner of at least 90 degrees. The ability to turn a corner at speed without danger to the passengers or car. Low center of gravity, short wheelbase, wide track, and hard suspension help cornering.

COUPÉ   Originally meant a vehicle "cut" by a glass partition behind the front seats that enabled the rear passengers to ride enclosed and the driver exposed. Today, a two-to-five-seater with smaller interior than a sedan. Usually a sporty type.

COWL   That part of a car's body between the engine compartment and the driver. It contains the instruments and heater or air-conditioning ducts.

CRANKCASE A pan or box that encloses the bottom of the engine, supports the crankshaft, and contains the oil for the engine.

CRANKSHAFT The main shaft of an engine with a U-shaped offset at each cylinder to which the connecting rod is attached. It delivers rotary motion taken from the reciprocating pistons and connecting rods.

CUBIC CAPACITY The volume of the cylinder between the piston top dead center and bottom dead center. Expressed in cubic centimeters or cubic inches. Known as swept volume capacity (U.K.) and displacement (U.S.).

CUBIC CENTIMETER European, metric, and competition measure of engine displacement: 1,000 cc = 1 liter, which equals about 61 cubic inches.

CUBIC INCH U.S. measure of engine displacement: 1 cubic inch = 16.387 cc.

CUSTOM CAR An automobile that has been restyled by its owner, or an all-new body fitted on an existing chassis.

CYCLECAR A term used to describe the very light production autos made prior to 1922. Usually made from motorcycle parts and generally powered by single- or twin-cylinder engines. Disappeared when genuine light cars appeared.

CYLINDER The hollow tubular cavity in the cylinder block in which the piston travels and in which combustion takes place.

CYLINDER BLOCK The basic component of the engine to which other engine parts are attached. It is usually a casting and includes the engine cylinders and the upper portion of the crankcase.

CYLINDER HEAD The detachable part of the top of the cylinder block that contains the spark plugs and valves. It seals the cylinder and forms the top of the combustion chamber.

CYLINDER TYPES "F" Head—Side exhaust valve and overhead inlet valve.

"L" Head—Both valves on one side of the cylinder.

"T" Head—Exhaust valve on one side and inlet valve on the other side of the cylinder.

"I" Head—Both valves located directly over the piston. Also called valve-in-head or overhead-valve engine.

DASHBOARD Term used to denote the auto instrument panel or firewall. Originally the board in front of a horse carriage to protect the driver from mud and debris that was dashed up from the horse's hooves. Now, the partition between the driver and the powerplant. (Fascia, U.K.)

DE DION AXLE The nineteenth-century axle principle of Count de Dion. The wheels tied by a transverse tube curved to clear the final drive unit rigidly mounted to the car's chassis frame. Drive to the wheels is by universally jointed half shafts. The tube moves vertically on a slide to allow the wheels to rise and fall independently. General use was dropped in 1914, but still is used on many sports and racing cars.

DEEP DRAWING Forming flat metal sheets into deeply hollow items, such as fenders, without tearing the metal.

DIE A production tool, in the shape of the desired part, for shaping metal by pressure in a machine in forging, stamping, or die casting.

DIESEL ENGINE An internal-combustion engine in which the fuel is injected into the cylinder near the end of the compression stroke and is ignited by the heat of the compressed air in the cylinder. No spark plug or carburetor is needed, and relatively inexpensive fuels can be used.

DIFFERENTIAL GEARS The gears that convey engine power to the driving axles and are arranged so as to permit the rear wheels to turn at different speeds as required when the vehicle is negotiating a turn.

DISC BRAKE A type of brake in which two friction pads grip a steel disc that is attached to the wheel, with one pad on each side. Used on race cars, sports cars, and better passenger cars. Also disk brake.

DISPLACEMENT See Cubic Capacity.

DISTRIBUTOR The moving part of the internal-combustion engine ignition system that directs the high-voltage current from the coil to the spark plugs in the proper firing order.

DOS-à-DOS A four-seater auto in which four passengers face each other or sit back-to-back. Seldom seen after the early 1900s.

DRAFTING See Slipstream.

DREAM CAR A one-of-a-kind futuristic, experimental automobile usually appearing at auto shows to stimulate interest in the manufacturer's products. Much design benefit spurs from dream cars and many reach the production stage.

DRIFT A balanced four-wheel slide in car racing, sustained through wide-radius corners by only the most skillful drivers.

DRILL A machine tool used for making holes in a variety of diameters for the entrance of bolts and screws or for lightening the structure.

DRIVE SHAFT   The shaft that transmits the engine power from the gearbox to the differential at the driving wheels.

DRIVE TRAIN   That combination of gears, clutches, shafts, etc., that transmits the engine power to the wheels.

DROPHEAD COUPÉ   See Convertible. Also called cabriolet on the Continent.

DRY SUMP   Type of internal-combustion engine in which the lubricating oil is stored either in a separate tank or cooling radiator instead of in the crankcase pan. The oil is pumped to and taken from the engine by separate pumps.

DYNAMO   Obsolete term for the electric generator. In general, a machine that generates electricity.

ECONOMY CAR   Generally, a car with a short wheelbase—under 100 inches—with an engine under 2.5 liters displacement and economical to purchase and operate. Also known as subcompact and mini-car.

ELECTRICAL SYSTEM   In electric ignition internal-combustion engines, those components required to convert the electricity produced by the generator into a high-voltage spark for the plugs. Includes: generator or alternator, points, condenser, coil, distributor and spark plugs plus wiring.

EPICYCLIC GEARBOX   A form of gear used by Benz in which small pinions revolve around a central or sun gear and mesh with an outer ring gear called the annulus. Type used in the Ford Model T. Also called planetary gears, sun-and-planet gears.

EQUIPE   French for team and used to mean race team in France. Same as Italian *scuderia*.

ESSES   In road racing, a continuous series of left and right turns, usually shallow.

EXHAUST   The system of exhausting the burned gases from an internal-combustion engine consisting of piping or tubing, silencers, and, at times, resonators. In highly tuned racing engines, attempt is made to fit exhaust pipes of identical length to each engine cylinder.

EXHAUST MANIFOLD   See Header.

EXPLOSION   The very rapid, almost instantaneous, burning of fuel and air.

FASCIA   See Instrument Panel.

FAST AND LOOSE PULLEYS   A system of transmission used on early Benz cars in which a countershaft carried a loose pulley for neutral and two fixed pulleys meshing with spur gears of different ratios on the axle. Moving the belt from the loose to a fixed pulley provided clutching action.

FASTBACK   A car that has an unbroken curved line from the top of the roof to the rear bumper as opposed to a drop in the line for a near-vertical rear window. In a fastback design the rear window slope follows the unbroken roof line and is often at less than a 45-degree angle.

FENDER   A guard or protective covering over a wheel of an automobile. Also, see Bumper.

F.I.A.   Fédération Internationale de l'Automobile—the world governing body of automobile racing.

FIBERGLASS   A very tough and durable plastic material with fibers running through the plastic. Used for race car bodies, many sports car bodies, and also enjoys considerable acceptance for passenger car bodies.

FIREWALL   See Bulkhead.

FLASH BOILER   A steam generator in which a long coil of tubing is located in the furnace and into which water is pumped and instantly converted into steam. "Flashes" into steam.

FLAT ENGINE   An engine in which the cylinders are lying horizontally, 180 degrees to each other at opposite sides of the crankcase. Also called horizontal, pancake, and opposed engine.

FLUID COUPLING   A form of clutch consisting of two vaned wheels housed in an oil bath. The driving wheel impels its force on the other via the dynamic action of the fluid. Also called fluid drive. Very smooth method of transmitting power.

FLYING START   Race cars traveling in formation at high speed before the race, and upon the green flag signal, the race begins with all cars moving.

FLYWHEEL   A large, heavy iron or steel disc attached to the rear of an engine crankshaft in order to provide sufficient centrifugal force to smooth the power impulses from the cylinders.

FOOTPRINT   Area of contact between a tire and the ground. Very important in tire safety and design.

FORGING   Steel or aluminum part pounded either manually or mechanically into the desired shape when hot to improve its strength.

FORMULA   A detailed specification regulating the classes of open-wheeled, open-cockpit, single-seat international race cars.

FOUR-STROKE CYCLE   An internal-combustion engine that requires two revolutions per cylinder or four piston strokes to achieve a power stroke: internal stroke, compression stroke, power stroke, exhaust stroke. More efficient than the two-stroke-cycle engine. Also called Otto cycle.

FOUR-WHEEL DRIVE   A drive system in which power is transmitted to four wheels instead of two. Has the advantage of added traction on rough terrain and muddy areas.

FRAME A bridge-like, structural base of a car that supports and positions the body and major mechanical items.

FRICTION TRANSMISSION A transmission system using two discs in contact at right angles (90 degrees). Variation in ratio is achieved by sliding the edge of one disc across the face, radially, of the other disc.

FUEL INJECTION On internal-combustion engines, a system that injects a precisely measured amount of fuel into the cylinder at exactly the right moment. Dispenses with the carburetor and increases engine efficiency.

GALLON One imperial gallon equals 4.546 liters.

One U.S. gallon equals .832 imperial gallon.

One U.S. gallon equals 231.18 cubic inches.

Six U.S. gallons equal five imperial gallons.

GASOLINE A highly volatile and inflammable liquid hydrocarbon mixture made from petroleum, coal, or natural gas. The principal fuel used in automobiles. (Called petrol in U.K.)

GAS TURBINE An internal-combustion rotating engine with one main moving part: the rotor with pinwheel-like blades attached. Air is compressed by the first rows of blades and delivered to the combustion chambers, from which the exhaust is directed to pass the remaining blades and to generate the power. Power is extremely smooth due to the absence of explosions and reciprocating parts.

GAUGE An instrument with face and hands similar to a clock that conveys a variety of information such as oil pressure, temperature, engine rpm., car speed, amperage, etc.

GEARS Wheels with meshing teeth to transmit power between rotating shafts. When the gear wheels are of different sizes, a change in speed ratio occurs. Gears are made of hard steel.

GLASS SALOON Vintage large closed vehicle with very large windows (U.K.); sedan (U.S.).

GRANDE EPREUVE In racing, a World Championship qualifying round for Formula 1 drivers. French for "major test."

GRAND PRIX A race that counts for points toward the World Championship of Drivers. Loosely used to promote any kind of race.

GRID In road racing, the starting lineup. Also starting grid.

G.T. Grand Touring from the Italian Gran Turismo. A car combining sedan and sports car features in which engineering is the dominant feature. Combines excellent road handling qualities with relative comfort. Made in two- and four-seaters with the rear seats always cramped.

GYMKHANA Hindustani word adopted by British officers for slalom. See Autocross.

HAIRPIN In auto road racing an extremely sharp 180-degree turn. Also called switchback.

HALF SHAFT A rotating shaft that transmits power from the final drive unit (differential) to a power wheel. Used in independent rear suspension and front-wheel drive. Two are required; one for each side.

HAND CRANK A crank handle for manually starting internal-combustion engines. Used till about 1930. Now obsolete.

HARDTOP See Convertible.

HATCHBACK A car of the fastback design in which the trunk lid includes the rear window, thereby opening into the rear of the car for stowage space. The rear seats often fold flat to provide additional trunk space. This type of car is often called a three-door design.

HEADER A section of the exhaust system that is attached to the cylinder heads to carry off the gases. Also called exhaust manifold.

HEAD RESTRAINT An extension of the back of the seat to reach up behind the head to reduce whiplash injuries in collisions by limiting the rearward movement of the head and neck.

HEATED INTAKE An anti-pollution device that helps vaporize the fuel to a cold engine. Hot air from the exhaust manifold heats the intake air going to the carburetor. System is thermostatically controlled.

HEAT EXCHANGER A device that transfers heat between two fluids through a separating wall. The automobile radiator is a heat exchanger that transfers the heat of the water to the passing air.

HEEL AND TOE A race-driving technique in which the driver places the toes of his right foot on the brake pedal with the heel on the accelerator so that he can simultaneously brake and blip the throttle for a downshift, thereby lessening the strain on the gearbox and drive train.

HELICAL GEAR A gear in which the teeth are cut at an angle to the shaft. The advantage is that there are usually two teeth meshing at all times, making for smoother and quieter operation.

HEMI Slang term for an engine with hemispherical combustion chambers which allow for larger and less shrouded valves. This improves the volumetric efficiency. Used in many sports and racing cars.

HEMI-HEAD A hemispherically shaped combustion chamber at the top of the engine cylinder. The hemispheric shape provides improved efficiency because the forces of the explosion are directed to the piston by the curved surface of the combustion chamber.

HESITATION Term used for an emission-related failure of an engine to respond promptly to pressure on the accelerator pedal. Caused by a very lean fuel-air mixture and retarded timing.

HIGH-TENSION LEADS   The high-voltage wires leading from the distributor to the cap of each spark plug.

HIGH-WHEELER   A motorized buggy that was popular in the U.S. and Canada between 1907 and 1912, using the same thin, metal-rim wheels as on horse-drawn vehicles.

HILL-CLIMB   A speed dash up a hill from a starting line to a finish line, one car at a time, racing against the clock.

HOOD   The removable or lift-up part of an auto body that covers the engine and allows access to it. (Bonnet in U.K.)

HORIZONTAL ENGINE   See Flat Engine.

HORSEPOWER (hp., bhp., French CV., German PS.)   The unit for measuring the power output of an engine. One horsepower is defined as lifting 33,000 pounds one foot per minute. The relationship or ratio of English hp., French CV., and German PS. is 15, 11, and 9 respectively.

HOT ROD   A production auto that has been modified by the owner for outstanding speed and acceleration through extensive changes to the engine, chassis, and body.

HOT-TUBE IGNITION   A very early system of internal-combustion engine ignition in which the air-fuel mixture was ignited by a small platinum tube, open at the cylinder end, that was screwed into the cylinder head. The outer end was closed and heated to a red hot temperature by a fuel-fed burner. When the air-fuel mixture in the cylinder passed into the tube, it ignited. This system was obsolete by 1900.

HYDRAULIC   A mechanical operation based on incompressibility of liquids, generally oil and sometimes water, and their ability to offer resistance when being forced into a small cylinder or through an orifice, thereby transmitting an increase in applied force. Hydraulic brakes and clutches use this principle.

HYDRAULIC VALVE LIFTER   Valve lifter using hydraulic oil pressure to operate and capable of maintaining zero clearance between metal parts. Thus, valve noise and wear are considerably reduced as are the periodic valve adjustments.

HYDROCARBON   Any compound composed entirely of hydrogen and carbon, such as petroleum products, which, when burned, constitute a principal ingredient of photochemical smog.

HYDROPNEUMATIC SUSPENSION   A suspension using both a gas and a liquid separated by a flexible bladder as a springing medium. Usually a sphere or cylinder with nitrogen above the bladder and hydraulic oil below the bladder.

HYPOID GEARS A type of differential final drive using a spiral bevel gear on the drive shaft, allowing it to be located below the center of the ring gear on the axle. This makes possible a lower floor in the car.

ICING Ice forming at the edge of the carburetor due to rapid evaporation of the fuel. This lowers the temperature of the air-fuel mixture and freezes the moisture in the air. The ice restricts the flow of the fuel-air mixture flow and usually occurs when the temperature is between 28 to 55° F. and the relative humidity is between 65 to 100 percent.

IDLER ARM One of the connecting levers in a parallel relay-type steering linkage. The arm is pivoted at one end to the chassis and at the other end to the transverse moving tie rod and center link joint. It serves to keep the tie rod and center link on a steady path throughout their back-and-forth movement.

IGNITION The timed exploding of the fuel-air mixture in a cylinder by either an electric spark or the heat of compression.

IGNITION SYSTEM See Electrical System.

INDEPENDENT SUSPENSION Suspension in which each wheel is sprung individually so that any disturbance on the wheel has no effect on the opposite wheel.

INDUCTION SYSTEM The system that delivers the fuel-air mixture to the cylinders for combustion. It includes the carburetor or fuel-injection system, intake manifolds, and intake valves.

INLINE ENGINE An engine having the cylinders in a straight line, one after the other. Also called a "straight" engine.

INSTRUMENT PANEL That part of an automobile on which are mounted the instruments or gauges and minor controls. Also called dashboard. (Fascia, U.K.)

INTAKE MANIFOLD An arrangement of tubes through which the fuel-air mixture is distributed from the carburetor to the cylinders.

INTAKE PARTS The passage in the cylinder head that connects the intake valve and intake manifold through which the fuel-air mixture flows to the combustion chamber.

INTAKE STROKE The first stroke of a four-stroke cycle internal-combustion engine. This downward movement of the piston from top dead center to bottom dead center creates a partial vacuum that draws the fuel-air mixture into the cylinder.

INTERNAL-COMBUSTION ENGINE Any engine, either reciprocating or rotary, in which the fuel is consumed in the interior of the engine rather than outside of the engine.

JACK A mechanical or hydraulic device to raise a portion of a car for changing tires or making minor repairs.

JACKING A cornering force acting on swing axle suspensions that tends to lift the body of the car through the solidly mounted differential. This forces the outboard wheel to tuck or jack under the car. If continued, this can upset the vehicle.

JET A calibrated nozzle in a carburetor through which fuel is drawn and mixed with air. Carburetors normally have several jets for idling through power in order to provide the proper amount of fuel for all conditions.

JOURNAL The section of an axle or rotating shaft that is in actual contact with the bearing.

KAMM TAIL Named for the German aerodynamicist W. Kamm, who discovered that drag begins to increase after the rear of a car's cross-sectional area is reduced to 50 percent of the car's maximum cross section. He then designed the sharply cut-off tail that is now found on all racing cars and many production cars.

KEY A small block inserted between a rotating shaft and a gear or pulley to lock them together so they rotate as a single unit.

KEYWAY The slot in a shaft and gear or pulley into which the key fits.

KING OF THE BELGIANS A luxurious open touring car named after King Leopold II of the Belgians, whose mistress, Cléo de Mérode, suggested the style to him. Style also known as Roi des Belges and Tulip Phaeton.

KINGPIN In solid axle and in some early independent front suspensions the kingpin was the vertical pin in the end of the axle around which the stub axle and wheel pivoted. It has now been replaced by the ball joint.

KNOCKOFF A single wing nut for fastening a wheel to the hub. Easily removed and replaced, it is struck (knocked off) with a mallet on the wings.

LACQUER A fast-drying pyroxylin paint often used to finish automobile bodies.

LAMINATED WINDSHIELD A windshield consisting of a thin layer of rubbery plastic sandwiched between two sheets of glass. When struck by the head in an accident, it bows out without puncturing, and the plastic holds the glass to prevent it from splintering.

LANDAU A cabriolet limousine in which only the roof behind the front side windows was collapsible.

LANDAULET A small landau with only two seats in the fixed-roof portion.

LAP One complete circuit of a race course.

LAP OF HONOR In auto racing, the final lap made by the winner at a slow speed to receive the applause of the spectators.

LAPPING   In auto racing, when a driver gains sufficient lead over his competitors to close up behind them and overtake them, he is lapping the competition by placing them a full lap behind him.

LATERAL ACCELERATION   The side movement created when an automobile corners, resulting in a centrifugal force that tends to pull the car outward. The tires resist this and therefore, if the turn is too sharp or too fast, the car will tend to roll over, depending upon the location of the center of gravity.

LAY-DOWN ENGINE   An inline engine that is angled from the vertical to reduce the hood line and/or lower the center of gravity. Also called slant, canted, or tilted engine.

LEADING ARM   An independent suspension system with the wheel attached to the end of an arm that swings in a plane parallel to the longitudinal axis of the car. The wheel is ahead of or leads the fixed pivot point of the arm.

LEAF SPRINGS   A number of slightly curved, flexible steel plates of varying lengths, mounted one atop the other. The ends are attached to the chassis, and the middle is fixed to the axle. Also called semi-elliptic springs.

LEFT-HAND DRIVE   Location of driver and controls on the left side of the automobile, as in all U.S. cars today.

LIMITED SLIP DIFFERENTIAL   A differential that uses cone or disc clutches to lock the two separate axle shafts. This forces both driving wheels to transmit the same drive torque regardless of the traction available. It still allows differential action under normal driving conditions but improves traction in mud and snow.

LIMOUSINE   A closed, chauffeur-driven automobile in which the driver is separated from the passengers by a glass partition.

LIVE AXLE   An axle that transmits power either by separate half shafts or by side chains, as opposed to a dead axle.

LOCOMOTIVE   An early nineteenth-century term for a heavy, steam-propelled road vehicle. Presently applies only to railroad engines.

LOUVER   A slatted air intake or air outlet. Slats used to capture and control the air flow.

LUBRICANT   Any substance, usually oil or grease, that can reduce the friction between moving parts, can absorb and carry away the heat, plus wash away the abrasive metal worn off the surfaces.

LUG NUTS   The nuts used to hold the wheels to the car.

LUXURY CAR   A well-appointed, well-equipped, well-designed and constructed auto varying in size from a compact to a large sedan with base prices from $6,000 upward to $13,000.

MAGNETO   A self-contained device that generates electricity, steps up the low voltage to high voltage, and distributes the high voltage to the proper cylinder at the correct time.

MAIN BEARING   In an internal-combustion engine, the special lubricated metal supports in which the crankshaft revolves.

MANUAL TRANSMISSION   A mechanism in the drive train with gears to vary the power and torque delivered to the driven wheels. It consists of a lever that the driver operates in conjunction with the clutch to change from one gear to another.

MEAN EFFECTIVE PRESSURE   The steady pressure which, if applied to each piston during each power stroke, would give the measured power.

MECHANICAL EFFICIENCY   The ratio of the power placed on the pistons divided by the actual power available at the engine crankshaft. The actual power at the engine crankshaft is always less, due to friction, heat losses, and the power used to drive the auxiliary equipment.

METALLURGY   The science of metals and the experimentation with alloys.

MINI-CAR   See Economy Car.

MIXTURE   The blend of fuel and air fed into the cylinder of an internal-combustion engine.

MOCK-UP   A full-size dummy of a car made of wood and clay, used for design studies.

MONOCAR   A term used for the ultra-light, single-seater cyclecars of the period before 1915.

MONOCOQUE   Literally a "single shell" method of chassis/body construction in which the two components are made as one. Also called unit construction and unitized construction. Results in a very high strength-to-weight ratio. The eggshell illustrates the perfect monocoque structure.

MUFFLER   A chamber in the exhaust system in which the exhaust gases expand, cool, and pass around baffles or porous plates that reduce the noise created by the exhaust. (Silencer, U.K.)

MULTIPLE DISC   A clutch with two or more clutch discs and pressure plates in order to reduce slippage and clutch wear with high-powered engines. Also permits a smaller clutch enclosure because of the smaller diameters.

N.A.C.A. DUCT   An air inlet duct design that draws in maximum resistance. The opening is generally flush with the body and does not protrude like a scoop. Named for the National Advisory Committee for Aerodynamics, responsible for researching the design.

NEEDLE AND SEAT   An assembly that controls the flow of fuel into the carburetor float bowl. The needle lifts off the seat to admit more fuel when the level in the bowl drops.

NITRO   Abbreviation for nitromethane, which is blended with the gasoline used in racing cars.

NOMEX   Trade name of the flame-resistant fabric used in racing drivers' clothing, such as coveralls, gloves, underwear, socks, and face masks.

NORMALLY ASPIRATED   An engine that intakes air or "breathes" without the assistance of a supercharger or turbocharger.

NOTCH-BACK   A car body shape with a roof line that has an abrupt, near vertical, drop at the rear window and returns to near horizontal at the trunk.

OCTANE   An arbitrary numerical designation for rating the anti-knock qualities of gasoline.

OIL COOLER   A small heat exchange similar to a radiator used for cooling the transmission fluid or lubricating oil.

OIL PAN   A removable bottom portion of the crankcase that acts as a lubricating oil reservoir.

OIL PUMP   An engine-driven pump that delivers oil, under pressure, to the engine's moving parts.

OIL RING   The lowermost piston ring that scrapes off excess oil from the cylinder walls and returns it to the oil pan via vents in the ring and piston.

OPPOSED ENGINE   See Flat Engine.

OTTO CYCLE   See Four-Stroke Cycle.

OVERDRIVE   A small auxiliary gearbox that provides an additional gear ratio. It causes the drive shaft to turn faster than the engine crankshaft or "overdrive" it. It is engaged manually when under way and reduces fuel consumption.

OVERHEAD VALVE   See Cylinder Types.

OVERSQUARE   An engine in which the cylinder bore is greater than the piston stroke. A "square" engine has the bore and stroke identical.

OVERSTEER   In a turn, the tendency of the rear of the car to slide toward the front of the car and possibly to overtake it, thereby turning the car around 180 degrees.

PANCAKE ENGINE   See Flat Engine.

PANHARD ROD   A lateral brace connecting the chassis with the live axle, providing lateral location of the axle. Also called track bar.

PETROL   British for gasoline.

PHAETON   In the early days of motoring, a light, open two-seater with spoked wheels and a hood. The four-seater was called a double phaeton, and the six- or seven-seater a triple phaeton.

PHOTOCHEMICAL SMOG   See Hydrocarbon.

PINION   A small diameter gear with a small number of teeth designed to mesh with a much larger gear wheel or a toothed rod (rack). Used in rack-and-pinion steering and for speed reduction with an increase in power.

PISTON   A partly hollow, cylindrical metal engine part that is closed at one end and fits into the engine cylinder. Connected to the crankshaft via the connecting rod and usually fitted with rings to seal it in the cylinder.

PLANETARY GEARS   See Epicyclic Gearbox.

PNEUMATIC TIRE   A circular tube of rubber and fabric, and sometimes also steel, attached to the rim of the car's wheel, having resilience due to its containing air under pressure.

PONY CAR   A sporty compact or subcompact car having better handling and speed than the average car but not in the real sports car category, although the styling usually approaches that of a sports car. Name derived from the Mustang, which was the first "pony car."

POPPET VALVE   A mushroom-shaped valve head operated by a cam.

POWER TAKEOFF   A device whereby power from the engine of a self-propelled vehicle can be used for another purpose besides propulsion, generally via belt and pulley.

PRE-SELECTOR GEARBOX   An arrangement that enables the driver to select a gear speed before he needs it and then depress the clutch pedal when he desires to use the selected gear.

PRIMARY CIRCUIT   The low voltage electrical circuit from the battery to the primary coil winding, through the breaker points and back to the battery.

PRODUCTION   Another word for stock. A car made in quantity for street use.

PROTOTYPE   The test model of a new car design that is to be produced in quantity.

PUSHROD   A metal rod connecting the valve lifter or camshaft with the valve rocker arm on overhead-valve engines.

PUSH START   A start of a car engine by engaging the clutch while the car is being pushed forward.

QUADRICYCLE   An early type of light, four-wheeled automobile using bicycle wheels and a frame of steel tubes.

QUALIFYING   In auto racing, the pre-race speed runs that determine the starting positions in the race. Cars run against the clock and the fastest start at the front of the starting grid or lineup.

QUARTZ-HALOGEN BULB   A bulb having a quartz envelope holding the tungsten filament and filled with an inert gas of the halogen type. The gas removes the tungsten deposits from the bulb wall and redeposits them on the filament. This prevents the blackening of the bulb surface and reduction in light output. More lighting power per watt of electrical power used is produced.

RACK-AND-PINION STEERING A steering system having a pinion gear at the lower end of the steering column that engages a rack or a toothed rod that connects to the wheel steering arms.

RADIAL PLY A tire in which the fabric cords run radially in a line from the wheel hub or straight out from the bead or around the tubular shape of the tire. Annular belts of fabric or steel mesh add rigidity. Advantages of this design are: more flexible side walls with a relatively stiff tread area and a larger and more consistent footprint on the road under all driving conditions.

RECIPROCATING Motion of an object between two limiting positions. Applied to piston engines because of the limited up-and-down motion of the pistons.

RESONATOR A small auxiliary muffler placed in series with the main muffler to assist it in reducing the exhaust noise.

REV. COUNTER See Tachometer.

RING GEAR One of the gears in the rear axle that transmits power to the differential from the drive shaft.

ROAD RACE An auto race run on a road course or simulated road course with esses, hairpins, etc., as opposed to a race run on an oval track.

ROADSTER A 1920–1940 description of a two-seater open car of sporty appearance.

ROCKER ARM A pivoted lever that transmits the action of the pushrod to the valve stem. (Pushrod upward action is converted to downward push on the valve stem.)

ROI DES BELGES See King of the Belgians.

ROLL BAR A loop or frame of tubular steel firmly attached to the chassis and rising above the driver's head. When the car rolls over, the bar protects the driver from being crushed by the vehicle. Generally fitted to race cars and competition sports cars.

ROLL CENTER That point about which the car body rolls when cornering.

ROTARY VALVES Valves contained in the cylinder head whose rotary motion opens and closes the parts to allow passage of the fuel-air mixture and gases.

ROTOR A small rotating device in a distributor mounted on the breaker cam inside the cap. It connects the high voltage of the coil to the spark plugs as it turns and makes contact with the proper spark-plug terminal.

RUBBING STRIP A chrome or resilient plastic strip on the sides of a car body as protection against minor damage.

RUNABOUT   An open sporting-type vehicle, lightweight, with two seats and with simple bodywork. Term used in the early 1900s in the U.S.

RUNNING BOARD   A long flat board under the car doors that acts as a footstep for the passengers.

S.A.E.   Society of Automotive Engineers. A group known for publishing research papers and defining various standards of measurement.

SAFETY RIM   A type of wheel rim having a hump on the inner edge of the ledge on which the tire bead rides. The hump holds the tire on the rim in case of a blowout.

SALOON   British for sedan.

SCAVENGING   Removal of the exhaust gases from the cylinder by special means: using the momentum of the exhaust gases in a long exhaust pipe or by a special blower.

S.C.C.A.   Sports Car Club of America.

SCUTTLE   See Bulkhead.

SEALED BEAM   A one-piece, hermetically sealed headlight in which the filament is an integral part of the unit, and the lens itself is the bulb.

SEDAN   A closed car for four or more passengers with either two or four doors. (Called saloon in U.K.)

SELECTIVE TRANSMISSION   The conventional manual transmission of today in which any gear may be selected at will as opposed to the very early progressive transmission in which the gears had to be selected in order.

SELF-STARTER   A device for starting an internal-combustion engine without muscular effort.

SEMI-ELLIPTIC SPRINGS   See Leaf Springs.

SEMI-TRAILER   A truck trailer with part of its weight supported by a truck tractor.

SHIMS   Thin strips of metal used as spacers between parts.

SHOCK ABSORBERS   A term used for what are really dampers. Fittings used to absorb the energy that the wheels convey to the springs. The dampers keep the springs from continuously rebounding. The majority of shock absorbers are hydraulic.

SHOES   Slang for tires.

SHRINK FIT   A tight fit obtained when the part to be inserted into a cavity is slightly larger than the cavity. The cavity part is heated and the shaft or part to be inserted is chilled, thereby enlarging the cavity and shrinking the part to be inserted. After assembly and both return to normal temperature, the parts grip each other tightly.

SILENCER   See Muffler.

SLALOM   See Autocross.

SLANT ENGINE   See Lay-down Engine.

SLEEVE VALVE   Consists of metal sleeves located between the piston and cylinder wall. When moved up and down, holes in the sleeves coincide with inlet and exhaust parts to provide passage for the gases at the right time.

SLIPSTREAM   A racing technique where a car follows the leading car very closely in order to gain speed. Reason: the total aerodynamic drag acting on the two cars close together is less than the drag that acts on each car when it is several car lengths from the other. Also called drafting.

SPARK PLUG   A device inserted into the combustion chamber of a cylinder on an internal-combustion engine that provides the electrical gap across which the high-tension voltage jumps. This creates a spark that ignites the compressed fuel-air mixture.

SPOILER   An aerodynamic device attached to a car either on the extreme rear or under the front bumper. Purpose: to prevent understeer or oversteer tendencies or to reduce drag. "Spoils" normal airflow around the car.

SPORTS CAR   An agile vehicle that is easily maneuverable, accelerates briskly, brakes positively, handles well, steers precisely, and gives a taut performance. It is tightly sprung and does not wallow and heave as does a conventional passenger car and is therefore not as comfortable.

SPORTY CAR   A car that looks like a sports car, has some of the sports car's qualities, but is not a true sports car.

SPYDER   In the early 1900s, a light two-seater car. In the 1950s the word was revived by some Italian manufacturers for an open two-seater sports car.

STEAM ENGINE   An engine using steam pressure to drive the pistons.

STOCK   See Production.

STOCK CAR   A racing car having the basic chassis of a commercially produced assembly-line model.

STRAIGHT ENGINE   See Inline Engine.

STROKE   The back-and-forth motion of the piston. The length of the motion of the piston from top dead center to bottom dead center.

SUBCOMPACT   See Economy Car.

SUN-AND-PLANET GEARS   See Epicyclic Gearbox.

SUPERCHARGER   An air compressor fitted to an internal-combustion engine to force the fuel-air mixture into the cylinders at a pressure greater than that of the atmosphere. Boosts the power of the engine.

SUSPENSION The assembly of springs, shock absorbers, torsion bars, joints, arms, etc., that cushions the shock of bumps on the road and serves to keep the wheels in constant contact with the road, thereby improving control and traction.

SWEPT VOLUME CAPACITY See Cubic Capacity.

SWING AXLE Type of independent rear suspension using half shafts that have universal joints only at their inboard ends on both sides of the differential. This causes a camber angle change of the wheel with up-and-down wheel movements.

SWITCHBACK See Hairpin.

TACHOMETER An instrument that indicates the number of revolutions per minute at which the engine is turning. Also rev. counter. Fitted on sports and racing cars, but rarely on passenger cars.

T-BONE In racing, to strike another car broadside.

TILTED ENGINE See Lay-down Engine.

TONNEAU An open vehicle with a bench seat in front and semicircular seat behind. A part of the back seat was built into the rear door. Used until about 1915.

TOOLING A collective term for factory equipment used to make the parts of the product.

TORPEDO A long open sports vehicle with an unbroken line from hood to windshield and from the windshield to the back of the car. Term used from about 1910 to 1920 in the U.S., and until 1930 in France and Italy.

TORSION BAR A rod in the suspension system that, when twisted from a grip at one end, functions like a spring.

TOURER An open car with seats for four or more passengers. Early models had no side weather protection but later tourers were fitted with detachable side screens and curtains. Made until about 1930.

TRACK See Tread.

TRACK BAR See Panhard Rod.

TRACK LAYING Said of a vehicle on which wheels are supplanted on both sides by usually endless belt systems that form their own roadway, as on a military tank.

TRANSMISSION The gear-changing or gear-shifting system through which engine power is transferred to the wheels. The purpose of gear-changing is to keep maximum engine power applied to the wheels at all times for all conditions, from start-up to high speeds.

TREAD Width of a car measured from the centerline of the wheels. Sometimes called the track. Also the pattern on the surface of a tire.

TREMBLER COIL IGNITION An ignition system using an induction coil and electromagnetic vibrator which breaks the primary circuit and induces the high-tension current in the coil secondary windings. Used by Benz and many others and replaced by the De Dion Bouton patent contact breaker. Developed by Georges Bouton in 1895.

TRICYCLE   A three-wheeled, early-type open automobile using bicycle wheels and a steel-tube frame.

TULIP PHAETON   See King of the Belgians.

TURBOCHARGER   A supercharging device driven by exhaust gases from the engine.

TURNING CIRCLE   The diameter of the circle described by an automobile when the steering wheel is fully turned in one direction (fully locked).

TURNPIKE   A major highway, generally much longer than roads connecting towns. Often used to describe a modern highway.

TWO-STROKE CYCLE   An internal-combustion engine that requires only one revolution per cylinder or two piston strokes (up and down) to achieve a power stroke. No longer used in U.S. cars but still found on old motorcycles and outboard motors.

UNDERSTEER   In a turn, the tendency of the front of the car to proceed relatively straight ahead instead of following the direction in which the front wheels are turned.

UNIT CONSTRUCTION   See Chassis.

UTILITY VEHICLE   Relatively new type of recreational vehicle built on a truck chassis. Includes two-and four-wheel-drive cars such as Jeeps, supervans, dune buggies, etc.

VALVE   Device that opens and closes the combustion chamber of an internal-combustion engine to admit the fuel-air mixture or exhaust the gases.

VALVE-IN-HEAD   See Cylinder Types.

VALVE STEM   That part of the valve that is actuated by the camshaft or rocker arm.

VEE ENGINE   An engine with cylinders arranged in two rows at an angle to the common crankshaft. Has a "V" shape when viewed from the front.

VICTORIA   A two-seater open auto with a large folding hood. Seldom used after 1900.

VIS-à-VIS   A four-seater in which two passengers faced the driver. Used around the turn of the century.

VOITURE LEGÈRE   A light car, especially a racing car falling between the heavy cars and the voiturette. Term seldom used to describe production cars. Not used after 1914.

VOITURETTE   Early two-seater touring car without a hood. Name first used by Léon Bollée and then applied to any small car until

1905. Term not used for twenty years until 1925, when it was only used for small racing types and not for production autos.

WAGONETTE Large car for six or more passengers in which the rear seats faced each other. Usually open, with entrance in the rear.

WATER JACKET The chambers that surround the cylinders and combustion chambers of an internal-combustion engine with the cooling water.

WEIGHT Dry weight—car without fuel, oil, or water. Curb weight —car with full tank of fuel, oil, and water.

WHEELBASE The distance between the centers of the front and rear wheel axles as viewed from the side of the car.

X-TYPE ENGINE An engine that has four rows of cylinders that form an "X" when viewed from the front.

Index